The Trial of a Khmer Rouge Torturer

ALEXANDER LABAN HINTON

Duke University Press | Durham and London | 2016

© 2016 Duke University Press
All rights reserved
Printed in the United States of America on acid-free paper ∞
Designed by Heather Hensley
Typeset in Arno Pro by Westchester Publishing Services

Library of Congress Cataloging-in-Publication Data
Names: Hinton, Alexander Laban, author.
Title: Man or monster? : the trial of a Khmer Rouge torturer /
    Alexander Laban Hinton.
Description: Durham : Duke University Press, 2016. | Includes
    bibliographical references and index.
Identifiers: LCCN 2016028000 (print) |
LCCN 2016029326 (ebook)
ISBN 9780822362586 (hardcover : alk. paper)
ISBN 9780822362739 (pbk. : alk. Paper)
ISBN 9780822373551 (e-book)
Subjects: LCSH: Kang, Kech Ieu, 1942—Trials, litigation, etc. |
    Tuol Sleng (Prison : Phnom Penh, Cambodia) | Trials
    (Crimes against humanity)—Cambodia.
Classification: LCC KZ1208.C36 K36 2016 (print) | LCC KZ1208.
    C36 K36 2016 (ebook) | DDC 345/.0235—dc23
LC record available at https://lccn.loc.gov/2016028000

Cover art: Cover photo by permission of the Documentation
Center of Cambodia / Sleuk Rith Institute. Photo by Terith Chy.

Man or Monster?

Man or Monster?

FOR
Nicole, Meridian, and Arcadia

Contents

1   The Accused, Fact Sheet, Public Version–Redacted

3   FOREGROUND
Monster

PART I   **CONFESSION**

41   INTERROGATION
Comrade Duch's Abecedarian

44   CHAPTER 1
Man (Opening Arguments)

68   CHAPTER 2
Revolutionary (M-13 Prison)

90   CHAPTER 3
Subordinate (Establishment of S-21)

103   CHAPTER 4
Cog (Policy and Implementation)

130   CHAPTER 5
Commandant (Functioning of S-21)

142   CHAPTER 6
Master (Torture and Execution)

168   ERASURE
Duch's Apology

PART II   **RECONSTRUCTION**

171   TORTURE, A COLLAGE
The Testimony of Prak Khan, S-21 Interrogator

176   CHAPTER 7
      Villain (The Civil Parties)

197   CHAPTER 8
      Zealot (Prosecution)

213   CHAPTER 9
      Scapegoat (Defense)

229   CHAPTER 10
      The Accused (Trial Chamber Judgment)

243   BACKGROUND
      Redactic (Final Decision)

288   EPILOGUE
      Man or Monster? (Conviction)

297   Acknowledgments
301   Timeline
303   Abbreviations
305   Notes
335   Bibliography
345   Index

The Accused, Fact Sheet, Public Version—Redacted

Extraordinary Chambers in the Courts of Cambodia (ECCC)
Information Sheet, Case 001
Case file No. 001/18–07–2007/ECCC-SC

Defendant

Name	Kaing Guek Eav, alias Duch
Date of Birth	17 Nov 1942
Place of Birth	Kompong Thom, Cambodia
Position in DK	Deputy then Chairman of S-21 (security center known as Tuol Sleng)

Allegations

- Crimes against Humanity
- Grave Breaches of the Geneva Conventions of 1949
- Murder and Torture (over 12,000 dead)

Procedural History

Arrest Date	31 Jul 2007
Substantive Hearings	30 Mar–29 Nov 2009 (72 trial days)

Judgment	26 Jul 2010
Final Decision	2 Feb 2012

Participants

Defense	Kar Savuth (Cambodia) & François Roux (France)
Prosecution	Chea Leang (Cambodia) & Robert Petit (Canada)
Investigating Judges	You Bunleng (Cambodia) & Marcel Lemonde (France)
Civil Parties	90 victims and their lawyers
Trial Chamber	Cambodian Judges (Nonn Nil, President, Sokhan Ya, Mony Thou)
	Intl. Judges (J-M. Lavergne, France & S. Cartwright, New Zealand)
Witnesses	17 fact witnesses, 7 character witnesses, 22 civil parties

ECCC (Khmer Rouge Tribunal)

• *Type*	International "hybrid" tribunal
• *Commenced*	2006
• *Temporal Jurisdiction*	Crimes committed during Democratic Kampuchea (DK)
	(7 Apr 1975 and 6 Jan 1979, the period of Khmer Rouge Rule)
• *Personal Jurisdiction*	Senior Leaders & Those Most Responsible

Source: ECCC, "Kaing Guek Eav"; ECCC, "Case Information Shehet, Kaing Guek Eav, alias Duch," ECCC, "Extraordinary Chambers in the Courts of Cambodia: ECCC at a Glance."

Monster

A Picture says a Thousand Words
—*Entry in Exhibition Comment Book, Tuol Sleng Genocide Museum (November 29, 2005)*

EVIL. Black ink staining white cloth. The word is written across the neckline of the man's polo shirt in a photograph at the Tuol Sleng Genocide Museum in Phnom Penh, Cambodia. A caption names him: "DUCH (original name Kaing Guek Eav aka Kiev)." Duch's head rises from the shirt collar, too large for his slight build. Pressed into a line, his lips conceal bad teeth. In the background, a man in a dark suit is a shadow behind Duch. Someone has scribbled in white marker across Duch's eyes, which glow, demonic. Another person has given him a small, pointy goatee, the kind associated with the devil. The picture is uncanny.

Some visitors to the museum would recognize Duch as the Khmer Rouge cadre who ran a secret security prison, S-21 (Security Office 21), at the site from 1976 to 1979. In the mid-1960s, Duch (b. 1942) had joined the Khmer Rouge, a Maoist-inspired group of Marxist-Leninist revolutionaries who had risen to power on the ripples of the Vietnam War. Upon taking control on April 17, 1975, they enacted policies leading to the deaths of roughly two million of Cambodia's eight million inhabitants, almost a quarter of the population, before being deposed by a Vietnamese-backed army on January 6, 1979.

During Democratic Kampuchea (DK), the period of Khmer Rouge rule in Cambodia, over 12,000 people passed through the gates of S-21, which Duch ran beginning in March 1976. Almost all of the prisoners were executed, many after being interrogated and tortured into making a confession. Evil. A picture is worth a thousand words, the saying goes. One look tells the story. What more needs to be said?

March 11, 2011, Tuol Sleng Genocide Museum, Phnom Penh

I look again. I stand in an exhibition room at Tuol Sleng staring at Duch's photo. Two years before, on March 29, 2009, the day before Duch's trial at an international hybrid tribunal commenced, I passed through this room and, without much thought, photographed the wall on which Duch's photograph hung. His image was unmarked. Over the course of 2009, the Extraordinary Chambers in the Courts of Cambodia (ECCC), more colloquially referred to as the Khmer Rouge Tribunal, held seventy-seven sessions that included the testimony of thirty-five witnesses and twenty-two victims.[1] Duch spoke extensively during his trial, making observations and offering his own version of events. Closing arguments concluded on November 27, 2009.

The verdict, delivered on July 26, 2010, was appealed by all sides, a process that is ongoing as I stand in the exhibition room. Like many others, I wonder if this sixty-nine-year-old man, who ran this camp where so much death and suffering had taken place, might end up walking free. Lurking in the background were other questions. Who is this man? Will his trial deliver justice? What sort of a person runs a place like S-21?

During the course of Duch's trial, I considered these questions as I attended dozens of trial sessions and interviewed court officials, civil society workers, and ordinary Cambodians from the city and the countryside. Sometimes during an interview, I would ask which moments in the trial of Duch most stood out. I received many answers. Some noted his ability to recite French poetry in the original or the time he chastised one of his former deputies for not telling the truth, bringing the man to tears. Others remarked on the testimony of the survivor and artist Vann Nath, whose description of S-21 undercut some of Duch's key claims; still more noted a startling turn of events on the last day of the trial.

Now, as I stand in front of the defaced photograph, I reread the caption that spells out Duch's name in capital lettering. It reminds me of a moment on the fourth day of Duch's trial, when he was given the floor to tell his story and discussed the origin of his name.

Wearing a white, long-sleeved dress shirt, the color associated with purity and clarity of thought and often worn by teachers and lay religious practitioners in Cambodia, Duch stood in the dock describing his path to M-13, the prison he had run during the civil war that preceded DK. His dark trousers were pulled high at the waist, covering a slight paunch.

When Duch had finished his remarks, the Cambodian president of the five-person Trial Chamber, Nonn Nil, asked him to be seated in the dock and turned the floor over to Judge Jean-Marc Lavergne, the international judge from France who sat to Nonn Nil's far left. Each time the Trial Chamber entered and exited the court, Judge Lavergne's height was apparent: he towered over the other judges. Judge Lavergne had a boyish face, brown hair, and glasses. In a soft, almost delicate tone that belied his size, he often asked questions about trauma, character, and suffering, perhaps in part because of his past experience working with victims as a judge in France. When necessary, however, he could be direct, probing, and challenging, especially when moral issues arose.

Judge Lavergne was the first person afforded the opportunity to directly question Duch during the trial proceedings. As he posed his questions, he sometimes gesticulated, exposing the sleeves of his blue-and-white-striped dress shirt beneath his undersized red court robe. If he at first asked Duch about the historical context that had led him to M-13, Judge Lavergne soon turned to other factors that had influenced Duch to become a revolutionary, including the teachers who had sparked Duch's interest in politics and his possible exposure to violence while imprisoned shortly after joining the Khmer Rouge.

After returning to the topic of the oath Duch had sworn to the Party, Judge Lavergne asked Duch if that was when he had changed his name. "My revolutionary name," Duch replied, "was the name they had me select in 1967 while I was secretly undertaking political study."[2] Judge Lavergne asked him to elaborate.

"This name," Duch replied, glancing at the court camera, "is commonly used by Cambodians and doesn't have any special meaning." Pausing for emphasis, Duch continued, "But for me, it did. I loved this name." His oratorical skills, honed during years of teaching, were on full display, leading some observers to comment that he sounded pedantic, rehearsed, or even disingenuous. He explained that when he was young, his grandfather had praised the work of a local sculptor who had this name.

Duch had also encountered the name in a primary school text. In one passage, he told the court, "The teacher instructs Duch to read from a book. Duch rises and stands straight, his head turned face forward and unwavering, as he reads carefully and clearly. It was the first essay in the text. So I was interested in the name Duch. It was a good name and a Khmer name."[3] Shifting back to 1967, he explained that when he was asked to select a revolutionary name, he chose

"Duch" because "I knew that the name Kaing Guek Eav was a Chinese name. I was becoming part of the Khmer Revolution so I had to use a Khmer name."

Then, raising his maimed left hand, fingers extended, Duch, as if having concluded a lesson, returned to Judge Lavergne's original question and summarized the key points of his answer: "Thus, with regard to the name Duch, in terms of its exact meaning, it is a name that I liked because I respected the work of the artisan Duch and I believed that the child Duch from the book was a good student." Duch punctuated each point with a wave of his hand in the air, then leaned back in his seat and turned off his microphone.

"So the reference," said Judge Lavergne, seeking clarity about the memory of events that took place more than 40 years before, is to a student "who is particularly disciplined, particularly obedient, who is always ready to answer questions asked to him, who is always ready to learn, who is always willing to do what he's told. Was that the reference?" Duch replied, "Your Honour is correct. I liked the name Duch because I wanted to be like this pupil who was orderly and disiplined, a student who feared, respected and obeyed his teacher, a youth who was waiting to fulfill his duty, whatever it might be, well."[4]

Returning to the time when Duch joined the revolution, Judge Lavergne asked him to confirm his reasons for doing so. "I was resolved to liberate the nation and my people so that they would be free from oppression," he replied. "I did not have the intention of committing crimes against my country. . . . My oath was [given to serve] the people."[5] When Duch finished his reply, he inhaled sharply and murmured "mmmm" as he nodded his head.

Duch noted that rather than harboring criminal intentions, he had been ready to fearlessly sacrifice everything to serve the revolution, whether it be imprisonment, separation from his parents, or even death. Beyond joining the revolution, Duch stressed, "the thing I loved the most was being a teacher." He paused, then inhaled and continued, "I hoped that, after the revolution had been won, they would not discard me but let me be a teacher again. This was my thought. I didn't know they would pull me in and have me do this sort of [criminal] work."[6]

Before the session ended for lunch, Judge Lavernge asked Duch which qualities his superiors saw in him when they chose him to run a security center. "The most important quality," he replied, "was loyalty to the Party. My patron, teacher Son Sen, knew me clearly, as did Elder Chhay Kim Hor and, later, Elder Vorn (Vorn Vet). They knew I was straight with them and would not dare to hide anything." The Communist Party, Duch then added, also looked for those who "paid attention and did their work responsibly and precisely."

He had begun to speak in short bursts with sharp intakes of breath; Duch then raised his voice and quickly finished, "For my entire life, if I'm not able to do something, I won't do it. But if I am able to do it, I do it meticulously and well."[7]

| | |

Meticulous. This word was often used to describe Duch. It seemed to fit in many ways. He arrived in court prepared, sometimes carrying stacks of documents with color-coded annotations. On occasion, he corrected lawyers or recited court document numbers by heart. His memory was unsettling, both for its detail and selectivity.

But as soon as it seemed possible to get a fix on Duch, his image suddenly shifted, like his name. The revolution was not the last time he would change it. At the end of DK, when the Vietnamese-backed army routed the Khmer Rouge, Duch fled in haste into the jungle, where he remained for years, continuing to serve the Khmer Rouge, who waged war against the new People's Republic of Kampuchea (PRK) government. He also returned to education, and he was teaching at a primary school in Samlaut district by 1985.[8]

In 1986, Duch changed his name to "Hang Pin," when he was sent to China to teach Khmer literature.[9] During the 1990s, he again returned to education, teaching at a high school and working in a district education office. Several of his children also became teachers. Duch claimed that he had begun seeking a way to leave the Khmer Rouge as his relations with the group had begun to fray in the 1990s, pointing to a 1995 incident in which he had been injured and his wife stabbed to death, during a robbery that he thought had been an assassination attempt.[10]

Duch had converted to Christianity the following year. During his trial he met with his pastor, who also served as one of his character witnesses. In 1999, photographer Nic Dunlop stumbled on Duch in a remote village.[11] He subsequently told Dunlop and journalist Nate Thayer: "It is God's will you are here. . . . I have done very bad things before in my life. Now it is time for *les represailles* [to bear the consequences] of my actions."[12] Duch said that he wanted to reveal the truth about S-21, whose existence Khmer Rouge leader Pol Pot had denied, claiming that it was a Vietnamese fabrication.[13]

Shortly thereafter, Duch was also interviewed by the representative of the UN high comissioner for human rights, Christophe Peschoux. During his trial, Duch claimed he had been deceived and "interrogated" by Peschoux, perhaps worried that his comments during this interview suggested he had been more actively involved in the day-to-day operations of S-21 than he would acknowledge during his trial.[14] He was soon detained and locked in jail, where he would remain for many years as negotiations to establish a tribunal dragged on.

As his replies to Judge Lavergne illustrated, Duch made a number of disquieting claims. A man accused of mass murder appeared to be portraying himself as a hero, almost a martyr, someone who embodied qualities that everyone would applaud: hard work, diligence, resolve, devotion to nation, trustworthiness, and the accomplishment of duties. This paradox often found expression in descriptions of Duch, including media stories at the start of his trial that ran with titles like "Man or Monster?"[15]

Given the salience of this question in popular discourse and as a key undercurrent of Duch's trial, I have chosen it as the title of this book. Beyond the apparent "either-or" choice the question demands, it has a second sense that asks to think critically about the framing and the opposition it suggests. More broadly, this question speaks to larger issues in the study of perpetrators, to arguments at the heart of this book, and, relatedly, to our humanity and everyday ways of thought. As I discuss in the epilogue, the question is provocative and haunting, offering two narrow alternatives to characterize a complex person—in a manner that parallels the reductive categorization and transformation of people into "enemies" that took place at S-21.

For many observers, both the heinousness of Duch's alleged crimes and their seeming incomprehensibility were heightened by the fact he was a teacher, a person immersed in learning and knowledge. This is particularly true in Cambodia, where teachers are highly esteemed. In fact, the Khmer term for "teacher," *krou*, is etymologically related to the root of the Sanskrit *guru*, sometimes connoting a learned "master." This is how Duch often described his *krou*, Son Sen, who he also described as his patron (*me-*), a term that means "mother" while also connoting the idea of a leader, supervisor, or master.[16]

Indeed, Duch's background as a star mathematics student and later teacher repeatedly emerged at the trial, suggesting that to more fully understand what happened at S-21 it was necessary to always bear in mind his background. Like Son Sen, who was Duch's teacher at the National Institute of Pedagogy in Phnom Penh, Duch joined the revolution as part of what he identified as a group of intellectuals. Indeed, many of the leaders of the Khmer Rouge, including Pol Pot, were intellectuals who had been teachers.[17] Duch's own teachers, including Chhay Kim Hor and Ke Kim Huot, helped inspire his interest in revolution and politics. Later, two of Duch's top interrogators at S-21 were former teachers, including one who also taught math.

His pedagogical practices had also seemed to suffuse his work. When describing interrogations, he depicted the back-and-forth exchanges with the prisoners almost as mind games. He said his goal was to critically ascertain the truth. He also seemed to handle the written prisoner confessions like student papers, annotating them extensively, sometimes in red. He explained, "I had been a teacher. I had used red ink to correct students, to assess students' points, and to provide my observations to students. So when I went to S-21, I maintained this idea of using red ink in order to differentiate from the black ink that prisoners wrote in."[18]

Perhaps most jarring of all was the fact that Duch decided to locate his prison on the grounds of a school. Classrooms were used for interrogation and prisoners cells. Prisoners were executed on site. Meanwhile, a short distance away, Duch converted a building into a lecture hall where he held political sessions and instructed his interrogators. This former teacher, who claimed to have been forced to become a torturer and executioner, chose to have these acts carried out in a place of learning.

I visited Tuol Sleng many times, looking for clues about this uncanny man and the acts of mass murder of which he was accused. Like me, tens of thousands of people—including tourists, diplomats, officials, researchers, survivors, and students—toured the compound. Some, moved by what they had seen, decided to graffiti Duch's photo, to articulate an understanding of him and the violent acts he had committed at the site. This book is my articulation of Duch, the extermination center he ran, and his trial, all of which are suffused with the uncanny. His story and trial say something about all of us, a link suggested by Duch's photo and these acts of defacement.

| | |

Now, as I gaze at Duch's defaced photo at Tuol Sleng, I glimpse a trace of this connection. At Tuol Sleng, many of the exhibitions, ranging from display cases to paintings, are bordered in black by a square wooden frame. Duch's photo, in contrast, is "frameless," lacking such a clearly visible border. Looking closely, I notice a background rectangular trim suggesting the photo is mounted from behind on a frame that is otherwise out of sight.

If a frame colloquially refers to a "structure surrounding a picture, door, etc.," it more abstractly suggests a "basic underlying or supporting structure of a system, concept, or text," including our ways of thinking about the world. To frame something is to place it in a surround, thereby sharpening the image, a notion that may be extended to the articulation or formulation of a "system, concept, or text."[19] As it "confers structure," a frame encloses that which is depicted within, as illustrated by the images framed in the Tuol Sleng exhibitions, including Duch's photograph. At the same time that the frame renders something visible, however, it also forms a border cordoning it off from, even as it nevertheless remains related to, that which lies beyond the border. When a frame foregrounds something, therefore, it simultaneously suggests a background pushed out of sight by the very existence of the frame and what is articulated within.

The faint trim surrounding Duch's defaced photograph therefore raises a series of questions that resonate with the issues of this book. How is Duch's photograph framed by the context of Tuol Sleng, the trial, and the understandings of passersby? How do these frames, as illustrated by the graffiti in his photograph, suggest an articulation of Duch as evil? To label him "evil," however, is to suggest a reductive explanation that naturalizes violence and directs our gaze away from the larger context of his actions.

Ultimately, much of the "evil"—and I place this term in quotes to note my hesitation in using it, due to the naturalization of violence it suggests, even as I recognize the severity of the violence the word conveys—that took place at Tuol Sleng was premised on the same, everyday ways we think, as we classify and assert a structuring order of the cosmos and the beings who inhabit it. In other words, the reductive frames that Duch and his associates brought to bear at S-21 parallel our everyday ways of thinking, including, as illustrated in Duch's photo, characterizing another person as "evil."

Indeed, this dynamic structured Duch's trial itself, as his subjectivity was framed in a variety of ways, including the rendering of a juridical status through the proceedings and the verdict. There is a large literature on "frames" and "framings";[20] I use the term in a restricted sense to refer to the ways our experience is organized so as to "point toward" a given articulation (and simultaneously to "point away" from that which is suggested as irrelevant even if related to what is highlighted): a frame is a surround that foregrounds an image and suggests an articulation of it.

The frame of a picture, like that of Duch's photo at Tuol Sleng, provides a way of visualizing this point. Indeed, we might think of the frame as being relatively "thick" or "thin," depending on the extent of structural pressures directing our gaze toward a more singular articulation of the foregrounded image. If the structural pressures may be social, cultural, economic, or religious, they may also be enmeshed with political power in contexts like S-21, Tuol Sleng, and even the ECCC.

These frames have both a public and a private life. On the one hand they are manifest in a variety of public institutions, such as cultural codes, collective memory, and social rituals. On the other the frames that are related to this public knowledge and related practices are learned by individuals, who internalize them, sometimes in highly variable ways, and then publicly reenact and retransmit them in their everyday practices. The degree of variation changes across time, place, and person. At times, given frames may be more widespread and somewhat less variable when sociopolitical pressures and institutional focus is brought to bear ("thick frames")—though such structural force is never complete and is met with a degree of resistance and variation, even if it often manifests in less public or "offstage" contexts.

| | | |

Tuol Sleng is suggestive about such "thick frames." At one time today's Tuol Sleng compound was part of S-21, where tremendous political pressures asserted the legitimacy of given DK frames for viewing the enemy. These DK "thick frames" are illustrated in the first half of this book. The Tuol Sleng Genocide Museum, in turn, reframes this past in a different way, one linked to a specific politics of memory in the PRK, the regime that replaced DK after the Khmer Rouge were deposed by over 100,000 Vietnamese troops following an off-and-on military conflict that began soon after the Khmer Rouge took power and escalated into outright war in 1978.

Startled by the sudden arrival of Vietnamese troops in Phnom Penh on January 7, 1979, Duch and his men fled the S-21 compound, leaving behind thousands of confessions, photographs, memoranda, execution lists, and other materials that came to serve as the archival basis for exhibitions at the museum at Tuol Sleng, which was established later in 1979, and more recently as a significant portion of the material evidence introduced in Duch's trial.[21] Even in 2011, the Tuol Sleng museum remained informed by this PRK politics of memory—in part because the leaders of the PRK continued to hold power and still linked their legitimacy to their overthrow of the DK regime. Indeed, this was part of the Cambodian government's motivation for agreeing to the establishment of the ECCC.

The Tuol Sleng Genocide Museum

As a guest tours Tuol Sleng, this PRK political frame is immediately evident. The genocide museum consists of four main buildings, lettered A–D, which

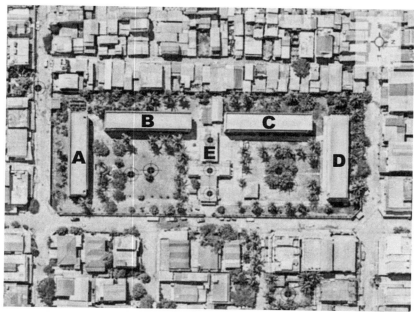

Aerial view of Tuol Sleng Genocide Museum. Photo courtesy of the Extraordinary Chambers in the Courts of Cambodia (ECCC).

are laid out in the shape of the two legs (A and D) and top (B and C) of a rectangle.

Each of the four buildings has three stories, though the primary exhibitions are located on the bottom floors. Guests usually proceed sequentially, starting with Building A. Duch's photo hangs in a second-floor room of Building D, in an exhibition area that is noted by signage but is not on this main tourist circuit. Buildings A–D enclose a fifth single-story building (Building E), which is not open to the public and now hosts Tuol Sleng administrative offices. During DK, some of the rooms in Building E were also used to process prisoners and included a room where, in 1978, several prisoner-artisans worked. At the time of Duch's trial two of these artist-prisoners, Vann Nath and Bou Meng, were still alive and testified, presenting their own perspective on life in the prison. Over the years they have also periodically returned to Tuol Sleng.

I see Vann Nath, whose health is poor, slowly walking along the path toward Building D, one arm knotted behind his back to clasp the other. Soon after the DK regime was toppled, Vann Nath returned to work at Tuol Sleng, painting portraits relating to S-21 that are among the most powerful exhibits at the museum. Now I watch him disappear into Building D, where his paintings still hang. He reemerges on the third-story balcony of Building D and gazes at the tourists below.

I think about how Vann Nath stands in a corridor along which young students walked in pre-DK times, then S-21 guards and prisoners, and now tourists. From a distance, the open entrances and windows of the classrooms appear blacked out and impenetrable, connected only by the exterior balcony passageways. The chipped grey-and-white concrete buildings are fronted by a courtyard of yellowed grass, palm trees, and clean yellow-and-red brick paths. Here and there, visitors sit on benches, chatting or in silence.

As usual, many of the Western tourists below are dressed in shorts and carry backpacks, water bottles, and cameras. I notice a child, perhaps five years old, get a smack from his father after dropping the family's guidebook. A group of Muslims, perhaps Cambodian Chams, a group directly targeted by the Khmer Rouge, are gathered in front of a sign near Building E, where people sometimes begin their visits before walking to Building A. In Khmer, English, and French, the sign describes how the prison was established by Pol Pot and his "clique":

INTRODUCTION TO THE TUOL SLENG GENOCIDE MUSEUM

In the past "TUOL SLENG" Museum was one of the secondary schools in the capital, called 'Tuol Svay Prey' high-School.

After the 17th, April 1975 Pol Pot clique had transformed it into a prison called 'S-21' (Security office 21) which was the biggest in Kampuchea Democratic. It was surrounded with the double wall of corrugated iron, surrounded by dense barbed wires.

The classrooms on the ground and the first floors were pierced and divided into individuals cells, whereas the ones on the second floor used for mass detention.

Several thousands of victims (peasants, workers, technicians, engineers, doctors, teachers, students, buddhist monks, minister, Pol Pot's Cadres, soldiers of all ranks, the Cambodian Diplomatic corps, foreigners, etc.) were imprisoned and exterminated with their wives and children.

There are a lot of evidences here proving the atrocities of Pol Pot clique: cells, instrument of torture, dossiers and documents, lists of prisoner's names, mugshots of victims, their clothes and their belonging's.

We founded the mass graves surrounding, and in particular, the most ones situated 15 Km in the south-west of Phnom Penh, in the village of Chhoeung Ek, District Dankgor, Kandal Province.[22]

Both the prose and the broken English translation highlight the fact that the museum has not been renovated in the manner of the contemporary Holocaust museums found in much of the Global North. Instead, the museum bears the imprint of the PRK regime, which, following the war, sought to enhance its domestic and international legitimacy by highlighting the atrocities of the "fascist" (and thus by implication not truly socialist) "Pol Pot clique." Tuol Sleng became "Cambodia's Auschwitz," a symbolic reminder of the suffering and death that occurred during DK. Indeed, Duch in some ways came to occupy a place similar to that of Adolf Eichmann, the Nazi bureaucrat who arranged the transport of the Jews to the death camps and came to serve as a symbol of Nazi atrocity.

Building A highlights this PRK atrocity frame. In front of it, the group of Chams stops before a memorial terrace with fourteen white, raised coffins. A sign, "The Victim's Grave," states: "The 14 victim's corpses have been found by, the army forces of the Front Union of Salvage National Kampuchea, through the building 'A' and carried its to bury in this place," noting that the corpses included "a woman victim. [T]hese victims were the last ones who had been killed by the agent of S.21." Again, the translation does not quite work, even if it strikingly connotes victimhood and atrocity.

This theme of atrocity is amplified in ground-floor rooms of Building A, where another sign explains that S-21 used them for torture and interrogation. Each cell contains a metal bed frame in the center of the floor and a few other items that were found at the site, such as iron shackles, ammunition cans that prisoners used to relieve themselves, and instruments of torture. For many years, visitors could see bloodstains on the white-and-tan checkerboard floor.

Black-and-white photos, marred by mildew, suggest what the cells looked like when Phnom Penh fell on January 7, 1979: dead prisoners, faces bashed in, lying on or next to metal bedframes to which they are shackled, in puddles of blood. The rooms have no electricity or light. The only illumination comes through the barred windows on either side of the cells, the iron rods casting shadows against the walls. The display contrasts strongly with the verdant vegetation that can be seen outside. A nearby sign on the lawn lists the security regulations at the prison, which threatened prisoners with admonitions such as "While getting lashes or electrification you must not cry at all." During the trial, Duch stated that this list, like some other Tuol Sleng exhibits, were fabrications.

Ahead, a Cambodian schoolteacher with a megaphone leads a class of teenage students, dressed in white-and-black uniforms, toward Building B. I think of Duch lecturing his students in prerevolutionary Cambodia, and then interrogators at S-21. The teacher leads the students past a series of photographic panels that, with the aid of terse captions, tell the story of DK.

The narrative starts with an attribution of guilt: a panel of "Kampuchea Democratic Leaders" that includes photographs of "Brother Number One" Pol Pot, the French-educated leader of the Khmer Rouge, and top associates of his, such as "Brother Number Two" Nuon Chea; Pol Pot's brother-in-law and later foreign minister Ieng Sary; and Duch's patron, defense minister Son Sen, another French-educated intellectual. In a group shot, several of the leaders stand in front of a limousine, dressed in black as they await the arrival of a foreign delegation.

The panel includes two photos of Duch that were discussed during his trial. In one, he stands before a microphone, a slight smile on his face, as he lectures at S-21. Photographer Nic Dunlop carried this photo with him in the Cambodian jungles, hoping he would one day find Duch. In the other photo, Duch stands, solemn, with his wife and the families of three of his S-21 comrades. The photos raise questions that were asked during his trial, such as how a person could raise children while running a center where entire families were killed and babies smashed against trees.

The time frame of the PRK narrative begins with "The Arrival of Kampuchea Democratic 1975," a panel that includes photos of children clapping for heavily armed and stern-faced Khmer Rouge who, after the long civil war (1968–1975), victoriously entered Phnom Penh on April 17, 1975. Little is said about the civil war itself, when Cambodia, caught up in the currents of the Vietnam War, was rent by violent upheaval.[23] Homes and communities were destroyed, and hundreds of thousands of Cambodians perished during this conflict, which was exacerbated by intensive US bombing. The Khmer Rouge movement gained momentum in early 1970, after Prince Sihanouk was deposed by General Lon Nol and joined the revolutionaries in a united front, calling on his peasant followers to fight Lon Nol's Khmer Republic. As the ranks and territorial control of the Khmer Rouge rapidly increased in the early 1970s, Duch was running M-13 prison and developing methods of interrogation he would bring to S-21.

Other photos in the first rooms of Building B highlight the massive socioeconomic changes the Khmer Rouge set in motion immediately after taking power. A large map of Cambodia with arrows depicts how the Khmer Rouge rusticated the urban population on taking power, warning the inhabitants that the cities might be bombed so they had to leave for a few days. They were not allowed to return. Meanwhile, the Khmer Rouge began to round up perceived

Pol Pot, also known as "Brother Number One," prime minister of DK and the leader of the Khmer Rouge. Photo courtesy of the Documentation Center of Cambodia (DC-Cam) / Sleuk Rith Institute (SRI) Archives.

DK leaders and members of the Standing Committee of the Central Committee of the Communist Party of Kampuchea (CPK). Facing forward, from left: Pol Pot (CPK secretary and prime minister of DK), Nuon Chea ("Brother Number Two"; deputy secretary of the CPK Central Committee), Ieng Sary (deputy prime minister for foreign affairs), Son Sen (deputy prime minister for defense), and Vorn Vet (deputy prime minister for economy). Photo courtesy of the DC-Cam / SRI Archives.

Duch speaking at S-21 meeting. Photo courtesy of the DC-Cam / SRI Archives.

Duch (third from left, not wearing a cap) and S-21 staff and families. Duch's deputy Mam Nai (Chan) is first from the left (the tallest man in the photo). Photo courtesy of the DC-Cam / SRI Archives.

Cambodians working on an irrigation project: "January 1, Dam, Chinith River, Kompong Thom Province, 1976." This photograph is thought to have been taken by a Chinese photographer during a visit by DK Minister of Social Affairs Ieng Thirith. Photo courtesy of the DC-Cam / SRI Archives.

enemies, including former Khmer Republic officials, civil servants, military, and police. Tens of thousands of people likely perished during this initial phase of forced evacuations and executions.

The evacuations and arrests were just part of a larger Khmer Rouge project of mass social engineering, which involved obliterating everything that smacked of capitalism, "privatism," and class oppression.[24] Broadly, the Khmer Rouge targeted Buddhism, the family, village structure, economic activity, and public education—key sociocultural institutions in prerevolutionary Cambodia. More specifically, they sought to eliminate corrupting influences from the past by banning nonrevolutionary art and styles, destroying and damaging temples, curtailing media and communication, ending traditional holidays and rituals, separating family members, homogenizing clothing, and eliminating private property, including photos and other mementos. A series of black-and-white photographs in a panel titled "Forced Work in Kampuchea Democratic" depict one dimension of the collectivization process, as large groups of Cambodians, with shovels, hoes, and baskets in hand, worked to build dams and canals, which were at the center of a DK attempt to create a pure, self-sufficient agrarian society.

In the new society, each person had to be reformed, like hot iron, in the flames of the revolution. The Khmer Rouge called this "tempering" people, literally "to harden by pounding" (*luat dam*). If hard labor in the countryside provided a key method of tempering, so did the Khmer Rouge practice of self-criticism.

A person's consciousness was to be reshaped during such processes until it aligned with the Party line, which colored the past in revolutionary red. Borrowing a Maoist metaphor that resonated with Buddhist conceptions of the wheel of life and two wheels of *dhamma*, the Khmer Rouge spoke of "the Wheel of History" (*kang bravattesas*) that, powered by natural laws that had been discerned by the "science" of Marxist–Leninism, moved Cambodia inexorably toward communism, crushing everything in its path.[25]

Achieving this goal required the creation of a country filled with a new sort of person who, after being "tempered" by hard peasant labor, criticism and self-criticism sessions, political meetings, and constant indoctrination, would develop a political consciousness that accorded with the Party line and history. Those showing signs of being unable to rid themselves of vestiges of the past—dwelling too much on one's former life, complaining, appearing unenthusiastic about the revolution, making mistakes, or missing work—were sometimes said to have "memory sickness" (*comngii satiaramma*).[26]

If the sickness was chronic or did not heal rapidly, it was "cured" by execution. Indeed, execution served as the most direct means of obliterating counterrevolutionary memories. After economic failures, suspected treason, and disagreements over the pace and direction of the revolution, the list of enemies widened, eventually expanding far into the ranks of the Khmer Rouge. At S-21, Duch and his cadre played a key role in this process, extracting confessions that implicated others.

|　　|　　|

At Tuol Sleng, I follow the students through the rest of the white-walled rooms of Building B. The victims, represented as depersonalized corpses in Building A, are given faces, though ones frozen in the frames of black-and-white mug shots. Most are set in checkerboard panels, a panorama of suffering and humanity. If a visitor looks closely, clues about the victims come into sight. Women crop their hair and wear black, revolutionary-style. No one smiles. The faces of some prisoners are swollen and bruised. Many have numbers affixed to their shirts. In a few cases, the pins are stuck into skin.

Some of the photos have been enlarged, including ones of foreigners, a little boy with an iron chain around his neck, dead prisoners lying on the ground. Other photos reveal blindfolded mothers and children, including an almost iconic photo of a mother holding a sleeping infant. A placard on her chest states her name, Chan Kim Srun, and date of arrest, March 14, 1978. She looks as if she is about to cry. There is almost no explanatory text. Lacking captions, the photographs are left to speak for themselves.

The students and I continue to Building C, which is masked by a cobweb of barbed wire. The bottom floor classrooms are filled with small, dark, brick-and-cement cells; the ones on the floor above are made of wood. A sign notes that the barbed wire was used to prevent "desperate victims" from jumping to their deaths, a point the guide also makes while telling the group about female prisoners who attempted suicide. A smaller sign with a bar crossing out a hand holding a pen instructs: "Do not write or paint on the photos and wall."

Through much of Building D, Vann Nath's paintings, based on what he witnessed, heard, or was told about by other prisoners,[27] provide a thread depicting the atrocities that took place at the prison. In one room, portraits of a baby being taken from a mother and a detainee being whipped are positioned next to a display case filled with instruments of torture: iron bars, rope and wire, shackles, a shovel, even an axe. In another painting, a forlorn and emaciated prisoner sits alone, shackled by the ankle, in a tiny brick-and-mortar cell. I look down at the floor and see the cement outline of the tiny cells depicted in the painting, the trace of a trace, classroom, cell, museum, art, memory. Vann Nath's paintings have dark backgrounds, against which are cast pallid, half-clad bodies in various states of pain and ruin. The visitors in the group are silent.

Torture is highlighted in the third room. Vann Nath's paintings depict some of the techniques. In one, a prisoner's head is immersed in water as an interrogator watches. Another shows a pair of interrogators at work. One takes a scorpion out of a cage while his partner uses pliers to pinch the nipple of a bare-chested woman strapped to a platform. Pointing to another painting depicting a cadre using pliers to extract a prisoner's fingernails above a small pool of blood, the guide says, "You can see how victim tortured like this. Very cruel."

The students continue on to the last room, the climactic ending. If the tour began with unrecognizable corpses (Building A), moved to photos of the victims' faces (Building B), and through the now empty cells in which prisoners were kept (Building C), to portraits and displays depicting the prisoners' bare

Chan Kim Srun (Sang) and
infant, S-21, 1978. Photo courtesy
of the DC-Cam / sri Archives.

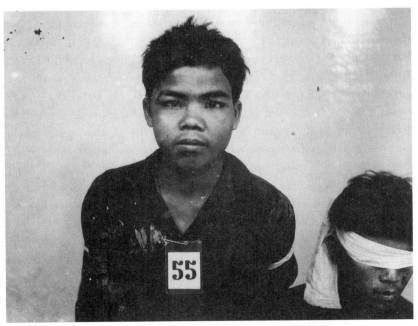

Unidentified prisoner, S-21. Photo courtesy of the DC-Cam / sri Archives.

life at S-21 in graphic detail (Building D), the visitors are last presented with tangible remains. For many years, the far wall included an enormous map of Cambodia made up of skulls, supposedly taken from every province in Cambodia after DK, with the country's rivers painted blood red. This sort of image has become iconic of Cambodia, which is often represented, like other sites of mass murder, by association with skulls or, in the case of Cambodia, by the phrase "the killing fields." After a controversy about the appropriateness of the map of skulls, the exhibit was taken down in 2002, though some of the skulls are still on display.

On the other walls of the room, Vann Nath's paintings illustrate how the prisoners were tied in a line and marched to a mass grave, where a Khmer Rouge executioner clubbed them on the back of the head and slit their throats. One painting, set at the edge of a pond overflowing with corpses, depicts a Khmer Rouge cadre bayoneting an infant who has been tossed into the air. A large photograph of a mass grave filled to the brim with the remains of the dead reinforces the message. Some visitors break down in tears.

| | | |

On exiting building D, I see a sign inviting guests to view temporary exhibitions on the second floor of Building D. The group of students ascends the stairway. I follow them into the second-floor corridor and the first room, where an exhibition, entitled "Vanished," is displayed. A series of panels tells the stories of the "new people": the urbanites and rural refugees the Khmer Rouge marked as less trustworthy, since they had not supported the Khmer Rouge during the civil war. A young Western tourist, a large water bottle dangling from her hand, gazes at a black-framed poster of a black-and-white family portrait photograph. In the next room, the group of students listens to their teacher as they view a second exhibition, "Stilled Lives," which broadens the story, telling about the experiences of the "base people" who had supported the Khmer Rouge during the war and often enjoyed higher status as a result, some serving as soldiers or cadre. The students continue on to a third floor classroom, where Vann Nath waits, as he now does on occasion, to tell them about his experiences at the prison.

The third room's exhibition, "Victims and Perpetrators? Testimony of Young Khmer Rouge Comrades," profiles several people who worked at S-21. I pause by photographs of a man I recognize, Him Huy, a former S-21 guard who oversaw the transport of detainees to an execution site.

Him Huy and S-21 guards. Him Huy (fourth from left) is in the center, with a gun slung behind his right shoulder. Photo courtesy of the DC-Cam / SRI Archives.

A black-and-white DK photograph of Him Huy wearing a Mao cap is juxtaposed with a 2002 color photo of him with his wife and infant in his rural village. His large hand is outstretched, gently holding the fingers of his child. Vann Nath told me that, at S-21, Huy was "savage" and had killed many people. "I didn't want to work there," Huy states in an accompanying panel. "I was ordered to do this; if I had refused, they would have killed me."

Duch made the same claim.

People's Republic of Kampuchea (PRK) Atrocity Frame

Duch's photo hangs in the fourth room. I gaze at it, consider how his photograph is framed within the museum, which was created soon after DK by the new PRK. This backdrop inflects not just Duch's defaced photograph but also his trial and the ECCC.

In advance of their invasion of Cambodia, the Vietnamese pieced together a small, pro-Vietnamese group of Cambodian communist leaders, made up of longtime Cambodian revolutionaries who had been living in Vietnam for years and Khmer Rouge defectors who had fled the DK purges, to create the Kampuchean United Front for National Salvation. This group, which included Hun Sen, the then young Khmer Rouge defector who has effectively ruled Cambodia since becoming prime minister in 1985, formed the nucleus of the PRK, which next came to power.

Almost immediately the new regime was beset by problems of legitimacy. The PRK government, initially headed by Heng Samrin, was closely linked to Vietnam, which had supplied roughly 150,000 troops for the invasion and wielded obvious influence over the government, including the appointment of its top leaders. While initially welcoming Vietnam's help in overthrowing the Khmer Rouge, many Cambodians remained suspicious of a country that was often viewed as a historical enemy coveting Cambodian land.

Some Cambodians also viewed the PRK regime with suspicion both because, like DK, it was socialist and because, like Heng Samrin and Hun Sen, a number of high-ranking officials were former Khmer Rouge.[28] Finally, the PRK government was increasingly threatened by new resistance groups and a resurgent Khmer Rouge army that, after arriving in tatters at the Thai border, was propped up by foreign powers.

Memory mixed with politics as the PRK regime set out to articulate a narrative of the recent past that would buttress their legitimacy both domestically and abroad.[29] Genocidal atrocity stood at the center of this story. The new PRK political narrative centered around the theme of a magnificent revolution subverted by a small group of evildoers, led by the "Pol Pot" or "Pol Pot–Ieng Sary–Khieu Samphan clique."[30] Inspired by a deviant Maoist strain of socialism, the narrative went, this clique had misled or coerced lower-ranking cadre into unwitting participation in a misdirected campaign of genocide.

As a result, most former Khmer Rouge cadre, including by implication many PRK officials, were said to be not ultimately responsible for the DK violence and suffering. Socialist discourses remained central to this narrative, as the PRK regime could still speak of how the revolutionary movement had "won the glorious victory of 17 April 1975, totally liberating our country" from "the yoke of colonialism, imperialism, and feudalism."[31] With a growing Khmer Rouge insurgency on the border, this PRK role as liberator had resonance for many Cambodians.

Besides civil war, the PRK regime faced other domestic problems, ranging from an economy and infrastructure in shambles to potential famine.[32] Entire government bureaucracies, including the health care and educational systems, had to be completely rebuilt. Staffing was extremely difficult since the Khmer Rouge had targeted civil servants, intellectuals, educators, and professionals. Only a handful of legal personnel had survived, a legacy that has contributed to Cambodia's contemporary judicial problems.

For the next decade, Cambodia remained entangled in the web of the Cold War. Linked through Vietnam to the Soviet bloc, the PRK regime found itself isolated by a strange coalition of Thailand and its anticommunist Southeast Asian neighbors, China, and the United States and other Western democracies. Revitalized by covert Thai-US-China support, the Khmer Rouge deftly played on Cold War fears. Former DK foreign affairs minister Ieng Sary soon became their top spokesperson. In a June 1979 interview he warned: "If Cambodia became a Vietnamese satellite it would have direct repercussions on Thailand." Ieng Sary also denied that the Khmer Rouge had carried out a genocide, stating that "in all of Cambodia perhaps some thousands" had been killed. Instead, it was Vietnam that was carrying out "a genocide of our race and nation."[33]

The United States and other Western powers did little to refute such denials, with diplomats often avoiding the use of the term "genocide" when referring to the Khmer Rouge.[34] Cambodia's seat at the UN was even awarded to the Khmer Rouge, creating a situation in which the DK delegation was given international legitimacy while the PRK regime became diplomatically isolated and was prevented from receiving needed international aid.

In this context, the Tuol Sleng Genocide Museum was established. Just days after Duch and his men fled, Vietnamese soldiers noticed a bad smell coming from the compound and were shocked to discover dead bodies and the trove of documentation that had been left behind. Under the guidance of Vietnamese experts, the Tuol Sleng Genocide Museum was quickly created to provide domestic and international audiences with evidence of the atrocities of the "Pol Pot clique." By mid-1979, groups of officials and journalists were being taken to the site, which soon opened to receive friendly foreign delegations and the Cambodian public.

The PRK regime asserted this atrocity narrative in a variety of domains, ranging from the construction of memorials to the creation of highly politicized schoolbooks, some of which taught young students to learn to read and write using short vignettes demonstrating the atrocities of the "Pol Pot clique." One lesson focused specifically on S-21. On the Tuol Sleng wall where Duch's photograph hangs, other photographs depict related PRK commemorative initiatives. Several show scenes from the August 1979 People's Revolutionary Tribunal, at which the PRK regime convicted Pol Pot and Ieng Sary in absentia of genocide. Another photo shows a woman with her fist pressed against her forehead as she speaks into a large microphone at a PRK genocide remembrance event, likely the annual "Day to Remain Tied in Anger" against the "Pol Pot clique." The woman sobs. Rows of skulls are displayed behind her. The eye sockets, dark and empty, stare.

| | | |

On the ledge of the single barred window in the room, I see a book with a red cover that invites visitors to "please comment." People from all over the world have written comments about their impressions of the museum, most of which are dated and signed. Many of the entries by Cambodians echo the PRK atrocity narrative, referring to the "Pol Pot regime/clique," describing its actions as "savage" or "cruel" (*khokhov*), and noting the person's anger and anguish (*chheu chap*).[35] I glance back at the Duch photo, notice that someone has written "despicable cruel one" in Khmer on Duch's white shirt just below the English "evil." From the vantage of this PRK atrocity frame, only a savage monster could have run a place where such terrible acts took place.

Human Rights Frame

Reading through the lined comment book, I find entries that range from a word or two to half a page or more. They are written in many languages, though most are in English and Khmer. If the English-language commentaries invoke atrocity, they often do so from a human rights frame that points toward an interpretation of them as mass human rights violations or crimes against humanity. Many of the comments reference the post-Holocaust refrains "Never forget" and "Never again." These invocations are often linked to humanitarian sentiments, not just recognizing the suffering of the victims but asserting an empathetic connection to them and moral desire to act.[36] The museum artifacts provide the point of connection that links the visitor to both victim and perpetrator. A man from the UK wrote: "I have never been so disturbed to see such inhuman suffering by the people. So barbaric. Let us be sure this never happens again."[37]

This refrain of "Never again" also appears in another theme found in the remarks of visitors to Tuol Sleng: global citizenship. While this term is fairly elastic, it connotes membership in the global community, with an accompanying worldly perspective and commitment to a set of transnational rights, duties, and obligations. These include a commitment to human rights and global concerns, ranging from international law to environmental issues and social justice. While humanitarian sentiments are often associated with it, global citizenship suggests a more cerebral approach, one involving understanding (versus the driving compassion of humanitarianism) and appropriate action, including the imperative of prevention.

Relatedly, many of the commentaries mention learning "lessons" from Tuol Sleng, which a number describe as an "eye-opening experience." From this perspective, Tuol Sleng serves a pedagogical role. Thus a woman from Oregon wrote: "Stunning in its absolute cruelty and efficiency . . . / I can only hope we (as a global community) take the lessons from this place and prevent such evil from consuming another innocent life."[38] Others discourse about geopolitics, human rights violations, perpetrator motivation, the obligations of the global citizen, and the possibility for justice and healing.

After the start of the Duch case, justice became a more frequent theme in the commentaries at Tuol Sleng. One of the longer entries in the comment book reads: "A fair & just trial with all evidence presented free of bias or emotion will give Cambodians & the world the closure required. A court trial is not about revenge, it is about truth, & from that truth according justice." On the side of the page, a person has written: "This is exactly my sentiment."[39] The focus on the end point of justice illustrates the future orientation of many of the commentaries, which move from the devastation of the past to a better future. In many cases, the Cambodian case is depicted as a particular example of the universal category of crimes against humanity, a point emphasized by noting the link to other cases of mass human rights violations.

Such invocations of "justice" dovetail with a set of discourses and practices at the Tribunal itself, which might be called the "transitional justice imaginary."[40] In this articulation, Duch's trial represents a manifestation of a larger process of humanitarian uplift by which authoritarian conflict-ridden states are transformed into their opposite, a progressive neoliberal democratic order characterized by human rights and the rule of law.

During the February 2009 initial hearing, Duch's lawyer, François Roux, explicitly made this connection, asserting that "seeking transitional justice" is at "the very core of what we're about here [in the court]."[41] To highlight his point, Roux quoted transitional justice scholar Pierre Hazan's comment that transitional justice seeks to rebuild societies torn asunder, a process in which people needed to "perceive the humanity of the other" to succeed. According to Hazen, Roux added, transitional justice was characterized by "the one key formula" of "truth, justice, forgiveness [and] reconciliation."[42]

If Hazen's point about "seeing the face of the other" played a role in Roux's defense strategy for Duch, transitional justice was the motor of the transformation of a failed past into a successful future. This assumption was frequently implicit in many remarks made during Duch's trial, as were the related humanitarian and human rights frames that also formed a strong current in the Tuol Sleng comment books.

| | | |

Now I return to the defaced photograph of Duch, reconsider the image, and look for more clues. Underneath Duch's name, a caption says the photo is from the "Documentation Center of Cambodia Archives." On an adjacent descriptive panel, which is large and surrounded by a black frame, is a title in yellow lettering: "JUSTICE AND RESPONSIBILITY." The text begins with a question: "Why has it taken over thirty years to bring the former leaders of the Khmer Rouge to justice?" While the panel includes photos from the PRK regime, it focuses on the path to justice, with the implicit framing of the Khmer Rouge atrocities as a human rights violation. It speaks of the "Khmer Rouge," as opposed to the PRK's focus on the "Pol Pot clique."

Part of the reason, the panel explains, is geopolitics. "Because the [PRK] was supported by Vietnam, an unlikely scenario developed in which both China (the main backer of the Khmer Rouge), Thailand (fearful of the Vietnamese troops massed near its border), and the United States (embroiled in the Cold War and still stung by its defeat in Vietnam) and its allies" sought to isolate the PRK regime and rearm the Khmer Rouge.

The PRK took steps to hold the Khmer Rouge accountable, the text notes, by gathering evidence and holding the People's Revolutionary Tribunal. However, in contrast to the PRK atrocity narrative, this human rights narrative notes that these initiatives "failed to meet international standards of justice," even as the panel adds that, during the 1980s, the PRK regime "called for an international tribunal, a call that went unheeded as the international community glossed over the 'unfortunate events of the past' in supporting the Khmer Rouge."

A peace settlement led to the withdrawal of Vietnamese troops from Cambodia in 1989 and a "1993 UN-sponsored election in Cambodia, which the Khmer Rouge ended up boycotting in favor of continued armed struggle." Meanwhile, "the United States and other members of the international community began to call for a tribunal. Due to a successful defection campaign, the Royal Government of Cambodia demurred in favor of reconciliation."

During the late 1990s, the situation changed when "a large number of high-ranking Khmer Rouge, including Ieng Sary, Khieu Samphan, Ke Pauk, and Nuon Chea, were allowed to defect to the government. Two others, the general Ta Mok and Duch, the former head of S-21, were captured and placed under arrest" in 1999.

In 2003, the panel continues, "the Cambodian government and the UN finally signed an agreement to establish the Extraordinary Chambers in the Courts of Cambodia (ECCC), which will be a 'mixed tribunal' comprising Cambodian and international legal personnel." Ultimately, due to political realities, "the ECCC has been given limited temporal and personal jurisdiction: it will only try crimes committed during DK and prosecute those Khmer Rouge who were 'senior leaders' and criminally 'most responsible.' Because of further delays, the ECCC only began operation in July 2006."

The photographs on display "depict some of the key moments in this long road to justice: the 1979 PRK tribunal, the signing of the 2003 agreement establishing the ECCC, and the site of the ECCC itself. Other pictures, such as the pictures of Khmer Rouge leaders and mid-ranking officials 'then and now,' raise important questions about justice and responsibility."

The panel concludes with a series of rhetorical questions: "Who, Cambodians are asking, should be held accountable for the violence that took place during DK? Why have the senior leaders of the Khmer Rouge been allowed to live freely for so long? And, will they, like Pol Pot (who died in April 1998) and Ta Mok (July 2006), die before they face justice or will they be tried for genocide and crimes against humanity?"

If this human rights frame foregrounds Duch in a legalistic manner, it may also suggest, like the PRK atrocity frame, an articulation of him as a monster since, by implication, only someone who was inhuman could commit crimes against humanity. Some Tuol Sleng visitors suggest the incomprehensibility of the atrocities they have seen through terse remarks such as "No words," "Why?" "Indescribable," "Words fail me," or "Speechless."

Other visitors seek to provide an answer to the "why" of atrocity by describing it in terms of monstrosity, as illustrated by the English-language commentaries that use terms like "madness," "inhumanity," "barbarities," "cruelty," "cretins," "horrors," and "evil." A woman from the Netherlands writes: "People who can do this to other people are no more than monsters!"[43] Still other commentaries tentatively grapple with "human nature" or the "capacity" for evil.

Indeed, this language and imagery of monstrosity is frequently used to describe genocidal perpetrators in films, the media, and the popular imagination, providing a seeming answer to the seeming paradox of perpetration: how can a human commit inhuman acts? Sometimes savagery is depicted iconically, epitomized by figures like the swastika-adorned Nazi or janjaweed "devils on horseback" and images of skulls, mass graves, gas chambers, and victims. Part of the power of the language and imagery of savagery comes from the fact that atrocity seems to contrast strongly with the normalcy of our lives.

Yet the self-evidentiary association of perpetrators with savagery helps to naturalize genocidal violence and direct explanation in two prominent directions. On the one hand the "savage" monster represents a lower, more animal-like state of development, one linked to the "barbaric" and "primitive" as the nadir of a scale that rises toward "civilization." As such, it appears "natural" that monsters will commit horrific and at times seemingly "irrational" acts without the deep moral concern of "civilized" people. In this explanation, violence becomes biologized as something that is "in the nature" of savage, monstrous beings. On the other hand the imagery of excessive cruelty may imply psychological deviance. In this framing, horrible acts of cruelty are perpetrated by sadistic monsters who derive an often sexualized gratification by inflicting pain and harm on others. Here, genocide and mass violence are naturalized as psychological dysfunction. These sorts of explanations circulated during Duch's trial, suggesting he was a monster.

Besides finding traction in folk beliefs about "nature," such explanations are, paradoxically, also comforting. For they lead us to answer the question "How could *they* do it?" in a manner affirming that *we* are not like that. Genocide is something that only other sorts of beings (savage and sociopathic monsters) would do. The word "evil" graffitied onto Duch's photo likely emerged from this sort of "shallow articulation" of the perpetrator as monster.

The monster trope is one that has appeared in a variety of contexts involving genocide and mass murder, perhaps most famously in controversies surrounding the Nazi bureaucrat Adolf Eichmann. He was captured in Argentina by Israeli operatives and placed on trial in Jerusalem in 1961. Many observers regarded him as a maniacal anti-Semite, a monster responsible for mass murder. Little explanation was needed. A similar sentiment was evident at the start of Duch's trial. Like those who scribbled on Duch's photo at Tuol Sleng, some people already viewed him as evil and took for granted that he had done horrible things, apparently with glee. In articles, essays, and casual conversations, Duch was often described in terms similar to those that would be inscribed on his photo at Tuol Sleng, as illustrated by headlines such as "Memories of Evil Stir as Duch Trial Open," "Monster of the Killing Fields," and "At last, Justice for Monsters."[44]

Hannah Arendt's groundbreaking work on the Eichmann trial argued that this sort of reductive explanation misdirects us away from other critical factors.[45] As opposed to being an anti-Semitic monster, Arendt controversially argued, Eichmann's great failing was his thoughtlessness, a failure to think that she referred to as "the banality of evil." If others have argued convincingly that Eichmann was in fact highly anti-Semitic and took the initiative (as opposed to being a passive pawn), Arendt nevertheless drew attention to a dimension of mass violence that had been overlooked.

In this book, I inflect Arendt's argument differently. The "banality of evil," I suggest, is not just a failure to think in exceptional circumstances but part of our everyday thinking. In particular, the everyday ways we simplify and categorize the world in order to navigate complexity—particularly renderings of us and them, self and other—directly parallels a key dynamic in the genocidal process.[46] Along these lines, I show how there were moral economies in circulation at the ECCC that framed Duch in different ways—just as the PRK atrocity and human rights frames suggested articulations of Duch's photo at Tuol Sleng.

This book considers how Duch was "graffitied" by participants and observers at his trial while also considering the ways the Khmer Rouge framed their victims at S-21. All of us, in a sense, are "graffiti artists." The frames and understandings we use to inscribe meaning on the world enable us to navigate our social worlds. We use them every day. They mediate our lived experience—including justice and genocide. They also mediate this book.

Our framings and understandings demand reflection, since they otherwise pass as "natural," as the graffiti on Duch's image revealed. In this sense, the "failure to think" is a constant challenge, an inevitable part of the everyday ways we think about, frame, and articulate the world. As we think, then, there is a need to critically reflect about how we are framing, including framings suggesting interpretations of self and other. Given the Judeo-Christian and often naturalized uses of the word "evil," perhaps we should consider not just the "banality of evil" but also the way the acts we call "evil" are intimately bound up with the "banality of everyday thought," our everyday ways of framing and categorizing the world—and all that, in so doing, we erase.

| | |

As I stand in Building D, looking at the graffiti on Duch's defaced photo, I wonder who assembled this exhibition. I glance back at the descriptive panel and reread it. This time I notice a single credit line at the bottom of the page, in a tiny, barely legible font. The credit reads: "Text by Dr. Alexander Hinton in *Night of the Khmer Rouge: Genocide and Justice in Cambodia* (2007)."

The Redactic

Like the other exhibitions on the second floor of Building D, the one with Duch's photo was sponsored by the Documentation Center of Cambodia (DC-Cam), a local NGO that worked for many years gathering documentation to support the trial of former Khmer Rouge leaders. DC-Cam transferred almost a million pages of documentation to the court, much of which served as evidence in Duch's trial. They also used this material to create exhibitions.

In 2000, I first visited DC-Cam while conducting research for a book. Youk Chhang, the director of DC-Cam, later invited me to serve as one of their academic advisors. We have since collaborated in different ways, including an original 2007 exhibition and related catalogue titled *Night of the Khmer Rouge: Genocide and Justice in Cambodia.*[47] Later DC-Cam informed me that they would be putting part of the exhibition on display in Cambodia. But I heard nothing further about the exhibition and had completely forgotten about the connection until the day I read the credit line of the panel, adapted from text I had written for the 2007 exhibition.

Suddenly seeing my name listed as the author of the text was thus an unsettling experience at an uncanny locale. The unexpected presence of my name is revealing in a number of respects, suggesting my own positioning in this project as well as a thread running throughout this book.

While the uncanny has been defined in different ways, it signifies a juxtaposition of the familiar and strange that is unsettling and even eerie. In his famous essay "The Uncanny," Sigmund Freud discusses the German term for uncanny, *unheimlich*. *Unheimlich* is the antonym of *heimlich*, which refers to that which belongs "to the house, not strange, familiar," while connoting something safely contained or even concealed.[48] For Freud, then, the uncanny involves a disruption of the familiar, as something normally hidden from (public/open) view is suddenly glimpsed, leading to a sense of unease. In the case of the Tuol Sleng exhibition with Duch's photograph, I felt the uncanny as I suddenly saw my name where it didn't belong, in an exhibition at Tuol Sleng that I was examining. Text that belonged in a given time and place suddenly burst forth in a radically different context; my words were familiar but strange.

Tuol Sleng is an uncanny place. Indeed, part of the power of the site comes from the unease it evokes. Visitors are confronted with immense suffering, imprisonment, torture, and death, experiences normally kept out of sight. If the uncanny is obliquely suggested by comments that there are "no words" to describe what has been seen, it is also more directly referenced by visitors who write things like "goosebumps," "R.I.P.," "horrific," "shocking," "upsetting," "chilling," "disturbing," and "evil."[49] Visitors sometimes remark on the stares of the victims in the photographs, which are themselves disturbing, providing a moment of seeming contact with people shortly before death, a moment usually unseen and repressed. And then there are the hauntings, the spirits said to inhabit the site. The uncanny also emerged repeatedly during Duch's trial—in sudden disjunctures, invocations of the spirits of the dead, the politics of the court, and Duch's comments and behavior.

The uncanny's suggestion of excess, overflow, and eruption leads to another notion that informs my analysis: the redactic. I juxtapose it to the didactic and to legalism (emphasizing the juridical, the rule of law, accountability, and deterrence), which are often asserted as two key objectives of tribunals.[50] What legalism and the didactic less frequently attend to is that which is elided by the histories, juridical process, and other articulations that mediate our understanding of the world.

Post-9/11, many people are familiar with redaction, or the erasure—often by blacking out—of names, words, or phrases in official documents when sensitive or classified information is involved. But the word "redact" has a broader range of referents. Etymologically, "redact" is derived from the Latin stem *redigere*, meaning "to drive or send back, return, to bring back, restore, to convert, reduce, to bring (into a condition), to bring (under a category), to bring into line."[51] Most simply, I use "the redactic" to refer to the process of "editing out." The term's etymology highlights that, more abstractly, the redactic connotes articulation (disparate parts brought together to create a whole), reduction (involving a diminishment), and conversion/calibration (something brought into accordance with a category).

All of these senses of the redactic relate to framing. A frame involves conversion and calibration since it is premised on a conceptual order. Framing also involves reduction, since, like the borders of a photograph, it foregrounds a certain image that is blocked off from a larger contextual background. The image highlighted by the frame points toward an articulation, a formation of meaning calibrated to accord with the operative frame while editing out what is deemed unnecessary, extraneous, or discordant.

An articulation of "Duch the monster," then, may emerge from both the PRK atrocity frame as well as the human rights frame. But such articulations, which are part of the banality of everyday thought, inevitably fall short, asserting an edited and truncated version of a more complex reality. This process, part of our everyday thinking, is also a critical aspect of the genocidal process as the members of the victim group, in a situation of socioeconomic upheaval and structural transformation, are thickly framed and categorized in a manner leading to a shallow articulation that reduces their complex histories to characteristics of a given type.

These articulations are haunted by the uncanny. The redactic suggests an act of force as excess meaning is "driven back" in the very attempt at formulation. As we inscribe meaning, we also redact, editing out a more complex reality that inevitably exceeds the confines of the articulation we produce. We are all redactors, since, through the act of constructing meaning, our articulations necessarily involve editing, a reduction and attempted conversion that always leaves something out, repressed excesses that may return—a haunting that is often uncanny, strange yet familiar, unsettling as it disrupts the taken-for-granted.

Thus Duch, as a complex human being, could never be fully characterized as a "monster." From the start of his trial, he seemed professorial and remorseful, qualities that did not accord with the assumed savagery and sociopathic behavior of a monster. Some people presumed he had to be lying. Nevertheless, for those who simply viewed him as a monster, Duch's actions were uncanny, as "Duch the monster" clashed with a familiar yet strange articulation of "Duch the man." The title of this book foregrounds this point with the question "Man or Monster?"—which is meant to provoke thought about the often oversimplified ways we think about people like Duch.

Another way to think of the redactic is to consider released classified documents about post-9/11 US interrogation and detention practices. In many of these documents, an enormous amount of text is blacked out. The redacted document provided an articulation of meaning, though one that was clearly diminished and left out key information, a haunting presence lurking in the dark, driven back behind the blackout yet still there, an excess of meaning waiting to overflow. The back-mounted frame of Duch's defaced photograph provides another way to visualize the redactic, as it is pressed over a space that can't be seen, suggested only by a trace, the edges of the frame.

The trace, a presence obscured by articulation, is labile, haunting, and a point of pressure. This pressure may grow, welling up like a plant pod readying to release its seeds or a medical suture under stress, and at times suddenly burst open—what is known in botany and medicine as dehiscence, a word etymologically suggests a sudden eruption, gaping, or yawning.[52]

If we are to deepen our understanding of a given phenomenon, we must become attuned to such traces and the uncanny, which hint at more complex realities that have been elided. In situations of potential or ongoing violence, of which DK is an extreme, such critical thinking entails consideration of the thick frames and shallow articulations of the other. In the court, in turn, juridical articulation may mask complex political and historical realities and, inflected by the thick frames of law, produce a shallow articulation of criminality. Likewise, in our daily life, we constantly use frames suggesting naturalized articulations of self and other that need to be destabilized and unpacked.

These dynamics are bound up with the banality of everyday thought, for reductions of the other that are taken to the extreme in genocide are present in our everyday lives. Arendt astutely noted the connection of the banality of evil to thoughtlessness. By foregrounding "evil," however, her phrasing connotes the exceptional. I suggest that such "thoughtlessness" might be supplemented by the notion of "the banality of everyday thought"—even if in both formulations (one focusing on the exceptional, the other on the everyday) what is called for is critical thinking, what might be called "reflexive articulation" and, as I discuss at the end of the book, "affacement."

In a sense, then, this book is an "anthropology of the redactic" that asks us to pay greater attention to that which is redacted by the frames and articulations that mediate our everyday lives. The uncanny remains a guidepost pointing to framing, articulation, calibration, effacement, and the redactic. A haunting presence, the uncanny is manifest in moments, large and small, when the banality of everyday thought is suddenly unsettled by what is just out of sight— such as my reading the single credit line with my name at the bottom of the "Justice and Responsibility" exhibition panel that suddenly placed me directly into the context of the frames mediating Tuol Sleng, the graffiti on the Duch photo, and the topic and site I was studying—places where the researcher is not supposed to appear or belong.

| | | |

Yet this book is also written differently from many ethnographies. Instead of foregrounding straightforward exposition and exegesis, I have sought to write an ethnodrama, an ethnography that includes elements of dramatic structure and uses language and narrative structure to raise questions and evoke ambiguities that are often glossed over in expository writing. After writing the book, I discovered that there is a small anthropological literature on ethnodrama that links it to anthropological concerns with representation, performance, and ethnographic narrative style. This literature, however, has largely focused on ethnotheater, or performative ethnography, which often is scripted and staged.[53]

In keeping with this orientation, this book has a dramatic structure that includes a protagonist (Duch), an agonist (his victims), key roles and characters (defense, prosecution, judge), a stage (the courtroom where the trial took place), and dramatic action (events unfolding before an audience). Indeed, each morning the start of the proceedings was marked by the drawing of curtains, and the proceedings are sometimes referred to as "the show." This book also includes monologues, dialogues, a plot-like structure, scene, suspense, and a denouement.

Moreover, even if this book includes exegesis, including this very discussion of ethnodrama, it draws on literary techniques, including poetry, to evoke and convey ambiguity, uncertainty, disruption, contradiction, and the redactic. I also place myself directly into the narrative, particularly in this opening and in the concluding chapters. In these respects, the book is linked to a tradition of ethnographic writing that seeks to experiment, blur genres, convey polyphony versus a singular voice of ethnographic authority, and encourage critique and reflexivity[54]—including the idea that all ethnography, like this book, is redactic, a point highlighting the need for us to constantly consider the banality of everyday thought and what is being edited out.

In accordance with its ethnodramatic structure, the book proceeds chronologically, moving from the start to the conclusion of Duch's trial, while occasionally going outside the "inner" courtroom to explore the related moral economies circulating in other places, including the Tuol Sleng Genocide Museum. Chapter 1 sets the stage with the dramatic opening of Duch's trial. The remainder of part I follows the action of the trial as it explored the origins and functioning of S-21. Along the way, Duch, witnesses, former S-21 cadre, and survivors of S-21 provided riveting testimony and commentary. Part II discusses the experiences of the victims and different articulations of Duch that circulated during his trial, especially juridical articulations, during the closing arguments and verdict.[55] I conclude by returning to where the book began: the Tuol Sleng Genocide Museum, the defaced photograph of Duch, and the notion of the redactic. In keeping with the theme of return, the conclusion is an ending that is followed by another iteration, an epilogue that backlights the book.

By structuring the book in this manner and using literary techniques and dialogue, I seek to give readers a sense of the trial and the people involved, as well as to highlight tensions difficult to convey in traditional scholarly writing. This structure also reflects my experience of the Duch trial, which often seemed like a performance, and resonates with the importance of the oral tradition in Cambodia, where the Khmer Rouge past is often recollected through narrative and story. This style is also more conducive to conveying a sense of the redactic and the uncanny, as illustrated by three poems, including an erasure poem redacted in black.

I conclude with a last unsettling. This chapter has been written from the vantage of an English-speaker. The word "evil" written on Duch's shirt served as an entry point to explore the frames and articulations circulating at Tuol Sleng and the broader concerns of this book. Most of the graffiti, however, is in Khmer, the Cambodian language. What do these messages say? The meaning is redacted to those who speak only English, remaining as an uncanny presence on the photo.

Here again we find a juxtaposition of the familiar and strange, an ethnographic encounter suggesting an excess, an articulation of moral understandings that falls short, leaving a surplus of meaning ready to unexpectedly burst forth. Invoking a Western adage, several visitors to Tuol Sleng commented on the photographs there: "A picture says a thousand words." There may be truth to this saying, but as the scribbles on Duch's photo illustrate, what is seen depends on the language a person speaks, on the frames mediating that person's articulations, and on what that person edits out.

I. Confession

Comrade Duch's Abecedarian

Apology.

Black ink.

Confession. Conversion. Christianity.

Duch. Eldest son. Star student. Loner. Math teacher. Meticulous. Khmer Rouge Revolutionary. Patriot. Party Member. Dutiful. Prison commandant. Brute. Eyes and ears of the Party. Obedient. Gave orders. Stoic. Fanatic. Torturer. Father. Cog in the machine. Believer. Mass murderer. Prisoner imprisoned. The Accused. Defendant. Criminal. Convict.

Enemies. Attacking from without. Burrowing from within.

First, extract their information. Next, assemble many points for pressuring them so they cannot move. 3. Propagandize and pressure them politically. 4. Pressure and interrogate by cursing. 5. Torture. 6. Examine and analyze the responses for further interrogation. 7. Examine and analyze the responses to make the document. 8. Guard them closely, prevent them from dying. Don't let them hear one another. 9. Maintain Secrecy.

Ghosts. Suspended between lives. Watching. Awaiting justice. Karma. An offering to the dead. Merit. Rebirth.

Cannot hesitate and have ideological doubts that hinder our task, even if that person is our brother or sister or someone whom we trusted.

Interrogation note to Duch: The Situation of Interrogating Ke Kim Huot alias Sot. On the morning of July 21, 1977, we pounded him another round. Electrical wire and feces ["shit"]. This time he cursed those who hit him very much, [and said] Go ahead and beat me to death. Had him eat two or three spoonfuls of feces ["shit"]. . . . by nightfall, we went at him again with electric wires, this time pretty seriously. He became delirious. He was all right. Later he confessed a bit as reported above. . . . Sot said he had nothing to answer to send to Angkar, and since he did not, he did not know what to say, that now he just waits for death, and he can close his eyes and die easily because he has sacrificed and was loyal to the party. . . . My operative line is to continue torture with mastery, because the enemy is breaking emotionally and is at a dead end. Along with this, I ask for opinion and guidance from Angkar in carrying out this task.

Joined the revolution to liberate the country.

Ke Kim Huot alias Sot. Duch's teacher, mentor, comrade, prisoner. Deum Sareaun. Ke Kim Huot's wife. Also a teacher. Interrogated. Tortured. Sexually abused.

The Line. Party line determining politics, ideology, organization, arrest, imprisonment, interrogation, torture, execution. "The crimes came from the Party line of the Communist Party of Kampuchea." Anyone considered an enemy was to be smashed.

Man or Monster? Mathematical calculation. "Make them think of their wives and children." Mastery.

Numbers. The S-21 Statistics list. 90 percent of the people are strong and firmly believe in the Party, the collective, and defend the party. 10 percent are weak. 1 percent very weak. 1 percent are enemies. Therefore . . . screen out the enemies no matter what.

The Objective of torturing is to get their answers. It is not done for fun. Therefore we must make them feel pain so that they will respond quickly. Another objective is to make them afraid. It is not done by individual anger to let off steam. Therefore, beat them to make them scared, but absolutely not to let them die. When torturing, it is imperative to check their health in advance and to inspect the whip. Do not get greedy and want to be quick; that leads to death and loss of a document.

Psychological functioning: obsessive, low self-esteem, depression, traumatic organization, disempathy, splitting, willing participant, need for mentors and strong belief, avoidance, narcissistic self-depreciation, negation, projection, repression, displacement, inhibited dream activity, reaction formation, somatization, avoidance, rationalization, denial.

Qualifications for joining the Party. 18 years or older. Already tested. Follows Party line, ideological and organizational stances of the Party. Good class pedigree. Clean morals and politics. Never involved with enemy. Clean personal history.

Revolution. Return. Revenge.

Smash. To crush or reduce to nothing. A Scream. Silence.

Torture by hand, rod, club, whip, electrical current, waterboarding, suffocation by plastic bag, pliers pulling out toe- and thumbnails, pouring salty water on wounds, eating feces, drinking urine, rape, exposure, poisonous insects, paying homage to the image of a dog.

Ugly habits. Talking to other groups. Not maintaining typewriters. Must be vigilant. It is careless, taking a pregnant woman to put in a new house. She cuts her belly open. When we get sleepy, put the enemy back.

Voice. Victim. Voiceless.

Wheel of History. Samsara. Wheel of Life.

No eXit. Hostage and Actor. Caught in the gears of the revolutionary machine.

You must be vigilant: First, Rough work—careless work → Conflict with the collective. Second, Morality with females.

Zero. Empty. No enemies. Unmarked.

Source: Most of this text is taken or adapted from ECCC documents from Duch's trial, including notes from Duch's interrogation lectures, a memo about the interrogation of a prisoner, and a psychological report on Duch.

Man

(OPENING ARGUMENTS)

"I wish to apologize."

Standing straight while reading a prepared statement held at eye level, Duch offered the first public apology by a high-ranking Khmer Rouge. "I do not ask that you forgive me here and now," he continued, glancing periodically at a dozen victims staring at him from across the courtroom. "I know that the crimes I committed against the lives of those people, including women and children, are intolerably and unforgivably serious crimes. My plea is that you leave the door open to me to seek forgiveness."[1]

Duch made this apology on March 31, 2009, the second day of his trial, while standing in the court's horseshoe-shaped dock. As he spoke, he pressed the tips of the four fingers on his left hand, mangled in a hunting rifle accident in the early 1980s, against the dock's small table for balance. Sitting behind him, a security officer watched Duch with half-closed eyes, Buddha-like. The apology was part of a 20-minute statement Duch made after the prosecution had completed its opening arguments.

In the 500-seat spectator gallery, located behind the court's tall, curving glass back wall, the audience listened intently. The room was packed with a range of people: ECCC officials, Cambodian students wearing blue shirts, Muslim Chams, NGO staffers, students from abroad, and Cambodians from different walks of life who wanted to get a firsthand look at this man who had run what had become the symbolic center of the Cambodian genocide.[2] A large contingent of domestic and international media was also covering the story.

Duch was separated from the people sitting in the front row of the gallery by just half a dozen meters and the protective glass wall. Everyone in the gallery gazed at Duch as he staked his claim to humanity, the former watcher now watched.

Day 1, March 30, 2009

BACKDROP

Duch's trial had opened the previous day to the flash of cameras as three photographers rapidly moved about the courtroom taking shots of him from different angles. Sitting in the gallery, I thought of how Duch's prisoners had their mug shots taken on arrival at S-21. But, as observers sometimes pointed out, those victims never had a trial. There were no courts during DK. The fact of arrest implied guilt, since the Party supposedly did not make mistakes. Wearing a long-sleeved dress shirt, Duch gazed back, unsmiling, at the photographers, his brown eyes lit by flashes of light.

Then Duch's trial began, as Judge Nil Nonn intoned: "In the name of the Cambodian people, and the United Nations, and pursuant to the Law on the Establishment of the Extraordinary Chambers in the Courts of Cambodia for the prosecution of crimes committed during the period of Democratic Kampuchea . . ."

The trial was to begin and end in controversy. Judge Nil, whose black hair was often disheveled, was himself involved. From the very beginning of negotiations between the United Nations and Cambodia over the creation of the trial, various parties had raised concerns about the corruption and politicization of the country's judiciary.

Judge Nil, who would efficiently lead the proceedings, had been appointed president of the Trial Chamber. His official court biography notes that he had been president of Cambodian courts in Battambang and Siem Reap province prior to joining the ECCC. A professor of law, he obtained his degree at Ho Chi Minh City University, receiving additional training in international law and human rights from organizations such as the United Nations Development Programme (UNDP).[3]

In 2002, a PBS documentary filmmaker had interviewed Judge Nil, who complained about criticism of the Cambodian judiciary even as he admitted taking bribes while serving on the Battambang court, "but only after a case is over." The filmmaker explains: "After all, he earns only $30 a month, not nearly enough to provide for his family. What else, he asks with that toothy grin, is he supposed to do?"[4]

While Judge Nil later denied having made these statements, he acknowledged in another interview that Cambodia's judiciary suffers from a range of problems, including lack of independence, government interference, and fair trial rights violations—even if such problems are also linked to insufficient resources, training, and experience.[5] He noted his determination to help fix these problems.

It was precisely because of such issues that the UN had initially advocated for an international tribunal. In the same 1997 resolution that requested that the UN secretary-general respond to any Cambodian appeal for assistance in holding a tribunal, the UN Commission on Human Rights expressed "serious concern" about a recent report of its special representative that was highly critical of the "continuing problem of impunity," including the Cambodian judiciary's lack of "independence," "impartiality," and proper "due process."[6] Such concerns about "international standards of justice" were echoed in the "Group of Experts" report, by diplomats, in subsequent UN statements, and in human rights and NGO reports and press releases.[7]

In early 2007, the Open Society Justice Initiative sparked a major controversy by revealing that the UNDP, which oversees donor funding for the ECCC, was carrying out an audit of the tribunal's finances, in part because of allegations that the Cambodian judges at the ECCC were sending kickbacks to their political patrons, charges the Cambodian government declined to investigate.[8] While an independent investigation found that as a result of a number of reforms undertaken during the following year, the ECCC had adequately addressed the issues raised in the UNDP report, corruption allegations continued to surface.[9] These issues were part of the backdrop of the Duch trial.

| | | |

All institutions have performative rituals through which they assert their legitimacy, and the Duch trial was no exception. Thus, in the first few moments of the hearing, Judge Nil quickly asserted the court's legitimacy by noting its foundation on international and Cambodian law and its jurisdictional mandate, which empowered him and his fellow jurists, whom he named, to oversee the proceedings.

Duch at an initial hearing, ECCC courtroom, February 17, 2009. Photo courtesy of the ECCC, by ECCC/Pool/Adrees Latif.

The domestic and international composition of the judges and the use of both international and Cambodian law were just two of many signs of the hybridity of the ECCC, a point also highlighted by Judge Nil's opening remarks. At a long table to Duch's front right sat Duch's defense lawyers, while to his far front left were the co-prosecutors. Immediately to Duch's left sat the civil parties, who were participating fully in the proceedings, something never before allowed at an international or hybrid tribunal.[10] Two long tables were positioned across the wall facing Duch. Eight court clerks and functionaries were stationed at the first table. Above them on an elevated platform sat the five judges of the Trial Chamber, all of whom, like Judge Nil, wore flowing red gowns and long white kerchiefs.

Three emblems hung on the high wall behind the judges. The flags of the UN and Cambodia were affixed to the left and right sides of the wall, respectively. Between them hung a larger white flag with the ECCC logo, a blue ink drawing of a wreath of olive branches—the symbol of the UN—partly encircling an Angkorean-era Cambodian judge sitting cross-legged on a dais and grasping with his right hand an upright sword.[11] On an outside band, the ECCC flag listed the court's official name, in Khmer, and abbreviations, in English and French; these were the three official languages of the tribunal. All of the judges wore this emblem, signifying the court's hybridity, on circular patches affixed on the left sides of their robes.

The hybridity of the court was also evident from the composition of the court personnel. Three of the five judges were Cambodian; the other two, sitting to the immediate right and far left of Judge Nil, who sat at the center of the table, were from New Zealand (Silvia Cartwright) and France (Lavergne). Cambodian judge Sokhan Ya sat to Judge Nil's left and Ottara You to his far right. Similarly, the prosecution, defense, and civil parties were a mix of Cambodian and international lawyers.

| | |

This hybrid structure was the outcome of a long process of negotiation that began when, following the April 1997 UN resolution offering international assistance,[12] the co-prime ministers of Cambodia, Hun Sen and Norodom Ranariddh, sent a June 21, 1997, letter to Kofi Annan asking for UN assistance in "bringing to justice" those responsible for the Khmer Rouge genocide.[13]

In response, Kofi Annan appointed a "Group of Experts for Cambodia" to explore the feasibility of holding a tribunal. On February 19, 1999, this group issued their report, which recommended establishing in a nearby country an ad hoc international tribunal, modeled after the international criminal tribunals in the former Yugoslavia and Rwanda to try former Khmer Rouge leaders "for crimes against humanity and genocide committed from April 17, 1975 to January 7, 1979."[14]

By the time the report was issued, however, the political situation in Cambodia had changed with the death of Pol Pot on April 15, 1998, amid the mass defection of his former followers. Ieng Sary defected with a host of Khmer Rouge soldiers in 1996. As part of a deal, he was given an amnesty and pardon.

Two other senior Khmer Rouge, Nuon Chea and DK head of state Khieu Samphan, both of whom would be tried in Case 002, defected to the government in December 1998. The last Khmer Rouge holdout, General Ta Mok, was arrested the following year, an event that signaled the end of the Khmer Rouge. Ta Mok joined Duch in prison, where he died, untried, on July 21, 2006.

In the name of reconciliation, the Cambodian government backtracked, alternatively suggesting that the country hold a truth and reconciliation commission, a domestic trial of just Ta Mok, and a predominantly national tribunal.[15] The negotiations that ensued between the UN and the Cambodian government were characterized by stops and starts as the two parties worked to create a new type of transitional justice mechanism, a "mixed" or "hybrid" tribunal, a model that would be used in East Timor, Sierra Leone, and Kosovo before the ECCC finally commenced.

The two sides signed a June 6, 2003, agreement establishing a hybrid tribunal that would be a special chamber within the Cambodian court system and use a combination of domestic and international law.[16] In addition to the five-judge Trial Chamber overseeing Duch's hearing, the ECCC has a five-person Pre-Trial Chamber and a seven-person Supreme Court Chamber (SCC), each of which has a majority of Cambodian judges but requires for a decision a supermajority that includes the vote of at least one international judge. In addition, there are Cambodian and international co-investigative judges, and civil parties and defendants may select Cambodian and, if they wish, international lawyers. The ECCC, consisting of seventeen Cambodian and twelve international judges and lawyers, began operation on July 3, 2006. It took almost three more years for Case 001, Duch's trial, to start.

| | | |

After completing his prefatory remarks, Judge Nil asked Duch to stand. With a court officer on each side, Duch walked to the dock, refusing at one point to take the arm of a guard. Judge Nil, speaking in Khmer, began to ask him a series of informational questions, to which Duch responded in a low voice:[17]

> QUESTION: What is your name?
> DUCH: My name is Kaing Guek Eav alias Duch. . . .
> QUESTION: What [was] your occupation before you were arrested?
> DUCH: I was a teacher. . . .
> QUESTION: Do you have a wife?
> DUCH: I have a wife. We got married on the twentieth of December 1975 but she died on the eleventh of November 1995.
> QUESTION: How many children do you have?
> DUCH: Four.

Like him, his children were teachers.

After finishing his background questioning, Judge Nil informed Duch of his right to be defended by a lawyer, to remain silent, to avoid self-incrimination, and to be informed of the charges. The irony was not lost on the observing survivors, who would complain about how well Duch was being treated in contrast to his victims.

Judge Nil next asked two court clerks to read excerpts from the "closing order," a document outlining the findings of the Office of the Co–Investigating Judges (OCIJ) and the charges against Duch. The closing order was the product of a long investigatory process that had begun almost immediately after the establishment of the court in 2006 and followed given procedural guidelines.

Like all courts, the ECCC is governed by specific statutes. In the case of the ECCC, three key documents delineate the court's mandate, jurisdiction, composition, and applicable laws. The June 6, 2003, agreement between Cambodia and the UN establishing the court laid out the broad parameters of the ECCC. The following year, these principles were codified in Cambodian law. On June 12, 2007, the court published a seventy-one-page set of "Internal Rules" that detailed how the principles were to be put into practice.[18] It took court officials almost an entire year to finalize this document, which, by the end of the Duch trial, had been revised eight times.

While blending in elements of the common law tradition, these three documents are premised on the assumption that, in accordance with Cambodian legal tradition and its French colonial influence, the ECCC would largely operate in accordance with the civil law tradition. In contrast to the common law tradition, which is found in Great Britain and many Anglophone countries, including the United States, civil law predominates in continental Europe and many of its former colonies, including Cambodia.

If the common law tradition is often characterized by the importance of evidentiary oral testimony, case-based legal precedent, and trial by jury, the civil law tradition emphasizes written texts, abstract law, and judicial inquisition. To put it another way, whereas in the common law tradition the jury evaluates the facts of a case and the judge arbitrates in terms of the law, in civil law courts judges usually do both. Along these lines, the proceedings at the ECCC are largely driven by the judges, and the role of the prosecutor is, if important, emphasized less than in common law practice.

The ECCC internal rules stipulate that the Office of the Co-Prosecutors (OCP) is entitled to conduct preliminary investigations. The case is handed over to the OCIJ once the OCP has gathered sufficient evidence to make an "introductory submission." At this time, the OCP transfers its "case file" of evidentiary material to the OCIJ.

The OCIJ conducts further investigations and continues to build the case file. Once the OCIJ investigation is complete, the OCP is invited to make a "final submission." The investigative process concludes with the OCIJ's "closing order," which calls for dismissal or indictment. If the case proceeds, the OCIJ transfers the case file to the Trial Chamber, which will commence the proceedings, pending any appeals.

As opposed to focusing on the evidence introduced during a trial as in common law systems, a civil law court, such as the ECCC Trial Chamber, will have the bulk of the relevant evidentiary material in hand by the start of the trial. The Trial Chamber judges then take the lead in structuring the proceedings, deciding what testimony and evidence will be introduced, questioning witnesses, apportioning time, and rendering a verdict.

Thus, in the Duch case, the OCP began its investigation on July 10, 2006, almost immediately after the court began operation.[19] A year later, on July 18, 2007, the OCP made its introductory submission to the co-investigating judges, Cambodian jurist You Bunleng and his French counterpart, Judge Marcel Lemonde. They detained Duch less than two weeks later, eventually charging him with "crimes against humanity" and "grave breaches of the 1949 Geneva Conventions." After the OCP made its final submission on July 18, 2008, the OCIJ issued the closing order indicting Duch on August 8, 2008, and transferred the case to the Trial Chamber. The closing order provided a rough outline of the facts that had emerged during the case, including information about the origins, structure, and functioning of S-21. At this point, the case file included twenty-one pretrial interviews with Duch.[20]

| | |

The victims proved to be a strong presence at Duch's trial. But they would have to wait before having their chance to speak. On the first morning of the trial, perhaps a dozen civil parties sat inside the courtroom behind their lawyers, on the opposite side of the room from Duch. Because there were not enough seats, the civil parties took turns, rotating between the courtroom and the gallery.

They listened intently as the closing order was read, tracing out Duch's path to S-21 and the brutalities that took place there. At several points the closing order referenced their experiences. Duch rarely looked up, his head bent, perhaps reading along.

At the end of the lunch break, I saw Chum Mey, who, along with Vann Nath, was one of a handful of prisoners who survived S-21. Chum Mey had been spared because he was a mechanic and could fix generators on the compound. Despite his age, Chum Mey remained agile and sharp, his mouth set in a determined line. He almost always carried a small notebook and wore a short-sleeved dress shirt, with a pen clip protruding from the pocket. He had been waiting years for this trial to begin.

During a break, I asked him what he thought of the proceedings. Smiling, Chum Mey told me that he was very happy with the way things were going. Then he paused, his smile fading, as he continued, "I cried and cried when they read the part [of the closing order] about how I was tortured with electrical shocks."

Chum Mey would return to the court almost every day until Duch was judged.

Day 2, March 31, 2009
JUSTICE AND HUMANITY (CHEA LEANG,
NATIONAL CO-PROSECUTOR)

"For 30 years, one and a half million victims of the Khmer Rouge have been demanding justice for their suffering," Cambodian co-prosecutor Chea Leang began her opening remarks at the start of the second day.[21] Her Canadian counterpart, Robert Petit, sat next to her, reading glasses pushed down on his nose toward his goatee.

"For 30 years the survivors of Democratic Kampuchea have been waiting for accountability," she continued, glancing up occasionally from her text on a podium. "For 30 years a whole generation of Cambodians have been struggling to get answers about their families' fate. Well today, in this Courtroom, before the Cambodian people and the world, at long last this process begins and Justice will be done."

It was a justice whose meaning would be contested.

| | | |

Chea Leang, her round face framed by short black hair, stated that while the Cambodian government had struggled with the legacy of DK, the international community had "long failed the people of Cambodia," even if it now had "finally recognized that justice must prevail and that there cannot be impunity for the worst of crimes. Even after 30 years."

Her remarks reflected those of Prime Minister Hun Sen and other CPP party members, who had noted the hypocrisy of the international community, which they alleged had long ignored their calls for justice. Chea Leang, who had received an MA in law from a German university,[22] was closely linked to the CPP, in part through her relation to her uncle, Deputy Prime Minister Sok An, a close Hun Sen ally, who had been the point person for the Cambodian side during the tribunal negotiations.

Suggestions that her choice as national co-prosecutor had been political were heightened when it was revealed that her office was effectively supporting the position publicly taken by Hun Sen opposing trials beyond Case 002 because of "Cambodia's past instability and the continued need for national reconciliation."[23] Later in 2009, she would be appointed prosecutor general of the Supreme Court of Cambodia even as she continued her duties at the ECCC.

Continuing, Chea Leang highlighted another tension in the meaning of justice. While Duch had to be judged from his crimes, she called on the judges to "determine before all how and why this man was allowed to commit those crimes. . . . History demands it."[24] More broadly, she noted, "it is the purpose of courts such as this one, to establish the truth, unflinchingly . . . so that mankind may learn and history may not be repeated." Throughout the opening arguments that day, the prosecution, defense, and even Duch himself would invoke these two senses of justice as law and as truth. Linked to these two notions of justice were different conceptions of humanity.

| | | |

During their two hours of remarks that morning, the co-prosecutors would foreground the origins, structure, and operation of S-21, Duch's degree of autonomy and criminal responsibility, and the profound dehumanization of his victims. Chea Leang began with a brief discussion of the rise of the Khmer Rouge and their attempt to create a pure new revolutionary society. From the start, the DK regime had sought to eliminate "perceived enemies and placed little value in human rights or life itself. As one of these infamous slogans so chillingly foretold 'To keep you is no gain, to destroy you is no loss.' "[25]

To quickly implement its radical program of social engineering, she argued, the Khmer Rouge established a system of control in which authority ran from the top down. This hierarchical system enabled the regime to eliminate its many perceived "hidden enemies burrowing from within." Security centers, where prisoners were detained and executed, were established all over the country. S-21 stood above the rest, serving as the site where the most important prisoners were sent and operating in coordination with the DK leadership.

Duch therefore ran the most important prison in Cambodia, Chea Leang went on. At least 12,380 people were killed there, she said, citing the low-end estimation based on evidence that was almost certainly lower than the real total, since documentation had been lost, and some prisoners were killed without being registered.[26] Over three-quarters of the victims were Khmer Rouge officers and soldiers who had been swept up in political purges. Most (70 percent) were male, though female cadre and the wives (4 percent) and children of inmates were also detained and executed there. The inmates were relatively young, averaging twenty-nine years of age, and most were incarcerated there for an average of sixty-one days before execution. As war with Vietnam escalated, increasing numbers of Vietnamese were arrested, making 3 percent of the S-21 population. At least 190 staff at S-21 came under suspicion and were arrested and killed there, as were a handful of foreigners.

These inmates, Chea Leang emphasized, were thoroughly dehumanized. The starving prisoners were shackled in cells and seldom given medical care or allowed to bathe. They had to request permission even to relieve themselves. At the end of her remarks, she displayed a self-portrait painted by Vann Nath. It depicts an emaciated prisoner wearing only shorts and sitting shackled by the leg in a tiny brick cell. He stares into space, forlorn and without hope.

In the gallery, Vann Nath was watching.

CRIMES AGAINST HUMANITY (ROBERT PETIT, INTERNATIONAL CO-PROSECUTOR)

After a break, International Co-Prosecutor Robert Petit picked up on the theme of dehumanization even as he shifted to a more explicit discussion of Duch's culpability. Like many of this court's international personnel, Petit had extensive experience in international justice, having worked in the prosecutor's office at the International Criminal Tribunal for Rwanda before moving on to work at the hybrid courts established in Kosovo, East Timor, and Sierra Leone. His appointment as a co-prosecutor at the ECCC was the culmination of his hard work.[27]

He had begun working at the ECCC from the start, assuming his post in 2006. He jointly oversaw the indictments of Duch and the senior leaders in Case 002 but later diverged from Chea Leang regarding the controversy about whether there should be additional trials; he was in favor of more.[28] In an interview, he stated that he hated bullies and had become a prosecutor because he "profoundly dislike[s] criminals and people who think they're above the law."[29] He seemed to regard Duch in this light. He spoke in a polite yet slightly clipped manner, alternating between fluent English and French, and pausing at times to let the translators catch up.

If Chea Leang's remarks outlined the broad textures of Cambodian life under the Khmer Rouge and the horrors of S-21, Petit used a more juridical frame that emphasized crimes against humanity, making periodic references to the Holocaust. "I would now like to continue to address the crimes committed at S-21," he began, glasses now off and bending slightly to read from the podium. "As the accused himself admits and as the mountain of documentary evidence clearly proves, torture was extensively practiced at S-21."[30]

He did not spare any details. "Victims were beaten with rattan sticks and whips, electrocuted, had toenails and fingernails pulled out, were suffocated with plastic bags forcibly held over their heads, and were stripped naked and had their genitals electrocuted," he explained.[31] I thought of Chum Mey, whose experience Petit again used as an illustration. Not only did Duch oversee the torture, he taught the interrogators how to do it.[32]

Duch left behind a huge amount of incriminating evidence, including 120 documents bearing his annotations.[33] Like the Nazis, Petit noted, Duch and his staff kept "meticulous records." The deaths of the prisoners were noted in hundreds of execution logs. Some died on site due to the harsh life conditions or torture. Most were executed with a blow to the back of the head and buried in mass graves, their throats slit. Even young children were not spared.

S-21 was a massive compound, encompassing numerous buildings in Phnom Penh as well as the Choeung Ek execution center, located seven miles south of Phnom Penh, and S-24, or Pray Sar, a "reeducation camp" based around the grounds of a prerevolutionary prison. An unknown number of cadre were "tempered" there. Over 500 of them, including children, were transferred to S-21.[34]

Duch, Petit continued, was directly responsible for these atrocities.[35] Duch, he stated, reported directly to Son Sen and later Nuon Chea, two of the highest ranking DK leaders. Duch's own deputies, in turn, reported directly to him. To illustrate, Petit displayed a chart showing Duch's connection to his superiors on the CPK standing committee and his subordinates heading different sections of S-21.[36]

Duch, he warned the court, was trying to assert that he was a "Chairman in theory," a cog in the machine who transmitted orders from his superiors to his subordinates. Duch's claim to have done little more than annotate confessions while largely delegating authority, Petit argued, was "simply not believable."[37] If anything, he continued, Duch "spent endless hours micro-managing S-21" as part of a "joint criminal enterprise," a legal categorization that made him responsible for the crimes committed by his subordinates "even if he himself never got his hands dirty."[38]

Ultimately, Petit suggested, Duch made voluntary and self-aware choices along a "pathway that brought him to the commission of the crime."[39] In running S-21, he was "devoted and merciless."[40] And after DK he remained a committed revolutionary for almost 20 years. This long history cast doubt on his cooperation with the court which may well have been a calculated move to get a reduction in his sentence in the face of overwhelming evidence.

To render justice for Duch's victims, Petit concluded, the court needed to "apply the law to the facts" as they sought the truth,[41] which resided in the "personal stories of each one of the victims of the Accused." Displaying a series of S-21 prisoner mug shots, Petit emphasized that the reality behind the lists and statistics consisted of these "people who had names, families, memories, hopes. They all deserve to be heard, to have their day in court and to have their stories told and remembered." By considering these stories, the court would not just "acknowledge the humanity of [Duch's] victims" and restore some of the dignity and voice they lost at S-21 but also "give back to us a bit of the humanity that we all lose [in] the face of such horrors."[42]

PENITENT (THE ACCUSED)

After breaking for lunch, Judge Nil gave the floor to the defense. Duch's international co-counsel, François Roux, requested that Duch be allowed to make a statement, particularly because "the victims have been waiting for a long time for the accused to speak." Duch, dressed in a white short-sleeved shirt, had spent the morning sitting in the dock. While listening to Chea Leang and Robert Petit describe the horrors of S-21, Duch had frequently looked down, sometimes slumping in his chair. Now it was his turn to speak.

Duch the teacher rose from his seat, ready with a reprimand. Gazing toward the prosecutors, as if lecturing students who had gotten the facts wrong, he said that he would like to start by "clarifying" their depiction of Cambodian history. It was, he stressed, Lon Nol who had first begun butchering peasants in 1966. After the coup d'état of March 18, 1970, both sides "competed in the race to kill Cambodian people." It was only after April 17, 1975, when the Khmer Rouge came to power, that they alone bore responsibility for the killing. Robert Petit stared back at Duch.

Outside, the skies thundered, and it began to rain.

Putting on his glasses, Duch began reading from a prepared statement. He started with evidence. The 1976 Party Statutes, he noted, clearly stated that the Party had "an absolute monopoly of leadership in all domains."[43] Nevertheless, as a member of the CPK, Duch had to accept "moral responsibility" for the crimes committed, including the deaths of over one million people. His voice quivered slightly as he said this number. Then he paused and glanced over at the civil parties before expressing "my regret and my deepest sorrow" for these crimes.[44]

After taking a deep breath, Duch acknowledged his "legal responsibility" for the crimes committed at S-21, ranging from torture to executions. He also wanted to apologize. While he realized that the crimes seemed unforgivable, he hoped that the victims would "consider my intentions" and "leave the door open for me to seek forgiveness."[45] As he spoke, his voice had become increasingly soft, his arms barely moving.

Whenever he thought about S-21, Duch said, he was "terrified and appalled" by "the activities which I was ordered to carry out, and the orders I gave to others" that led to the death and suffering of so many, including "women and children." Though he had been "a hostage, a mere puppet," he understood that people regarded him as "a cowardly and inhumane person." He had failed to find an alternative in this "life and death [situation] for me and my family." And so he continued to have "the deepest sorrow and regret, and I feel ashamed."

In light of his crimes, Duch declared he would do what he could to help facilitate the proceedings. He would cooperate with the court, since this was "the only way for me to help bring [relief] and condolences" to the victims. He also could confirm the reality of S-21, which Khmer Rouge leaders had denied. Finally, Duch said, he would answer the questions of the judges, prosecutors, and even the civil parties.[46]

Having completed his statement, Duch set down his glasses and clasped his hands. Glancing alternatively between the judges and the civil parties, he said that he wanted to express "the remorse that I have felt all my life. I was not satisfied with my work."[47] His voice sounding more confident, like the teacher who had at first chided the prosecutors, Duch explained that at several points he had tried to avoid working at S-21. He had been shocked and terrified by the spiraling arrests, thinking "My days are numbered."

On a personal level, Duch said, the revolution had also been costly. "I lost everyone around me," he pointed out, including two siblings and six nephews and nieces. In the year after the end of DK, he came to understand that in light of all those who had died during DK, "my own life meant nothing. . . . So for a whole year I could not do any work. I just lay in bed."[48] In the end, he realized the only thing he could do would be to make "offerings and pray for forgiveness from the victims, and from my parents who gave birth to me and wanted me to grow up as a good child." Despite his desire to "follow the good path," Duch lamented, "I fell onto the wrong path."

His contrition was supposedly so deep that, on his birthday each year, he would do something "to commemorate my remorse. This year I made a painting."[49] He offered the picture to the judges, who asked that it be displayed. The black-and-white, hand-drawn image with annotations could barely be made out. It depicted the end of DK, he explained. At the top stood the communist sickle. Below were three torsos set on a raised dais, like Buddhas. Pol Pot, Duch said, was in the middle on the highest dais. To his right and left sat Nuon Chea and Ta Mok. Below them, in neatly drawn stacks, were four piles of skulls representing their many victims. Duch had also created a legend explicating the meaning of each image. The one-page sheet resembled a lesson plan, though it was difficult to read the small, precise script. Like Duch, the text was slightly blurred, just out of focus.

Which Duch was authentic, many observers wondered. The math teacher who had scolded the prosecution? The contrite Duch who at times seemed on the verge of tears as he read his prepared statement and acknowledged his responsibility? Or Duch the unwilling executioner who was ultimately powerless and victimized by the regime but still felt remorse and sought atonement? And then there was the Duch suggested by the prosecution, the ruthless, calculating man only cooperating to get a reduced sentence.

FALL GUY (KAR SAVUTH, NATIONAL DEFENSE CO-LAWYER)

Duch's national defense lawyer, Kar Savuth, did not bring clarity.

International co–defense lawyer François Roux had praised Kar Savuth for defending a former Khmer Rouge despite himself having been imprisoned by the group. "He is a credit to the profession," Roux told the court. "Could he possibly imagine that one day he would find himself as a lawyer defending, representing the director of S-21[?]"[50]

Kar Savuth, who had started defending Duch shortly after he was arrested in 1999, always spoke before Roux during the trial. At times, Kar Savuth's lack of international legal training became apparent. Perhaps to compensate, he spoke in a booming voice, gesticulating with his right hand or tapping the podium for emphasis. He often listed his points numerically, reading them one by one. His straight-forward style seemed to play well to some Cambodians. Kar Savuth was also somewhat controversial, having served as an advisor to Hun Sen.[51]

Duch, Kar Savuth stated, was a scapegoat. "What is the purpose of prosecuting the leaders of the Khmer Rouge regime?" Kar Savuth asked rhetorically.[52] It was meant, he said, to bring justice, prevent the return of the Khmer Rouge, uphold the sovereignty of Cambodia, and satisfy the victims and the souls of the dead.

The UN-Cambodia agreement, however, had restricted the jurisdiction of the court to "senior leaders" and "those most responsible." If someone other than a senior leader or a person most responsible were to be tried, it would be unjust and unacceptable to the victims, living and dead. Duch did not fit these jurisdictional categories. Accordingly, Kar Savuth asked the court to terminate the proceedings.[53] Petit gazed across at him, hands clasped in front of his mouth as if to hold back a sharp reply. Several civil party lawyers were intently taking notes.

To support his argument, Kar Savuth asserted there were at least 196 Khmer Rouge prisons, each of which was led by someone like Duch who was required to interrogate and torture prisoners.[54] Either the heads of all of the prisons had to be tried, Kar Savuth suggested, or Duch should be released. Not to do so would be to treat Duch unfairly, he noted, something that would violate Article 31 of the Cambodian Constitution, which guaranteed equal rights. This violation, combined with the court's lack of personal jurisdiction, constituted a violation of Cambodia's sovereignty.

Kar Savuth concluded by returning to the prosecutor's assertion that the trial was not only for the Cambodian people but for all of humanity. What lessons are being learned, he asked, when the court tries someone who is outside its jurisdiction? "Please consider this fact," Kar Savuth asked the judges, "before Duch is prosecuted as a scapegoat."[55]

If Kar Savuth's larger point might ring true for some, the court had long ago decided the issue of jurisdiction. Petit would directly challenge Kar Savuth on this point and on Kar Savuth's claim that the court violated Cambodian sovereignty. When Judge Nil asked Kar Savuth to clarify his position the following day, Kar Savuth backtracked,[56] even as he reiterated his argument that Duch was neither a "senior leader" nor one of "those most responsible."

REPAIR (FRANÇOIS ROUX, INTERNATIONAL CO-DEFENSE LAWYER)

François Roux took a different path.

A longtime human rights activist with a history of defending conscientious objectors and others engaged in civil disobedience,[57] Roux seemed an unlikely candidate to defend Duch. Over time, however, he developed an interest in international law that led him to defend four accused Rwandan perpetrators as well as participate in the defense of 9/11 suspect Zacarias Moussaoui. With boyish hair, parted on the left, Roux's lips were often pressed and slightly upturned, almost in a patient smile. He liked to invoke philosophy or poetry to highlight a point.[58]

While Kar Savuth had argued for Duch's release, Roux sought a lighter sentence. His comments echoed much of Duch's written statement, including his passing remark that, while accepting responsibility, Duch was ultimately "a hostage, a mere puppet in the criminal regime."[59]

Roux noted that the defense and prosecution agreed on many of the facts in the case. The key issue, which Petit had touched on, was the sincerity of his apology and of his claim about his lack of autonomy. The co-prosecutors, Roux continued, had failed to discuss "the twin pillars of terror and secrecy. It was because of the terror that every link in the chain of command acted zealously to please superiors who were the ones who issued orders."[60] Since Duch took responsibility for giving orders, the court needed to acknowledge that he himself received orders, which he then transmitted.

Although obedience did not excuse Duch's acts, Roux claimed, it should be considered a mitigating factor. How many people in Cambodia, Roux asked, had acknowledged such a role in the killings? To do so in public and before the victims, as Duch had done, was not easy.

From the time that Roux had first met him in 2007, Duch had said that he recognized his responsibility and wanted to talk about what had happened. When asked if he would like to participate in a "reenactment," a civil law proceeding in which the accused returns to the scene of the crime, Duch responded affirmatively, asking only that he be left alone for a while at Tuol Sleng and that he be allowed to speak to some of his former prisoners and guards. When he did so, Duch wept. How could anyone doubt Duch's sincerity, Roux asked? "What other than justice . . . could have organized this meeting between Duch and his former victims."[61]

There is no doubt, Roux continued, that the prosecution's description of the tragic events at S-21 "arouses all our compassion for the innocent victims." But everyone also needed to think about "the one that today is confronting his past," an act that took "a certain amount of courage."[62] By allowing Duch to seek forgiveness, address his victims, and provide answers, the court would help restore his humanity. Duch would at times fall short, since he "remains a human being" and, like all of us, has "a bit of trouble admitting certain things that are extremely painful."[63]

Toward the end of his remarks, Roux told the civil parties: "You have your full place in these hearings. You will be able to ask Duch the questions that you wish to ask him."[64] Then he issued a warning. Duch might not be able to answer all of their questions, including their main question: why? "I'm not sure that Duch on his own has the answer to this tragic question," Roux explained. "Why these scenes? The unthinkable scenes, these unbearable scenes at S-21? Why these scenes that de-humanize the victims?"[65]

Roux concluded by noting that perpetrators like Duch also had been de-humanized by the atrocities. "Will we," he asked, "be able at the end of these hearings . . . to return to the victims all of the humanity? But to also be able to allow those or the one [who] had exited humanity to return to humanity? This is the stake for our court."[66]

Duch had become a tragic character, almost a victim. The trial was his path to redemption.

Day 3, April 1, 2009
VOICE (SILKE STUDZINSKY, INTERNATIONAL
CIVIL PARTY CO-LAWYER)

"What is the meaning of 'participation'?"

At the start of the next day, International Civil Party Co-Lawyer Silke Studzinsky posed this question after being given the floor.[67] Due to a Trial Chamber ruling, the civil parties had not been able to make an opening statement. When Duch apologized, they had to remain silent. When Roux addressed them at the close of his remarks, they were unable to reply. Now they had the opportunity to be heard on the issues of the day, beginning with the legality of Duch's detention.

Studzinsky, dressed in an oversized black robe, was a German lawyer who had a background in criminal defense and civil party representation in Germany and other European courts.[68] Since early 2008 she had been working with civil parties in Cambodia as part of her work with the German Civil Peace Service. She had a long-standing interest in gender-based violence and would later push to have alleged forced marriage and sexual crimes investigated in Case 002. Only one such alleged crime, a rape during interrogation, had appeared in the Case 001 indictment. At many points in the trial, Studzinsky would give Duch a piercing look, her dark eyes sharpened by eyeliner.

Shuffling through her notes, Studzinsky pointed out that the civil parties had only learned on the first day of the trial that Duch would be afforded an opportunity to speak. Participation, she stated, was closely linked to "the right to be heard," including the right to "respond to the accused and to express their concerns and views." This was basic to their fair trial rights.

International jurisprudence supported this argument, she claimed. In a case at the International Criminal Court the Pre-Trial Chamber had afforded civil parties an opportunity to make opening and closing remarks. If Duch had the right to make opening remarks, then so did they. "Bringing justice to the victims," she concluded, meant allowing them to "express their view on what [they] thought about the apologies that the accused expressed yesterday, and on what he said, that he is a victim."[69]

| | |

Studzinsky's comments reflected the perception of many civil parties and their representatives that their status had been under attack from the start, despite their having been empowered with unprecedented rights at the ECCC.[70] Her remarks also raised a complex issue. As opposed to splitting civil and criminal cases, as is often done in common law courts, the two may be conjoined in civil law. Victims thus may be a party to the court proceedings. This right is explicitly given in the Cambodian Code of Criminal Procedure, one of the key sources of inspiration for Article 23 of the ECCC's Internal Rules, which states that civil parties may "participate in the criminal proceedings" by "supporting the prosecution" and seeking "collective and moral reparations."[71] To become a civil party, a person had to have suffered "physical, material or psychological" injury related to one of the crimes in question.

This empowerment of civil parties, which dovetailed with recent trends in international law, was often cited as one of the original contributions of the ECCC, even a historic one, since civil parties had for the first time been given unprecedented procedural rights.[72] Almost immediately, however, questions emerged about how far civil party rights could be taken.

What exactly, as Studzinsky had asked, does "participation" mean and entail? If, as a Victims Unit statement noted, the "rights of Civil Parties are comparable to those of the accused, including the right to participate in the investigation, to be represented by a lawyer, to call witnesses and question the accused at trial, and to claim reparations for the harm they suffered," then how might these civil party rights impact the rights of the accused? The defense lawyers repeatedly highlighted this issue.

THE CIVIL PARTIES

By the start of the Duch trial, ninety-three people had brought suit as civil parties, most of whom were family members of people who had been killed at S-21. They were represented by fifteen lawyers and, in accordance with the recent rule changes, divided into four groups, roughly organized in terms of the intermediary organization with whom they were affiliated.

Thirty-eight of the civil parties were in Group 1, composed largely of civil parties being assisted by DC-Cam, which had arranged for their representation by Cambodian lawyer Ty Srinna and two international lawyers, Karim Khan (UK) and Alain Werner (Switzerland).[73] They were working pro bono. Despite empowering civil parties with full participatory rights and emphasizing fair trial rights, the ECCC failed to provide any compensation for the civil party lawyers. This was part of what some considered a larger pattern of neglect of the civil parties.

Although Internal Rule 4 explicitly called for the creation of a Victims Unit as part of the court's efforts to empower civil parties, the ECCC Victims Unit was barely operational by early 2008 and remained understaffed and underfunded for much of the next year. It eventually received a needed infusion of funding support from the German government, which contributed 1.5 million euros to it on November 6, 2008.[74]

Forty-four civil parties attended the first day of Duch's trial.[75] Artist-survivor Bou Meng was there. So was Chum Mey. Vann Nath, and an S-21 child survivor, Norng Chanphal, would testify as witnesses. Bou Meng and Chum Mey were both in Civil Party Group 2, which was in part organized by the umbrella human rights coalition Cambodian Human Rights Action Committee and was represented, among others, by Studzinsky and Cambodian lawyer Hong Kimsuon. Unlike other international civil party lawyers, Studzinsky had salary support that enabled her to live and work full-time at the tribunal.[76] The lawyers in Civil Party Groups 3 and 4, in turn, received some assistance from the foreign intermediary organizations around which the groups were formed, Avocats Sans Frontières and the Paris Bar Association.[77]

During the first two days of the Duch trial, the civil parties quietly watched and waited. I had spoken with Bou Meng and Chum Mey a few times. The contrast between them was striking. Despite being ten years younger than Chum Mey, Bou Meng looked much older. Perhaps this aging was in part because of the years Bou Meng spent in the sun as a farmer, while Chum Mey worked as a mechanic in the city. But Bou Meng's toothless grin and poor hearing were no doubt also linked to the beatings he endured at S-21.

From the start, it was clear that there were tensions with Duch. On entering the court on the first day, Duch had greeted the civil parties, palms pressed at chest level, along with the rest of the court. Later I noticed Duch waving at or giving a small salute to Bou Meng and Chum Mey, as if they were comrades. Chum Mey halfheartedly saluted back; Bou Meng waved his hand slightly.

Bou Meng just shook his head when I asked if he was okay with Duch's greeting. "We don't know each other" (*at squal knea*), he told me, invoking a Khmer term that can mean one has met or is acquainted with another person but can also signify having a friendly relationship with that person. Chum Mey, in turn, later told me, "I saluted back because it would be rude not to do so. . . . But I have joined in a petition to the court requesting that he stop greeting the civil parties." He was referring to a March 26 request Studzinsky had made on behalf of twenty-three civil parties from Group 2 asking that Duch cease from making gestures toward the civil parties that might be interpreted as seeking their forgiveness or sympathy.[78]

Perhaps that was why Duch had saluted Bou Meng and Chum Mey. Maybe he hadn't heard. Or maybe he didn't care. In the days that followed, however, Duch stopped trying to greet the civil parties.

RESPONSIBILITY AND REMORSE

The contestation over civil party rights continued on Day 3, focusing on a motion for Duch's release. He had first been detained, Roux noted, on May 10, 1999. In 2007 he had been transferred to the ECCC. Now it was 2009. This meant that Duch had been under arrest for roughly ten years. This violated both Cambodian and international law forbidding prolonged detention without trial. Accordingly, the defense requested that he be released and credited for time served and illegal detainment if sentenced.

Roux noted the irony of this request in light of Duch's apology.[79] It didn't matter. In the end, the law had to be applied, even if it was difficult for the civil parties or the public to understand. "Dura lex sed lex," he said; "The law is hard but it is the law."[80] Moreover, it was also difficult to imagine, he added, that a person could be detained for almost ten years without trial. The law required Duch's release. Roux emphasized: "Nothing less than the integrity of the Tribunal is at stake."[81]

Speaking for the OCP, Chea Leang noted that the ECCC was independent and therefore that the illegality of Duch's prior arrest was out of its jurisdiction. A Pre-Trial Chamber decision had affirmed this point. Moreover, to free Duch would risk not just his flight but his safety, since Cambodian victims were angry "and [might] take revenge on him."[82] Duch, who had been carefully listening, his face impassive, glanced at the audience in the gallery.

When Chea Leang finished, the civil party lawyers rose to speak. Roux interjected, invoking Internal Rule 82, which stated that if an accused made a request for release, the "Chamber shall decide after hearing the Co-Prosecutors, the Accused and his or her lawyers."[83] Since no mention was made of the civil parties, Roux concluded, "the civil parties do not have a place, a role to play in such a discussion."[84] Later he would address them directly, saying: "We will hear you. We will hear what you have to express to us but, please, do not venture onto areas which are not yours."[85]

After conferring, the Trial Chamber allowed the civil parties to comment on the scope of Rule 82. Studzinsky asked the judges to recall the Pre-Trial Chamber's decision of March 20, 2009, affirming the right of the civil parties not just to be physically present but to "participate in detention appeal hearings," since they impacted their right to reparation. Swaying slightly as she spoke, Studzinsky asked the Trial Chamber to "be consistent" with this decision.[86] Even if civil parties were not explicitly mentioned in Rule 82, the judges needed to consider "the spirit of civil party participation," since "one of the fundamental rights of participation is the right to be heard."[87]

FACT

While Studzinsky was speaking, the French international lawyer for Group 3, Martine Jacquin, had been patiently standing. With short blond hair and square-framed glasses, Jacquin headed the Avocats Sans Frontières office in Cambodia and, in addition to representing civil parties at the ECCC, had been working to develop a grassroots network of pro bono lawyers to assist Cambodia's poor.[88] She wore a black sash over her shoulder. It was "surreal," she noted, that the day after "Mr. Duch expressed remorse and regret and a request for forgiveness . . . he applies for release" based on legal arguments.[89] There should be "a minimum of recognition of the suffering of civil parties which is due here. In that light, Mr. Duch's application is unconscionable."[90]

She noted that the previous day the prosecution and defense had discussed how to present to the court the list of facts on which they had agreed. This list, largely drawn from the closing order, included 351 factual allegations.

According to Petit, the defense had agreed to 157 of these facts and not disputed 81 others, meaning that 238 of the 351 allegations were uncontested.[91] Of the remaining 112 facts, the defense had disagreed with 21 of them and either partly agreed or commented on the others. Petit had stated that it was important to explicitly note these facts "to indicate where the debate lay between the parties. It will come as no surprise . . . that most of the disputed facts rest with the part of the indictment dealing with the responsibility of the Accused."[92]

The initial plan had been to submit this list through written submissions. Jacquin insisted, "we should read out the factual analysis one-by-one." This would provide a sort of response to Duch's opening remarks and also highlight the points of agreement and disagreement. She concluded, "I think it is important for Mr. Duch to realize the gravity of the events that have brought him here today and these facts are of particular [importance] to the civil parties who [lost] their loved ones and whose lives were destroyed."[93]

The civil parties would win on this particular issue. The next day, however, the court ruled against their request to make opening remarks or to comment on Duch's motion for release. While the court noted Pre-Trial Chamber decisions "with interest," Internal Rule 82.3 was a "conscious decision by the ECCC plenary shaping civil parties' participation" that took into account the "balancing of the rights of civil parties with the need [for] a fair and expeditious trial."[94]

However, for the remainder of the third day, Duch had to listen as parts of the closing order detailing his alleged crimes were stated in public. Standing before a podium, Petit began reading the agreed facts from a list sorted into topics like "Establishment and Structure of DK," "The Policy of Smashing Enemies," "Conditions of Detention at S-21," "Systematic Use of Torture during Interrogation," and "Executions at Choeng Ek."

> "Paragraph 3. S-21 was chaired for most of its existence by Kaing Guek
> Eav alias Duch. Agreed. . . ."[95]
> "Paragraph 30. Duch was feared by everyone at S-21 [not contested] . . ."[96]
> "Paragraph 168. S-21 personnel performed medical experimentations on
> prisoners. Agreed. . . ."[97]
> "Paragraph 235. Over 12,380 detainees were executed at S-21 [not
> contested] . . ."[98]
> "Agreed Paragraph 254A. [O]n one prisoners list Duch handwrote, 'To
> the attention of Uncle Peng. Kill them all. 30 May 1978. . . .'"[99]

"Paragraph 260. Children of S-21 prisoners were taken away from their parents, killed within the S-21 compound and buried north of the prison [not contested]...."[100]

The process took two hours. Duch sat with his reading glasses on, following along on a paper copy, with the pages neatly stacked on the table before him. At times he licked the tip of his finger and flipped a page. Yellow marker in hand, he was annotating.

After the final factual allegation was read, Roux stood and informed the court that "Duch acknowledges the facts that have been read out concerning the executions." However, Duch was requesting "that we use the term 'S-21' and not the term 'Tuol Sleng' that he does not recognize because it's a term that was only given after the fact." What concerned Duch, Roux explained, was that he had been the head of S-21, whereas "Tuol Sleng is a word that was given after the arrival of the Vietnamese troops."[101] The defense said nothing about the other facts.

But another Duch was starting to emerge: Duch the mathematician, the model defendant, meticulous and always ready with a comment or clarification.

| | | |

The stage is set. The protagonists are ready. And the structure of the drama is taking shape. At the center stands Duch: tragic hero in search of redemption, evil villain without remorse, something in between, or all of the above?

In the gallery, the audience waits for answers. Who is Duch? What did he do and why? Was his apology sincere? Can he be forgiven? And might justice and humanity somehow be found?

For this performance, the marquee is flashing red: "Duch: Man or Monster?"

Revolutionary

(M-13 PRISON)

"Who Does the Hitting?"

On the sixth day of Duch's trial, François Bizot, the first witness called to testify, recalled posing this question to Duch while a prisoner at M-13, the prison camp Duch ran during the civil war. Over the course of his three-month detention in 1971, Bizot and Duch had established a rapport, after spending hours together during Bizot's interrogation. Bizot was never beaten, but he had heard that other prisoners were abused. He was unprepared for the answer given by the dedicated revolutionary he had come to know. It brought Bizot face-to-face with the paradox of perpetration, how a seemingly ordinary person can commit inhuman acts.

In response to this issue, during the first substantive phase of the trial, which focused on M-13, the parties asserted divergent articulations of Duch, which often revolved around portrayals of Duch as man (the defense) or monster (the prosecution and civil parties). Duch appeared eager to contribute to the process, sketching a portrait of himself and his past that was streaked, like the walls of Tuol Sleng, with black and white.

In many ways, the civil law system provided the Trial Chamber with greater flexibility than common law in matters ranging from evidentiary standards to procedure. Given Duch's apology and stated intention of cooperating, the court allowed him to speak at length, respond to questions posed by the parties, and make "observations." He appeared happy to do so.

Teacher, Torturer (Duch on M-13, April 4–6, 2009)

At the start of Day 4, Judge Nil explained that although M-13 operated during the civil war and therefore was outside of the court's temporal jurisdiction, the Trial Chamber needed to examine M-13 in order to understand "the context of S-21," since M-13 established precedents bearing on "the operation and functioning of S-21" and related to "the personality of the accused."[1] After instructing Duch to be seated in the dock, Judge Nil asked him to "describe the establishment and the location of security office, M-13."

Duch stood and rubbed his palms together several times before responding with a request: he wanted to tell the court about his path to M-13. As he spoke, he unclasped his hands and held them apart, as if holding a segment of a timeline, then quickly moved his left hand toward the right as he said, "[to tell] my history from before onwards [to M-13]."[2]

"The Trial Chamber permits you to do so," Judge Nil responded. "Please proceed."

Duch remained on his feet, hands clasped just below his belt, fingers fidgeting, perhaps nervous, perhaps trying to hide his maimed hand. "Your Honors of the Trial Chamber, with respect," he began. "My interest in politics first began in 1957 and continued until October 1964, when I decided to become a revolutionary."[3]

If Duch started by talking quickly with sharp intakes of breath, his voice tone modulated, and he began to speak with emphasis, accentuating key words and phrases, letting significant pauses hang in the air. His oratorical skills quickly became clear, the practiced teacher settling into a rhythm as he began to lecture the court, the Cambodian people, and the world about history and the role he played in it. "I believed this was a proper decision for my life," he continued. "I renounced everything for the revolution in a manner that was sincere and absolute."

With these words, Duch took center stage as a man of noble qualities who, through circumstance and poor judgment, became trapped in a vortex of violence. His story had an honorable beginning, one characterized by selflessness, devotion, and good intention. It began, he claimed, as a journey to help liberate his country from oppression.

The Khmer Rouge rose to power in the context of a war with the moral claim that they would liberate the country from foreign influences. Duch himself was born on November 17, 1942, in the midst of World War II. If French colonial rule was increasingly resented in Cambodia and elsewhere in Indochina for its taxation, fees, and corvée labor requirements, it also had laid the seeds of nationalism by building infrastructure, ranging from roads and railway links to schools and media, which facilitated communication and helped make possible an imagined community of Cambodian nationals headed by a small but growing educated elite.[4] Japanese influence and the weakness of Vichy rule provided a catalyst for the nascent anticolonial movement.

By the turn of the decade, as Duch was beginning his schooling and France attempted to stave off Cambodia's independence by enacting democratic reforms, a number of Cambodians were taking up arms against French rule, including a growing number of leftist fighters allied with communist Vietnamese revolutionaries.[5] The Khmer People's Revolutionary Party, a precursor of the CPK, was established in 1951. By 1952 leftist revolutionaries controlled almost a sixth of Cambodia. Their momentum, however, was undermined when Prince Sihanouk procured Cambodia's independence in 1953, and they were left with nothing at the 1954 Geneva Conference, which formally ended French colonial rule. Duch was 12 at the time.

A divide in the Cambodian communist movement, albeit a fluid one, can be traced to this moment. Some of the revolutionaries retained ties to or took refuge in North Vietnam, only to be purged when they returned to Cambodia in the 1970s. Others, including Pol Pot, Ieng Sary, Khieu Samphan, and Son Sen, eventually drew closer to China after studying in France during the late 1940s and early 1950s before returning to Cambodia. A number of these revolutionaries, many of whom occupied key posts on DK's Central Committee, would later date the origins of the CPK not to the founding of the Khmer People's Revolutionary Party but to the First Party Congress, held in secret in the Phnom Penh railway yards from September 28 to 30, 1960.

In a key speech given on September 29, 1977, to commemorate the seventeenth anniversary of this meeting, Pol Pot claimed that it was then that the revolutionaries formulated their political line, established the Party Statutes, and elected the members of the Party's Central Committee, which included him. This 1977 speech is important, since it provided a moral warrant for the revolutionary struggle, including the ongoing fight against perceived traitors and counterrevolutionaries. According to Pol Pot, those who attended the 1960 Party Congress used "scientific analysis" to understand "the real nature of Kampuchean society at that time." The resulting political line held that Cambodia was "enslaved by imperialism."[6]

In addition to this "contradiction" between Cambodia and foreign imperialism, Pol Pot asserted, the country was also plagued by internal class contradictions, particularly those between the peasants, constituting the vast majority of the population, and the groups who exploited them, such as "capitalists" and the "feudal" and "semifeudal" landowners.[7] Accordingly, the revolutionaries determined that they would seek to "arouse the peasants" so that they "burned with class hatred and took up the struggle."[8]

| | | |

Duch was an ideal recruit. He was born, the only male among five children, in a rural village in Kompong Thom province. His family was poor and ethnic Chinese, a background that may have contributed to a sense of devaluation, disempowerment, and humiliation.[9] While growing older, Duch became aware of his family's difficult financial situation, including his family's land problems and indebtedness to a usurious uncle,[10] precisely the sort of "contradiction" that the Khmer Rouge believed would draw recruits to the movement. Duch started school late but excelled in his studies, especially mathematics.

As Duch noted, his interest in politics dated to 1957, when at age 15 he became more fully conscious of the family's economic plight and of a possible solution to the exploitation they suffered: communism.[11] A Chinese official visited Cambodia that same year, providing Duch with a more positive identification for his ethnic background. "I felt proud to be Chinese,"[12] he recalled. At this time he also began to be influenced by one of his first teachers and mentors, Ke Kim Huot, who assisted poorer students and spoke out about corruption and social injustice.[13] Ke Kim Huot, who later became the head of a DK sector before being purged, may have continued helping Duch as Duch advanced in his studies, which eventually brought him to Phnom Penh, where he passed his baccalaureate exams in 1964.[14]

A number of Khmer Rouge used teaching to recruit students. While studying in Phnom Penh, Duch met two teachers who would become future mentors, Son Sen and Chhay Kim Hor.[15] A roommate at the Buddhist pagoda where Duch stayed recalled that Duch was already preaching about communism.[16]

In 1965, Duch took a position teaching mathematics at a junior high school in Skoun, a provincial town in Kompong Cham. By this time he had already joined the revolutionary movement, and his activities reflected it. Former students recalled him as "meticulous" and demanding yet "smooth" and "gentle and kind"—someone who treated the students with respect even as he assisted them by purchasing books and school supplies, establishing a student co-operative, taking in some of the poorest students, and giving extra lessons for free.[17] No one remembered him being overly strict or easily angered.[18] While Duch was not overt about his political leanings, students recalled, he spoke about class structure, carried a copy of Mao's "Little Red Book," and distributed communist leaflets to interested students.[19] All said he was a popular teacher.

While slowly building a base of student followers, Duch continued to deepen his association with the Khmer Rouge. At one point in early 1967 he even decided to work as a laborer to experience the difficulties firsthand.[20] In June or July of that year, he participated in a CPK political study session where his former teacher Chhay Kim Hor was instructing. They examined documents related to the party line, including texts on CPK policy, the 1960 Party Statutes, and the proper view of party members.[21] In October, Vorn Vet, another high-ranking Khmer Rouge cadre who would end up at S-21, invited Duch to join the Party.

| | | |

Duch remained on his feet, hands clasped and head swiveling to gaze at the different parties, while describing these events to the court on the first morn-ing of testimony on M-13. When he approached the moment when he joined the revolution, however, Duch began to gesticulate for emphasis before sud-denly crossing his arms tightly across his chest, his maimed hand pressed be-tween his forearm and chest, out of sight. He bowed slightly as he recalled the moment of his induction: "I stood before the Party flag and raised my hand."

Suddenly, Duch lifted his right hand, which was curled into a fist, to his temple, dropping his left arm to his side, as if he had been transported back in time and was standing at attention. "[I raised my hand] to show respect and swore to be faithful to the Party, the [oppressed] classes, and the people of Cambodia for the rest of my life," he said as he stared into the distance, lost in a moment of nostalgia. His curled fist still pressed against his temple, he re-peated: "to serve the Party, class, and the people for the rest of my life, without fear and ready to make any sacrifice."[22]

Then Duch abruptly crossed his arms once again, the moment past. "This was the goal of joining the Party back then." But, however briefly, those in the audience felt as if they had caught a glimpse of his revolutionary fervor. It was unsettling, since he seemed over four decades later to be able not just to recall the occasion of his induction into the Party but to summon the passion he felt toward it, an ardor that helped propel him toward M-13 and then S-21—and now to his seat in the dock.

Duch shifted back to lecture style almost seamlessly, as if the moment had never occurred. He explained that he joined the movement "to liberate the nation, my own people from any oppression. I did not have any intention to do criminal activities. . . . I strived to commit myself to the revolution. I was not afraid of being imprisoned or . . . dying. . . . [My spirit] to sacrifice was always constant."[23]

He was soon tested. On January 5, 1968, Duch was arrested, along with his mentor, Chhay Kim Hor, and Nat, the first chief of S-21, and sentenced to twenty years in jail. He would be released after two years, though not before observing the harshness of prison life, which—though he himself was not beaten—could include torture or illegal execution.[24]

This was a pivotal time in the revolutionary struggle. In 1963, just as Duch was finishing his studies, Pol Pot and Ieng Sary, who had been teaching in Phnom Penh, fled into the countryside. Son Sen, the former director of the Pedagogical Institute, followed them a year later. "We had to live in the countryside," Pol Pot explained in his 1977 speech, "in order to directly mobilize the peasant masses."[25] There, cadre worked directly with the peasantry since "the people had to understand our reasoning. Our policy had to conform with their interests for them to give us their support. We talked to them, had meetings with them. Sometimes they agreed with us, sometimes they didn't. We came back again and again." If, at first, some people didn't see "the true nature of U.S. imperialism," they eventually "ended up seeing it more and more clearly and uniting with us to combat it, to win independence, peace and neutrality."[26]

While such retrospective political histories must be read with caution, Pol Pot's remarks shed light on the key focus of Khmer Rouge agitation: US imperialism. During the mid-1960s, the US involvement in Vietnam escalated. The conflict had strong ripples in Cambodia, as the United States began bombing North Vietnamese troops who were passing through Cambodian territory. Cambodia's economy eventually began to destabilize. These events helped funnel one stream of recruits to the movement. A rebellion, sparked by anger at a new government rice policy, broke out in the Samlaut region of Battambang province in 1967. The Khmer Rouge used the occasion to launch their armed struggle in early 1968.

If Pol Pot asserted that the situation at that time was "like dry straw in the rice fields" needing only "a small spark to set it on fire," the reality was more complicated. There is no doubt that Khmer Rouge propaganda about imperialism and neocolonialism was more resonant in the midst of the upheaval caused by the Vietnam War. But their gains were nevertheless modest. Perhaps the key event that turned things in their favor was the March 1970 coup d'état against Prince Sihanouk. Duch claimed that the "Khmer Rouge would [have been] demolished" if it hadn't been for the coup, which handed the Khmer Rouge "a golden opportunity" and large numbers of new recruits.[27]

The coup also led to Duch's release on April 3, as Lon Nol freed a number of political prisoners so as to contrast his rule to that of Sihanouk. Duch swiftly rejoined the revolution, going to southwest Cambodia in August 1970, where he served as a political instructor at a military base. Less than a year later, in July 1971, he was asked to direct M-13, a new security office under the supervision of Vorn Vet (through mid-1973) and subsequently Son Sen (through 1975). Duch claimed to have protested that he just wanted to teach, but his superiors insisted he take this position. When asked why his superiors wanted him to head M-13, Duch explained that it was because of his "sincerity to the party" and meticulousness.[28]

At M-13, Duch refined many techniques he would use at S-21. The mission of M-13 was to "beat and interrogate and smash" prisoners,[29] most of whom who were initially supposed Lon Nol spies. As things got "complicated," the prisoner population expanded to include other groups, including "class enemies" and suspect cadre. Male prisoners were shackled, and all suffered from poor hygiene and insufficient rations.

Duch explained that torture was a common practice at security offices in Cambodia, and M-13 was no exception. Indeed, the only reason prisoners were kept alive was for interrogation.[30] The goal was to produce confessions. Initially, less abusive "cold methods" might be used. If prisoners were not cooperative, they would be beaten, often with a bamboo cane. Some prisoners were tied to poles. Duch admitted to interrogating and torturing two prisoners and to experimenting with new tortures.[31]

He claimed that prisoners were only killed on the authorization of his superiors. Executions, which typically involved striking victims on the back of the head, usually took place in secret. Allegedly following the advice of his mentor Chhay Kim Hor, Duch used peasants to do the killing, since they could "do it better" than intellectuals.[32] More broadly, he noted that he preferred to recruit young peasants because of their pure class origins and because his own background as an intellectual could raise questions. Many of these cadre came from the villages near M-13, to which Duch said that he and his staff had close ties. He was both boss and teacher, indoctrinating recruits into Khmer Rouge ideology and practice and training them for their duties, including torture.

Everyone, including Duch, was required to participate in "livelihood" meetings at which cadre would speak about their previous work, reflect on their good and bad qualities, and criticize their weaknesses before being criticized by others.[33] These sessions might last half or even an entire day. "We had to do livelihood meetings," Duch explained, "like we needed food. We cannot avoid eating food." The purpose was "to build a new political view . . . in line with the Party line. . . . We built our collective stance and got rid of our personal stance."[34] When participating in livelihood meetings, he recalled that he might talk about how he had studied the Party line yet not paid enough attention to catching spies or improving his staff.[35]

While Duch was running M-13, the revolution was turning in favor of the Khmer Rouge. In 1970–1971, many of the best trained units of Lon Nol's army had been destroyed by Vietnamese communist troops after two poorly conceived offenses. The United States continued to support the Lon Nol government, including the use of intensive bombing. From October 4, 1965, through August 15, 1973, the United States dropped at least 2,756,941 tons of ordnance on Cambodia during 230,516 sorties on 113,716 sites.[36] At M-13, Duch ordered the construction of trenches into which the cadre and prisoners jumped during B-52 raids. By the beginning of 1975, the war had all but been decided. Operations began to shut down at M-13 prior to closing on April 30, just two weeks after the Khmer Rouge took Phnom Penh.

| | | |

Duch told his story over two half days as he sat in the dock making observations, offering clarifications, and answering questions from the judges and then the prosecutors and civil parties. As he did so, clues about this man and his path to S-21 continued to emerge.

The defense was afforded the opportunity to go last in order to respond to what had been said. Roux honed in on the argument that Duch was a cog in the machine. How much choice did Duch have? Roux suggested very little. Secrecy was paramount. From the moment he joined the revolution, Duch was "trained to keep secrecy," even when doing something as basic as distributing flyers.[37]

The Khmer Rouge had related sayings, including the "four nots: Not to speak, not to know . . . not [to] see, and [not to] hear. So they had us try to continue to conceal everything."[38] Duch carried out his duties at M-13 in accordance with this principle of secrecy and instructed his staff that "confidentiality must be the first priority."[39] Even the burial sites at M-13 were kept secret. When Roux asked if it was then correct to say that everyone in the hierarchy "had to keep secrecy" and knew that if they did not their lives "could be endangered," Duch replied affirmatively."[40]

Roux turned to fear and obedience. Earlier in the trial, Judge Lavergne had read a pretrial statement Duch had written for the investigating judges titled "The Influence of Terror on Me." In the tract, Duch stated that he hated the work and killing, which he likened to being forced to walk in excrement.[41] He claimed to have responded to the situation by focusing on discerning the truth of the confessions. Later he would say that the confessions were perhaps "40 percent" accurate but that there was "no scientific method to verify the truth."[42] This uncertainty terrified him, since it introduced unpredictability into the process.

Duch also said he had tried to help some M-13 prisoners, like Bizot, by seeking their release. He succeeded in freeing 10 prisoners, even if he acknowledged it was like "a drop of water . . . in a pond."[43] He also split M-13 into the two branches, M-13A and M-13B, where prisoners with lesser crimes were put to work and could potentially be released. Despite his strong dislike of his work at M-13, Duch claimed, "I had to do it."[44]

The third part of Roux's argument focused on moral restructuring, as illustrated by the livelihood meetings. The larger purpose of the meetings was to "build [kâsang] a new political view" that accorded with the party line and principles. This included "respect[ing] the organizational discipline," even if this entailed running a death camp.[45]

With this last argument, Roux's articulation of "Duch the Man" clearly came into sight. Duch had joined the revolution for the best of purposes, carrying out his duties with precision, sacrifice, and noble goals. He became caught up in a Khmer Rouge movement that demanded absolute obedience from its followers, a coercion reinforced by terror. In this context of fear and the larger tumult of the civil war, the Khmer Rouge sought to reshape the minds of followers like Duch to transform them into obedient devotees.

Roux gave the last word to Duch. "At that time," Duch told the court, there was no other path than "to respect the discipline of the Party."[46] As human beings, he continued, we sometimes have to do things not to our liking. To console himself, Duch said, he sometimes reflected on the final lines of a nineteenth-century French poem that he had memorized: "The Death of the

Wolf," by Alfred de Vigny. Speaking slowly in heavily accented French, he recited it to the court:

> Weeping or praying—all this is in vain.
> Shoulder your long and energetic task the way that destiny sees fit to ask.
> Then [as I do] suffer and so die without complaint.[47]

"It means," he finished with a wave of his hand, "When God assigns you something, what can you do?" A long silence ensued as Roux let the court ruminate on Duch's ability to recite—in the original and from memory—French romantic poetry.

What greater evidence was needed of his humanity?

The Double (François Bizot on M-13)

Such moments at the Duch trial were uncanny, unsettling the articulations being asserted. Here, an accused torturer and executioner, the sort of person thought to epitomize the opposite of that which is called "civilized," was making a strong claim to it by reciting one of its highest forms, poetry.[48] This moment would be mentioned later in the trial, as when one of the civil parties recalled the long silence that followed Duch's recitation: "Everything went dead. We could even hear the sounds of a mosquito if there was one in the chamber.... And during that three minute time, everything was ... so quiet."[49] Duch's reading of the poem was, he suggested, a farce.

Many of the participants in the proceedings would return to Duch's seeming duality, which Bizot, who took the stand after Duch had recited the poem, noted gave rise to an "ambiguity" about Duch that Bizot found deeply troubling.[50]

Just before Duch recited these lines of poetry, for example, he had discussed the torture of Sok, a former prostitute, who was subjected to a method of cold exposure Duch had devised: forcing women to stand in the breeze after submerging themselves in the nearby river so that their clothes were soaked. The woman in question had been accused of spying, and he "wanted to know how many people came along with her."[51]

After using the cold exposure technique on Sok, Duch noticed the silhouette of her breasts and hips, which he and his staff found arousing. He ceased use of this torture because he was uncertain that he and his men could "refrain" from violating the Khmer Rouge moral code. Duch noted that even after the cold exposure, Sok had not wavered in her response that she had come alone, so he believed she was telling the truth. Nevertheless, his superiors "decided to smash her," a decision he implemented.[52] At that time, Duch continued, carrying out such Party orders was "an obligation," even if doing so was now considered a crime.

It was precisely this sort of moral claim that made Bizot uneasy, as Duch's actions were informed by an ethic. In making this suggestion, Bizot was not excusing Duch's actions, which he viewed as criminal. But there appeared to be a moral logic at the root of what he did, something common to all human beings.

| | | |

Bizot's view of Duch emerged over the course of his three-month detention, which began in October 1971, when Bizot, a young anthropologist, and his two research assistants were captured.[53] Over the next few days, Bizot found himself facing a Khmer Rouge tribunal in which he was accused of being an American spy and spat on by a dozen village girls. Following a mock execution, he was marched, blindfolded, to M-13.

At that time the camp, which was relocated several times, consisted of four raised huts, open on one side and holding a total of perhaps fifty prisoners, who were shackled by the ankle. Bizot recalled that the modest site was "covered with a tangle of palm leaves; it was bounded by a stream and the edges of a poorly defined clearing. There were some shrubs, some undergrowth and several tall trees: they marked the forbidden perimeter in the heart of a bamboo plantation that a handful of men could easily control."[54] Duch's staff included perhaps a dozen men, including young guards from local villages.

Bizot was greeted by one of Duch's deputies, an older man who refused Bizot's request to bathe and ordered him shackled. Bizot remembered this deputy as a "coarse and brutal fellow" of whom he was very frightened and around whom even the guards were cautious[55]—someone more in keeping with the stereotype of a monster.

Shortly afterward, Duch arrived. "Do you want to wash?" he asked, with a "smile that exposed teeth and gums. . . . [His] light skin and the crowded, uneven teeth betrayed his Chinese origins. He looked young, not yet thirty. . . . But his authority was total."[56]

Bizot recalled that Duch's face would suddenly flash from happy to tense and that he often spoke softly and slowly, revolutionary-style, with his head slightly raised, while "looking down so far that his eyelids appeared to be shut."[57] He also appeared gaunt and in poor health. Nevertheless, he commanded respect from the guards, who admired him for his revolutionary commitment and tireless work, which often consisted of reviewing documents on a small portable table set in front of the guard's hut.[58]

At M-13, Bizot was chained to a bamboo post in a storage shed, separate from the other prisoners, and occupied a relatively privileged status. The prison conditions were difficult. Hygiene was poor. Many prisoners fell ill, often with malaria, and were sent to a sick hut, where some died. And the prisoners were always hungry. Duch explained to the court that most of the prisoners at this time had been arrested for spying and that M-13's mission was to interrogate and "smash" these enemies.[59]

Duch interrogated Bizot himself. After explaining that he was facing serious charges, Duch gave Bizot paper and a pen and asked him to write a "statement of innocence," which included biographical details "about my studies, my life, my father and mother, why I was in Cambodia and, thereafter, I was supposed to swear about my innocence."[60] Doing so was extremely difficult and emotional, bringing tears "to my eyes as I signed" what might be "the last trace I had managed to leave behind."[61] Bizot would be asked to redraft this statement more than a dozen times.

Bizot's statement became a baseline for interrogation. Duch's method of interrogation was to "test" Bizot about these declarations along with what he had said at the people's tribunal and what Bizot wrote in a notebook he had requested from Duch, which Bizot filled with "childhood memories, drawings, poems, observations on Buddhism, mantras, [and] my curriculum vitae."[62] Conversing in a firm but polite tone, Duch had probed Bizot's claims as he sought to verify whether Bizot was a scholar of Cambodian Buddhism, as he claimed, or a CIA agent.[63]

Throughout the process, "Duch proceeded by watertight deductions, with the calm of scientific procedure, advancing to the truth only if he had distinguished it from fallacy," with the ultimate aim of making "a final decision on my autobiography—as an innocent or guilty one."[64] Even when Bizot, who was greatly angered by the unjust accusations, became upset, Duch "never lost his calm and, technically speaking, maintained his position as inquisitor. I could be sure that whatever I said would be rapidly dissected and weighted as a symptom of my duplicity, my supposed talents as a spy."

At times, Duch found contradictions in Bizot's accounts. When Bizot had gone before the people's tribunal, for example, he had acted as if he didn't understand English, which he worried would confirm allegations he was a US spy. When providing biographical details, however, Bizot noted that he had lived in England. In the midst of one of their sessions, Duch suddenly laughed and then asked, "Now tell me why you don't speak English, when you spent more than a year in England."[65] Bizot admitted his lie and the reasons for it, but Duch told Bizot: "this inconsistency in my dossier was a very serious matter and bothered him greatly. What had occurred in England that I wished to cover up?"[66]

Duch's interrogation techniques seemed to be inspired by several streams of moral understanding. As an intellectual, he appeared to have a commitment to truth and knowledge and the scientific principles by which they might be discerned. The "science" of Marxist-Leninism accorded with this perspective.

Duch's interrogation methods also resonated with Buddhist rationalism, which emphasized the analysis of evidence (*ceak sdaeng*) to discern truth from falsehood (*khos-treuv*) and moral right from wrong (*bon bap*).[67] It was this sort of moral underpinning of Duch's ideals—which ultimately were used to justify highly immoral acts—that Bizot found paradoxical.

Over the course of Bizot's seventy-seven-day imprisonment at M-13, he grew to establish a bond, not quite a friendship but a sort of familiarity and rapport, with Duch. Duch sometimes told Bizot about his past or experiences as a math teacher. But it was not a relationship of equals. Bizot lived in fear and uncertainty, knowing he might be executed at any time. Duch the inquisitor was his only hope for survival. Each of Bizot's answers could thus mean the difference between life and death. The interrogations involved a back-and-forth, as Duch tested Bizot's statements and Bizot had to anticipate and adjust his answers to fit criteria that could prove or disprove the accusations. In this sense, the interrogations somewhat resembled the livelihood sessions or Khmer Rouge practice of giving biographies, which had to accord with the Khmer Rouge articulation of reality.

Duch's words therefore had enormous import and impact on Bizot. For example, Duch could, through nonverbal or indirect speech, suggest how Bizot should answer a question in a manner that might lead to exoneration. But his words could also devastate. One day Duch attended a meeting that he had told Bizot would be very important to Bizot's fate. On his return, Duch avoided Bizot's gaze and spent a long time with his guards before approaching Bizot "without lowering his eyes. Then I heard his voice, enunciating every syllable, suddenly cutting like steel: 'You have been exposed! Your calculations have been totally thwarted!'"[68] Bizot collapsed to his knees at the death sentence. Duch rushed over to help steady Bizot, his expression suddenly changing as

Duch's "mouth broke into a laugh, and he gazed at me. 'But of course not . . . did you believe me? Come on, it was a joke! You are going to be set free.'"[69]

The relation between Bizot and Duch shifted once again after the news of Bizot's release, though Bizot remained cautious even after his shackles were removed. Duch and Bizot began to have discussions that focused on abstract issues as opposed to Bizot's biography, culminating in a long fireside conversation the night before Bizot's departure from M-13. They spoke of the Khmer Rouge revolution, which Duch explained was necessary to free Cambodians from the oppression of US imperialism and its lackey, the Lon Nol government. As he spoke, Duch's voice trembled, making Bizot "aware of the strength and authenticity of his dedication. But he spoke clearly and eloquently, never raising his voice, his eyes lowered and his mind concentrated."[70]

At one point Bizot suggested that there were many similarities between Khmer Rouge ideology and Buddhism. If *dhamma* served as the guiding principle of Buddhism, Angkar and its party line seemed to serve a similar role. The Khmer Rouge emphasis on discipline (*vinay*) and renunciation (*leh bang*) directly dovetailed with Buddhist traditions. And the Khmer Rouge even used the term for religious education and prayer (*rean sout*) to refer to self-criticism sessions.[71] "This has nothing to do with it!" Duch responded. "Buddhism is the opium of the people."[72]

Even if Duch's power at M-13 and control of Bizot was always in the background, Bizot and Duch were talking more as equals than before, which gave Bizot the opportunity to ask Duch a lingering question. Earlier during his imprisonment, Bizot had passed by a prisoner who had been granted extra privileges and was sharpening a rattan stick. When Bizot asked, in jest, if the prisoner was going to beat prisoners with the stick, the man replied, "No, no, no, I'm not the one who does the hitting."[73] Bizot, who had been kept separate from the other prisoners, was startled by this response. Duch had never struck him, nor had he seen any prisoners being interrogated. He assumed that Duch's harsh deputy must be the one who abused prisoners.

As he and Duch poked at the fire with sticks, Bizot asked about the beating of prisoners. Duch responded that the prisoners were accused of spying and could endanger the revolutionary struggle. So they had to be interrogated. When Bizot again asked "But who does the beating?"[74] Duch cut him off, saying "Ah! . . . I can't stand their duplicity. The only way is to terrorize them, isolate them, and starve them. It's very tough. I have to force myself. You cannot imagine how much their lying infuriates me!"[75] Duch explained, "When I cross-examine them and they resort to every ruse to avoid talking, denying our senior officers potentially vital information, then I beat them! I beat them until I'm out of breath."

For Bizot, this moment became a sort of existential landmark. To this point, he had largely viewed Duch in terms of an articulation of "Duch the Man," the devoted revolutionary fighting a struggle that was ultimately moral and just. But suddenly this articulation collapsed, as he was overwhelmed by the realization that Duch also tortured prisoners, something only done by brutes. Previously, he explained, "I considered that I was on the right side of humankind and there were monsters and, thank heavens, I would never be amongst the ranks of them. There was a difference due to history, to one's sensitivities, and that this had to do with a condition of nature and not everybody could be a monster."[76]

This was a mistake, Bizot suggested, which diverted one's gaze from the fact that under tragic circumstances, anyone might end up like Duch. Indeed, Duch "looked very much like many friends of mine, a Marxist, a human being who was a Marxist who was prepared to surrender his life for his country [and] for the revolution. He believed in this cause and the ultimate goal of his commitment [to] . . . the well-being of the inhabitants of Cambodia. He was fighting against injustice."[77] From this moment on, Bizot had to deal with the realization that he, too, could in the right circumstances do horrible things.[78]

Bizot freely admitted that he and Duch had established a bond as they recognized one another's humanity, with Bizot coming "to see the man behind the henchman" and Duch "to see the man behind the spy, the man behind the prisoner."[79] This growing recognition of the face of the other, perhaps further enhanced by their young ages and identifications as intellectuals, disrupted the deeply dehumanizing conditions that exist in places like M-13.

While there is no universal and monocausal dynamic, a transference between interrogators and prisoners sometimes takes place as each person projects onto the other. In some cases, the person being interrogated may come to identify with the interrogator, not just because his or her sense of self and identity may be diminished but also because attunement and empathetic understanding may be key to survival. Looking back, Bizot recognized that something along these lines had taken place between him and Duch, as Bizot gradually came to understand Duch and even empathize with his suffering as he carried out duties he disliked. Bizot had served as a double, a mirror that said " 'I feel, I share; I make your dread and your fate my own.' I was freeing him from his own fear and was able . . . to hide from him the detestable image

('Do you have no pity') that his other victims all project on to him. My face became his own, and that forbade him from killing me."[80]

Bizot's reflections about his experiences at M-13 dovetailed in many respects with those of the defense. At the end of Bizot's testimony, Roux asked some final questions related to Duch's plight at M-13. Bizot acknowledged that Duch did not appear to have decision-making powers about executions and also lived in a "terrifying atmosphere of fear and death."[81] Duch often had the look of someone who lived in a state of suffering, something not surprising, given the "constant presence of executions, of killing, and of torture."[82] Roux also read a passage from Bizot's memoir, *The Gate*, recounting how, as they were about to separate on Bizot's release, Bizot turned to Duch and said, "Thank you, Comrade. I owe you my life." Duch replied, "I only acted in accordance with my conscience and with complete conviction."[83]

THE MONSTER (PRISONERS AND GUARDS ON M-13)

If Bizot ultimately affirmed Duch's humanity, he also revealed an excess that unsettled this articulation of Duch the man. Even before Bizot left the stand, Duch faced questions about what, exactly, he had done at M-13. Duch acknowledged that prisoners were beaten as part of the M-13's mission to "smash" spies and other enemies. M-13 was not an exception in this regard. In Cambodia, Duch said, torture had a long history and was commonplace, even "inevitable," in police offices and prisons.[84] So were executions.

Duch had observed this firsthand when he was sent to Prey Sar prison in 1968. He knew from reading a Vietnamese (*yuon*) book that mentioned torture that he might be abused; but, he insisted, "I was ready to receive such torture. As a revolutionary instructor I was not afraid."[85] Moreover, such crimes were part of the reason that "we, the sons of the motherland, had to defend the people" and transform society.[86]

At Prey Sar, the inmates "were shocked and terrorized for every breath they [took]."[87] He knew of prisoners who were illegally executed. Prisoners were also kicked and beaten. While Duch said that he himself had been verbally abused, he was never tortured—though Bizot recalled him saying that he was beaten on the head by the police. It was in prison that he also met Chan (Mam Nai), a fellow teacher who would serve as a deputy and interrogator at M-13 and S-21.[88]

When Duch was assigned to work at M-13 in 1971, he knew little about torture beyond the method of beating a person with a whip. This meant that he had to experiment. He acknowledged that he tortured two people, including

Nget Sambon, a man who wrote for a newspaper and had traveled to the Liberated Zones. Duch beat and interrogated him for almost a month in order to "experiment."[89] Duch's description of his experiment with Sok, the former prostitute, suggests how he may have proceeded.

Through such experimentation, Duch began to refine the torture and interrogation methods he would bring to S-21. Physical torture usually involved beatings with tree branches, though sometimes prisoners were tied to poles or exposed to cold.[90] He knew about waterboarding and suffocation by plastic bags, but the interrogators lacked the materials to use these methods. Duch acknowledged that the torture techniques used at M-13 "were designed or improvised by me myself . . . [not] by the superior or upper echelon."[91] His superior Chhay Kim Hor had just stressed the importance of secrecy when using torture. Duch also began drawing on his teaching skills to train staff in interrogation and torture methods.

Bizot's testimony had raised questions about Duch's claim that he was largely uninvolved with the torture. In particular, Judge Lavergne wanted to know if Bizot's recollection that Duch had told Bizot that Duch became angered and beat prisoners until he was out of breath was true. Duch replied that Bizot must have been referring to the interrogation of the second man he had beaten, an accused spy named Kao Bun Heang. At the time, Duch explained, he had malaria and "felt dizzy." During the interrogation, "two comrades from Hanoi" arrived and beat the man until he confessed. His lies made Duch, who was already sick and emotional after observing the beating, "very angry and I was walking towards him about to beat him. Then I grabbed a whip or stick. Then the guy begged me and then I could not beat him because I was out of breath myself already. Then I let him be taken to his rest place."[92] When Judge Lavergne noted that his explanation still diverged from that of Bizot and asked him, "Is it true or it is not true?" Duch replied that he could not comment since the event had taken place over thirty years ago.

| | | |

The haze of time and memory would only deepen when the final three witnesses, all of whom were from villages near M-13, took the stand. The first, seventy-two-year-old Uch Sorn, told the court he could only see "shadows" but, when the camera zoomed in on Duch, affirmed that Duch had been the chief of M-13.[93] Duch, in turn, did not recognize Uch Sorn.

Arrested in 1973 when he was on his way to purchase pigs for a Buddhist ceremony, Uch Sorn was accused of being a spy and taken to M-13. By this time, M-13 had moved to a new site in Amleang subdistrict near a lake and was surrounded by a bamboo fence. Chan Khan, a former M-13 guard who testified a few days later, recalled that the fence was surrounded by ditches and spikes to prevent escape.[94]

Uch Sorn testified that the main M-13 compound included several meter-deep pits, in one of which he was detained. Conditions were harsh. Each pit contained perhaps 20–30 people, who were shackled by the ankle and slept on their backs. When it rained, the prisoners got soaked. The inmates received little food, and many became sick or died. They were bathed infrequently and were required to urinate into bamboo tubes.

Uch Sorn, who as a local villager had the possibility of release, was eventually granted extra privileges and put to work. Among other things, he dug trenches that were used as mass graves. He recalled that if the bodies were not buried deep enough, dogs would sometimes dig up the remains.[95]

Given his duties and ability to move around, Uch Sorn sometimes witnessed prisoner abuse. At a mass grave he had dug, for example, he observed the execution of a man and a woman, who, "chained [by] the neck . . . were brought to the rim of the pit" into which they fell after being struck by a hoe. The woman, he recalled, was kicked unconscious "into the pit and they buried her while she was still breathing."[96] Earlier he heard Duch warn the prisoner, "I only kill . . . enemies."[97]

On another occasion, Uch Sorn saw five prisoners tied, naked, to posts. Duch's deputy, Chan, shot the middle prisoner in the head. Afterward, Uch Sorn "cleaned the brain and the blood which was spattered [about]."[98] He surmised that the execution was perhaps intended to scare the other prisoners.

Such incidents were part of a broader pattern of abuse. The guards kicked, beat, and yelled at inmates. Uch Sorn glimpsed interrogators using pliers to extract the fingernails [correct] of detainees, who screamed from the pain. He also observed Meas, one of Duch's men who would move to S-21, submerge a bound prisoner in pond water.

Uch Sorn also saw Duch use a whip to beat a woman. After a while, Duch's guards came and beat her until she began to have a seizure. At this point, Duch "slapped his butt and he laughed."[99] He recalled that, at M-13, he "was so afraid of [Duch], I did not even dare to look him straight in the face." But this was no longer the case, since Duch had become "a tiger without teeth." Noting that the prisoners were treated worse than animals, Uch Sorn wondered how Cambodians could have done such things to their own people.

When Judge Lavergne asked Duch to comment on Uch Sorn's testimony, Duch acknowledged that it was "fundamentally true," before disputing the details. He had never beaten a woman in this manner. And it would have been impossible for Uch Sorn to observe this, since interrogations were conducted out of sight. Further, it was unlikely that Meas would have submerged a prisoner, since others would have seen it. At M-13, Duch continued, pliers weren't used, and there were only three pits, which held no more than 10 people, and victims didn't die there, just during "the smash." He did allow that a prisoner had been shot once and that it was possible that dogs had dug up the mass graves.

Following up on Uch Sorn's earlier question, Judge Lavergne asked Duch why Cambodians had killed fellow Cambodians. Duch explained that it "was about political issue[s]. First . . . it was to smash the enemy spies and it was the class struggle in the liberated zone. . . . And the class line, the proletariat class line was introduced, that's why Khmer killed Khmer blindly, because of that principle."[100]

| | | |

Things did not become clearer during the subsequent testimony on M-13. If everyone seemed to agree that Duch was a devoted revolutionary, they diverged on the degree of his zeal. On the one hand the defense and Bizot depicted him as a reluctant revolutionary, one who did bad things out of necessity but took no pleasure in these duties. On the other hand the prosecution and civil parties portrayed Duch as a zealous executioner, an image that ran through the accounts of the witnesses from the Amleang area near M-13.

Perhaps the most extreme version of this articulation—Duch the monster—was expressed by the next witness, Chan Voeun.[101] In 1974, Chan Voeun was assigned to M-13, where he served as a guard. Like Uch Sorn, Chan Voeun stated that the pits were used to detain prisoners, who were chained by the neck and suffered from the difficult conditions. He recalled that once after a hard rain there was a flood, and some of the detainees drowned, an accusation Duch denied.

But what stood out in much of Chan Voeun's account was the brutality of Duch and his men. He claimed to have seen prisoners "stripped naked and beaten during the interrogation."[102] When Judge Lavergne asked, "And who conducted the interrogations?" Chan Voeun replied, "It's him, Duch."[103] According to Chan Voeun, Duch "alone had the rights to torture prisoners. He did the torture personally by himself, for instance, by taking a cloth, dipping it in kerosene and wrapping it around a stick and burning the bodies of the prisoners who had their arms tied behind them and were hanging from a tree branch and swinging up and down."[104] Duch also allegedly beat prisoners with whips and clubs and "submerged them in the water in the stream adjacent in the prison site, causing the prisoner to go unconscious."

Duch's brutality included sexual violence. Chan Voeun recalled seeing Duch torch the breasts of a female prisoner: "That's what I saw with my own eyes. I stood and watched it."[105] Duch also supposedly shot and executed Chan Voeun's uncle, Soy, who had been tied to a post. "Let me tell you the truth," Chan Voeun said, when he claimed that Duch shot his uncle with "two bullets from the AK rifle. . . . One hit his left shoulder and the other one left his chest and he died. . . . [Duch] killed him in front of me."[106]

In Chan Voeun's view, abusing prisoners was something that made Duch "happy like a madman."[107] When administering torture, for example, Duch sometimes laughed and seemed "happy like he had gone crazy in doing the torturing."[108] Duch was "a very mean and vicious person. If Duch wanted someone dead, he had to die." Duch's subordinates, Chan Voeun continued, feared "Duch as if he were a tiger and did not dare glance at his face. If Duch spoke jokingly, you had to be vigilant. If he spoke with a straight face, it was okay."[109]

Chan Voeun acknowledged that he had a conflict with Duch, who had arrested him after he allowed three prisoners to escape. Eventually he managed to escape himself, fleeing to his cooperative, where he was afforded some protection, since the Khmer Rouge did not want to upset the base villagers. But there were limits to such tolerance. At one point villagers from Amleang were accused of secretly stockpiling weapons, presumably for a revolt, leading to the arrest of perhaps 30 of these "spies."[110] Duch would apologize for "the crimes I committed [against] the people of Amelang who once supported me, who sent their children to me to be educated . . . to become the very honest people [who would be] so loyal to the Party." But he also noted, "I never wanted to work this kind of job."[111]

Chan Voeun, however, was a fraud. "Your Honours," Duch said, "first of all, let me inform you that Chan Voeun was not a staff of my office of M-13. Let me show you the evidence as follows."[112] He proceeded to cite specific documents and page numbers to highlight contradictions in Chan Voeun's pretrial statements. Judge Lavergne cut Duch off, asking him to respond specifically to Chan Voeun's accusation that Duch had burned the breasts of the female prisoners. Duch replied that Chan Voeun had combined truth and falsehood in his account, drawing on what he had heard from others.

Duch, his anger rising, proceeded to take issue with almost all of Chan Voeun's allegations. As he spoke, some observers might have recalled Bizot's recollection of Duch's remark that he became furious when people did not tell the truth. "This is a fabrication," Duch concluded. "I cannot accept his testimony."[113] When Judge Lavergne asked Chan Voeun if he stood by his statements, Chan Voeun, in seeming disbelief, asked why Duch denied that he worked at M-13.

| | | |

Duch did recognize Chan Khan, the last M-13 witness. In 1973 Chan Khan, a thirteen- or fourteen-year-old boy from a nearby village, was assigned to work at M-13 as a guard, though he sometimes did agricultural work or escorted prisoners to dig graves. When asked if he recognized Chan Voeun, Chan Khan affirmed that Chan Voeun was the guard "who allowed the prisoners to escape."[114]

Like all of the witnesses, Chan Khan had difficulty remembering things and also at times seemed, like Chan Voeun, to contradict his earlier statements. But he clearly recalled prisoner abuse. He saw the whips and bamboo rods used to beat prisoners, who, after interrogation and torture, sometimes returned "with swollen bodies and blood all over."[115] If he did not witness executions by shooting, he did see the poles where prisoners were tied and shot. And he confirmed that a handful of prisoners had drowned during the flood.

He remembered Duch as "strict" and hardworking, someone who was "firm and serious." Chan Khan was frightened of Duch, and none of "the guards dared enter his office . . . [or] dared joke with him [as] we would joke with the others, and he was very meticulous in his work."[116] Duch carried a pistol and smoked. Chan Khan also observed him "laugh like crazy."[117] Chan Khan noted that the staff worked in fear at M-13, because "during that period everyone was being followed and monitored, so we had to be vigilant all the time and we had to be careful of what we said or we would be dead."[118] Today, he said, he felt ashamed of having worked at M-13 even if he would have been killed if he had tried to escape.

If Chan Khan claimed that it was not possible to refuse an order to work at M-13, Duch painted a somewhat different picture when asked to make observations. After noting how moved he was to see "my former guard," Duch stated that he had good relations with local "referral villages" that had long supported the revolution and willingly sent children to work at M-13. Duch recounted that he did background research to find recruits who had "good biographies" before making a request to his superiors for the assignment, though ultimately the villagers had to consent.[119] When Judge Lavergne pressed him on his recruitment of children, Duch was evasive and even critiqued the Judge for asking about something "I have explained already."[120]

Duch would later have a more testy exchange with international civil party lawyer Karim Khan, who, in a challenging tone, asked Duch to expand on the difficult prison conditions at M-13. M-13, Duch told Khan, "was a prison that was not just harsh but . . . cruel and heinous. It is a place where humanity was smashed."[121] Then he noted that Khan was a "new face in the Court," suggesting he was engaging in repetitive questioning. At another point in their exchange, Duch said with a trace of sarcasm that M-13 "was not a school building. It was a Khmer Rouge prison."

Later the discussion would return to Duch's training of the recruits, for whom he said he felt affection. He used his teaching skills to educate recruits about "the revolutionary way"[122] as he sought to instill an "absolute stance toward the enemy," as well as the strictness required to interrogate and "smash" prisoners.[123] Education, he continued, was different during this period. Recruits were not taught Buddhist principles of nonviolence or about the Universal Declaration of Human Rights. Instead, they were taught about class and stance. Anyone who deviated from this principle would be "beheaded."[124]

Subordinate

(ESTABLISHMENT OF S-21)

Red slashes divide the faintly lined manila paper displayed on the monitor. Dates mark a circulation: 2/9/1977, 10/15/77, 17/10/77, and finally 11/11/77. A signature just above the second date reads: "With respect! Duch. 15.10.77." The two large sloping red letters that spell out Duch's name contrast with the rest of his tight script. He underlines his name.

At the top of the page, someone has written in black: "The Answers of Long Muy=Chuon, Head of the Khmer-Chinese Translation Group, Office K16." The equal sign signifies an alias. Each Khmer word is marked underneath by an even red line. Just to the right, someone has made a large check, also in red. There is also a page number: 66.

In the center of the paper, two more lines of text, written in black, provide additional clues about the document: "About the traitorous activity of Long Muy=Chuon." The text is enclosed by a rectangle, its straight red edges unwavering amid the noise of the competing script and the small rips, tears, and punctures marring the surface. Like the graffitied photograph of Duch, this cover shot of a confession was created in a room at Tuol Sleng. It also appeared during Duch's trial soon after the discussion shifted to S-21. Duch would use a victim's confession as evidence.

Beginnings

"Can you tell the court about your memory of the establishment of S-21?" Judge Nil asked, after instructing Duch to sit in the dock. "You take the floor."[1]

Duch seemed to embrace such moments, as if back in the classroom lecturing. He did so within a context of authority and principles, first education and mathematics, then S-21 and the Party line, next church and God, and now the court and law.

"Mr. President. S21 was a combination of security forces from Division 703 and cadre from M13," Duch began, speaking slowly. He wore headphones and was dressed in a pristine white polo shirt.

As Duch continued, his voice became louder and he gesticulated, even waving a document at one point, more like a teacher than a defendant accused of mass murder. Over the next three trial days, the details of his path to the leadership of S-21 would come into focus through his own expositions, his testimony about M-13, and details from questioning.

According to Duch, M-13 began to shut down at the start of 1975 as the civil war drew to a close.[2] He learned about the Khmer Rouge victory on April 17 by radio. Soon thereafter, on April 30, he received orders to release the remaining M-13B prisoners, perhaps 100 in total. The handful of prisoners at M-13A were transferred or executed.

After M-13 shut down, Duch waited for orders, even as Son Sen gave him a motorbike, a status symbol in the new regime. "After April 17," he recalled, "the Communist Party had ordered everyone out of the cities. The workers were evacuated. So, too, were the civil servants and the capitalists. Even the barbers. Everyone. No one was left. The only ones who came to live in the city were units of the revolutionary army."[3]

"In May," he continued, "after I had finished my work at M-13. . . . I rode my new motorbike to the house of Brother An," who had served as the secretary of Sector 15 of the Special Zone. Earlier, Duch had explained that the Special Zone, composed of Sectors 15 and 25 and the Phnom Penh area, had been created in 1971 due to tension between General Ta Mok and "the intellectuals."[4] The Special Zone was headed by Vorn Vet, Cheng An's longtime boss, who was Duch's immediate superior when Duch started working at M-13. Son Sen later became the deputy secretary of the Special Zone in 1973, even as he oversaw Khmer Rouge military strategy.

After the war, Cheng An was transferred to the Ministry of Industry, where he would continue serving under Vorn Vet. In May 1975, Cheng An had returned to the Special Zone to gather cadre. "Everyone was going to Phnom Penh," Duch recalled. He was "perplexed" because he heard nothing.[5] So, when Duch arrived at Cheng An's house, "I begged him, 'Can I come work with you in industry, Elder Brother?'"[6] Cheng An seemed to reply favorably but asked Duch to wait a week and then come meet him again. "I was so happy," Duch recalled. But, in the end, Cheng An sent a messenger with a letter that said: "Comrade, Angkar won't allow you to come work in Industry. Instead you must continue to wait for Angkar to assign your new duties."[7]

Duch repeatedly pointed to his request as an illustration of his reluctance to do security work. He also stated that after a prisoner revolt at M-13 in 1973, he asked Vorn Vet for a transfer, a request that was also denied.[8] Alan Bates, a member of the prosecution team, pressed Duch on this point, asking if he had said to Cheng An "'I don't want to work in security. I don't like it?' Or did you say to him, 'I don't like having to give orders to kill people'?"[9] Duch answered, as he often did, by invoking a Cambodian proverb: "If you break open the crab you'll show the shit."[10]

"I didn't dare tell Elder Brother Cheng An that I hated security work," Duch explained. "Instead, I said, 'I really want to work with you, Elder Brother, in Industry.' Cheng An and I had mutual understanding. I loved and trusted him and he loved and trusted me. . . . I was like a loyal German shepherd."[11] Under the Khmer Rouge, Duch continued, "this was the way we spoke with the level above. I would never dare 'Break open the crab to show the shit.'" Those who did, Duch would often say, would be "beheaded."[12]

Accordingly, during DK, cadre had to calibrate their speech, expressing things in a roundabout fashion, never directly criticizing the regime or a superior and never expressing one's desires too directly for fear of being accused of "individualism." If one revealed the "shit," the unseemly and unspoken—what had been redacted from the Khmer Rouge ideological articulations, an excess that lay under the surface with the potential to dehisce—one would be dead, just like the crab. "So we had to find a different way of saying it."

In many ways, this sort of calibration resonated with preexisting Cambodian norms related to status, whereby one is expected to protect the face and honor of those with whom one has social ties and obligations, particularly in formal contexts where face is at stake.[13] During DK, however, the stakes intensified in a context in which, increasingly, every action taken or word said was carefully observed for signs of subversion and could be a pretext for execution.

In such a situation, the pressure for compliance rose dramatically as each person constantly self-monitored and monitored others, a practice ritually enacted through criticism and self-criticism sessions but operative across a variety of everyday contexts. During DK, Cambodians invoked a number of slogans suggesting this panoptic situation in which the "all-seeing Party" constantly watched everything people did and said, including "Angkar has the eyes of a pineapple," "Hear nothing, do nothing, see nothing," and "Remain deaf and mute."

People were constantly watched—at work, in the communal mess hall, at meetings, and even in the family circle at night, when Khmer Rouge spies crept about. Sometimes parents even came to fear that their children, exposed to intensive Khmer Rouge indoctrination, would inform on them. On occasion they did. According to Khmer Rouge ideology, everything, including family ties, had to be subordinated to the revolution. One of the ultimate tests for a cadre was to demonstrate a willingness to cut off sentiment toward someone to whom he or she had previously been close, whether a friend, teacher, relative, or family member.

Duch himself would confront this situation at S-21, as his former workers, comrades, and even his brother-in-law passed through the prison gates. By likening himself to a German shepherd or "instrument," analogies he used repeatedly, he sought to convey the situation of fear and coercion in which he acted. Like a German shepherd, "we had to be loyal to them" and serve as a "pure instrument of the Party" that would "not dare to betray the party. If the Party pointed us to the left, we'd go left. If the Party pointed to the right, we'd go right."[14]

Such analogies suited the defense argument that Duch disliked police work and was merely a cog in a larger system of violence and terror, in which he had to continually demonstrate his trustworthiness. While this assertion may have been true in part, he would also make statements suggesting he enjoyed a degree of agency, initiative, belief, and privilege in the new regime. Thus, even as he asked to work under Cheng An at the Ministry of Industry, he also asked permission to marry. The request was granted, though a date was not immediately set. His fiancée also worried that because he was an intellectual and had not yet been assigned a position, he might be arrested. It was only after he started working at S-21 that they married, on December 20, 1975.[15]

| | | |

Finally, on June 20, 1975, Duch and several of his top M-13 cadre were called to attend a political study session in Phnom Penh.[16] The training began on

June 24 and lasted about two weeks. During the first four days, the trainers lectured the attendees on the political, ideological, and organizational line of the Party. Topics ranged from the definition of the enemy to class structure and political consciousness.

At the time, there was a sense of euphoria about the revolutionary victory, a theme that pervaded the sessions. Duch recalled that the participants were told they needed to continue to sacrifice for the new revolutionary society and work hard to rebuild the country.[17] While no documents remain from the training session, Khmer Rouge radio broadcasts at the time provide a sense of the pride, hope, and ambition of the new government, which claimed to have defeated the United States. One broadcast, which aired on the second day of the training session, asserted: "The three main characteristics of the Cambodian revolution which were the determining factors of the 17 April 1975 great historic victory are that of resolute struggle, independence and mastery, and willingness to endure all hardships and overcome all obstacles."[18] These characteristics, a focus of the training session that Duch attended as well, would enable the new regime "to defend and build a new radiant, prosperous Cambodia."

These efforts were initially directed to reconstructing a country devastated by war. The task was likely apparent to Duch and his colleagues as they arrived in Phnom Penh, which was largely deserted and was being cleared of debris. They may have listened to a broadcast two weeks earlier extolling a military unit that had played a key role in the final assault on Phnom Penh and had then been charged with "cleaning up" the capital, where "heaps of foul, smelly garbage littered every street corner; grass grew wild; [and] barbed wire barricades obstructed" movement.[19] "Seeing this filthy, unhygienic and disorderly" situation, the broadcast continued, "Our brother combatants and cadres vigorously and determinedly plunged into an offensive to tidy up and clean the area." This unit may have been Division 12, which would become Division 703 and provide the vast majority of S-21 staff.[20]

"Cleaning up" was also a key metaphor for the new society, which was contrasted to the Lon Nol regime. A May 10, 1975, commentary began: "Seventeen April 1975 was the historic day on which our Cambodian people . . . achieved total victory over U.S. imperialism and all its stooges," who had been responsible for introducing "rotten culture to poison our people" even as "injustice, corruption, hooliganism, burglary, banditry, and prostitution" became "a natural and even legal way of life."[21] In contrast, the broadcast proclaimed, "A new Cambodian society is being established—the cleanest, most fair society ever."

In such early DK broadcasts, several aspects of the Khmer Rouge vision for DK are apparent. If revolutionary zeal had defeated US imperialism, it would now be used to purify and reconstruct the country. Military metaphors were a recurrent feature of DK ideology. This "battle" to "clean up" society did not just refer to physical localities or society as a whole: it was also a battle waged on the individual level. This meant any person "going the wrong way by mistake or past habits will be given a gradual moral and political education" until "totally reformed and purified."[22]

Like the cities, the debris of the mind needed to be cleansed in order to build a pure new revolutionary being, one "forged" in the flames of revolution. Each person had to continually "sharpen" his or her consciousness, an unceasing process. Anyone, even a high-ranking leader, could regress. Everyone therefore had to engage in self-criticism.

Thus, after the June 1975 training lectures and small group discussions had concluded, Duch and his colleagues turned to writing their revolutionary autobiographies. He explained that they had to describe their "view of the revolution and our biography. We prepared these documents for about three days . . . [after which] we read our own biography to all the comrades in the group . . . [who then] would pose questions and we would have to respond."[23] Each year, Duch had to attend such a training session, which would serve as a model for the political study sessions held at S-21. At the conclusion of the training, he was told to await assignment at the Phnom Penh train station.

| | | |

Just over a month later, on August 15, 1975, Son Sen met with Duch to discuss the establishment of S-21. He was joined by Nat (In Lorn), the commander of Division 703, which had operated as Division 12 during the civil war in the Special Zone. As part of his duties, Son Sen managed Sector 15 of the Special Zone, where M-13 was located.[24] If Duch had initially reported primarily to Vorn Vet, Son Sen increasingly took over this supervisory role after the middle of 1973.[25] Given his position in the Special Zone and as head of the Khmer Rouge General Staff, Son Sen also appears to have served as Nat's superior and patron.

By the time of the August meeting, Son Sen ranked seventh in the Khmer Rouge leadership and had been appointed head of the general staff of the DK army, which had been formally established a few weeks earlier. At this time

Division 12 was renamed Division 703 and placed under the command of Son Sen's office.[26]

Duch explained that Son Sen "had a lot of power" because he was in charge of security and defense.[27] Duch surmised that Pol Pot had given the order to establish S-21 and then charged Son Sen with implementation.[28] Son Sen, in turn, assigned two subordinates he trusted and who had experience to run this key security center. Duch noted that Son Sen's office, where he sometimes went to meet, was located relatively close to S-21.

This sort of a hierarchical pyramid of personalized relationships, whereby superiors appointed trusted followers to key posts, was a key feature of the DK sociopolitical order.[29] Later, the Khmer Rouge leaders would purge entire networks, or "strings" (*khsae*), of "traitors." To avoid having one person in the link assume too much power, however, leaders would often seek to balance someone's influence by appointing others to key posts. This may very well be a reason why, even as he appointed Nat chairman of S-21, Son Sen assigned Duch to serve as his deputy with responsibility for overseeing interrogations. Indeed, Duch often spoke disparagingly about Nat and his men, even describing their relationship as one of competition. A second officer from Division 703, Hor (Khoem Vat) completed the three-person leadership team.[30]

In response to a question from Judge Nil about the meaning of the acronym S-21, Duch explained that at the August 15 meeting, "Teacher Son Sen, my boss [*me*], said, 'We should not use the word "police" [*nokorbal*]. It's a name used by the Vietnamese. King Sihanouk's group also used this word for their despicable police. Instead, we used "security" [*santebal*] . . . or those who take care of peace and security in the country.'"[31] The S in S-21 thus stood for "security" or "security office." Duch added that Nat suggested using the code "21," Nat's communication number.

Even though the location of S-21 had not yet been determined, Son Sen instructed Duch and Nat to prepare. "Comrade Duch," he said, "Bring your [M-13] cadre forces from Amleang to Phnom Penh. As for you, Comrade Nat, continue the police work being undertaken by Division 703 until it is finished."[32]

Division 12 (703) soldiers had been at the forefront of the battle to take Phnom Penh.[33] After the city had been evacuated, its soldiers were charged with cleaning up the city, including the rounding up and detention of former Lon Nol soldiers. As part of this work, Division 12 (703) had opened a prison on the grounds of the former Ta Khmav psychiatric hospital, which remained in operation under Nat's authority until November 3, 1975.[34] Duch would soon visit the site.

At the August 15 meeting, Son Sen had instructed Duch to begin collecting documents from Lon Nol government buildings and the homes of the regime's top police and military officers. During the next month, Duch traveled about the city searching the homes of Lon Nol and his former generals, as well as Lon Nol's army headquarters and security offices.[35] Along the way, he gathered some books related to teaching. "The work I was really interested in was teaching," he lamented. "But I couldn't be a teacher."[36] Son Sen, Duch added, laughed when he found out. Duch acknowledged finding other books as he moved about Phnom Penh, including books on Leninism and Stalin, the KGB, the CIA, and torture.[37] He claimed that he didn't have much time but acknowledged sometimes reading about communist theory and torture.

In October 1975, Nat assigned Duch to oversee the interrogation of Ta Khmav prisoners in the house of a former general located near Ponhea Yat High School, which would eventually become the central compound of S-21.[38] "So my duties started from there," he informed the court. "The establishment of S-21 started from [October 1975]."[39]

Over the coming months, S-21 changed locations several times. To clarify the shifts, Duch had drawn a map, which Judge Nil had displayed on the court monitor.[40] Written at the top of the document, in French, were three lines: "Bureau S.21 / Secteur Phnom Penh / Maisons et bureaux successifs de Duch." The middle of the second line was underlined. The map was a lattice of straight lines, cutting out long square blocks from a cross-section of downtown Phnom Penh. Several of the streets were named: "Rue 310," "Rue 360," "Boulevard Monivong." In the center of the diagram was a larger rectangle, double the size of the others, inside which was written "B."

The map was full of small, precisely drawn numbers, each boxed in a small square. They ran 1–7, and several were paired with the prime symbol: 3 / 3', 4, 4', and so forth. This symbol, which is used to differentiate units otherwise alike, was an apt choice to describe an institution dedicated to differentiating friend from foe, a place where a comrade could suddenly be marked as an enemy. Duch would explain that each of the seven numbers represented one of his offices, while the corresponding prime designated the site of his residence at that time. At the bottom of the page, the numbers were stacked in three rows of four, creating a sort of legend; each number was connected by a precise dashed line to the corresponding location, marked by a small box containing the number.

The map had mathematical undertones, offering an abstract model of reality composed of numbers, geometric shapes, and straight lines. Duch's map

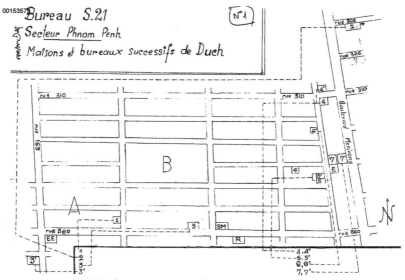

Duch's diagram of the locations of his office and home and the main S-21 compound. Photo courtesy of the ECCC.

was also redactic, asserting an articulation of the past removed from the real-world complexities that nevertheless remained ready to burst forth. What, for example, happened to the people who traversed the streets, houses, and buildings represented on the map? While Duch would provide answers to such questions, he preferred to keep the discussion more abstract, placing himself in the middle step of a three-part calculation running from his superior to himself and then to his subordinates.

With the map projected onto the computer screens, Duch led the parties on a tour of the early history of S-21. "Your Honor. This is location A," he began, pointing with the tip of his clear plastic pen to the A on the map, which was near the corner of Streets 360 and 163 in the heart of Phnom Penh.[41] "Only a few victims were detained and interrogated here," he continued. "At that time I was not married. I stayed in house number 1 here." He pointed to one of the small boxed numbers, connected by a dashed line to the numeric legend. There was no corresponding prime: his house and office apparently were the same.

During this first phase, Duch explained, S-21 had two major shifts. First, in late November 1975, Nat moved the prison to the national police headquarters from Location A, a residential house where it was difficult to run the interrogations.[42] The new site, however, was more exposed, and S-21 was relocated to its original site in January 1976.[43]

As he spoke, Duch explained the meaning of the letters and numbers on the map.[44] The number 3′ marked the house where he and his wife had first lived shortly after marrying. They would move several times before settling into a house near Monivong Avenue, next to his office (7 and 7′). His previous office was later used by Chan to interrogate Vietnamese prisoners of war. The letter R marked the spot where Hor's men met trucks delivering detainees.

Duch's map illustrated how the S-21 compound moved several times before coming to be situated in a compound (Location B) that was much larger than the contemporary grounds of Tuol Sleng suggest. Large villas have since been constructed on parts of the former S-21 compound, including mass graves. Other people now live in houses once used by interrogators.

During these first months, the operational structure of S-21 began to take shape, largely an amalgam of organizational practices developed at M-13 and at Nat's prison at Ta Khmauv. Division 703 provided hundreds of cadre for the operation, which included units devoted to guarding, photography, documents, logistics, medical care, administration, typing, economics, and cooking.

If Nat oversaw S-21, Comrade Hor ran its daily operations. Hor, who was in his midtwenties, had joined the revolution in 1966 and led a special forces battalion of Division 12 during the civil war, during which he lost an eye. He was known as strict and feared by staff.[45] Among his other duties, Hor, together with his deputy Phal, ran the military units in charge of guarding the prison and arresting and executing prisoners.[46] Duch described Phal as "a good cadre," clarifying that Phal was "absolute" (dach khat). Continuing his pattern of lecturing the court on Khmer Rouge history and ideology, Duch explained that this revolutionary phrase was used for those who were "absolute in smashing the enemy."[47] Of all the cadre from Division 703, Phal stood out the most in this regard.

Yet another cadre from Division 703 with a fierce reputation, Peng, worked under Phal in running the guard and special forces units.[48] Duch said that while the internal guards were tasked with regular guard duties, the special forces guarded the perimeter of S-21, received and registered incoming detainees, responded to any threats, and oversaw the transport and execution of prisoners.[49] They also sometimes arrested people.

Given his experience at M-13, Duch was assigned to run the interrogation unit. If he at first focused on gathering and writing briefs for his superiors about the Lon Nol regime documents, he increasingly concentrated on two tasks that would continue to occupy much of his time during DK: training interrogators and reporting to his superiors about confessions.[50] He brought perhaps 10 cadre from M-13 to work at S-21. Most were assigned to the interrogation unit, including his former assistants, Chan and Pon.[51]

Both would play important roles at S-21. Nat initially used Chan as a clerk, but Duch later assigned him to serve as his own assistant and subsequently placed him in charge of interrogating Vietnamese prisoners of war since Chan spoke Vietnamese. Pon (Hoeung Song Huor), who, like Duch, was a Sino-Khmer math teacher, was assigned from the start to interrogate important prisoners at S-21 because he was "very skilled."[52] Thirty years after DK, Duch remembered the names of most of the other M-13 cadre he brought to S-21 and recited them to the court.[53] Besides the M-13 cadre, the interrogation unit included soldiers from Division 703 and a small number of secret forces from Phnom Penh.[54] Eventually S-21 grew to include more than 2,000 staff.

| | | |

From the start there was tension and competition between Duch and Nat. They had served in the revolutionary ranks since the end of 1965, and Duch seemed to resent the fact that Nat had been selected to lead S-21. "He wasn't on my level in terms of theory," Duch noted. "I beat Nat on theory. As for communist theory, or what we now call dictatorial class proletarian theory[,] I also beat Nat. Thus, at the meetings to discuss the creation of S-21, I directed Nat but did not lead the proceedings. Thus I managed Party work that he should have handled."[55] Each time he said "beat," he used the metaphor of "eating" (*si*), a colloquial term that suggests consumption even as it is extended to things like corruption ("eating" bribes) or games (Team A "devouring" Team B).

Despite the DK regime's attack on individualism, interpersonal relations often had this kind of competitive structure, particularly in institutional contexts like S-21. When a civil party lawyer asked Duch whether cadre competed to display their good qualities at S-21, he replied affirmatively. The Khmer compound term they used for "to compete" combined the terms for school testing (*bralang*) with another term meaning "to vie" (*branang*).[56]

If, in the past, students competed in terms of test scores, DK cadre now vied to display the highest revolutionary spirit. "With great respect, Mr. President," Duch began, using highly formal speech registers, "There was competition in DK. Who did they compete with? They competed with the [revolutionary] movement."[57] Such competition, he continued, was evident from notes interrogators had taken during training sessions. Just as the revolutionary workforce was to strive to meet the nationwide production goal of "3 tons per hectare," so too should the interrogators work hard to get "clear" confessions. Moreover, each person competed against the movement to "build" him or herself. The stakes were high since poor performance could lead to arrest.

There are numerous hints of such competition at S-21, including the relation between Duch and Nat that emerged in Duch's negative descriptions of Nat. If Duch described himself as passive and merely concerned with fulfilling his duties at S-21, he portrayed Nat as responsible for creating the machinery of death at S-21, one that emerged out of the "police office of Division 703. The methods of torture, detention, interrogation, and smashing people used were characteristic of [their practices]."[58]

Speaking softly, slowly, and politely, Duch depicted Nat and his unit as coarse and brutal. In contrast to Duch, Nat "liked police work." Nat and his Division 703 soldiers were also "really proud" of their method of "smashing," including the practice of "killing prisoners by slitting their throats."[59] In contrast, Duch didn't "pay much attention to the smashing. . . . [But] if the party ordered it, it had to be done."[60] The more Nat appeared a monster, the more Duch appeared a man.

Nat's crudeness was just another indication of a flawed character that extended to his revolutionary consciousness. During S-21's initial phase, Duch noted, "the purges focused on former Lon Nol officials, soldiers, and police."[61] Nat, however, used the occasion for his own personal benefit, using the pretext of searching for former Lon Nol regime leaders to visit his girlfriend. Nat also disregarded the chain of command, unilaterally arresting and executing people, including people from his own unit. Such violations of the Khmer Rouge moral code (sexual offenses and "individualism") and the DK party line (being deceptive and disregarding orders) stood in direct contrast to the way Duch described himself.

It was precisely because he embodied the ideal qualities of a revolutionary (selflessness, morality, honesty, loyalty, and obedience), Duch suggested, that the DK leaders trusted him with sensitive security work. In contrast, Duch's superiors distrusted Nat and Division 703. If Duch was not directly ordered to spy on Nat, Duch understood implicitly that he should do so. "I was not just their eyes and nose," Duch told the court, "I was their German shepherd."[62]

In the end, Duch won the competition with Nat and rose in rank. During March 1976, Nat was transferred to the General Staff, and Duch replaced him as chairman of S-21. When asked why he was promoted, Duch offered several reasons, explaining that he was more skilled at interrogation and training cadre due to his experience at M-13 and as a teacher. But, ultimately, their superiors "didn't trust Nat but trusted me. After Nat had left, my boss, Teacher Son Sen, always said to me, 'Nat is full of tricks.' . . . I was honest with them. If a stalk of bamboo stalk is segmented, I was like the leaf of an onion that is [smooth and] undivided. I was straight with the Party and would rather die than tell a lie."[63]

Duch added that he tried to escape security work, suggesting to Son Sen that Chhay Kim Hor, a longtime cadre and a mentor of Duch, replace Nat as head of S-21. Son Sen replied, " 'Duch, what's this? What's so important about S-21?' . . . I didn't dare say anything else."[64] Nat would return to S-21 as one of its last prisoners. An unnamed photo of Nat hangs at Tuol Sleng, one taken after he was executed. His neck is cut and his stomach eviscerated.[65]

Cog
(POLICY AND IMPLEMENTATION)

In a haze of dark grey, the black lettering is barely visible.

The image is unfocused, and Duch is dissatisfied. "This document is black and white. It's hard to read," he complains. "I requested the color version. With your permission, Mr. President, can the clerk please display the [correct] color version?"[1] Duch doesn't like imprecision.

His request is granted. The clerk places the color document on the monitor, shifting it until centered. What had appeared to be uniform black and white is revealed to be a jumble of handwriting, inked in different shades of red and black.

At first the document, encased in plastic, won't stay in place. It begins to rise, as if a page is starting to turn, a story about to be revealed. A hand appears and presses down, flattening the document into place. The document starts to bulge again, then stops. I think of the plastic bag torture, a prisoner's last breath.

The boxed script in the center of the document can now be read: "About the traitorous activity of Long Muy=Chuon."

Duch sits in the dock wearing glasses as he slowly but meticulously begins to lecture the court on S-21. A man accused of mass murder has become his nation's history teacher. The current lesson centers on the chain of command. Long Muy's confession is both text and evidence, part of the lecture plan.

Earlier, Duch had explained that his promotion coincided with a major shift in DK security policy. If the first wave of interrogations and executions at S-21 had centered on former officials and officers of the Lon Nol regime, they now began to focus on internal enemies.

This change was formalized at a March 30, 1976, meeting of the DK leadership, the minutes of which are titled: "Decision of the Central Committee Regarding a Number of Matters" (hereafter "March 30, 1976 Decision"). As the title suggests, the topics range widely, concerning everything from a requirement for weekly reporting to the establishment of national holidays. The first item, however, specified four groups (the Zone Standing Committee, the Central Office Committee, the Standing Committee, and the General Staff) having, "The right to smash, inside and outside the ranks."[2]

According to Duch, this decision was orchestrated by Pol Pot. "It was short but firm," he explained. "Everybody recognized his style. So whatever Pol Pot decided, it was clear that this would be the line [*meakea*]."[3]

More broadly, the document illustrated the DK chain of command, which was strictly vertical, as orders flowed from top to bottom, with no horizontal communication allowed. At the apex, "Pol Pot was the one who initiated the idea," Duch explained. "Son Sen implemented it. . . . Nuon Chea was the one who would do the follow-up."[4] Duch repeatedly referred to the March 30, 1976 Decision as evidence that the order to smash internal enemies had come from the highest levels of the Party and that only four offices were invested with the authority to order executions. S-21 was not among them.

The security center stood on "two legs."[5] The first was the General Staff, where S-21 had the status of a battalion. S-21's logistical and medical operations were run in coordination with the General Staff. Duch and his leadership team also attended annual study sessions at the General Staff until 1977. S-21's "other leg" was the Party Center.

Only the Standing Committee, Duch told the court, had the right to send people to S-21. And only Duch received the list of names of the condemned, which he would pass down to his subordinates for arrest. Similarly, Duch reported to the Standing Committee. If he had violated this command structure, he would have been "beheaded."[6] "There are a huge number of surviving documents that demonstrate this," he stated. "I intend to report to you, Mr. President, about some of these documents that I used to report to the upper level [back then]."[7]

Duch was reporting to the judges in a manner that echoed his reporting to the Party Center. Indeed, he often greeted them using the same honorific (*ti korop*), "With respect," which he had used when sending reports to his DK superiors. Moreover, he now planned to use documents that had served as evidence of prisoners' guilt and had often been extracted through torture to prove his own innocence. Long Muy's confession was the second of five such documents Duch discussed.

| | | |

"Mr. President, with great respect" (*ti korop*), Duch began, as the color version of the cover of Long Muy's confession record was displayed on the monitors. A stack of photocopied documents, neatly arranged, lay on the table before him. He held one in his hand, which he opened with the fingers of his maimed hand: "This document shows you how I reported to the upper level, to my boss."[8] The first step, he continued, was to send this sort of document to Son Sen.

"This is my handwriting," Duch noted. The monitor zoomed to several lines of text, written in red at the bottom of the page, underneath which Duch had signed his name on October 15, 1977. "Elder Brother, with respect" (*ti korop*), Duch began, as he read the words he had penned over 30 years before. The passage consisted of three points, each highlighted by a small yet precisely written number that was circled and then followed by a period and dash.

"One," he continued, the document shifting on the monitor as the court clerk tried to center it. "The forces he [vea] reported this time were all from Sector 22, both from the revolutionary ranks and the network of Kok Minh Tang at Peareang. Two. The highest [ranking] force this contemptible one [vea] implicated was despicable [a-] Tum." Duch paused, inhaling slightly as he added that "despicable" Tum was the alias of Siet Chhe, the former head of Sector 22 who had been working as Son Sen's deputy at the General Staff. A protégé of Pol Pot, Siet Chhe lost favor and was arrested at the end of April 1977 and sent to S-21.[9]

Duch resumed: "Three, this contemptible one said that Comrade Ieng Si Pheng was a revolutionary. He then spoke about his stance [comho]." After reading Ieng Si Pheng's name, Duch added that the name was Chinese. Long Muy, Duch explained, had stated that Ieng Si Pheng was not part of a CIA network. In contrast to the polite honorifics Duch had used to address his superiors on the cover of Long Muy's confession, Duch referred to Long Muy with the diminutive pronoun *vea*, a Khmer term used for objects, small children, and animals. At S-21, prisoners were always mentioned in this dehumanizing and objectifying manner. "So," Duch said, "I reported to my boss about the three points . . . then I signed my name, 'With respect, Duch' on October, 15, 1977."

Long Muy's confession was shifted on the screen, zooming to three lines of annotation in the upper middle of the page. The large lettering, which sloped slightly and was scribbled in thick red ink, contrasted with Duch's script, tightly written and linear, exactly following the barely visible lining of the manila paper page. "After receiving this document from me," Duch explained, "My boss Teacher Son Sen wrote: '1—This might be important. 2—This despicable one is part of a string of Chinese translators. 3—I haven't yet read it. Please let me send this to Elder Brother first.' So this is what my superior, Son Sen[,] wrote to Elder Pol [Pot]. He signed it [with his pseudonym] Khieu [and dated it] October 17, 1977."

Directing the court's attention to a few words on the upper left-hand corner of the document, Duch read: "Special. Attention Comrade Khieu. Contact the East [Zone]." This script, with the largest lettering and placed highest on the page, was written in a reddish-orange pen and highlighted with underlining. "This is Pol Pot's handwriting," Duch clarified. "Pol Pot had made a decision for Brother Khieu to contact the East [Zone] about this document." On the opposite corner of the page, there was a large check mark. "This is a sign made by Pol Pot," Duch said, chuckling softly. "The biggest person of all read the document and made a check."

Yet another layer of the document's meaning came into focus: the DK pyramid of power. It radiated downward. Duch noted two words and a date written in Son Sen's red underneath Pol Pot's order to send the document to the East Zone: "Sent already, November 11, 1977." A plastic pen moved into the frame and rested just below the date, a punctuation to Duch's presentation. He concluded: "This document shows that I, the Chairman of S-21[,] reported directly to the level above, to Son Sen, and then it went from Son Sen to Pol Pot, then Pol Pot ordered Son Sen to contact the east. Please, I'm done with this document." The camera zoomed out. The confession vanished from sight.

More than thirty years later, Duch was again annotating Long Muy's confession. It encapsulated the central argument of his defense: he was a cog in the machine, an obedient "dog" serving as the eyes and nose of his masters, an "instrument" of the party, a desk bureaucrat. He explained that as the head of S-21 he had two main tasks, which he had been doing since M-13. First, he conducted political training. Second, he annotated confessions and provided summaries to his superiors, who in turn issued orders, which he conveyed to his subordinates. Furthermore, most of the violence that took place at S-21 had originated with the work of Nat and Division 703.

After taking the helm of S-21, Duch retained Nat's governance structure, with Hor serving as Duch's deputy and managing daily operations. When Duch received orders, he relayed them to Hor, who implemented them. Duch never lost an opportunity to note that he only acted with the authorization of his superiors and did not know the details of what happened in the prison because he was in his office. His actions, he stated, followed the "organizational line" of the Party, which was illustrated broadly by the March 30, 1976, directive about the authority to "smash" enemies and more proximately by the text written on the cover page of Long Muy's confession.

If Duch used Long Muy's confession to demonstrate his limited role in the chain of command, Duch's use of the confession's text, likely extracted under torture, as exculpatory evidence was unsettling. For a second time, Long Muy's humanity was being diminished, first at S-21, now in this legal setting. A number of related questions, if edited out of the immediate discussion, welled up just below the surface, struggling to burst forth. Who was Long Muy? What was his path to revolution and arrest? And what happened to him at S-21? On these issues Duch remained silent.

While we can never fully answer such questions, it is possible to reapproach Long Muy's confession, to turn the page, and to read it in different ways and seek glimpses of what was redacted. One place to start is with dates, which situate his path within the larger flow of violence at S-21 as noted in documents such as prison logs. Among the thousands of entries, one records the day of Long Muy's arrest: July 16, 1977.[10]

| | | |

What happened from the time Duch took office in March 1976 until the time Long Muy was arrested? A clue is provided by the March 30, 1976 Decision. This document was issued just a month after DK radio reported that airplanes belonging to the "U.S. imperialists" had bombed the town of Siem Reap, resulting in damage, injuries, and deaths.[11] The explosions appear to have increased the DK regime's fear of internal subversion.[12] In particular, suspicion seems to have fallen on Koy Thuon, the former secretary of the Northern Zone and Standing Committee member who now served as commerce secretary. Duch was appointed chairman of S-21 shortly after this incident.

And, early in the morning on April 2, just after the March 30, 1976 Decision, grenades exploded and shots were fired near the Royal Palace in Phnom Penh. A leaflet was also reportedly found that read "The Master Sergeant Is About to Come Out and Fight."[13] Again, there is uncertainty about what happened. Within days, however, combatants from Division 170, a former East Zone unit, had been arrested and sent to S-21, where they were interrogated.[14] Their confessions implicated their superiors and raised suspicions about the loyalty of East Zone cadre, in particular Chan Chakrei, a former monk who was leader of Division 170 and now served as Son Sen's deputy at the General Staff.

Chakrei was arrested on May 19 and interrogated for four months at S-21 until he confessed to plotting against the DK leaders and being a member of a counterrevolutionary network linked to the CIA.[15] At S-21, Duch gave him the Roman numeral I; the deputy secretary of Division 170, Ly Vay, received the designation II. Chakrei's confession implicated a number of East Zone cadre, including the political commissar of the East Zone military, Ly Phen (IV), and the secretary of East Zone Sector 24, Suas Neou (Chhouk) (VIII). More broadly, the purges raised questions about one of the most powerful members of the Standing Committee, Sao Phim, secretary of the East Zone.

As people confessed, they implicated others who, if named several times, might be arrested. S-21 began to swell with prisoners. By November, 241 members of Division 170 had been detained.[16] Wave after wave of these perceived "networks of traitors" passed through the gates of S-21. They came from all branches of the government: the Party leadership, zones, military, government ministries, and S-21 itself.

During the trial, Duch said little about this broader process of purging: he focused on his role in running S-21 and the command structure. He did not discuss the names, faces, or stories of the thousands of victims. As he did with Long Muy, Duch usually only mentioned an individual to support his contention of having been a cog.

Thus, Duch told the court a story to illustrate that although he "did not pay much attention to the smashing," if ordered to do something he had to comply. One day, he continued, his superior ordered him to observe the execution of Chhouk and another prisoner in the early morning dark. He watched by flashlight as the two men were "smashed." Duch reiterated that the executioners from Division 703 were "proud" of their work and their method of cutting the neck of prisoners "to ensure the victim was completely dead."[17]

A number of prisoners, Duch continued, referring to the map he had drawn, were "smashed at Location A" inside the S-21 compound. Another time, for example, "Teacher Son Sen, told me, 'Comrade Duch, exhume the corpse of despicable Phan [Li Phel] and take a photograph, then send it to me.' I was angry and cursed to myself . . . [but] if he used me like this, what could I do?"[18] Li Phel had been killed just three days before, so his corpse had not yet started to swell and decompose, but it stank and had to be washed. Duch concluded that Son Sen had asked him to do this because our "boss trusted me but not Nat or his [Division 703] men" and wanted to confirm that Li Phel was dead. Duch's superiors would make similar requests about the corpses of other high-ranking cadre who ended up at S-21, including Nat.

Duch mentioned Koy Thuon more frequently. Even before the February 1976 bomb attack, Koy Thuon had come under suspicion. Soon after the March 30 "smash" directive, he began to be stripped of his duties and was effectively placed under house arrest on April 8, before being sent to S-21 in early 1977.[19] Koy Thuon's arrest was significant to Duch for a number of reasons. Court documents tied Duch to Koy Thuon's interrogation, one of only two cases in which Duch admitted being directly involved. He stressed, however, that he never tortured Koy Thuon, instead using "cold tactics." In fact, he seemed to relish the fact that he had been able to outsmart this senior leader and get him to confess.

Duch gave his description of Koy Thuon's interrogation, as he had those of Chhouk's execution and Phan's exhumation, with little detail, just enough to support his defense. He used these stories, as he had Long Muy's confession, as exculpation. If horrible crimes had been committed under his watch, they were not intentional but the result of duress. This distinction between act and intention, the *actus reus* and *mens rea* in legal discourse, was a key criterion by which the Trial Chamber would judge him.

Circumstance

For the first month of his trial, Duch dominated the floor while laying out his claims. The establishment of S-21, he said, illustrated how he was thrust into a preexisting house of horrors, the worst practices of which originated with Nat. Duch, in contrast, dutifully performed his tasks but no more. Rarely did he draw connections to M-13. Reluctantly, he said, he assumed the helm of S-21, where he withdrew to his office, annotating confessions and writing reports out of earshot of prisoners' screams. Duch argued he was merely a conduit, one link in the chain of command. Even as he dominated the early stages of the proceedings, other parties sought to disrupt his claims.

Throughout the proceedings, the prosecution argued that Duch, as opposed to being a passive cog, had been an active and willing participant who, as the head of S-21, had wielded enormous power. His state of mind and authority could be discerned in a number of ways, ranging from his initiative to surviving documentation.

If, on being appointed chairman, Duch retained much of the security center's organizational structure, he implemented key changes that put his mark on S-21. Among the first was its relocation to the grounds of Ponhea Yat High School (renamed Tuol Svay Prey High School during the Lon Nol regime), site B on Duch's map and roughly coterminous with the grounds of the Tuol Sleng Genocidal Museum.

Duch noted that the S-21 compound was much larger than the site of the current museum. One can no longer see, for example, the wooden buildings of Tuol Svay Prey Primary School, which were separated by a fence from the back of Ponhea Yat and used as workshops by S-21. The place where the special unit took control of incoming detainees (R on his map) as well as Duch's home and office (7 / 7′) were located several blocks from the central compound. He claimed to have spent most of his time working there, rarely visiting the central prison compound.

Within the Ponhea Yat grounds, Buildings B, C, and D were used for detention, while the old administrative office (Building E) was where prison mug shots were taken, document lists made, and artists like Vann Nath and Bou Meng put to work. Duch added that the Special Prison, where Koy Thuon, four Westerners, and other important prisoners were held in slightly better conditions than the regular prison, "was to the south of Building A but where the Vietnamese or Yuon were interrogated was to the east" (location 6 on Duch's map).[20] Toward the end of DK, the Special Prison was moved to Building A.[21]

Duch acknowledged that the idea to relocate the central office of S-21 to the school grounds "was initially my idea, but was approved by my superior, Professor Son Sen, and the purpose was to facilitate the detention and the interrogation" of prisoners.[22] When asked about the individual cells within the compound, Duch explained they were built in Buildings B and C, another change he initiated.[23] This time, however, he did not inform Son Sen. Duch acknowledged he had the authority to make such a decision, adding that he never bothered to examine the cells after they were constructed.[24]

Duch also took the initiative when finding new staff. Soon after the establishment of S-21, he received Son Sen's permission to recruit young combatants from Kampong Chhnang province. These recruits, Duch explained, were from base areas, in contrast to many Division 703 soldiers who were from upper-middle peasant class backgrounds and therefore not entirely trustworthy.[25] Duch claimed most of the perhaps sixty youths, ranging in age from twelve to seventeen, were too young to take on significant duties. A few served as messengers; most were put to work gathering "morning glory to feed the rabbits."[26]

The prosecution confronted Duch on this point, reading statements he had given in a pretrial interview in which he acknowledged that some of the youths had served as guards or distributed food. Duch had explained that the Party line (*meakea*) held that only the poor and lower-middle peasant classes were trustworthy and that the youths he recruited were "clean and pure, the children of the poorest peasants."[27] Moreover, they were susceptible to indoctrination, "like a white piece of paper upon which they could write or draw whatever they wanted."[28] Using his teaching skills, Duch claimed to have transformed these impressionable youths into devoted and fearless revolutionaries.

While we don't know exactly what Duch taught, a few clues exist, including the testimony of himself and his cadre, notebooks recording his lessons, and a photograph. As the focus of the trial shifted to the implementation of CPK policy at S-21, International Deputy Co-Prosecutor William Smith requested that the photo be displayed. In it, a youthful Duch sits at a table before a microphone, its metallic grill glowing against his dark shirt, heart-level. He holds his head high, eyes wide open, lips full and teeth exposed, perhaps in a smile, maybe in a scowl. The fingers on his left hand are slightly raised, as if playing a piano, for emphasis. Duch seems at ease and in his element, as he did thirty-one years later when lecturing the court.

Duch explained that he alone at S-21 had the right to "hold the mic" and educate cadre about the "political and educational stance toward the enemy."[29] His teaching followed from the CPK "line" (meakea), which held that "the enemy must be smashed," as illustrated by the March 30, 1976 Decision. In accordance with the CPK "organizational line," Duch was responsible for implementing policy in his unit, which included, he said, referring to the photograph, "authority over this microphone that is at the school at Street Number 95 . . . opposite to my house."[30] He added that he had indicated this location with the letter *E* on the map he had drawn. If Duch initially held such training sessions in an old church building, the new political study school, which seated 50–60 people, was built near his home, in case he had to take one of the frequent calls from Son Sen.[31] Once again, he had taken the initiative.

In Khmer, the term "line," meakea, might be better translated as "the path" or "the way." It is related to the Buddhist term for the Eightfold Path, which, if followed, leads to self-awareness and the end of suffering. The Khmer Rouge often used Buddhist language in their ideology, since many of their rural followers had been educated in or spent substantial time in pagodas. According to the Buddhist "way," a devotee could find liberation exercising proper wisdom (right view and intention), ethical behavior (right speech, action, livelihood), and consciousness (right effort, mindfulness, and concentration). By extension, the Khmer Rouge "way" provided a path to salvation, now couched in terms of class struggle and freedom from oppression but requiring each cadre's thoughts, efforts, actions, and view to accord with the Party's meakea. A person who did so was said to have a proper revolutionary "stance" (chomhor). According to Duch's annotation on Long Muy's confession, Long Muy had claimed that Ieng Si Pheng manifested such a proper stance.

When asked how the "line" was different from "policy," Duch explained that the line was general while policy was more specific. The line was more like a first principle from which all else, including policy, followed. He noted that the "line" had first been established at the 1960 Party Congress.[32] It was refined at later congresses, according to Duch, but determined by Pol Pot.[33] "The line is the line," Duch stated; if "very strict," it was almost something "sacred" that could not be "touched" or "violated."[34]

The CPK "line" and related "policy" were disseminated in several ways. Khmer Rouge documents fell into three categories: open materials such as Revolutionary Flags and Revolutionary Youth and radio broadcasts that included political speeches, revolutionary songs, slogans, and political tracts; confidential internal tracts like the March 30, 1976 Decision; and internal party texts, including the CPK statutes. Duch claimed he knew nothing about the most confidential documents.[35] However, S-21 received the magazines, which Duch distributed to his personnel, from Son Sen's General Staff office. But Duch said he didn't pay much attention to the magazines and his political instruction was more influenced by study sessions and the CPK statutes.[36]

Each year, for example, Duch attended a political training session. From 1975 to 1977 these were led by Son Sen, since S-21 was under the General Staff. After Son Sen had left for the battlefield in late 1977, Duch attended a 1978 study meeting conducted by Pol Pot.[37] Duch recalled seeing high-ranking cadre, including Ieng Thirith, Ta Mok, and Son Sen's wife, Yun Yat, taking notes as Pol Pot lectured for three days. As with the 1975 training session that Duch attended, the participants then met in small groups for three more days before writing and examining each other's biographies. The entire process took about 10 days. Duch observed that, to prevent jealousy, none of the participants were allowed to talk to Pol Pot. Being in the presence of Pol Pot, the highest ranking leader, Duch recalled, was a bit strange but felt good.[38]

Soon after the study sessions, Duch organized an S-21 meeting for the group leaders at which he presented what he had learned, thereby disseminating the party line.[39] The structure was largely the same, with lectures, small group discussions, and the examination of revolutionary biographies. Duch "held the mic" at these meetings, with the exception of the 1977 session, which Son Sen led. Besides these annual meetings, S-21 cadre held regular livelihood meetings and self-criticism sessions at the group level. While Duch allowed the group leaders to run such meetings, he continued to train the interrogators. He noted that one of the training sessions at the General Staff included discussion of the CPK statutes, which he studied extensively and incorporated into his political education at S-21.[40]

Indeed, Duch said he paid most attention to the Party Statutes. The first section of the Party Statutes outlines the "fundamental principles and political stances of the Party," beginning with the declaration that the CPK is the party of the "worker class" and holds an "absolute monopoly in every sector" as it continues "to move forward toward Communism" while defending "the results of the revolution."[41] In undertaking these tasks, the CPK would be guided by Marxist-Leninism "in accordance with the concrete situation of Kampuchea" and with the "principle of connecting principle with the concrete, absolutely, along the principles and stances of dialectical materialism and historical materialism."[42]

Judge Lavergne asked Duch if the ideological content of such DK political documents "corresponds to your convictions at the time. Whether this was the objective that drove you."[43] Duch responded with a discussion of historical materialism and class struggle, describing how a society passed through a series of stages (a primitive stage to slavery to capitalism to socialism) culminating in communism. He started to "appreciate [this] theory when I was studying at the elementary mathematics class; at that time [my geography] teacher, Mr. Gao Laing," had discussed how the relations of production were "based on a slogan," which Duch repeated in Khmer and French: "To each according to his abilities and from each according to his needs."[44] Duch, who mentioned this principle at several points during his trial, added: "I really like the theory, so after[ward] I studied a secret document, the Leninist theory, it shows the development of the society follows that trend, and I believed in it."[45]

Noting that some scholars referred to the Khmer Rouge as Maoist, Duch claimed that the regime instead should be viewed as "Pol Pot-ist," a blend of Marxist-Leninism, Maoism, and other influences adapted to the Cambodian context.[46] Because of DK's large peasant population, the country couldn't follow strict Marxist-Leninism, which holds that communist revolution is propelled by the worker class. As was done in China and Vietnam, the Khmer Rouge reworked this theory to foreground the peasantry as revolutionary catalysts.[47] If the DK regime was influenced by Maoism, especially the Gang of Four's implementation of the Cultural Revolution in the People's Republic of China (1966–1967), Pol Pot's perspective on class differed from Mao's in various ways, such as the status of monks and religion, the monarchy, and former elites. In contrast to Maoist China, which included four classes (workers, peasants, petty bourgeoisie, and capitalist-nationalists), Duch said, Pol Pot's revolutionary society just had two: the workers and the peasants.

This view was manifest in key DK symbols such as the flag, which consisted of three yellow temple towers set against a red background. The larger middle tower, Duch explained, represented the Party, while the two smaller ones stood for the two classes. The DK Constitution noted that the red represented "the revolutionary movement and the valiant struggle by the Cambodian people," while the "yellow temple is the symbol of the national traditions of the Cambodian people who are defending and building the country."[48]

The national coat of arms, in turn, depicted a network of rice paddies (peasants/agriculture) split by a canal running from a factory (workers/industry) with smokestacks in the distance, an image slightly reminiscent of the tracks leading to Auschwitz. Likewise, the DK national anthem spoke only of workers and peasants.[49] Mao "kept four classes and Pol Pot only kept two classes," Duch stated, so "the Pol Pot theory or doctrine is not the same [as] Maoist theory."[50]

Duch attributed much of the DK violence to this Pol Pot-ist view of class structure, "which was even crueler than the theory of [the] Gang of Four."[51] He began to understand this fact when the cities were evacuated and the CPK began "the screening and the purges of those classes."[52] The supreme Buddhist patriarch and key Lon Nol officials were "within the hands of [Division] 703," while novice monks were disrobed and intellectuals targeted in the attempt to transform everyone into a worker or a peasant.[53]

Duch's "shock" intensified in January 1977, when the purge of Koy Thuon and his Northern Zone followers commenced. Duch had ties to many of these cadre, with whom he had worked in the late 1960s. He wondered why these "people who sacrificed their lives, their flesh and blood for the revolution, [and] the Party" had now been accused of treason.[54] In the end, he claimed, Pol Pot "only trusted Ta Mok's clique" as he set out to implement his vision of a two-class state.

Such events left Duch "speechless. Lots of people's lives were lost. I was shocked but I couldn't say anything. It was beyond my speech. People started to disappear, even my superiors."[55] Why, he asked, "did I not escape if I saw these terrible things. Where could I run to? To the west to Thailand? Could I escape? No, I could not." He continued: "The idealistic society that I truly wanted is a society that is based on the slogans that I mentioned earlier."[56]

Duch described his response as stoic, as he carried on in a dignified manner while in a hopeless situation. He continued to try to live according to the Marxist-Leninist adage "Everyone tries their best, but what they get is based on what they need, not what they want," fulfilling his revolutionary duties while living like his comrades—even if he acknowledged receiving a few small perks, such as his motorbike, cigarettes, and a special ration of two dishes of food rather than the usual one.[57]

Even as he offered such explanations, Duch would frequently express remorse, apologize, and accept responsibility. Thus he concluded his remarks about Pol Pot–ism by acknowledging: "I was a coward [because] I did not contest but went on carrying [out] their orders," in part to ensure he and his family survived. "Therefore," he continued, "I committed all kinds of crimes, serious crimes," including annotating confessions and training his subordinates to have "a very absolute class stance."[58]

These qualities were foregrounded in the DK Party Statues, which extensively focused on "stance." Each of the ten criteria used to select cadre, for example, referred to a "strong revolutionary stance" on matters of (1) "the party line," (2) "proletarian ideology," (3) "internal solidarity and unity," (4) "the lines of organization, leadership, and work of the Party," (5) "revolutionary vigilance, maintaining secrecy, and defending revolutionary forces," (6) "independency, mastery, self-reliance," (7) "examining personal histories and revolutionary life views," (8) "class," (9) "clean life morals, and politically clean" background, and (10) "the capability to build oneself and be receptive to future leadership."[59]

When asked to explain the criteria, Duch focused on the first, which the Statutes define as having "a proper and tough political stance, orderly, not rightist, 'not leftist,' in fulfilling specific political tasks of the party which one is implementing, one after another, and especially in the national defense and national construction of [DK]."[60] According to Duch, this Statute meant a cadre had to make a "clear division between the parties and the enemies" on the one hand and on the other to veer neither to the "left" nor to the "right."[61] A cadre who turned to the "left" and was too assertive in implementing the party line risked antagonizing the masses; one who failed to carry out his or her duties, in turn, might be accused of being a "rightist" subverting the revolution. "The good leaders were those who did not do surplus things but did not miss or did not fail to complete what's assigned," Duch explained. "So that's the main purpose: whatever we were assigned . . . we had to make sure [to do] it."[62]

Duch's remarks suggest the highly public and performative dimensions of DK life, particularly within formal contexts like S-21. Everyone was both watcher and watched, seeking to assert him or herself as a true revolutionary while simultaneously assessing the "stance" of others based on whether the person walked a "straight" revolutionary path. If such evaluations took place daily, they were also formally conducted as cadre wrote their biographies, participated in livelihood sessions, and engaged in criticism and self-criticism, activities that the Party Statutes required be "routine" as a way to "struggle to build the Party internally in eradicating and altering faults and various confusions."[63]

Each person was a microcosm of the revolution, constantly in need of purification. Thus the Party Statutes called for cadre to continuously engage in "revolutionizing oneself" by being "on the offensive, forging himself in the heat constantly, always agitating, attacking, and pushing constantly, inside the great, hot, and deep revolutionary movement."[64] Constantly building oneself and therefore the revolution, when based on a proper stance, was one of the two key criteria for membership in the party. The other was having a "good class pedigree" along with "good and clean life morals," being "good and clean politically," and having a verified "clear personal history."[65] The young Amleang and Kompong Chhnang cadre working at S-21 fit this profile. As an intellectual, Duch had to work harder to assert his proper revolutionary stance, particularly after intellectuals and former associates were arrested.

This indeterminacy about revolutionary status was a catalyst of DK violence, one that gave it meaning and form. Each cadre had to act in a manner that accorded with the qualities of an ideal revolutionary. Such articulations, as I have shown, reduce complex realities to more simplified forms. The surplus meaning that has been redacted pushes back, potentially unsettling and perhaps even being viewed as dangerous. In some ways, the Khmer saying Duch invoked, "If you break open the crab, you show the shit," highlights this point, as he explained that no one dared "break open" the shell that covered over that which was unsaid and unclean.

Cadre sought to avoid breaking open "the shell," or the stylized and idyllic version of revolutionary reality so forcefully asserted during DK. In such a setting the stakes were high, and cadre had a number of motives for performing well, both negative (fear of demotion, punishment, and execution) and positive (pride in being a proper revolutionary, status, and advancement). Each cadre therefore had to work constantly to forge himself or herself and behave in accordance with the party line.[66]

A strong stance on the party line also entailed remaining "vigilant" and able to distinguish friend from foe. Vigilance, Duch explained, meant that a cadre needed to carefully guard against attempts to destroy the revolution, both directly through assassination and indirectly though circulating anti-regime flyers or insulting the leaders, as when longtime revolutionary Hu Nim was overheard referring to Pol Pot and Son Sen pejoratively. Such behaviors "broke open" the crab shell, suggesting the revolution was not what was claimed. Interestingly, the CPK Statutes describe internal opposition through the metaphor of fractures, stating that such activity, ranging from "immoral acts" to violations of discipline, "causes fracture in internal Party solidarity and . . . a break in secrecy, endanger[ing] the Party, the revolution, and the people."[67]

Though the punishment for such infractions ranged from criticism to expulsion from the party, it often resulted in arrest. Thus Hu Nim was sent to S-21. He, like Long Muy, was caught in the internal purges that began to take place in mid-1976. While the purges were partly shaped by the paradox of a fundamental status indeterminacy that was operative in a situation in which a highly idealized image of a revolutionary was asserted, they were also informed by other factors, including DK class structure and ideology, power struggles, and, as Duch noted, Pol Pot and the DK leadership's growing suspicion and paranoia[68]—partly fueled by alleged plots revealed in S-21 confessions.

| | | |

In this regard, Duch's testimony often focused on three incidents that followed the March 30, 1976 Decision. The first was the purge of Chan Chakrei, Chhouk, and East Zone military cadre that got under way after the April 2 explosions. To illustrate his plight and the suspicion of the CPK Standing Committee, Duch recounted his story about being ordered to attend the execution of Chakrei and the exhumation of the corpse of Li Phel. Duch also pointed to these early executions so as to place himself in the middle of a chain running from the Standing Committee to the hands-on implementation on the ground at S-21. It was as if he were a relay point.

Thus, Duch acknowledged creating a list of enemies just before Chhouk's arrest but said he was ordered to do so, foregrounding the decision-making process. "Sous Neou, alias Chhouk," Duch explained, "was the secretary of Sector 24 of the East Zone. He was implicated in several confessions. When the Standing Committee was about to meet again, my superior ordered S-21 to gather information and extract key points from the document[s] concerning" Chhouk.[69] Duch noted the process was time-consuming. He and interrogators and typists familiar with confessions implicating Chhouk perused confessions "for three days and three nights with little sleep" to compile the requisite information.[70] Duch claimed that such detailed documentation was necessary because of Chhouk's high position in the East Zone, which was headed by longtime revolutionary Sao Phim, whose consent was needed before arrest.[71]

Another time, Son Sen asked Duch to compile a list of suspected enemies in two East Zone military units formerly led by Chakrei. So Duch examined various confessions and "gathered the names of the people who were implicated in Division 170 and 290." Son Sen invited Duch to attend "an open meeting of the General Staff" at which a decision would be made. Several high-ranking cadre attended, including Son Sen and Siet Chhe, whose alias, Tum, was mentioned on the cover of Long Muy's confession. Before replacing Chakrei at the General Staff, Siet Chhe headed Sector 22, which is where Peareang is located and, like Chhouk's Sector 24, was a part of Sao Phim's East Zone. Siet Chhe would also end up at S-21, where he was severely tortured. Nat, who was working under Son Sen at the General Staff at the time of the meeting, also attended.

During the meeting, Son Sen "read out the names who were implicated in the confessions" and asked Duch if he had any comments. He seemed to take pride in being recognized in such a manner, even if he quickly noted, perhaps realizing that being given the floor in such a meeting suggested more than a minor role in the decision-making process, that Son Sen "only asked in a more friendly manner. In reality I was not entitled to make any comments in such a meeting."

Duch added: "The right to arrest was the right of the secretary of the General Staff. . . . No one else had the right to arrest those people, other than Son

Sen himself. So this was the organizational line."[72] Before an arrest could be made, however, the leaders of the units to which the suspects belonged had to agree that there was sufficient evidence. In such a highly visible and performative context, it is difficult to imagine that unit leaders would fail to consent, since doing so could call into question their own revolutionary vigilance and stance. Indeed, mass arrests of cadre from Divisions 170 and 290 soon followed, with many sent to S-21.

| | | |

A similar pattern ensued following the arrest of Koy Thuon (alias Khuon) in early 1977. Like Chakrei, Koy Thuon had a reputation for womanizing. When asked by the prosecution about a *Revolutionary Flags* tract on morality, Duch explained it by referencing Koy Thuon, with whom there had been "many of those issues," the last of which led to his arrest after he was "alleged to have [had an affair] with another person's wife and killed the husband. It was very well known. So the CPK removed [Koy] Thuon according [to] the statute that any cadre who commits an offence will be removed."[73]

Duch spoke frequently about Koy Thuon, the second of the two people whom he admitted interrogating, even if Duch stated that he never beat him. At times, he seemed to emphasize such points to suggest that he was somehow more humane than the common interrogators, who beat prisoners regularly. He said of Koy Thuon that, as opposed to the usual diminutive pronouns, "I unconsciously called him Brother."[74] Duch noted that he tried to avoid contact with Koy Thuon because Koy Thuon was smart and, if Duch lingered, "my weakness would be revealed" to him.

Duch claimed that he "did not dare analyze [Koy Thuon's] confession" but instead only made annotations that assisted Son Sen's analysis of the interrogation, which Son Sen directed.[75] At times, Duch recalled, Koy Thuon was quick to anger when being questioned and sometimes broke a glass or pen.[76] Duch would ask Koy Thuon to calm down before starting to interrogate him again. With a smile, he would say to Koy Thuon, "Brother, why did you do that? Do not think that I am fooled by way of your anger and I would beat you to death [so that your] confession was cut off." He told Koy Thuon, "I already promised that if you wrote anything in the confession I would be serving as your messenger to transfer these confessions to the Party. So you [have] no other alternative [than] to send your confession to the Party . . . through me."[77] This seemed to Duch to placate Koy Thuon.

Koy Thuon, Khmer Rouge leader and DK minister of commerce, shackled at S-21 in 1977. Photo courtesy of the DC-Cam / SRI Archives.

Koy Thuon's arrest worried Duch because Duch was also an intellectual and had joined the revolution in the Northern Zone, an association that could cast doubt on Duch's loyalties. This concern was heightened when Koy Thuon's followers in the Northern Zone, including personnel from Divisions 310 and 450 of the military, began to be arrested en masse, along with those who had worked under him at the Ministry of Commerce.

Duch said that these arrests left him "very shocked. I tried to change [Son Sen's] opinion by saying, 'Brother, they don't seem to be the right people.' He threatened me on the other end of the phone line: 'Duch, it is based on Khuon's confession!' I said nothing after that."[78] Duch said he just thought to himself, "Oh, those poor people who sacrificed everything they had to liberate their country and their people, now they come here to be imprisoned and die, because they are considered traitors to the Party." He noted, "I was strongly attached to the North[ern] Zone cadres. I shared the same cell in prison with [many] of them in 1968."

In 1978, Duch claimed, his shock turned to hopelessness. First, Nget You, an ethnic Chinese cadre who "had supported [DK] and the CPK from the beginning," was sent to S-21.[79] Duch said he thought, "'Oh, my days are numbered now.' I was terrified."[80] He had trouble focusing on his work and began spending time in the room where Vann Nath, Bou Meng, and other prisoner-artisans worked.[81]

Finally, on November 2, 1978, Duch lost all hope when he received news that "three big packages" were on the way.[82] When the prisoners arrived, hands tied behind their backs with nylon string, he saw his former bosses from the Special Zone, Vorn Vet and Cheng An, along with the secretary of the Northwest Zone, Kong Sophal. His longtime colleague Chhay Kim Hor, with whom he sometimes drank Chinese beer, was also arrested around this time.[83] Nat was sent to S-21 in December. Duch said that he became "hopeless." On January 2 or 3, as the DK regime neared collapse, Nuon Chea removed the AK-47s from S-21 and ordered Duch to execute the remaining prisoners. "I thought, 'It's my turn now,'" Duch recalled. "I could not work or do anything. I stayed at home day and night."[84]

| | |

By describing events like the purges in this manner, which linked the story of S-21 to himself and his defense, Duch made himself seem not just human but almost sympathetic. By his account, he had joined the revolution for noble reasons and carried out duties he abhorred diligently and effectively.

This defense would be challenged by witnesses, starting with the testimony of Craig Etcheson, an academic who had written a book about DK and had been advocating for the creation of a trial since the 1980s. Given his familiarity with DK history and documentation, Etcheson had been hired by the OCP, for which he wrote a 66-page document titled "Overview of Hierarchy of Democratic Kampuchea."[85]

Roux highlighted this background, warning the bench that Etcheson "is not really an expert. . . . He is here the voice of the prosecution."[86] Roux also sought to disrupt Etcheson's testimony, which outlined the larger contours of the DK violence and S-21's role in it, by repeatedly raising procedural issues.

Etcheson agreed with the defense that during DK, control was highly centralized, with Pol Pot and the CPK Standing Committee making all key policy decisions and forbidding horizontal communication. Etcheson illustrated the pyramid-like, vertical structure of DK through the use of charts. The first showed the Standing Committee at the apex of the country's zones (in 1975, the Southwest, West, Northwest, North, Northeast, and East) and autonomous regions (Sectors 103 and 106), though he noted that the Northern Zone was split up with the creation of the Central Zone following the arrest of Koy Thuon.

Each zone, he continued, "was governed by a three-person Party Committee composed of a secretary, a deputy secretary usually responsible for security, and a member usually responsible for economics."[87] The structure was replicated by a series of subdivisions, with each zone including sectors, districts, and subdistricts. Each of these tiers had security forces, with the district playing a key role in this regard. Accordingly, there was a network of prisons throughout the country. The military, operating under Son Sen's General Staff, had a similar hierarchical structure, with forces at the zone and sector level.[88]

Etcheson also afforded significance to the March 30, 1976 Decision, which explicitly stated that the government "must be totally an organization of the Party."[89] This meant, according to Etcheson, "it was the intention of the standing committee that it would have total control over the government."[90] The Standing Committee, he continued, "devised policy for all sectors and organizational units of Democratic Kampuchea and monitored the implementation of that policy throughout the country." They did so from a Phnom Penh administrative hub known as Office 870, which included a network of suboffices designated by the letter *K*. The K offices also had a semihierarchical structure, with the top one, K-1, serving as the key organizational office and as Pol Pot's residence.[91] Long Muy had worked at one of these offices, K-16, as a Chinese translator.

Etcheson noted that, in contrast to an impersonal bureaucracy consisting of qualified personnel, the DK administration structure was highly personalized, with bosses seeking to staff their offices with those to whom they had ties.[92] In Cambodia, interpersonal relations are often structured in terms of this sort of a patronage system, in which, ideally, a superior provides benefits and protection to subordinates who offer loyalty and support in return.[93] Duch made a number of suggestive remarks in this regard, including his comment that Son Sen had given him a motorbike, a status symbol in DK. Thirty years later, he often spoke almost with reverence about this man who had assigned him to oversee the execution of over 12,000 people at S-21, describing him as "very clever" and referring to him respectfully as "master" or "Teacher (Kruu) Son Sen."[94]

Duch acknowledged that he had enjoyed the protection of Son Sen and later Nuon Chea, since he was viewed as their loyal "German shepherd" guard dog.[95] He in turn protected his cadre from M-13 as large-scale purges of S-21 cadre got under way. Likewise, "whoever was a long-standing subordinate ['grandchild'] of Comrade Hor was not touched either. This is because in the ranks of the CPK, if subordinates ['children'] obeyed their bosses ['mother'], then the bosses would protect their followers ['children']."[96]

As is common when describing Cambodian patronage ties, Duch used idioms of kinship that, by implication, should endure like a parent-child bond, with the subordinate/child respecting and obeying his or her superior/ parent, who provides him or her with protection and advancement. In Cambodia, these networks are often referred to as "strings" (khsae) and a patron sometimes likened to a tree that gives shade.

Most of the cadre purged at S-21, Duch noted, lacked protection. The dozen or so cadre from Phnom Penh who had been transferred to S-21 "came without their superior ['mother']." They lacked "resolve" in their interrogations and sometimes contested decisions, so Nat reported on them. Lacking patronage, this group was gradually purged, first by Nat and then by Duch until just one remained.[97]

Many more cadre from Division 703 were purged. These purges began under Nat after the previous secretary of Division 12, Sok, was executed. Afterward, "his subordinates were monitored and tracked by the upper echelon . . . [and] would not be able to escape from being purged." When, for example, they made a mistake, such as beating a prisoner to death before a confession was obtained, or were perceived as challenging, Hor, Nat, and later Duch would file a report, which often resulted in the person's arrest.[98] In contrast, if a person had protection and made a mistake, that cadre might not be killed.[99] "So," Duch concluded, "when the superior was arrested, it was just a matter of time before his subordinates were also arrested. It [was a] principle."[100] This is why Duch feared for his life after Vorn Vet, Cheng An, and Chhay Kim Hor were arrested, since he was linked to their networks.

The purge of Division 703 at S-21 illustrates a frequent DK dynamic in which "those who lost their superiors, those whose superior[s] were smashed," became suspect and were frequently demoted, transferred, or purged. Given that patronage relationships are personalized and premised on an idealized affective relationship in a patron-client dyad, they may also be characterized by instability and mistrust. Patrons may worry about providing their followers with too much power and authority, which could tempt clients to seek to displace the patron.[101] This uncertainty is one reason nepotism was common in the DK administrative ranks, since family bonds were considered more trustworthy.

One way to guard against betrayal is to balance the authority of a subordinate. Thus, at first Nat and his troops were favored because of their valor in the fight to take Phnom Penh and were entrusted to carry out the critical task of "cleaning up" the capital. However, according to Duch, Nat soon fell out of favor because, as Son Sen once told Duch, "Nat is full of tricks" (*sâmbour lbech*), including making arbitrary arrests.[102] When S-21 was established, Duch was placed there as a counterbalance to Nat.[103] Eventually, Nat was separated from his base of power and transferred to the General Staff, where Son Sen could watch him. Duch noted that a similar thing happened after Chakrei fell under suspicion.[104] Similarly, when the top leadership no longer trusted Koy Thuon, they transferred him from his base of power in the Northern Zone to the Ministry of Commerce. Then he was placed under house arrest before being sent to S-21.

Such transfers often removed a suspect cadre from a decision-making post, as authorized by the March 30, 1976 Decision, which might have allowed that person to protect followers. In cases where a high-ranking cadre retained power and authority, things became trickier. Thus, to arrest an East Zone cadre such as Chhouk, the Standing Committee had to present sufficient implicating evidence.

The cadre with the authority of arrest in such situations had to proceed with caution, however, to avoid falling under suspicion themselves. In some situations, it would behoove such a cadre to assent to arrests as a validation of his or her revolutionary line and stance. Sao Phim may well have traversed such a delicate path in allowing the arrest of followers like Chakrei and Chhouk who had been clearly implicated. Ultimately, in 1978, Sao Phim himself was targeted for arrest, leading him to commit suicide. Soon thereafter, a massive purge took place in the East Zone. Duch noted that the Khmer Rouge strategy of gradually purging a network before taking a big boss was inspired by a Ho Chi Minh adage: "Before cutting the bamboo, one must trim the thorns."[105]

This general pattern, in which the suspected leaders and their "strings" of followers were jointly purged, took place throughout DK. During his testimony, Etcheson presented a number of graphics illustrating how the process unfolded, indexed partly by the number of cadre sent to S-21 from a given unit over time. He began with a chart illustrating how the number of cadre arriving at S-21 from Division 310, linked to Koy Thuon and the Northern Zone, began to spike in December 1976, just before Koy Thuon's arrest. Division 310 cadre continued to be purged throughout 1977, a pattern that mirrored the broader purge of Koy Thuon's Northern Zone network. At least 855 people from Division 310 were sent to S-21.[106] Other suspect units were also purged in high numbers, including another unit affiliated with the Northern Zone, Division 450 (467 arrests), Division 703 (406 arrests), and Division 502 (399 arrests).[107] The arrests were often part of a spiral in which those arrested implicated others, leading to further arrests.

Etcheson next turned to the purges of DK government ministries, which were widespread and at times so extensive that some ministers "actually complained that it was difficult for them to carry out their responsibilities because of so many people from their ministries being seized by security forces."[108] Ministries headed by leaders who had been purged, such as Koy Thuon's Ministry of Commerce (386 S-21 arrests), were hit particularly hard. Other units that were extensively purged included the Ministry of Public Works (532 people arrested), the Ministry of Energy (268 arrests), and the Ministry of Railways (251 arrests).[109]

Following one of Roux's procedural complaints, Judge Cartwright asked Etcheson to describe the zone purges. Etcheson replied that, while purges occurred in all DK zones, three zones were particularly hard hit: Koy Thuon's Northern Zone, the Northwest Zone, and Sao Phim's East Zone. Using a color coded graph, Etcheson noted that these purges peaked at different times, with the Northern/Central zone peaking in the second quarter of 1977, the Northwest Zone in the third quarter of 1977, and the East Zone in the second quarter of 1978. "More than 1,000 cadres from the East Zone and more than 1,000 cadres from the Northwest zone were sent to S-21," Etcheson said.[110]

After yet another procedural complaint from Roux, Judge Cartwright asked Etcheson to describe the position of S-21 in comparison to other DK security centers. Even though there was an extensive security system throughout the country, Etcheson argued, S-21 was unique in at least three respects. First, S-21 alone operated on a nationwide basis. Second, the population of prisoners sent to S-21 included the highest-ranking cadre in the country, including members of the Standing Committee. Third, S-21 was uniquely linked, via Son Sen, to the uppermost "node of the [DK] power pyramid."[111]

Duch, who had been taking scrupulous notes, leaned back in his chair un-smiling, hand tightening on the armrest, as Etcheson claimed that "leading cadre from the zone, sector, and district echelons, along with high-ranking military leaders and ranking leaders of government ministries, almost invari-ably ended up at S-21 when they were purged. I have seen no evidence that would suggest this was the case with any other security office."[112]

| | |

Etcheson's claim undercut one of Duch's main lines of defense—that S-21 was just one of many DK security centers. During several days of testimony, Etcheson also took issue with other parts of Duch's defense. As opposed to being a passive, reluctant cog, Etcheson suggested, Duch was an active, will-ing participant and an innovator. This more dynamic role was evident in a number of ways, including Duch's reports.

Earlier, Duch had acknowledged that reporting was one of his key tasks at S-21 and that he developed new ways of doing this after becoming chairman. The methods of reporting, he had explained, developed over time based on "the ability of the chairman in addition to the requirements of the purges by the [CPK] from one stage to the next."[113] While making this admission, he emphasized that he simply relayed information to the upper echelons who did the analysis, made decisions, and gave orders.

Other documentary evidence, however, challenged the notion that Duch was largely passive. In the minutes of a September 9, 1976, General Staff meeting concerning "The Problem of Leaflets That Were Picked Up," for ex-ample, he is listed as a participant, along with "Brother 89" (Son Sen), Pâng (the head of Office 870), and Comrade Pin, the secretary of Division 703.[114] The minutes record Comrade Pâng's "surmise" that the content of the 12 leaflets was the same as ones that earlier had been thrown near the Chinese Embassy and included antirevolutionary texts. Duch is recorded as adding that, after the previous leaflets were distributed, "we arrested the contempt-ible Sâmbat. We questioned the contemptible Leat and the contemptible Mat, who said that the leaflets came from Phuon of Division 170." Here, Duch pointed to the likely culprit.

Speaking next, Son Sen then stated, "It's necessary to examine units of 170, units of 703 and other units that are camped in the vicinity," while warning that "these activities are part of an overall enemy plan. We have to be on guard against an enemy assassination" and urging the participants to "heighten the outlook of revolutionary vigilance in view of the increasingly very sharp contractions and the ever strong class hatred of the enemies of the Kampuchean revolution."

During his questioning of Etcheson, Senior Assistant Co-Prosecutor Bates displayed another document from a meeting held a week later, on September 16, 1976, in which Duch appeared to play an even bigger role. This was a period of intense activity as Chakrei and other high-ranking cadre associated with the East Zone were confessing and naming alleged coconspirators. The record of this meeting, titled "Minutes of the Meeting with Comrade Tal Division 290 and Division 170," are detailed in small black typescript that is blurred in places and in shorthand that is somewhat difficult to follow.[115] The document lists several participants, including Son Sen, some of his key staff, Duch, and Comrade Tal, the head of Division 170.

In the document, Brother 89 (Son Sen) notes that Chakrei's confession implicated a number of people from Sector 24 "who had been in contact with Viet Nam and the Soviets to attack our revolution this 30 September 1976. Now we have arrested Chhouk, the secretary of 24[,] and his cronies. These guys have already confessed that Chakrei's replies were indeed correct." Here, as with the September 9 meeting minutes, the CPK leadership's growing fear of perceived assassination plots, internal subversion, and external coup plots is apparent. Cadre (from Sector 24) and military units (Division 290) associated with two of the purged senior cadre, Chakrei and Chhouk, are targeted for arrest.

Bates directed the court's attention to a section heading in the minutes titled "Comrade Duch Had a View." The text that follows notes that two cadre from Division 170, after meeting, agreed it was necessary to "take" another twenty-nine "names," which are then listed in two columns on the document. S-21, the minutes state, was involved in the decision-making process about these twenty-nine "names," as well as eleven more people identified at a September 15 meeting. "Based on the reasoning made clear by Sâ-21 and the Division," the minutes continue, "which have seen concrete and continuous activities, and based on the principle stipulated by the Organization that Chakrei's links ["strings"] must be taken, the meeting agreed to take these 29 more," as well as "two women, namely Chakrei's wife and cousin."

Bates asked the court clerk to then read the last two sections of the minutes concerning the "operational" and "concrete methods" to be taken. The first involved maintaining secrecy when making arrests, an objective that would be facilitated by consultation and discussion "with Sâ-21 as regards operational methods." The "Concrete Methods," in turn, specified that "Sâ-21 and the Division [290] must cooperate and seize right from the motorpool," while S-21 and Division 170 "must consult about the details of the concrete measures to take all 40." As soon as the clerk finished reading, Roux interjected that there was a translation problem. Bates objected to the timing of Roux's "interventions just when we are discussing key evidence."[116]

Bates asked Etcheson for his assessment of the minutes. "According to this document," Etcheson replied, "the accused person liaised upward to the very apex of authority in the [CPK] and then reached down through Son Sen into an operating division to assist in the planning and conduct of what became a very large-scale purge in the military, connected with the affair of Chan Chakrei." Further, Etcheson said, the document demonstrated that the Party Center authorized horizontal communication between "S-21 and the targeted units that are necessary to implement the planned purge."[117]

Duch offered a different reading. "I attended the meeting," he began, "so I know the details."[118] First, as he routinely did, he noted that everything was done in accordance with the March 30, 1976 Decision, which gave the General Staff the authority to "smash" the military ranks. This meeting had been led by Son Sen, the chief of the General Staff, he continued, and included his deputy, "Brother 81" or Siet Chhe (Tum)—the same person listed on the cover of Long Muy's confession—as well as Nat and the head of Division 170, Comrade Tal.

Duch claimed that Son Sen had departed after leading the first part of the meeting, leaving Siet Chhe in charge. It was Siet Chhe who asked if Duch had an opinion. Because Duch was "not part of the committee . . . I told him no, I did not have any opinion."[119] The meeting then continued. Duch admitted: "I was the one who sent the names to them" and later "ordered people to beat [them] to get a confession."[120] But here, as usual, he depicted himself as a middleman. Thus, he continued, he sent these confessions to "Brother 89, who was my superior. . . . That's how I reported, based on the chains of command and based on the designations of the Party."

Duch added: "And Mr. Etcheson, who is an expert, please don't forget that Brother 89 was there and nobody would make a decision [other] than 89, and when Brother 89 left he designated the chairmanship of the meeting to Brother 81."[121] This remark reflected Duch's broader irritation with Etcheson, whose testimony Duch at one point referred to as "nuts" (chkuot), a comment that led to a rebuke from Judge Nil.[122]

Later, when Kar Savuth asked Duch to comment on Etcheson's testimony, Duch assessed its strengths and weaknesses in a manner that seemed like a cross between Khmer Rouge biography writing (of good and bad points) and a school grade. The two good parts of Etcheson's analysis, Duch said, were Etcheson's acknowledgment of the importance of the March 30, 1976 Decision and the verticality of communication and top-down structure of the DK chain of command.[123] Much of the rest of Etcheson's analysis was weaker, including his translations, his suggestion that S-21 prisoners had been released, and his use of inculpatory evidence—including nine exchanges between Duch and Sou Met in 1977, which, like the September 1976 meeting minutes, Etcheson argued, suggested Duch had a more active role in the purges than he acknowledged.

Roux also challenged Etcheson about the limits of Duch's autonomy, repeatedly returning to the theme that he was simply an instrument of the DK leadership, which was increasingly driven by paranoia. In this context, how, Roux asked, was it possible to claim that Duch was an innovator rather than someone just doing his best to implement the party line? "My understanding," Etcheson replied, "based on long study of [DK] in general and the operations of S-21 in particular . . . is that the accused was very much an innovator, a creator, a developer, and an institutionalizer of the method of making very detailed confessions that are extracted over long periods of time" and often seemed to implicate every person a victim "has ever met and can remember."[124]

A cycle ensued, Etcheson continued, whereby these lists were used to make further arrests, resulting in confessions that generated more lists, leading to an "exponential growth in the number of accused traitors and in the number of victims of purges." It was Duch's "zeal" that led him to create this methodology, which, even if it had to accord with the Party line, nevertheless demonstrated the "creativity, inventiveness," and revolutionary ardor with which Duch carried out his duties. Indeed, Khmer Rouge ideology exhorted cadre to do so in accordance with the Party line of "independence-mastery," which encouraged innovation and dynamism in implementing revolutionary tasks.

But, Roux countered, "Did they have the choice?"

In life, Etcheson responded, "one always has choices."[125]

Commandant
(FUNCTIONING OF S-21)

The gate swings open to night. Duch, dressed in dark trousers and a charcoal grey safari shirt, walks into the frame, smiling broadly. He wears a wristwatch and a pen in his shirt pocket, symbols of status. Behind him, a second photographer snaps a shot of perhaps two dozen revolutionaries sitting at a table, large white bowls filled with food set before them. No one looks at Duch.

Men, women, and children are crowded in rows along the table, a long rectangle that seems to extend out of the gate and into the night. The women crop their hair revolutionary-style. Some hold small children in their laps. A girl, perhaps five or six years old, stares at her bowl of food as she prepares to take a bite. Another child, a boy a few years older, sits close to the camera, his mother's arm around him. He rotates his head, the only one looking as the photographer focuses the lens and snaps the shot, a flash in the night. The boy clasps a spoon tightly as he stares, uncertain.

S-21 is just a ten-minute walk through the darkness away, where inmates like Long Muy lie shackled in silence and starving while Duch and his comrades eat. Duch would describe them as the living-dead, trapped not in a prison but a "place to store people before killing [them]."[1]

Thirty-one days into Duch's trial, Deputy Co-Prosecutor Smith requested that this photograph be displayed. The proceedings had shifted into a new phase focusing on the functioning of S-21, one Smith referred to as "the main part of this trial," since it dealt with issues such as whether or not Duch had acted under fear or "duress, whether or not he had any choice."[2]

Smith's questioning was focusing on Duch's daily life. Duch reported that he worked long days.[3] He arose early and began his duties by 7 A.M. He took a break from 11 A.M. until 2 P.M., when he took a nap and had a light lunch, often just fruit. After a dinner break from 5 to 7 P.M., he continued to work in the evening, sometimes not stopping until midnight. Duch said he spent most of his time during these twelve-hour days annotating confessions at his residence, though he had to oversee the management of S-21 and provide training, most often for interrogators. He said he avoided the prison, which he found troubling, instead choosing to "close my eyes [and . . .] ears."[4]

The S-21 compound included a large mess hall where perhaps a hundred or more cadre could dine. Duch ate lunch and dinner there, sitting at the same place each day with two former M-13 cadre, Chan and Pon. Sometimes Duch engaged in chitchat, but he usually just tried to "finish the meal quickly so that I could return home and rest."[5] Trying to demonstrate that Duch was not nearly as removed from the daily operations of S-21 as he suggested, Smith noted that Duch ate each day with "Pon, the chief interrogator, and Mam Nai, one of the chief interrogators, and also [your deputy] Hor on occasion."[6]

Pressing this point, Smith asked for the dining photo to be displayed. "Mr. Kaing Guek Eav, can you look at this photograph?" Smith requested. "It's a photograph of you having a meal. Can you describe the photograph?"[7] Duch replied that this was not a picture of the canteen but instead one of the offices he occupied (number 4 on his map) in the early stages of S-21.

He lived in an adjoining villa with three of his messengers, one of whom, Phorn, was in charge of Duch's two telephone lines. "When he received a call from the upper echelon," Duch recalled, Phorn "would run and come call me to answer the phone."[8] Duch sometimes summoned Hor or Pon to a meeting by phone but spent most of his time on the phone talking to Son Sen, with whom he spoke perhaps an hour each day.[9] If he needed to leave S-21 to meet Son Sen, he could take his motorbike, though he had access to Nat's Jeep. Duch noted that vehicles reflected status during DK, with "medium cadre"

Duch, standing (back left), at a celebratory meal following the marriage of Nun Huy, S-21 Committee member and S-24 (Pray Sar) head, to Prok Khoeun. Photo courtesy of the DC-Cam / SRI Archives.

Wedding of S-21 Committee member Nun Huy and Prok Khoeun. Khoeun worked at S-24 until 1977, when she became deputy of a "hot group" of female interrogators. Both were arrested and sent to S-21 in 1978 after Huy's radio operator fled. Photo Courtesy of the DC-Cam / SRI Archives.

like him permitted to use motorbikes and division commanders like Nat a jeep. High-ranking cadre drove cars.[10]

The photograph of the meal at his office, Duch explained, was likely taken on the "day we married Comrade Khoeun and Comrade Huy." Directing the court's attention to two figures sitting at the end of the table by the open gate who seem in danger of falling into the night, Duch affirmed that the person next to Huy was "Khoeun, yes. It's the curly hair."[11] Huy, his face silhouetted against the black, peers into the dark.

In most cases, Duch elaborated, cadre from Division 703 were married in groups, a common DK practice, after which Duch would invite the newlyweds to his residence for a celebration. Khoeun and Huy, however, were the only couple wed on this day.[12] More broadly, Duch claimed that it was Khmer Rouge policy for a married couple to be together once every 10 days, which was part of a larger attempt by the regime to disrupt traditional family structure (whereby marriages were usually arranged by parents) and co-opt related affective ties.[13] Duch noted that after he and his wife married in December 1975, they abided by this principle as well.[14]

Comrade Huy, Duch had explained earlier in the trial, was the third member of the S-21 committee and oversaw S-24, or Prey Sar, a large "re-education" camp that was part of S-21—much as M-13 had been divided into a prison and a work camp. S-24 was created by Nat's Division 703 police office. If the inmates of this "prison without walls" had originally come from Division 703, they later came to include people under the authority of the General Staff and other suspect units.[15] S-24 differed from M-13B in one key respect, Duch explained: with the exception of 30 combatants from an East Zone tank unit, all the prisoners were eventually killed. Witnesses would dispute this claim.

S-24 inmates were closely monitored and required to do hard labor, even pulling plows at times. The S-24 prisoners did rice and vegetable farming, sometimes by moonlight during an agricultural "offensive," and also labored to build dikes and dig canals. Crop yields were used to supply S-21 and "support the units at the center."[16] In 1978, S-24 produced a surplus that Duch sent to his superiors because "I wanted to help the other units. I also wanted to promote the reputation of Prey Sar and S-21."[17] The OCP and civil party lawyers would use this action as further evidence that Duch cared little for the starving prisoners and that as opposed to being a reluctant and passive actor, he carried out his orders with zeal and sometimes even exceeded them.

The S-24 prisoners were referred to as "elements," whose status was unclear, and they were subdivided, "based on [their] true nature and [stance],"[18] into three groups," those needing light, moderate, and heavy "tempering." Their "re-education" was carried out through hard work, even as the "elements," particularly those in the third group, were closely monitored for signs of subversion, which might be gleaned from weak performance, attitude, or comments. While it was almost impossible for a prisoner to move from the third group to the first or second, prisoners were sometimes reclassified as in need of more tempering. In the end, Duch said, they were all "smashed." While he accepted responsibility for the deaths, he noted that he delegated decision-making authority to Huy, who, like Hor, had a standing order to execute prisoners. Duch became more involved when S-24 staff or prisoners were sent to S-21, often after they had made a "mistake."

Comrade Huy had such an incident. In December 1978, just a month before the end of the regime, Comrade Huy's radio operator fled. Duch explained that the Khmer Rouge held superiors accountable for subordinates, so Huy was punished. Duch recalled that he and Hor had been monitoring Huy, concerning whom there had been earlier incidents. The gravity of the escape necessitated filing a report with Nuon Chea, who, Duch said, ordered Huy's arrest. Duch summoned Huy for a meeting at Baku, a small compound centered around a former residence of Lon Nol at which S-24 cadre stayed, and Huy was arrested there along with his wife and son.[19]

| | | |

Such arrests, which Duch claimed to delegate to Hor, usually involved deception. Many prisoners had been told they were being sent away for study or work. Duch acknowledged that, as illustrated by the minutes of the September 16, 1976, General Staff meeting planning the arrests of Division 290 combatants, he was sometimes consulted about arrests, which had to be secret. With higher-level cadre, particularly those who knew about S-21, a more elaborate pretext might be necessary. Duch admitted being present for some of these arrests, which occasionally took place at his residence, though he added that his superiors made the arrest decisions.[20]

Prior to his arrest, for example, Koy Thuon had been escorted to Duch's house by Comrade Pang, who ran Office S-71. This administrative office was a key part of Office 870, a moniker referring to a cluster of key offices serving the CPK leadership, including the K offices, which reported to Pang.[21] Sometimes Pang was charged with the delivery of S-21 confessions. Around March 1978, Vorn Vet came to S-21 with a letter from Nuon Chea authorizing

Pang's arrest. Vorn Vet and Duch deliberated and decided that Pang would be arrested the next time he came to pick up a confession.[22] When Pang arrived, he didn't suspect anything. Duch then pointed at him, at which point Pang began to shout and protest as Hor handcuffed him.[23] From Office 870 and Office S-71, 209 cadre were sent to S-21, including Long Muy. We don't know the details of his arrest beyond the date, July 16, 1977, and the involvement of the General Staff.[24]

Whatever their route to S-21, prisoners like Long Muy, Pang, and Huy arrived at the gates of S-21, which Duch had marked on his map with the letter R. Duch usually just received a phone call informing him that prisoners were on the way. The S-21 "special unit," in charge of securing the perimeter of the prison, would be dispatched to the reception point, where they took control of detainees. On a handful of occasions, Duch said, members of this unit traveled outside the prison to arrest people, though this required a special pass.[25]

As they passed through the gates of S-21, the detainees began to be transformed. Since the Party did not make mistakes, the detainee's guilt was assumed. If, prior to their arrests, prisoners like Long Muy had worked among comrades, they were now marked as traitorous enemies who had been "burrowing from within."

Bound and blindfolded, the prisoners were escorted into the S-21 compound, and were registered and photographed (at Building E in the current Tuol Sleng complex). They were stripped of their black revolutionary garb, with the men often left in their shorts or underpants. High-ranking prisoners were sent to the nearby Special Prison within the S-21 compound. The prisoners were assigned to cells, usually starting in communal cells where they would lie in rows, ankles shackled to an iron bar. Those deemed important or undergoing interrogation would often be sent to one of the small individual cells Duch had ordered built.

Duch acknowledged that the prisoners were treated like animals, people halfway to death, since they were kept alive only to confess.[26] They ate like animals, being given just a few spoonfuls of food each day. On these starvation rations, the prisoners became malnourished, weak, and emaciated. They got lice and skin diseases. Some fell sick and were treated by ill-trained medics. Every few days they would be hosed down, a "bathing" given primarily so the floors could be cleaned. The prisoners had to sit in wet clothes until they dried. If a prisoner died in the night, the body was left until morning.

Detainees lost the ability to engage in common human acts, including talking to others or moving about. The prisoners had to lie on their backs on tile floors, where they slept without bedding or mosquito nets. If they wanted to defecate into an old ammunition can or urinate into a plastic bottle left next to them, prisoners had to ask the permission of the guards, who sometimes beat them. Duch said it was shameful the way "young people addressed the senior people [as] 'contemptible,'" a derogatory term of address that was part of a larger set of dehumizing idioms used at S-21.[27]

All of the detainees met the same end: execution. The majority were men; roughly a fifth were women.[28] Some of the women were revolutionaries, but the majority, like Comrade Khoeun, had been arrested along with their husbands. The female detainees were separated from the men, allowed to wear their clothes, and left unshackled.[29] Sometimes they were put to work on the premises.

Children often accompanied their parents to S-21. According to S-21 documentation, 1.1 percent of the detainees were children, a figure that Duch, doing the math, said was too low, given that a single surviving document recorded the executions of 160 children.[30] And, he added, the names of children were not recorded, a practice dating back to Nat. Duch explained that "if the husband was arrested, then the wife had to go too. It was unavoidable—and the children too."[31] This was done in part out of fear that the children "might [take] revenge."[32]

Later Smith displayed a photograph of a mother and child. The mother, in her early to midtwenties, stares back at the camera. A number is pinned to the collar of her light-colored shirt: 320. Part of her shadow can be seen, a silhouette of black on the white walls. Her infant lies on the floor of her cell, barely in the frame. He stares upward, arms outstretched and eyes half open.

"In all good conscience," Smith asked, "how could you have ever, ever, thought that these were the faces of the enemies?" Duch, as always, had an answer. He noted that the groups designated in the March 30, 1976 Decision, determined who was an enemy. "It was not S-21, it was not me, it was the upper echelon who made decisions," he explained. "So when there's an order, decision, we had to follow. If we failed to do that, we would be beheaded."[33]

Cambodian civil party lawyer Hong Kimsuon later asked how Duch felt when he returned home from work to spend time with his family even as children were being "smashed" at S-21. Duch, noting that if he had been arrested his family would have followed, replied, "I thought of my baby and that's why I needed to survive."[34]

As he described his life at S-21, Duch distanced himself from the violence. He repeatedly stated that he delegated the management of the prison to Hor and was "not close to the situation," "did not pay attention," or was "not there to see."[35] He said he never visited the central prison, made only a handful of trips to the Special Prison, and sometimes visited the sculpture room to watch the artists—an activity that again suggested he was a humanist, a lover of art and poetry, who was condemned to work at S-21.

Duch cautioned that much of what he was saying was his "presumption" based on these limited visits to the compound, his experience at M-13, what he had learned from former guards and survivors, and his reading of academic books like David Chandler's *Voices of S-21*. "Personally I could only think of how to avoid being close to that location," Duch would say.[36]

Instead, Duch stayed at his office, meeting regularly with his deputies to ensure the smooth functioning of the security center even as he spent most of his time annotating confessions and training interrogators. When S-21 was first formed, Nat had tasked Duch with training the Division 703 interrogators so as to integrate them with Duch's M-13 interrogators.[37] Duch also managed the interrogation process. When he took the helm of S-21, he assigned Hor to oversee this day-to-day operation of the interrogation process, even as Hor consulted Duch regularly.

The structure of the interrogation process was a fusion of the practices of Nat's Division 703 police office and Duch's M-13 unit, though the methods evolved over time. From the early stages of S-21, the interrogators were divided into three categories, each characterized by a particular approach. The "cold group" relied on verbal interrogation or "politics." The members of the "hot team," in contrast, used physical violence. "Their hands were hot," Duch explained, "so they would beat the prisoners immediately if the confession [was] not extracted."[38] A "chewing group" combined the "hot" and "cold" tactics over longer periods. Each team had five or six members.[39]

After Nat's departure, Duch created a fourth group at the Special Prison, charged with interrogating important prisoners. He placed Pon, who was effective and had been well trained at M-13, in charge of this group even as he paid close attention to and in a few cases became directly involved in the interrogation of high-ranking cadre.[40] Chan was not assigned to a specific group but assisted as needed and eventually headed the interrogation of Vietnamese detainees. Later, after a woman was sexually abused, Duch ordered the creation

Group of S-21 interrogators. Photo courtesy of the DC-Cam / SRI Archives.

Hor, Duch's deputy at S-21 (front left). One unconfirmed documentary source names the other three men (from left to right) as Noeun (documentation), Pon (a key interrogator), and Duch's deputy Mam Nai (Chan). Photo courtesy of the DC-Cam / SRI Archives.

of a five-member female team to interrogate female prisoners. Most of the members of this unit were the wives of leading S-21 cadre, such as Comrades Hor, Mut (head of the "chewing" team), and Nun Huy.[41] Nun Huy's bride became an interrogator before being purged. The female prisoner who had been abused was Deum Saroeun, Duch's former teacher. Ties were often close at S-21.

On arrival, prisoners like Long Muy were classified and taken to their cells, in his case most likely in the general prison. Depending on their importance, prisoners were either executed shortly thereafter or detained for interrogation. According to Duch, Hor then decided when, how, and by whom they would be interrogated. While Duch said that he was "unclear on this matter because I did not witness it," he was able to offer some "conclusions" about the interrogation routines.[42]

Before questioning, the interrogator would notify the guard on duty that a prisoner was slated for interrogation. The guard would unshackle and bring the prisoner to the cellroom door, where the prisoner would pass into the interrogator's authority and be walked to the interrogation room. This room included a chair, desk, and shackles—as well as instruments of torture, including objects, such as knives, that were displayed as a "deterrent."[43] Duch "presumed" that the prisoner on entering the room "would be shackled [with] arms untied." If the "prisoners agreed to confess and to write their confession, then they would be allowed to sit on the chair," to which their legs would be shackled, and "write their confession."[44] Those who did not would be questioned.

The initial questioning was done by a "preliminary interrogation team." This team would only ask questions to grasp the essence of the confession, and then Hor would make a decision," alone or in consultation with Duch, about whether to send the prisoner to "the cold group or the hot or the chewing [group]."[45] Interrogators worked three shifts daily from 7 to 11 A.M., from 2 to 4 or 5 P.M., and from 7 to 10 P.M. [46] Once the detainee was assigned to an interrogator, things began "with just soft questioning" to enable the interrogator to "understand" the prisoner. More specific questioning would follow. If this "cold method" was not successful, "the hot method would be introduced."[47]

Duch acknowledged the use of four "hot methods"; the most common was beating by club or whip. Prisoners were also shocked with electrical currents and occasionally waterboarded, a practice used by previous Cambodian governments, which involved pouring "water into [the] nostrils of the prisoners."[48] Duch said that the fourth practice, suffocation by means of a plastic bag placed over the head, had been originally suggested by Vorn Vet but was not frequently used.[49] Under questioning, Duch acknowledged that practices like the extraction of the toenails and fingernails of prisoners, a torture to which civil party and S-21 survivor Chum Mey had been subjected, took place but were unauthorized.[50] Others, like the use of poisonous insects, depicted in a Tuol Sleng Genocide Museum painting, did not occur.

Duch admitted to personally using physical violence on an S-21 prisoner only once, when Nat was still the prison head. At the time, Duch said, Nat asked him to interrogate Chhit Iv, who had "defeated" his interrogator. "So I went in to interrogate [Chhit Iv], and finally he gave in. So I slapped him."[51] This was done according to the "code of interrogation," which allows a "small torture just to remind the person not to lie again." Also, he suggested, he slapped the prisoner to prevent Nat from doing worse to Chhit Iv, a former police chief who had interrogated Khmer Rouge under the Lon Nol regime. Besides this one case, Duch said that he had only participated in the interrogation of a few key prisoners held at the Special Prison, including Koy Thuon.

At times, Duch seemed boastful about his interrogation skills. He noted that he only had to use "one single cold method to interrogate Koy Thuon" in contrast to other interrogators.[52] "I could control my emotion . . . and my action," he stated, "but the younger interrogators were not in the same situation. They would be extreme."[53] As a result, torture was used "the majority of the time. . . . I think all of the confessions involved the use of torture," most often by beating.[54] There were exceptions, including Comrade Pon, who was "in good control of his violence," though he was still not as skilled as Duch.[55]

Other interrogators, Duch noted, were the opposite. "It depends on the nature of each individual. Some people were cruel and some were less cruel."[56] One of the most infamous interrogators was Comrade Toy, a Division 703 cadre Duch described as "the hottest person in the [hot] group."[57] If the interrogation of a prisoner was proving difficult, Hor might reassign the person to Toy, whose "nature was to resort to torture" and who got results.[58] Siet Chhe, the person named on the cover of Long Muy's confession, was sent to Toy and soon confessed to raping his daughter, a confession that seemed to Duch at that time as "too extreme."[59] Duch added that Toy also competed "to gain my favour" through his efforts.[60]

What emerges in Duch's recollection of interrogation and torture at S-21 is a picture of extreme violence and few limits. To obtain confessions, interrogators beat prisoners with abandon. They also innovated. Duch recalled that one interrogator invented a method in which a prisoner would be forced to assume a stress position and pay homage to a picture of a dog with the head of Ho Chi

Minh or Lyndon B. Johnson, both of whom had died before DK. Duch was impressed by the results and encouraged other interrogators to use it.[61]

Problems arose, however, when interrogators abused detainees to the point where they were no longer able to respond due to incapacitation, which sometimes required medical treatment.[62] Duch, at work in his office, showed little concern unless cadre made "mistakes" such as beating a prisoner to death—though he sometimes tried to "cover the mistake" by requesting his superior to excuse the interrogator as a favor.[63] The cadre who sexually abused Duch's former teacher was merely transferred, though Duch claimed he was angered by the incident.

| | | |

Even as he noted the abuses carried out at S-21 by cadre like Toy, Duch acknowledged he was also partly to blame. After all, he said, he had trained Toy and the other cadre in the hot method: "it was my education."[64] During the first month or two after the establishment of S-21, he trained interrogators for up to a couple of hours a day. Later, new interrogators would learn by observing senior interrogators, while Duch focused on "politics" and "the directions for searching out the enemies."[65] His instruction focused, among other things, on the need to maintain "an absolute stance," viewing the prisoners "as the enemy."[66]

The second key point was the structure and chronology of the confessions. "Once the prisoners had confessed," Duch said, the interrogator cadre had to ask them to write their biographies, from the time of their involvement in their traitorous activities, with dates and details, as well as "the names of those who were implicated in the confessions."[67] If a prisoner was illiterate, the confession would be tape-recorded and transcribed. Sometimes prisoners, particularly important ones, would be required to write and rewrite their confessions.

By 1978, Duch was holding brief training sessions for small groups of perhaps 5–10 interrogators. These would take place a few times a month, varying depending on the flow of prisoners to S-21, for just a half or a whole hour. They were based on the notion of "fast attack / fast success," or the idea that the interrogators would take what they had been taught and use it later in the day.[68] He likened the process to a "circle" of practice and theory, each strengthening the other. He said that his pedagogy was inspired by Pol Pot, who said that "when you walk, the sharp sword is the one that is used, not the one in the sheath. So you had to use it to cut and then you had to sharpen it."[69]

Master

(TORTURE AND EXECUTION)

"Statistics List"

The block lettering is printed in a white square, pressed on all sides by black. The notebook cover resembles a door with a single pane of glass onto which words have been stenciled in thick, dark ink. Someone has partly shaded the block print, further staining the white. In places, the rims of the lettering are smudged or bleed inside and out, an imperfection, a danger to be boxed in by sharp lines.

On the cover of the notebook, the full title reads "The Statistics List of Security Office S-21." Below an abbreviation provides a subtitle: "Politics : Ideology : Organization." Some scholars simply refer to the notebook as the "Torture Manual."[1]

But this title directs attention from the text's broader meaning, which, if concerned with torture, is about much more. Perhaps English-speaking scholars use this colloquial title because the Khmer "Statistics List" does not seem to make sense as the title for a set of lesson plans about interrogation. But it did in Duch's world.

Statistics are models, trends extracted from a sampling of facts that provide a snapshot of a more complex reality such as a state, community, or population. Sorting what is disorderly, statistics use classification and categorization to reveal an arrangement that can then be further analyzed, explained, and used to predict future trends. Statistics are another modality of articulation that redacts, driving back as it obscures, leaving an excess of meaning. The very juxtaposition of "statistics" and "torture" is uncanny, as are the pages within.

| | |

"Be determined not to sleep while interrogating!"

The notebook begins with this disconcerting exhortation, written in block lettering on graph paper. I imagine Long Muy sitting, bloodied, beaten, and chained on the floor of his interrogation cell, while his torturer dozes, exhausted by the effort of beating his prisoner. The slogans continue:

"Be determined not to hesitate when interrogating Enemies!"

"Be determined to mount an offensive in interrogation to send answers to the Party without fail!"[2]

More broadly, this text, consisting of notes taken by unidentified cadre from mid- to late 1976 onward during training sessions led by Duch, is concerned with "facts" discerned from past interrogations, ranging from cadre performance to detainee responses. These facts are parsed in terms of the "thick frame" of the CPK party line, which provides classificatory schemes for labeling people (for example, in terms of class and stance) and evaluating behavior. Based on this information, recorded in numbered and subdivided lists, the notes also provide an explanation of the past, identify problems and strategies for the present, and create expectations for the future. In doing so, the notes outline a model of enemy subversion and strategies for uncovering plots and preventing the regime's downfall. "We are the Party's Special Branch,"[3] the notes records, highlighting the importance of the work.

The first set of lessons illustrates the central aim of interrogation: extracting information revealing treason and networks of coconspirators. Taken in the months following the arrest of Chakrei, these entries assert the existence of a "Free Khmer" network operating in the countryside and headed by East Zone secretary Sao Phim and his deputy Chhouk, the head of Sector 24. "Evidence" of this network's "intention to smash our cadres, i.e. the Communist Party of Kampuchea," has been demonstrated by "tracts, propaganda and sabotage," as well as "revolt by military force."[4] By means of interrogation, the composition of these networks has begun to be uncovered in places like East Zone sectors 24 and 25 and Division 170, as well as the broader linkages to "enemies" such as Vietnam and capitalists.

At another point, the lesson discusses "what was gotten out of" a group of a dozen prisoners who were "pounded." Their forced statements detail an alleged June 1976 meeting at which committees were established to carry out treasonous activities. The heads of the committees assigned to "distribute tracts" and "shoot and throw grenades" are named, as well as their location (Chhouk's Sector 24). In addition, the notebook records the names of the leaders of the Free Khmer network in Division 170.

Elsewhere, the lesson plan discusses the sorts of questions needed to obtain such information. Sometimes the queries are quite broad, meant to establish a chronology of treason. A section titled "Questions to pound on while interrogating Ngim" lists 12 topics to be covered, such as leadership history and structure, internal and external links, networks of traitors, horizontal communication, and "personal histories from beginning to end."

The "direction" of questions could also be specific, as when attempting to ferret out the details of the June 1976 meeting: "Were the meetings actually conducted or not? Who attended? What dates, Where?" or "What were the instructions in the meetings?"[5] Such investigation, in turn, yields "The names of those we suspect," "People who must be questioned," and "Directions to pound and find enemies boring holes from within the units."[6]

Just asking the right questions is not enough. Interrogation has to be carried out with a proper revolutionary stance. Duch's lessons again move between the broad and the specific. One section lists the Statutes of the Youth League, which require members to have, among other things, "A high renunciation of material ownership, power, views, ideology" and "Absolute obedience."[7]

Cadre are also required to engage in criticism and self-criticism to further hone their stance. In this spirit, Duch offers an "Evaluation of positive and negative points" and "Areas of improvement in the future" during an "Experience meeting on the work of the offensive: July 27, 1976."[8] The "Positive Points" include "Active combating, patience, carrying out our instructions to [the best of] our abilities, endeavoring to accomplish duties as assigned, whether the enemy's response are clear or unclear."

At times, the "Negative Points" seem odd and are often unsettling, even as they provide a glimpse into the S-21 torture chambers. In terms of "organizational discipline," Duch told his students, "we beat prisoners without considering it in detail, in particular comparing their responses to those who are networked with them." Another example concerns their performance when told to "attack" in their interrogations: "We did attack, but we gave more weight to torture than policy. . . . We still use loud voices when interrogating, and when the enemies answer exactly what we intended to ask, we are happy and laugh, causing the enemy to immediately catch our weakness."[9]

The remedy, Duch states in his lessons, is for interrogators to understand the sources of past mistakes, which result from not maintaining a firm revolutionary stance, as well as the related proper methods and principles for interrogation. It is from such discussions that the "Statistics List" has gotten the moniker the "Torture Manual." The language is often one of borders, interiority and exteriority, penetration and extraction, darkness and light. Each prisoner harbors a secret to be revealed.

A proper interrogation, the lessons make clear, involves an assumption (the guilt of the prisoners), belief (in the CPK and its party line), a "direction" (a set of questions related to a history of treasonous activities), and an objective (bring this hidden plot and a network of conspirators to light). "Our core duty," Duch tells his cadre, is "to interrogate, analyze and to extract responses" from "those arrested by the party."

These prisoners, he continues, "have been strongly active in the bases in all kinds of opposition activities," which have been identified "by way of reports from our Special Branch, which the Party has examined and followed-up."[10] Here Duch suggests that S-21 reports are not merely passive bureaucratic filings but instead help drive the process. Since the prisoners are guilty by virtue of arrest, the notebook states, "we cannot hesitate and have ideological doubts that hinder our task, even if that person is our brother or sister. . . . The most important thing is for us to absolutely believe in the Party."[11]

To carry out their core duty effectively, interrogators must combine this correct ideological stance with proper use of a two-pronged approach in their questioning. The first is "politics" or seeking to "propagandize and put constant and repeated pressure on [the prisoner] at all times." Torture, the second method, is supposed to be "supplemental," though, the lecture notes, "past experience is that our comrade interrogators mostly fall into torture."[12] Indeed, the notebook records, "torture cannot be avoided. It only differs as to whether it is a little or a lot."[13] Everyone, Duch is stating in his lecture, is tortured because it is assumed that when "politics" is used a detainee will "confess at the very lowest level."

From the start, the interrogator should expect resistance, deception, and "reactions." For example, prisoners "use tricks to confuse us," such as when they "complain and plead to us. They pretend to be docile and say that they did not betray us."[14] At other times, those being interrogated have "reactions, curse us, and say that we mistreat them and that they are not traitors." This situation is dangerous, Duch's lessons warn, since the reactions may raise "doubt that they may not be enemies."[15] A subsection titled "Why the enemies have reactions" adds that "ideological doubts" can also arise and the interrogator may begin to "have hesitations with them. Sometimes we are enraged at them, and that makes us lose our mastery ... [and makes] them think about other things," including "life and death."[16]

"Mastery" (*mâchaskar*), a key DK concept connoting action according with ideology, is invoked throughout Duch's lessons. Indeed, one lecture stresses the importance of studying "the movement of three tons per hectare," which meant, in the context of S-21, to "attack without hesitation" and "get results quickly to report to the Party."[17] As Duch noted during his trial, interrogators competed to outperform others in their "attacks" and the "results" obtained.

If prisoners resisted, there were "counter-strategies" that, if combined with a proper stance, would provide interrogators with the mastery needed to overcome these "tricks" and get a confession. Initially, Duch's lecture suggests, prisoners engage in "all kinds of non-stop reactions." The purpose of the preliminary investigation, he suggests, is to introduce the prisoner to the disciplinary structures operative in the interrogation room and to "constantly observe their expressions and behaviours." The "precaution" better enables the interrogator to deal with prisoner reactions, such as trying to provoke or even strike the cadre. At such times, the notes state, a cadre should "walk away and do not become short-tempered and beat them. We do whatever necessary to have mastery."[18] The goal was to "break" the prisoner.

When in control, the interrogator could use "politics" more effectively. Duch's lessons provide a long list of the "forms of propaganda" used in past interrogations, including "coaxing and soothing" prisoners, offering them food and suggesting they might be reinstated; "threatening, distracting, breaking them skillfully, arranging small scenes to make them docile and hopeless, seeing that they cannot resist any longer"; manipulating their feelings by making them think of their families; and suggesting their guilt was minor, thereby giving false hope.[19]

Torture should be used as necessary but remain secondary. "The objective of torturing," Duch instructs, "is to get their answers," to "make them feel pain so that they will respond quickly," and to "make them afraid."[20] He offers a number of caveats, reminding his interrogators that torture "is not done for fun" or "to let off steam." A prisoner might be beaten "to make them scared, but absolutely do not let them die." Interrogators had to monitor their prisoner's health and their use of physical violence. "Do not get greedy and want to be quick," he cautions, since this "leads to death and the loss of a document."[21] The death of a prisoner, in other words, had nothing to do with the loss of a human life: it was only significant insofar as it meant information was lost and the Party did not get "results."

Duch's lessons also discuss the process of confession. "If they do not answer everything or if the answers are not clear, do not despair," he advises. "There has never been an enemy who confessed the first time . . . it develops gradually."[22] Interrogators should have patience, control, and mastery and avoid influencing the prisoner's answer: "It is imperative to let them talk or write and to not interrupt them or correct them immediately to what we want, what we know, or what we want them to say."[23] Instead, the cadre should stick to "the points that the Party instructs us to ask" about the "details of background, character, interrelated [traitorous] activities, and purposes of conducting the activities."[24]

The confessions had to follow a specific style. In a lecture on "Methods in making Documents," Duch specifies that prisoners must "write about their traitorous lives in a smooth and clean narrative that is practicably clear and has reason, [has] bases for espionage and infiltration inside us, in a step-by-step process according to their plans."[25] What they wrote had to be written "by themselves with their own words, their own sentences and their whole ideas." Once they had finished a draft, the interrogator should "press on the weak points and put pressure on them. We give them reasons that they still lie, hide, exaggerate or subtract from the story. The writing and paper must be neat and clean."[26] Afterward, the document had to be "signed in acceptance of responsibility, clearly dated and must show whether it is the first or the second response, so that the Party can grasp their ideological development."[27]

To make the Party "comfortable" with the confessions, Duch advises, "do not press on names, do not lead them to talk, or beat them to say what we want."[28] A good document is one in which "our comrade interrogators are skillful in analyzing, detailing matters, raising doubts, and tackling their weak points."[29] The work is one of "intense struggle" between "an enemy who uses every trick to conceal their treasonous activities, their network and their leaders" and "our comrade interrogators," who are "talented at burrowing in and closely questioning in order to penetrate the mysteries inside their minds."[30]

Interrogation, the lecture concludes, is part of the Special Branch's "work of class struggle. That is, it is aimed at smashing the oppressor class, digging their trunks and roots out to defend the Party," the revolution, and the political "line of independence and mastery."[31] Interrogation did so by "[digging] out the mysteries of the enemy, no matter how dark, and smash[ing] their trickery, their organizational networks, and their plans. . . . We never stop."[32]

Interrogation

The "Statistics List" and other surviving S-21 notebooks are revealing about interrogation, both in terms of the models they offer of how questioning should proceed and confessions should be produced and in terms of the "problems" encountered. During a meeting on July 27, 1976, for example, Duch notes an incident in which, after a prisoner had become "exhausted and sleepy," the interrogator "gave them liquor to drink which slowed down our work."[33] Another lesson discusses "the problem of enemy escape," which might result from negligence, as when someone "in Brother Pon's group forgot to lock the shackle bar."[34] (Duch would clarify to the court that no one escaped from S-21.) Duch chides the interrogators about carelessness or being "absent-minded," as when cadre would "walk away and leave an enemy alone" or "throw away Special Branch paperwork.[35]

Discarding paperwork could also violate secrecy, a topic frequently mentioned in Duch's lectures. A subsection states that secrecy is part of the meaning and "soul of Special Branch work."[36] Thus prisoners must be guarded closely, "because if they escape they will talk about their confession." Interrogators should not "go around talking about the enemies' responses to other groups, offices, ministries or families." Documents should not be left scattered about but instead "burned" so they do not "fall into the enemy hands."[37]

Interrogation also apparently sometimes involved a degree of boredom or aversion, as when cadre fell into "clock watching" or worked "irregular hours."[38] Indeed, some of the lectures highlight how interrogation was bureaucratized and routinized. The notebook includes a section on "The system of making routine daily reports" in which Duch tells the instructors to include specific types of content (focusing on "important leaders" and "examples to make it clearer") and style, including the drawing of "lines with your pencil before writing. Write to the point and the essence."[39] A final report, in turn, should include a "daily diary," an "organization table," a "table of outlined responses," and "remarks of the group chief."[40]

Such routines were meant to produce confessions having a uniform structure and focus, which almost always included a cover sheet, a chronology detailing a history of subversion, details of alleged subversive activities, and a list of the prisoner's "string of traitors." In many ways, confessions resembled the revolutionary biographies cadre periodically wrote, with the confession listing the date when the prisoner allegedly joined an enemy network at the point in the cadre biography where the cadre would have specified the date when he or she "joined the revolution." The confessions also often included annotations, letters, and detailed summary reports.

The process of getting to this end point, however, was inconsistent, as interrogators combined "directions" and techniques given by Duch and their team leaders with their prior experience and proclivities to "break the prisoner" as the confession "moved forward" toward a "clear confession."[41] This process could be disrupted in a variety of ways, including "moral violations." Instead of questioning female prisoners about "political matters," Duch remarks in a lecture, interrogators "instead asked about [the] women's morality according to their sexual desires. While the Party's instructions were to beat female prisoners with the whip, to absolutely not beat them with hands only, we violated this."[42]

Several incidents of sexual or "morality" violations, which were officially forbidden by the regime, took place at S-21. One former S-21 interrogator who testified during Duch's trial, Prak Khan, once told me that while he didn't recall most of the people he interrogated, he remembered a young woman named Nai Non, with whom he "fell in love."[43] She was beautiful, he said, and the male cadre had no contact with single women. Plus, he added, he was young, and his hormones were flowing.

For the first few days, Prak Khan told me, he interrogated her using "politics," asking about her activities and network. When she did not confess, he said, he threatened her with a whip and then banged hard on a table, causing her to urinate on her clothing. She immediately agreed to confess. But she was illiterate, so he had to write much of the confession. He said that he sent seven or eight drafts of the confession to Duch, who kept telling him that her confession was not yet "clear." In the end, Prak Khan interrogated her, day and night, for perhaps three months. While he said that he pitied Nai Non and did not violate her, other interrogators did violate prisoners, both male and female, during interrogations.

With regard to the "agreement of fact," Duch had only partly agreed with the closing order statement, which had said: "Rapes were committed at S-21." He said only one such incident had occurred, when an "interrogator inserted a stick into teacher Deum Sareaun."[44] This incident stood out for several reasons. First, Duch said that he was "shocked" by this violation of the rules of interrogation.[45] He filed a report and waited for his superior's reply. None was forthcoming. So he "asked that the interrogator be removed from interrogating female detainees."[46] It was at this time, he said, that he decided to form the group of female interrogators.

Duch explained that he took no further action against Deum Sareaun's interrogator because she had been his primary school teacher and Duch was afraid of appearing "individualistic."[47] Nevertheless, he said he had been "very angry" about her abuse, even as he "tried to hold back my emotion" so that his superiors and subordinates would not "degrade my performance."[48] During DK, proper revolutionary stance and loyalty required demonstrating that one had cut off one's emotions from former family, friends, and teachers. If he had intervened, Duch suggested, he would have lost face and perhaps come under suspicion. "Everyone was afraid," he remarked, "and only thought about his or her own life."[49]

Perhaps this is why Duch also did nothing when Deum Sareaun's husband, Ke Kim Huot, was forced to eat excrement at S-21. Ke Kim Huot had also been Duch's teacher and had joined the Khmer Rouge, eventually becoming the head of Sector 7 in the Northeast Zone before his arrest on July 13, 1977.[50] Ke Kim Huot would remain imprisoned at S-21 for almost a year. His interrogation began the month of his arrest and continued into April 1978.

The long interrogation suggests that Ke Kim Huot resisted even though he was tortured from the start. In a July 22, 1977, report on "the contemptible Sot's confession," the preliminary interrogation team notes that Ke Kim Huot has "spoken about the situation some" but has "not yet confessed," even as they "request opinion and instructions, urgently!"[51] The report explains that Ke Kim Huot "admits participating in activities of the popular movement" but "speaks very deceptively about it," and "on joining the CIA, he confesses nothing." The report then discusses Ke Kim Huot's "health and torture."

IV. REGARDING [HIS] HEALTH AND TORTURE

1. On the morning of 18.7.77, we decided to do torture. We told him the names of those who had implicated him. In doing this, we did not grasp his weak points. We were forceful, but the results were zero. My analysis is that I observed his spirits fall somewhat. While being tortured he did not react, and when we brought him back for interrogation again, we [still] got nothing. On his health, he ate a little gruel, and cannot sleep well. Our medics are treating him.

2. On the morning of 20.7.77, we pounded him one more round. This time he reacted, cursing, saying he was not a traitor. Those that implicated

[him] were all traitors. . . . His health got weaker, but there was nothing remarkable.

3. On the afternoon of 21.7.77 we pounded him another round. Electrical wire and shit. This time he cursed those who hit him very much, [and said] Go ahead and beat me to death. Had him eat two or three spoonfuls of shit, and he asked about Hing, Neou, San, and Ranh.

4. By nightfall, we went at him again with electric wires, this time pretty seriously. He became delirious. He was [all right]. Later he confessed a bit as reported above.[52]

The report then lists five cadre who Ke Kim Huot had been told had implicated him as a CIA agent, including Deum Sareaun. Ke Kim Huot, in turn, "said he had nothing to answer to send to Angkar . . . that he now just waits for death, and he can close his eyes and die easily because he had sacrificed and was loyal to the party."[53] The report concludes by stating that the team's "operative line is to continue to torture with mastery, because the enemy is breaking emotionally and is at a dead end," even as it once again requests "guidance from Angkar."[54]

In the end, Ke Kim Huot would produce a confession that accorded with the script of treason demanded at S-21. During the trial, Duch noted that Comrade Toy had annotated Ke Kim Huot's confession,[55] suggesting that he had been passed along to S-21's interrogator of last resort, one who tortured with abandon. Even as he moved toward his final confession, written on April 29, 1978, Ke Kim Huot appears to have performed a last act of defiance. An undated version of his confession states that while he was teaching from 1956 to 1958, Duch was among "the students who studied hard, especially by asking me questions and paying attention to my explanation about politics and democratic view."[56] In a March 7, 1978, version of his confession, Ke Kim Huot ranks Duch number 11 in his "list of those who participated in traitorous activities with me."[57] Ke Kim Huot was executed on May 10, 1978, less than two weeks after his final confession.[58]

Ke Kim Huot's confession suggested that a wider range of tortures was used at S-21 than Duch had admitted. After Duch confirmed that Ke Kim Huot had been forced to eat excrement, Judge Nil asked Duch about other forms of torture, including forcing prisoners to drink urine (Duch replied that he didn't know but believed this took place) and making them "pay homage to an image of a dog," a form of torture that Duch acknowledged and that is mentioned in a 1978 lecture notebook. Duch explained that he sought to educate his cadre "to distinguish the position of the enemies and friends. So they were told not to regard any detainee as a friend by addressing" him or her politely. As an example, Duch spoke of Chum Mey, "who was addressed by the very young interrogators as 'a-' [despicable].... I think it was very humiliating... [and] by making the detainees pay homage to a picture of a dog, it was severe."[59]

The fact that Duch authorized the interrogation of Ke Kim Huot, Deum Sareaun, and so many other former friends and colleagues raised questions about his character and motivations. In Cambodia, teachers are highly esteemed, and students are expected to show them gratitude and respect. Duch's seeming indifference increased doubt about the genuineness of his professed remorse, an issue Judge Lavergne explored. "Have you ever imagined," he asked Duch, "what these prisoners could have felt [while being tortured]?" "Have you ever imagined what would be felt by a person whose head was placed in a plastic bag?"[60]

Most of Duch's replies avoided issues of feeling, offering indirections or specifications that veered from the intent of Judge Lavergne's line of questioning. But at times he seemed to get genuinely upset, as when he answered repeated questions about the extreme violence of S-21. He sometimes looked down, sighed slightly, and spoke very slowly, as if the words wouldn't come out. At one point he broke down and began to sob while discussing one of his former teachers. "The accused, collect your emotions," Judge Nil instructed.[61]

Judge Cartwright, questioning him later the same day, asked: "Today, in this courtroom, you appear to me to be deeply ashamed and regretful of your part in the obtaining of confessions using torture. Is that correct?"[62] "Your Honour," Duch replied. "I do not deny it." When she inquired why, then, he had not been concerned at the time and primarily focused on his tasks, he responded that his failure to assist anyone was "beyond cowardice because I betrayed my friends, because I was afraid of being killed."[63]

Besides raising questions about Duch's state of mind, Ke Kim Huot's confession was also suggestive about the interrogation process. Even though they were in an extremely one-sided power dynamic, those being interrogated had a degree of agency and resisted, sometimes refusing to confess even when severely tortured. A few prisoners tried to commit suicide, including Sous Sopha, who picked up and swallowed a screw, due to the "carelessness" of a guard. Since Sou Sopha was considered an important prisoner, Duch "ordered a medic from the general staff to operate on him, and when he recovered then we continued the interrogation. So all this was done in order to get the confessions."[64]

The Confession of Ya

The word "confession" suggests a teleology, focusing on an end point, and a prisoner's lack of agency. While many of the S-21 confession portfolios are incomplete or did not survive, some, like Ke Kim Huot's, include multiple versions and detailed notes, sometimes even correspondence between the interrogators and Duch. In contrast to the Long Muy cover page, which Duch used to argue that he was merely a middleman, such documentation implies a more active role, an issue the prosecution would press.

To highlight this point, the prosecution discussed in detail the confession of Ney Saran, known as Ya, the former secretary of the Northeast Zone. In September 1976, following the interrogations of Chakrei and Chhouk, Ya was summoned to Phnom Penh. His arrival coincided with a September 20 announcement that Pol Pot was stepping down as prime minister for health reasons.[65] Ya was arrested at Duch's office the same day under the pretext of a medical consultation.[66] His young wife and child soon followed.

Duch explained that Ya had been implicated in a number of confessions. But, more broadly, his arrest was related to a "bitter" dispute between on the one hand Ya and Keo Meas, another senior party member arrested shortly after Ya, and on the other Pol Pot and Son Sen concerning "the stance toward Vietnam."[67] Anyone perceived as deviating from the party line regarding Vietnam, Duch emphasized, was considered a traitor. Ya had long-standing ties to the Vietnamese, having, among other things, overseen during the civil war military logistics involving contact with Vietnam, headed a region adjoining Vietnam, and been involved in unsuccessful border treaty negotiations between the countries. Besides being suspect for his ties and supposedly "soft" stance toward Vietnam, Ya is thought to have expressed reservations about some CPK policies regarding class structure, the evacuation of Phnom Penh, the use of violence, and rapid collectivization.[68] Pol Pot's "resignation" may very well have been a ruse to sow confusion as Ya and Keo Meas were arrested.[69]

Duch noted that Ya was a full-rights member of the CPK Central Committee, ranking number 10.[70] As in a few cases involving high-ranking prisoners, Duch acknowledged that he participated in Ya's interrogation. However, in keeping with his defense, he said the interrogation actually involved three people: himself, Pon ("the interrogator"), and Son Sen ("the one who supervised and made corrections"). Once again, Duch positioned himself as an intermediary.

The prosecution pushed Duch on this point, highlighting annotations and notes he had made on drafts of Ya's confession. At the start of the interrogation,

Pon wrote a note informing Ya that on the previous morning the security office had held a meeting in which Ya had been named as a coconspirator accused, along with Chhouk and Keo Meas, of establishing a Workers' Party of Vietnam network. Pon's note then asked Ya about his traitorous activities with Keo Meas and Chhouk, including letters to Chhouk.[71] According to this note, Ya replied, "If you force me to answer using torture, I'll say anything."

In this first phase of back-and-forth, the parameters of the confession are established, as the interrogator suggests the "direction" the confession should go. The prisoner resists and contests the accusations (Ya writes a five-page letter of protest), while already aware that torture is a possibility. Next, Ya was provided with more details about the "direction" his confession should take: Duch wrote a four-page letter elaborating on the alleged plot to establish an alternative party linked to Vietnam. The letter begins by offering false hope, suggesting that Ya has only temporarily been detained due to his "missteps" in following the "influence of people who used to be trustworthy."[72] You are aware, Duch's letter continues, in a more menacing tone, "that the Soviets and Vietnamese are bones stuck in our throat which have to be scooped out and thrown away."[73] Cadre were judged not just by their words, but by their revolutionary stance and behavior, Duch writes. To demonstrate their stance, cadre had to reveal to the Party "whatever is inside us."[74] He concludes by urging Ya to confess, the sooner the better; but "the choice is yours."

Ya's torture began the next day. In a September 25, 1976, letter that the prosecution displayed on the court monitor, Pon reports to Duch that, following instructions, "we began the torture in the morning by whipping approximately 20 times with small rattan. In the evening, we tortured by whipping 20–30 times with three woven strands of electric wire."[75] This torture was supplemented by "propaganda" that included showing the prisoner Duch's four-page letter and excerpts from other confessions regarding "secret contacts with Vietnam." Ya was told, "There is only one path: confess to the Party." Pon notes that Ya "started to respond and confess verbally," writing a one-page letter by hand.[76]

Again, we see the process by which the interrogator gives cues to the prisoner about how the confession should be written, showing excerpts of previous confessions that model language and prose. Ya was literally beaten into making a one-page confession. The next day Duch visited Ya in his cell. His visit was recorded in another memo sent by Pon to Duch, which notes that Duch asked Ya if his wife and children knew what had happened to him. When the prosecution asked why he had brought up the issue of Ya's family, Duch explained: "Brother Ya had a young wife—25 years younger—so the upper echelon" requested Duch and Pon to raise the issue so "Brother Ya would consider the wife's situation."[77]

Here Duch used a tactic mentioned in his interrogation lectures: lying to prisoners and manipulating their emotions by mentioning their family and friends. It appeared to work. That evening, after Pon informed Ya he would be tortured, Ya agreed to confess. Pon instructed him to "write up a systematic account of your traitorous activities from beginning to end."[78] In the second iteration of his confession that followed the next day, Ya wrote eight pages admitting he had conspired with Chhouk and Keo Meas, who, like him, were under the influence of Vietnam. However, he concludes this confession by stating that he still follows the party line and offering his respects to "Brother Pol [Pot], Brother Nuon, and Brother Phim." He signs his letter "a real communist soldier, ready to die."[79]

Over the next two days Ya continued to develop his confession. In a version dated September 28, he discusses his alleged history of conspiring with Chhouk. In a notation added to the cover sheet of this version, Duch records that he has sent the original and two copies to his superiors.[80] More detail had been demanded.

The next day, Pon sent Ya a letter praising him for "initial steps" outlining his "contacts with Brother Chhouk," while noting that "there were still some shortages" about which "Brother Duch" had requested elaboration. In particular, Duch had requested that Ya provide more detail on "secret meetings" that included discussion of "actual conversations, plans and objectives."[81] In a one-page reply, Ya discusses an initial meeting with Chhouk in which they walked through "thick forests" while discussing how to build up counterrevolutionary forces.[82] Ya was required to date and sign Pon's memo after affirming that his replies had not been coerced.

This dialectic between the interrogator and the interrogated, in which the former indirectly instructed the latter on how a confession should be written, continued. Later in the day on September 29, Pon sent another memo to Ya requesting still more information, including names of contacts with Vietnam. "Brother Ya," Pon begins. "According to Brother Duch's instruction, can you confirm and detail your traitorous activities? What was your support? Forces from outside the country, how? Forces inside the country: other than Sector 24, what other forces did you rely on?"[83]

In Ya's reply, fewer than a dozen pages and designated Confession Four, he once again seeks to protest. Instead of signing off on Pon's memo as before, Ya adds that while he has not been coerced, "my responses since the night of the 28 September 1976 were made after I was severely and strongly tortured." This led Duch to take out his marker.

The prosecution requested that Duch's response be displayed. In it, Ya's caveat has been redacted: his loose scrawl is struck through by red lines. Next to what Ya wrote is a note Duch made, dated September 30, 1976; the prosecution asked Duch to read it to the court. "I wrote [to Ya]," he began, speaking quickly. " 'Do not write the words that I have crossed out in red. You don't have the right to report to Angkar. I have the right.' "[84] Duch skipped over two additional lines; they read "I have reported it already. I have reported clearly. Do not play tricks, wanting to deny. You cannot."[85] Duch explained to the court that his superiors had ordered Ya's torture, "so there was no need for [Ya] to write it in a confession."

On September 30, after Duch made this annotation, Pon rewrote the memo, backdating it to the previous day. The new version looks exactly like the original, as if copied by tracing. But Ya's comments have been edited out in the redacted version, which shows only his affirmation that what he has written has not been coerced. There is no sign of Duch's comment or the redaction.

But there are hints if one opens "Confession Four." On the pages within, someone, most likely Pon, has made extensive comments, markings resembling a teacher's comments on a student paper or edits on a manuscript. Confession Four begins with the heading "Relationship between Comrade Brother Phim and I," notes that Ya and Phim were born in the same region, and details their encounters from the 1950s onward.

On the first page, where Ya speaks of how "Brother Phim stayed at my house [in Phnom Penh]," Pon comments, "In Phnom Penh, how did you get orders and instructions from Brother P like this?"[86] Just below, where Ya states, "From what I knew [Sao] Phim had disappeared at one point," Pon writes above: "From whom?" When Ya mentions a meeting, Pon asks what it was about and who attended, telling Ya: "Just write about the traitorous work."[87] And so Pon's editing process continues, with underlining, inserted remarks, parentheticals, and other questions and comments made in the margins.

What is most striking are the large sections of text, sometimes as much as half a page, which Pon has crossed out. Next to one of these redactions, Pon directs: "You have to write about betraying the Party. Do not write like this again."[88] In another place, he crosses out two paragraphs and comments: "You should clearly differentiate between the slaves of the Vietnamese and true revolutionaries."[89] Elsewhere Pon adds in parentheses above text where

Ya alludes to subversion: "The plan to shoot Brother Pol and Brother Nuon at the Independence Monument."[90] Throughout, Ya is given explicit directions about what to write. Failure to do so would mean torture.

This threat was made more menacingly as Ya continued to resist. On September 30, after Ya refused to follow the "direction" of the interrogation cues, Duch wrote a note to Pon with the header "IX [Ya] reacts, denying contacts with Vietnam" and the confession number crossed out. After reading the text, Duch tells Pon, he has "decided not to send it to Angkar . . . from experience, only hot methods will work with this Ya. We cannot play friendly with him. Impose them on him."[91]

The following day, in a note written on graph paper, Duch informs Pon that he has consulted with Angkar, which "has decided that if this fool Ya continues to beat around the bush and hide his traitorous links and activities, Angkar has decided that he can be killed. Do not let him play games with us any more."[92] Duch complains that Ya is "looking down" on S-21 and the Party and that it is okay to "use hot methods strongly and for a long time," while reiterating "even if you make a misstep and he dies, you will have done nothing wrong."[93] Below, Pon writes, "Brother Ya, Please read and consider this letter seriously."

When the prosecutors confronted Duch with this memo, he asserted that his message had been part of "a strategy to bluff" and scare Ya, part of a "game" or "trick."[94] Cambodian Deputy Co-Prosecutor Yet Chakriya asked Duch if he had been angry. Ya refused to confess and had lost patience with him. "You could say that," Duch replied and added that it was "the upper echelon [that was] no longer patient" with Ya.[95]

These threats seemed to work. On October 1, Ya wrote his fifth confession, responding to a series of specific questions based on his previous responses that instructed him "to make your report precise and practical in sequence supported by logical reasons and incidents."[96] Ya's confession includes more details and begins to conform to the more standardized form of S-21 confessions, with each page dated and signed at the bottom.

This is the latest version of Ya's confession that remains. Most likely he produced additional versions before being executed shortly after completing the last one. Apparently portions of his confession were later read out, along with excerpts from the S-21 confessions of other senior leaders, before cadre gathered at the Olympic Stadium in Phnom Penh.[97] In 1997, shortly before his death, Pol Pot still tried to rationalize the DK violence by alleging plots, including one led by Ya, who "had been a Vietnamese agent since 1946."[98]

Articulation

After Ya's death, his name continued to appear in confessions. If, in 1976, Duch sometimes lectured his interrogators about the "Khmer Serei network" and the purge of some cadre linked to the East Zone and Vietnam, by 1978, as war with Vietnam intensified and after two years of purges, Duch's discussions of alleged plots frequently focused on Vietnam.

Two interrogator notebooks from this time illustrate this shift. Both refer to networks that had been uncovered. A lecture dated July 28, 1978, for example, states that after Koy Thuon's "connections were solved, the movements have made leaps in every sector."[99] Sector 7, which Ke Kim Huot (alias Sot) had headed, is provided as an illustration. The notes refer to "despicable-Sot" and a dangerous "disguised enemy" who had "embedded as cadre."[100]

Another key event recorded in the notebooks was Sao Phim's suicide on June 3, 1978, and the subsequent smashing of "despicable Phim's network," described as "equal to 17 April 1975."[101] On June 6, 1978, Duch instructs his interrogators about "the meaning of the great victory [over despicable] Phim and his clique and the future direction of the work of the Special Branch." Sao Phim, Duch asserts, was the secretary of the Workers' Party of Kampuchea (WPK), an organization allegedly run by CIA operatives in partnership with Vietnam. Among the CIA operatives linked to the WPK, Duch names Koy Thuon, Ya, and Keo Meas. Meanwhile, a large-scale purge of the East Zone commenced, as "we swept away his connections in the base."[102]

By July 7, Duch had woven the alleged plots and traitorous networks uncovered at S-21 into a more singular articulation, detailed in a 24-page document titled "The Last Joint Plan."[103] Handwritten, the text resembles a school lesson, with headers and sublists, most of which are no more than a sentence or two. The first section, "Introduction," consists of two points, the first of which discusses the answers of Chhouk. A third point has been scribbled out.

"The Last Joint Plan" lays out a history of subversion, listing nine CIA networks operative before 1970 and involving cadre trained in Hanoi, intellectuals, the Khmer Serei, Soviet students, capitalists, and longtime revolutionaries like Ya.[104] "The Last Joint Plan" describes how such counterrevolutionaries infiltrated the revolution and lists their alleged subversion, ranging from murder and abduction to sabotage, rumor, banditry, rebellion, and coup attempts. The document concludes with a section noting the WPK's alleged founding by Keo Meas and Ya and the involvement of a variety of "leaders of the treacherous party," including Koy Thuon and Tum (Siet Chhe).

Like the interrogator notebooks, "The Last Joint Plan" provides Duch's articulation of the alleged conspiracies in which S-21 prisoners were involved. The supposed networks, subversive activities, and histories of treason delineated in this document provide a baseline that Duch's interrogators could use to guide their questioning and the process of calibration between interrogator and prisoner. As the process of Ya's interrogation illustrates, the sought-after articulation demanded that prisoners adjust the details of their lives to fit the presupposed schema of treason, one thickly framed by the Party line.

Duch stated he never believed the entirety of a confession. Thus, even as a confession harmonized with the sought-after articulation of treason, it was never complete, since confessions redacted complex life histories and associations, producing "strings of traitors" that always included an excess: the neverending lists of imagined counterrevolutionaries not yet arrested.

Duch's use of the cover page of Long Muy's confession also had this sense of an excess of meaning that has been redacted from the narrow legal articulation of obedience to authority that Duch asserted. Who was Long Muy? What had he done and what happened to him at S-21? While such questions can never be fully answered, we can catch hints in the trial record and related documentation.

"The Last Joint Plan," for example, lists "the Chinese residents" as one of nine counterrevolutionary groups established before 1970. This group, the document states, originated with expatriates from China who created the Kok Min Tang (Kuomintang; KMT) and subsequently "controlled, managed and established all Chinese associations, schools and hospitals" in Cambodia.[105] They later went underground and "conducted seemingly revolutionary activities" while maintaining links to Vietnam, the CIA, and China.[106] Nget You (aka Hong), the longtime revolutionary whose arrest greatly worried Duch, is listed as the "chief of the Chinese community," which "The Last Joint Plan" states was "wiped out in Feb 78."[107]

Nget You is also mentioned in the Chan notebook, under the heading "Attack the KMT." Duch's S-21 lecture of March 22, 1978, given shortly after Nget You's March 13 arrest, urges his interrogators to continue research to find the KMT: "Capture them at all costs. Do not keep them. We [must] attack the KMT until they dissolve. . . . We must dig it out trunk and roots."[108]

A March 17 entry, in turn, states that the regime faces three "conflicts," including one with the KMT, which is controlled by "Imperialist America." In this lecture, Duch notes that "we got one back in 76 or 77," when a "despicable

Chuon" was interrogated. Noting the KMT's links to Chiang Kai-shek, the lesson claims that "KMT = CIA," while warning that the group has "plans to kill Brother with poison or with a bomb" and thus that "[we] must get them all."[109] Over two dozen Chinese cadre, including Nget You, were sent to S-21 in March 1978 alone.[110]

The "Chuon" to whom Duch refers may have been Long Muy. Indeed, Duch's first notation on the cover of Long Muy's confession states that the prisoner's "forces" were from Sector 22 and were connected to the KMT network in Peareang. Duch's second remark links Long Muy to Siet Chhe (Tum), the former head of Sector 22 who is listed in "The Last Joint Plan" as a WPK leader. He was arrested on April 30, 1977, just a few months before Long Muy. Long Muy's problematic ties to the Chinese network and the East Zone (which included Sector 22) are highlighted by Son Sen's remark that "this man is a string of the Cambodian-Chinese" and Pol Pot's instruction to contact "the East."

If Duch never discussed the pages of Long Muy's confession, the document was included in the court record, and other sections—including a typed version over 50 pages long—survive in archives. The version in the court record is written in clear, precise script and concludes with the date (August 29, 1977) and Long Muy's signature and thumbprint. A brief notation at the end of the document lists the interrogator as Oeun.[111]

According to court documents, Long Muy was arrested a little more than a month earlier, on July 16, 1977, at the Office of the General Staff.[112] Like Ya, Pang, and others, Long Muy may have been tricked, perhaps sent to the Office of the General Staff on a pretext. On his arrest, he was likely handcuffed, and perhaps blindfolded, before being led to S-21's reception area, where he would have been photographed and required to give background information before being taken to his cell. There he would have been shackled and would have lived in abject conditions.

One day Oeun may have arrived at Long Muy's cell and escorted him to an interrogation room. He might have seen blood on the floor or instruments of torture lying about. He would have been chained to the floor before questioning began, perhaps with a command to confess his traitorous ties to the CIA. Like most prisoners, he probably replied by professing his innocence, at which point he may have been beaten or tortured.

While more than one Oeun worked in the interrogation unit, Long Muy may have been questioned by Vong Oeun, who himself was arrested and interrogated at S-21 in early 1978. It is impossible to assess the accuracy of S-21 confessions, which mix truth and fiction. In any event, Vong Oeun's confession states that, among other offenses, he "tortured enemies, causing loud screams of pain [to] penetrate from one room to another, thus causing enemies to become nervous and feel uneasy," and "committed villainous acts such as undressing women and piercing their vulvas with sticks."[113] This statement may reveal more about the moral violations at S-21 than any actual act done by Vong Oeun; nonetheless, Duch repeatedly stated that almost every prisoner was tortured. It is almost certain that Long Muy was as well.

As the interrogation proceeded, a process of calibration between Oeun and Long Muy would likely have taken place, as Long Muy reconstructed his past to accord with the structure and content his interrogators sought. Extrapolating from the questions in the "Statistics List," Long Muy may have been asked to discuss the following topics.

1. The backgrounds of the KMT in Peareang
2. The leaders of the KMT
3. The leaders of Sector 22
4. The KMT's contacts with Vietnam
5. The Office K-16 translator unit network
6. The origins and background of the KMT
7. Plans prior to the coup and up to 17 April 75
8. Plans after 17 April 1975 and up to 77
9. The leaders' contacts with Vietnam and the CIA
10. Personal histories from beginning to end
11. The ways the KMT contacted other groups of conspirators[114]

Long Muy's confession follows the prototypical structure that emerged from such S-21 questioning, outlining how he secretly embedded himself in the revolutionary ranks, plotted and carried out subversive activities, and conspired with traitors. The information is pieced together, like so many S-21 documents, along the lines of a school plan, with sections, topic headings, descriptive material, and numeric lists.

The handwritten version of Long Muy's confession begins by providing basic biographical information, such as his age (33), birth date (September 21, 1944), marital status (married), birthplace (Snay Pol village in Peareang district, Prey Veng province), and position (head of the K-16 office translator group), before turning to his "traitorous activities."[115] The document notes that Long Muy's father, Liv Hann Pen, was born in China. He fled to Cambodia, for fear of the Chinese Communist Party, and soon thereafter supposedly joined the KMT. He would have nine children.

The second section of Long Muy's confession discusses the organization and counterrevolutionary activities of the KMT, noting that his father came to work in the market at Snay Pol village, located in Peareang, the district with the largest concentration of ethnic Chinese in Cambodia. Long Muy lists the names of alleged leaders and members of the KMT and their anticommunist stance. At a 1957 meeting, Long Muy's confession states, a meeting was held at which it was decided all the teachers in the Chinese schools should have a KMT stance and use books produced in Taiwan and Singapore. The KMT leader at the time, Li Chriel, supposedly told the assembled group: "We must fight communism without fail."

Long Muy's confession contains double-edged critiques of the Khmer Rouge, claiming that his father complained that communism was "unjust, lacking free rights . . . time to rest, and enough food to each so that everyone becomes so thin that just the bones are left." Later, the confession says, Long Muy began to work as a teacher, before his cousin helped convince him to join the Khmer Rouge on May 1, 1969. That cousin, Yann Pheng, was also known as Ieng Si Pheng; this name is listed in point 3 of Duch's annotation on the cover of Long Muy's confession.

After joining the revolution, Long Muy's confession states, he worked in Peareang, colluding with other KMT members to undermine the Khmer Rouge and connecting to Tum, the secretary of the region. In 1972, for example, Khmer Rouge soldiers needed provisions. Kuomintang leaders, the confession claims, instructed "their members [to] pack insufficient amounts of rice without dishes, containing nails, tree leaves, and sandy soil"[116] and to seek to bid up the price of rice and refuse to sell it to Khmer Rouge soldiers, who might starve.

During the civil war, the confession continues, the KMT allied with the CIA, for whom Long Muy allegedly became an agent in 1973. The supposed objective was to "burrow deeply inside and thwart the revolution" by propagandizing against the Khmer Rouge and engaging in sabotage. His confession lists many more examples and asserts that the KMT network extended to many ministries.

In Office K-16, Long Muy's confession states, he and his associates sought to subvert the revolution by "breaking up the solidarity between Kampuchea and China, humiliating the Communist Party by raising the issue of the maintenance and destruction of state property, and provoking trouble among office chiefs."[117] As the head of the translation group, Long Muy was allegedly able to further undermine DK-Chinese relations by failing to prepare his subordinates. The inability of trainees to grasp what was being said supposedly created tension and angered Chinese guests. A September 1, 1977, version of Long Muy's confession lists 85 members of his "group of traitors."

At different points in Long Muy's confession, someone has drawn a vertical line alongside a passage or underlined text, presumably to highlight content deemed significant, such as a subversive act or a mention of a coconspirator. A thick red mark highlights a passage discussing how the KMT-CIA group started using the name "Labor Party of Kampuchea," an alternative moniker for the WPK. Another highlighted passage discusses Long Muy's supposed recruitment of two cadre into the WPK. At another point, someone has drawn a vertical line next to a part of the confession where Long Muy discusses his wife, who was also arrested. He quotes her complaining that "there will be no one [left] to work [if] Angkar continues to arrest such a large number of people."[118]

Long Muy's confession provides one articulation of his life, mixing fact and fiction and framing events to fit the S-21 confession schema. In an attempt to learn more about this former prisoner, DC-Cam interviewed some of his family and friends. Long Muy's brother Tai confirmed the authenticity of the confession, noting that only Long Muy could have known the names of so many people from their village. Some details "were true and some were untrue" or distorted.[119]

Long Muy's father, for example, had immigrated to Cambodia to flee the Chinese communists and later sent Long Muy to school before he returned to teach in his home village from 1963 to 1966. His father began to worry that his son was becoming politicized after he fell under the influence of Ieng Si Pheng, a community leader who had gone to school in China, where he had learned in depth about Maoism.

While Long Muy had alluded to his revolutionary activity during the civil war, his family didn't learn that he was a cadre until just after April 15, 1975. Two of his three brothers subsequently joined the movement. Long Muy went to see his family a few times, including a visit in 1976 when he informed them he might study in China. He gave his family two photographs of himself in front of Wat Phnom in Phnom Penh. In one, a blotched black-and-white photograph, he stands in dark revolutionary garb, head raised slightly and lips set in a defiant line, as he stares into the distance. He wears a traditional Cambodian scarf around his neck. Behind him two Buddhist spires rise into the air. He is alone.

Long Muy's family never heard from him again. Ironically, they were able to fill in some of the gaps in their knowledge about his revolutionary life by reading his confession. Tai remembered his brother as someone who "hoped to develop . . . [and] was true to the country but was charged with betraying it." He noted: "the documents answer my questions. I know where he died. I feel released from [my] anger."[120]

Execution

Almost everyone who passed through the gates of S-21 perished. Given the political line that "the enemy had to be smashed," Duch stated, the detainees were "treated as dead people" whose end had been briefly delayed.[121] Usually prisoners were executed within a month or two after confession. S-21 records, for example, state that Long Muy was executed on October 23, 1977, almost a week after his wife had been killed and over two months after the latest date on materials in his confession portfolio.[122] In some cases, such as that of Ke Kim Huot, execution was delayed for longer periods.

In keeping with his defense strategy, Duch claimed that Son Sen's General Staff made the decision "to smash" in accordance with the March 30, 1976 Decision. The management of the execution process, he said, was overseen by the three-person S-21 committee, though he acknowledged being "overall in charge."[123] The decision-making meetings often just consisted of Duch and Hor, since Huy resided at S-24 and could not attend the daily meetings. Since there was a standing order to execute prisoners and Duch was in regular communication with Son Sen, Duch and Hor often decided when detainees, particularly those deemed less important, were killed.

The timing of executions was influenced by logistical concerns, which sometimes resulted in a spike in numbers. Prisoners were executed en masse, Duch noted, during the purges of Koy Thuon's network (early 1977), of Division 920 (October 1977), of the West Zone (April 1978), and of the East Zone (late 1978).[124] "We had to make sure," Duch explained, "that the premises were not too overcrowded."[125]

Duch admitted he was able to save a handful of people from execution, though he claimed his power was limited. Thus S-21 could "keep someone for helping [with] the work at the office,"[126] though S-21 then became accountable for that person, and Duch's superiors might still order their execution. Perhaps fifteen prisoners, including artists and a dentist, were "used" in this manner. Glancing briefly toward the civil parties, Duch noted, "I see Mr. Chum Mey here in the Court [who was one of them]."[127]

More controversial were documents suggesting that many more S-21 prisoners had been released, including S-21 release manifests that Duch claimed were a ruse developed by Nat to hide arbitrary executions.[128] Duch's argument was in keeping with his repeated claim that all of the S-21 prisoners, with the exception of the prisoner-workers, were executed. For if Duch had had the authority to release prisoners, his claim to be a mere cog in the machine would have been undercut.

Duch also suggested he once staved off the death of several prisoners by preventing them from being poisoned. At the time, Nuon Chea gave Duch a dozen capsules to administer to detainees while instructing him not to tell anyone. Duch speculated that Nuon Chea may have done so to test the medicine after a confession alleged a plot to poison Pol Pot. Without telling anyone, Duch discarded the medicine and "cleaned inside the capsule with a cotton bud" before replacing the powder "with paracetamol,"[129] to eliminate the possibility the capsules were poisonous. Later, he informed Nuon Chea that the medicine had had no effect. Duch noted that while all prisoners were destined for execution, he didn't want them to die by his "own hands." Distinguishing his administrative role from that of the executioners, he explained, "I tried not to be involved in the killing of those people directly."[130]

As this incident suggests, not every prisoner was executed in the same manner. Some were killed during medical experiments and procedures, which Duch claimed began under Nat. These practices included drug trials and medical operations on live prisoners to teach students about anatomy.[131] At least 100 prisoners also died after S-21 medics drained the "blood in their body and they died."[132] Their blood was given to injured soldiers. Son Sen once complained that the transfused blood had caused rashes, so Duch said he ordered that the prisoners "be well selected before their blood would be drawn and injected into any combatant, to avoid any disease or infection."[133] The lethal blood drawings only ended after the head medics at the hospital and at S-21 were arrested.

If prisoners sometimes died from torture, injury, starvation, malnutrition, illness, or suicide, most were executed at the edge of a mass grave. S-21 used three main sites during the course of DK. Initially, many S-21 prisoners were executed on the grounds of Ta Khmau, the former psychiatric hospital that Nat's unit began using as a prison at the end of the civil war.[134] The use of this site ceased a few months after Duch assumed the helm of S-21.

Son Sen later informed Duch that the site was being transferred to the Ministry of Social Affairs. To maintain secrecy, Duch ordered Hor to exhume and cremate all of the corpses, literally reducing them to ash in an act that epitomized the sense of "smash" in Khmer: crushing something to bits. With the exception of some corpses already buried underneath two big canals, Duch told the court, "No bones were left."[135] Four vacationing Westerners who had been sent to S-21 after sailing into Cambodian waters were similarly "smashed" when Pol Pot allegedly ordered that, after being killed, they be "burned to ash" in car tires so that "nothing would remain."[136]

After S-21 was relocated to Ponhea Yat High School, prisoners were executed near or on the grounds of the compound. While executions took place on the Ponhea Yat High School grounds throughout DK, Duch on his own initiative searched for another site, due to concerns about the potential for epidemics, given the rising number of detainees.[137] He selected Choeung Ek, a Chinese graveyard located just outside Phnom Penh, only afterward getting Son Sen's consent. The prosecution and civil party lawyers would later point to this act, like the selection of Ponhea Yat and Duch's unilateral decision to build individual cells, as evidence of Duch's initiative. To ensure secrecy, he had a fence built around Choeung Ek.

The majority of Tuol Sleng prisoners were killed at Choeung Ek, where a special unit carried out the executions. When asked if he had taught them the method of execution, Duch, invoking a Khmer adage, replied, "I [did] not need to teach crocodiles how to swim, because the crocodiles already [knew] how to swim."[138] During the civil war, he explained, Hor had led a company of special forces who had engaged in direct combat. Afterward, this unit had worked under Nat, where they learned methods of execution later used at S-21. Duch recruited some of these combatants as interrogators. Others were selected as executioners, given that they were accustomed to and skilled at killing.[139] A small group of these men remained stationed at Choeung Ek, where they would dig and later fill the mass graves.[140]

By the time they were taken for execution, prisoners like Long Muy would be emaciated and severely weakened. While again claiming that he was not certain exactly how things had proceeded and had learned the details after DK, Duch said that such prisoners were told that they were "moving to a new home," a pretext meant to keep them calm even as their arms were tied behind their backs and they were blindfolded and instructed to remain silent.[141] In the evening, the prisoners were driven to Choeung Ek in Chinese trucks, which were covered. Special forces personnel, including a driver and three guards, accompanied them.

On arriving at Choeung Ek, the prisoners were placed in a small hut. One by one, they were removed and their names recorded. By torchlight, they were then led, still bound and blindfolded, to the edge of the mass grave. The executioner would then strike them on the back of the head with an axe and slit their throats. Always ready to cast aspersion on his predecessor, Duch claimed that Nat had been quite "proud of killing prisoners by slitting their throats."[142]

Afterward, the prisoner's handcuffs would be removed. Duch acknowledged that, following Son Sen's orders, he once reluctantly traveled to Choeung Ek to observe the process. "I went there for a very short time," he told the court. "I did not dare look at the pits. I did not go and look in the house where the prisoners were kept."[143] He claimed that he got most of his details for his report to Son Sen from Hor. He had little contact with the executioners because "they were afraid of me."[144]

Duch said the families of S-21 detainees were sometimes also sent to the prison. The spouses were usually executed at Choeung Ek, sometimes after also being interrogated; their children, who were quickly separated from their parents after arriving at S-21, often met a different fate. While Duch rebutted a survivor's claim that children had been dropped from the top floor of the prison (since this would have violated the rule of secrecy), he acknowledged that children were held by the legs as their heads "were banged against a tree."[145] This method was used at Choeung Ek, though Duch speculated that children might have been executed in the same manner as adults at S-21 to avoid making too much noise.

At the end of a long day of questioning about the executions, one in which Duch repeatedly emphasized his distance from the process, Judge Lavergne asked him if this detachment was due to avoidance or a lack of concern. Did the prisoners have "any kind of human reality for you? [Or was] your job just executing simple mathematical operations such as addition and subtraction, or was it simply to make sure to guarantee the quality of the confessions? Was that all your work was about?" Duch replied that he had "tried to avoid seeing the place that could affect my emotion. . . . I was terrified, shocked and moved, but there was [a] . . . small feeling deep inside me, that kept me moving on."[146] Referring to the photo of himself leading an S-21 study session, he admitted that even if he now felt shame, "I was rather proud at that time for maintaining the class stand firmly."[147]

Erasure
DUCH'S APOLOGY

(Khmer Rouge Tribunal, 31 Mar ▮ ▮09

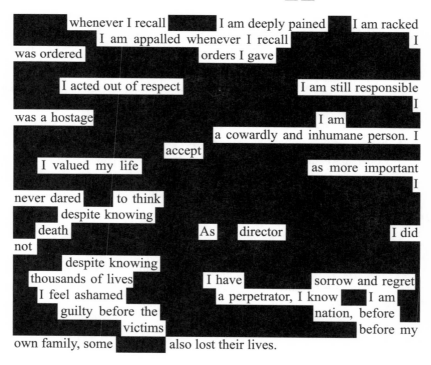

whenever I recall ▮▮▮ I am deeply pained ▮ I am racked
I am appalled whenever I recall ▮▮▮▮ I
was ordered ▮▮▮ orders I gave ▮

I acted out of respect ▮▮▮ I am still responsible
▮ I
was a hostage ▮ I am ▮
a cowardly and inhumane person. I
accept ▮
I valued my life ▮ as more important
▮ I
never dared ▮ to think
despite knowing
death ▮ As ▮ director ▮ I did
not
despite knowing
thousands of lives ▮ I have ▮ sorrow and regret
I feel ashamed ▮ a perpetrator, I know ▮ I am ▮
guilty before the ▮ nation, before
victims ▮ before my
own family, some ▮▮▮ also lost their lives.

II. Reconstruction

Torture, A Collage

THE TESTIMONY OF PRAK KHAN, S-21 INTERROGATOR

Background

Name: Prak Khan
Age: 58 (born 7 Jan 1951)
Nationality: Khmer
Occupation: Merchant (banana seller) and Farmer
Family: Married, 5 children
Joined Revolution: 1972
Education: Literate (8th grade), a bit of French
Duties at S-21: Guard, then Interrogator, "Chewing Group"
Number of Interrogations: 51
Preliminary Statement: February 2, 2008
Trial Testimony: July 21–22, 2009

Prak Khan: Observation

I never told
my bitter background to
anybody in
my village, not even
my wife. They only
know me as a
banana seller.

Work Schedule

5:30	Wake up and do labor
6:45	Bring the enemy to the interrogation site
1:45	" " " " "
5:30	Afternoon team meeting
6:55	Bring the enemy to the interrogation site

Prak Khan: Observation

Prisoners who entered S-21, I never saw them leave.

We did whatever was necessary

First, beating.
Second, electric shock.
Third, head in the bag.
Fourth, piercing and removing the nails.
The idea, Duch instructed
was to avoid having wounds
all over their bodies.

We used whatever we had

electric wires hands whips pliers shit branches needles fists plastic bags

Lost Confession

Some beat them to death
some gave them electric shocks until death
some suffocated them in bags to death.
After these events, Duch called us to meetings
at the political school near Duch's house
on the matter of allowing the enemies
to conduct sabotage.

Chewing Group

There were three groups:
hot, cold and chewing.
The hot group would apply the hot method
and the cool group would use politics.
As for the chewing group

usually the prisoners were
already tortured
had wounds and injuries
on their bodies
confessions yet to be
extracted.

Trial Exchange: Humanity

Prosecutor: Did you think of prisoners as animals?
Prak Khan: I would like to exercise my right to remain silent.

Prisoners who committed suicide

Some used pencils or ballpoint pens
to stab themselves
broke glass, used the pieces
to stab themselves.
Some used lanterns
to burn themselves
Some jumped
from the buildings

Trial Exchange: Character

Prosecutor: What type of person was Duch?
Prak Khan: studious, enthusiastic, meticulous.

One Night

Duch and five or six others
tortured the woman
from 9 at night to 3 in the morning
I can't remember her name
I was on guard outside.
I stood and watched.
She did not confess,
so the torture went on
beatings and then electric shocks
until she lost consciousness.
Duch administered the shocks.
I saw it with my own eyes.

I was there at the entrance
The door was open.
I saw it.
Duch used torture, beating, electric shocks
took off her shirt, leaving the trousers
Duch was the leader
He interrogated, beat her
until he got tired.

Political Study: Objectives

1. First, extract their information.
2. Next, assemble many points for pressuring them so they cannot move.
3. Propagandize and pressure them politically.
4. Pressure and interrogate by cursing.
5. Torture.
6. Examine and analyze the responses to make the document.
8. Guard them closely, prevent them from dying. Don't let them hear one another.
9. Maintain Secrecy.

Duch: Observations

This witness, Prak Khan. I never saw,
never heard of the name or the face of this person.
He was minor staff.
I was in the leadership at S-21.
My duty was to annotate.
I only interrogated one detainee.
Prak Khan said the drawing of blood
was done on 1,000 or even more.
I calculated the number.
There were probably 100 or so
people whose blood was drawn.
The person who ordered
the blood to be drawn
was my superior, Son Sen.
There are more examples of such
falsified evidence.
The child being thrown

I don't believe it.
There were no
three story buildings
at that location.
He should have
documents to support
what he claimed.
I categorically deny
the testimony of
this Prak Khan
is not true a
fabrication.

Sources: The text used in this cento is taken from the testimony of Prak Khan at the ECCC (Days 48–49), as well as his statement to the OCIJ; the S-21 "Statistics List"; and a May 10, 2012, article in the *Phnom Penh Post*, "A Tuol Sleng Interrogator Speaks Out."

Villain
(THE CIVIL PARTIES)

Humanity Lost (Civil Parties Closing Arguments, November 23, 2009)

"The law triumphs over the evil."

On the first day of closing arguments in Duch's trial, Silke Studzinsky, the international co-lawyer for Civil Party Group 2, made this statement, paraphrasing words famously uttered by British prosecutor Lord Hartley Shawcross during his closing address at Nuremberg: The Nuremberg Trials, Studzinsky continued, "were not guided for the sake of revenge but by the strong resolution that such heinous crimes never ever occur again."[1]

The Nuremberg Trials became a "cornerstone in the history of civilization and the foundation of international and internationalized tribunals dealing with mass atrocities beyond comprehension."[2] If Shawcross's hope that such genocidal violence would never take place again had not come to pass, the judicial precedent at Nuremberg was increasingly used to prosecute perpetrators as part of a "worldwide struggle against impunity." The ECCC, Studzinsky noted, would "close one of the numerous impunity gaps in history."[3]

This court was of particular significance, she added, because of the unprecedented status it conferred on the victims, which was a "first" and would serve as an "example" for the participatory rights of victims in the future.[4] She quoted Jean Améry, who was tortured by the Nazis, to suggest how the direct survivors of S-21 in her group, including Bou Meng and Chum Mey, had been shattered: "Jean Améry [wrote that] ... anyone who has been tortured remains tortured.... Faith in humanity, already cracked by the first slap in the face, then demolished by torture, is never acquired again."

| | |

Studzinsky was referring to testimony that Chum Mey and Bou Meng had given immediately after Duch had testified about CPK policy and the structure and functioning of S-21. While challenged at times, Duch's voice had dominated the proceedings as he gave his version of his path to S-21 and his role in the violence that took place there. Then, for the first time, the survivors of S-21 were given the floor to tell their stories and explain what transpired at S-21 from their perspective, providing a glimpse of what Long Muy and other prisoners experienced.

Vann Nath was the first to take the stand. He told the court how in 1975 he and his family, along with the other inhabitants of Battambang City, had been relocated to the countryside. Like Cambodians throughout the country, they were forced to perform agricultural labor for long hours on increasingly meager rations. On December 30, 1977, Vann Nath was arrested. He was taken to a pagoda that had been converted into a detention center, where he was accused of being a traitor and tortured.

Eventually Vann Nath was trucked to S-21. He said that after arriving there, he lost all hope on seeing how the guards "degraded us. It's indescribable, the way they treated us, the prisoners. Sometimes ... while we were asleep they suddenly woke us up and if we could not sit up on time then they used their rubber [tire] thongs to kick our heads."[5]

Vann Nath was shackled in a communal cell, where the prisoners subsisted on a few spoonfuls of rice gruel twice a day. In these conditions, prisoners rapidly weakened, making them susceptible to rashes and ailments. They began to smell. Over time, they barely looked human. The starving prisoners would eat insects if they could catch one, a difficult task since they were closely watched and beaten if they moved about or conversed. The prisoners "didn't care" if a companion died because "we were like animals." He thought only of thirst and hunger and "thought that even eating ... human flesh would be a good meal."[6] Meanwhile, the guards kicked and beat the prisoners without hesitation.

About a month after Nath's arrival, a guard called his name. When they unshackled him, he could barely stand. With assistance, he managed to walk down the stairs. Because he was handcuffed but not blindfolded, he observed

S-21 Prison survivors. From left to right: Chum Mey, Ruy Neakong, Iem Chan, Heng (Vann) Nath, Bou Meng, Phan Than Chan, and Ung Pech. Photo courtesy of the DC-Cam / SRI Archives.

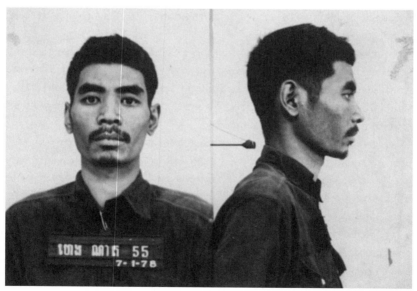

Vann Nath, age 32, at S-21, 1978. Photo courtesy of the DC-Cam / SRI Archives.

Prisoner in a mass cell at S-21. Photo courtesy of the DC-Cam / SRI Archives.

prisoners being taken for interrogation. He was brought before Duch. As he looked around, Vann Nath noticed several artisans at work in the room, including Bou Meng. Duch asked Vann Nath if he could paint. He replied affirmatively but noted that he had not painted for several years. Duch handed Vann Nath a photograph of a man and instructed him to copy it. It was a picture of Pol Pot.

Since Vann Nath "smelled like shit," Duch permitted him to rest a few days and to shave and bathe.[7] The guards provided him with a cotton scarf and some clothes. He was also given rice, which he could barely chew. When he started to copy the portrait, he was extremely nervous. He also found it difficult to paint in black and white and asked to switch to color. Duch granted his request but warned that the important thing was for "the Angkar [to] be pleased with the painting."[8] Vann Nath succeeded in making this happen. In 1980, he was shown an S-21 execution list that included his name, crossed out in red ink, with the annotation "keep for use."[9]

While conditions were better in the small artisan workshop where Vann Nath began to work, he frequently heard the screams of prisoners and caught glimpses of the violence.[10] For example, one day at the workshop a guard asked him for cement mix. Later, he saw the guard escorting a prisoner who had cement on his head.[11] On another occasion, he witnessed a desperate female prisoner commit suicide by jumping off a prison building.[12]

Most afternoons or evenings, Vann Nath stated, Duch stopped by the workshop, located in Building E. He remembered Duch as "clever," "intelligent," and "vigilant," someone whom guards and prisoners alike feared. "So every time he entered" the workshop, Vann Nath said, "I had to stand up and [wait] for his instructions."[13] When asked if Duch looked scared or anxious, Vann Nath replied this was unlikely, because "S-21 was his location" and Duch "was in control of everything."[14]

After Vann Nath finished providing an overview of his experiences at S-21, Judge Nil asked him to comment on his art as it was displayed on the court monitor. "The drawings," Vann Nath noted, consisted of three types: "First, what I saw with my own eyes. Number two, [what] I only heard [about]" but could imagine. "And number three, [what] I heard from prisoners [with whom] I shared the [workshop] room."[15]

The first works displayed were black-and-white sketches depicting Vann Nath's experiences in the Battambang prison and S-21. The first featured thick wood blocks being used as clamps to shackle prisoners in Battambang. The second depicted prisoners, necks tied in a length of rope, being led into S-21. Another showed Vann Nath on his knees before Duch, who lounges, leg crossed, on a couch. Each image was projected for a moment and then vanished. The courtroom was silent.

Vann Nath was next asked to comment on his color paintings, many of which now hang at Tuol Sleng. Two of these, including one of an emaciated prisoner shackled by the leg in a tiny red brick cell, illustrated the harsh detention conditions at S-21. Others depict scenes of violence, including images of prisoners having their fingernails extracted, enduring waterboarding, and being sexually mutilated. In one, four cadre wearing Mao caps whip a prisoner who lies on his stomach, arms tied behind his back, which is covered with red welts. Bou Meng, Vann Nath explained, had described this scene, in which the guards "took turns beating him up. So I made this painting for Bou Meng."[16]

Later, Vann Nath told the court how, as the artisans were finishing their work one night, Peng had suddenly said, "Contemptible Meng, get out," and marched him away. Perhaps two weeks later, as Vann Nath painted in the workshop, he heard the sound of chains "being dragged along the corridor and then at the door we saw Meng. . . . He was pale and his hair [had grown] longer."[17] Bou Meng was also emaciated and had bandages covering wounds. "I can still remember it clearly," Vann Nath recalled.[18]

Duch had been there as well and had kicked Bou Meng in the head. He said, "Contemptible Meng, what have you promised to me?" Bou Meng, Vann Nath continued, "sat right in front of me, kneeled down and apologized to every one of us." Duch then asked the artisans if Bou Meng should be used as an artist or "to make fertilizer." Vann Nath requested that Bou Meng be forgiven, though he was uncertain what Bou Meng had done. Duch warned that Bou Meng would be watched and this was "the last time he could correct himself."[19]

By the end of Vann Nath's testimony, the trajectory of Duch's trial had shifted. Up to this point, Duch's voice had dominated the proceedings. Now a survivor had spoken. Vann Nath provided a face and a voice, through both his testimony and his paintings, for the almost anonymous mass of victims, like Long Muy, from whom Duch claimed to have kept his distance.

Vann Nath's account also diverged from Duch's in important ways. While Duch claimed to have visited the workshop occasionally, Vann Nath placed him there on a regular basis, suggesting that Duch was more present than he had admitted. If Vann Nath heard prisoners screaming in pain, then how could Duch, who was also at the workshop, not have heard these cries as he had asserted? Similarly, Vann Nath's stories and paintings suggested that a wide range of tortures were used at S-21 in contrast to Duch's claims. Vann Nath also testified that he had watched Duch kick Bou Meng in the head, suggesting Duch was downplaying his own involvement in the prison violence.

| | | |

Vann Nath had testified as a witness; the next two survivors to take the stand, Chum Mey and then Bou Meng, did so as civil parties. Like Vann Nath, their testimony highlighted the brutality of S-21 and cast doubt on some of Duch's exculpatory claims.

Chum Mey, a mechanic, described how, on October 28, 1978, after being told he was being taken to repair vehicles, he was instead handcuffed and blindfolded at the entrance to S-21. As he was marched into the compound, Chum Mey pleaded with a guard, "Please look after my family." The guard "kicked me and I fell on the ground, and he said, 'you motherfucker, Angkar needs to smash you all. You don't need to think about your family.'"[20]

Chum Mey was registered in a room just inside the terrace of Building E, a process that included being photographed, measured, and asked for biographical details. "The method was so hot," he told the court. "It was always hot. . . . We were [scolded] . . . called contemptible."[21] Afterward, Chum Mey was stripped to his shorts and taken to a small cell, where he was shackled. The only objects in the two-meter by one-meter cell were an old ammunition case and a plastic bottle he was instructed to use to relieve himself. "There was no light," Chum Mey noted, "because all the windows . . . were closed. So both day and night it was all dark."[22] He was closely watched and had to request permission to do something as basic as changing the side on which he slept.

Later Chum Mey was taken to a new room for interrogation. "I was ordered to sit," he recalled, and then "my legs were shackled and the handcuffs taken off." When his blindfold was removed, he saw a typewriter resting on a table, which was next to a chair and a pile of wooden rods. He also saw "fresh blood nearby."[23]

Then the interrogation began. Addressing Chum Mey with pronouns connoting dominance and disdain, Seng, his interrogator, asked, "Look! You, contemptible one [aeng], tell the truth! How many people, contemptible one, joined the CIA and KGB with you?"[24] Chum Mey pressed his palms together [sampeah] in respect. Seng responded, "Contemptible one, don't *sampeah* me, your superior. I [your superior] am not a monk!" Chum Mey then told Seng, "Sir [lok], I am not familiar with the terms CIA and KGB." Because he had used the term "Sir," Seng gave Chum Mey 50 lashes. When Chum Mey tried to refer to him with the term "Comrade" (*mitt*), he received another 50 lashes. Finally, he asked what he should call them and was told "Elder Brother" (*bâng*).

As in Ya's interrogation, this exchange illustrates the process of calibration that took place at S-21, as singular articulations of the enemy other were forged in accordance with the thick frame of the DK Party line and ideology. The interrogator asserts his dominance over his prisoner and signals what is inappropriate (using counterrevolutionary language and behaviors, such as trying to *sampeah* or asserting a revolutionary bond by referring to the interrogator as "comrade") and appropriate—in this case using *bâng*, a term that acknowledges the interrogator's superiority, which Seng also highlighted through his use of first person pronouns signaling his superiority and contempt for Chum Mey.

Chum Mey had to sit with his legs extended and ankle shackled. Leaning to the side and raising his hands to illustrate, Chum Mey told the court that once, when the beating was particularly severe, he had tried to block a blow.[25] "They broke my little finger," he repeated three times, moving his raised pinky finger back and forth.[26]

While he told the court about how he was beaten, Chum Mey became more animated. "Later," he continued, "they used a pair of pliers and pulled out my toe nail. I was trembling in pain."[27] As he said the word "trembled," he quivered his hands in the air.

Perhaps ten days later, Chum Mey was tortured by electrical shock. "The electrical wire was [not administered using some sort of telephone machine like] Duch said," Chum Mey stated, pointing briefly toward the defense table. "The electrical wire was attached to the wall with a direct current. . . . It knocked me senseless . . . my ears just heard a thumping sound, tut, tut, tut, tut, tut."

Chum Mey took a deep breath before starting to name his interrogators, using a derogatory prefix (-a) as he enunciated each with emphasis. "The people who beat me were . . . despicable Seng, despicable Tet, and despicable Hor. And little Hor had a scar here on his cheek,"[28] Chum Mey said, rubbing a spot below his right eye. He had done research, he noted, and discovered all three men were dead.

Pausing, and then without looking at Duch, Chum Mey raised his hands in a perfunctory sampeah aimed in the direction of the defense and said, "I'd like to tell Mr. Duch that he is lucky he didn't beat me. If Mr. Duch had beaten me, he would no longer see the light of day."[29] Duch, slumped in his chair, glared. The only trace of a reaction was the twitch of a hand, an intake of breath, and a blink of the eyes. Chum Mey gazed at the Trial Chamber judges, a barely suppressed smile on his face, as the court momentarily fell silent.

"Uncle Chum Mey," Judge Nil finally interjected, "Please be well-behaved and make sure that you are more ethical and try to avoid attacking any individual because it is more about the legal proceedings."[30] While the court appreciated his testimony, Judge Nil continued, Chum Mey should avoid being unkind and "try your best to tell us the truth and, of course, the Chamber will use your testimony as evidence in our decision. So let's leave it for the Chamber to make the final judgment." He concluded by inviting Chum Mey to continue with his story, focusing particularly on the S-21 detention conditions.[31]

Even as he raised his hands to sampeah Judge Nil and spoke respectfully, Chum Mey was defiant. "If I don't tell the truth," he replied, "then [Your Honours] maybe wouldn't learn about the stories, hard as they are . . . because when I was entered that place, there were no cool methods [as Duch said] and derogatory remarks were [made] to me, like 'the mother-fucker' and 'contemptible one.'" Once, Chum Mey noted, "despicable" Hor instructed Seng to watch as Hor scolded Chum Mey, saying, "Contemptible Mother fucker, so you won't answer."[32] Demonstrating how Hor rolled up his sleeves, Chum Mey told the court that Hor then beat him so hard that he broke several rods.

"So I'd like to tell your Honour," Chum Mey concluded, once again offering a sampeah to Judge Nil, "This is the truth. If I didn't tell the truth, then it would be a problem."³³ Smiling at Chum Mey, Judge Nil offered a gentle rebuke: "Thank you very much, Uncle, for your testimony but when you stated something that is about—for example, you referred to Duch, that if Duch beat you during the interrogation then he would not live today, I think this is not really appropriate to say in the Court."³⁴

"They beat me like this," Chum Mey said, resuming his story, "for twelve days and nights."³⁵ At first, Seng interrogated him alone. Later he sometimes alternated with Tet. Chum Mey's ears became sore from being pulled as he was taken to and from his cell. "I was so scared," he recalled, "I didn't dare look at their faces."³⁶ Chum Mey was beaten every day. "They always had a bunch of the [bamboo or rattan] sticks ready at the corner of the table . . . after I was interrogated and beaten, then the person came back to type. . . . They asked me about the KGB and CIA. That was the main focus; nothing else. And if [I] answered about other things then I would be beaten."³⁷

The beatings only stopped when Chum Mey confessed to joining the CIA and KGB; but, he noted, "It was a fabrication because I was beaten so severely, so I just implicated other people."³⁸ His interrogator did not provide specific names, instead asking "me to think about the people, my network, and how many of my associates [had] joined the CIA or KGB."³⁹ Chum Mey said he didn't know what happened to the 68 people he listed.

Like Vann Nath, Chum Mey was saved because, as a mechanic, he had a skill needed at S-21. He was transferred to a communal cell and assigned to fix sewing machines and typewriters, among other things. While he worked, he observed dead prisoners being carried to be buried by a nearby tree.⁴⁰ He could also hear the screams of people being tortured. "I heard the guards laugh and the prisoners cry," he told the court. "When Mr. Duch says that he didn't hear any [screams], I don't believe it because I worked in the back of the compound . . . and I could hear the cries, yelling, and swearing."⁴¹

| | | |

In many respects, Bou Meng's account paralleled that of Chum Mey. Bou Meng also described how he was tortured and forced to confess at S-21. His interrogators asked, "Who introduced you into the CIA network and what was their name?" Bou Meng kept telling them he didn't know: "I could not

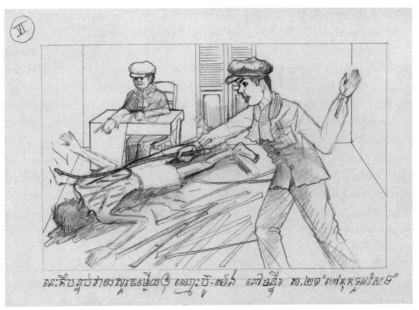

Bou Meng being tortured by whipping at S-21. Drawing by Bou Meng. Photo courtesy of the DC-Cam / SRI Archives.

Bou Meng being tortured by electrical shock at S-21. Drawing by Bou Meng. Photo courtesy of the DC-Cam / SRI Archives.

think of any mistake that I made. I did not know what the CIA or KGB network was; then how could I respond? So they just kept beating me."[42]

Bou Meng's back became covered with wounds, which a guard would sometimes poke or pour gravel onto. "There was no medicine," he told the court. "There was a bowl of saltwater and they just poured that saltwater on my back and it was so, so painful because of my open wounds."[43] He noted, "I have a lot of scars on my back as evidence from that torture."[44] Later the judges would request to see the scars.

Bou Meng was eventually transferred to work in the same workshop as Vann Nath. Duch gave Bou Meng a small photograph of Pol Pot and instructed him to paint a 1.5- by 3-meter black-and-white portrait of the DK leader. At times while Bou Meng painted, Duch sat "nearby me, watching me, sitting on a chair with his legs crossed," sometimes instructing Bou Meng to make small modifications, such as making Pol Pot's throat slimmer.[45]

In the end, Bou Meng painted four portraits of Pol Pot as well as one of Mao and another of a dog with Ho Chi Minh's head. While Duch did not personally abuse Bou Meng, Duch threatened Bou Meng that if his portrait did not resemble Pol Pot, Bou Meng would be used as "human fertilizer."[46] At another point, Duch ordered Bou Meng and another prisoner-artisan to fight. "I was not happy with that," Bou Meng said. "He did not treat me like a human being."[47]

| | |

If the testimony of the first three survivors suggested that Duch was minimizing his role, that of the fourth, child survivor Norng Chanphal, threw the issue into sharp relief. In 1978, soon after his father's arrest, eight-year-old Norng Chanphal and a brother accompanied their mother to Phnom Penh, where she was taken with her children to S-21 and arrested.

Norng Chanphal and his brother were separated from their mother and lived in a workshop on the compound. Once, when he was at the rear of the workshop, Norng Chanphal recalled, he glanced at his mother's cell and saw her holding the "bars of the window, looking at me." He thought she wanted to say something, but she was far away. "I looked at her for a moment," he told the court; "then I never saw her again."[48] After telling this story, Norng Chanphal began to weep, as he, like the other three survivors, had done at various points while testifying. At the end of DK, he and his brother remained at S-21 after the staff had fled and were eventually discovered by Vietnamese soldiers.

Once the prosecution and civil party lawyers had finished questioning Norng Chanphal, Judge Nil asked Duch for observations on Norng Chanphal's testimony. Duch acknowledged Norng Chanphal's suffering but wanted "to make some clarifications."[49] Initially, he continued, he had not believed that Norng Chanphal's father was imprisoned at S-21. But after seeing his father's biography, Duch acknowledged he had died there. Norng Chanphal's mother was another matter, since there was no supporting documentation. Because "at S-21 no child was spared," Duch concluded, "Mom Yauv, the mother of Norng Chanphal, [died] elsewhere."

Judge Cartwright asked the defense for clarification, noting "the statement made by the accused has left me unsure of whether he agrees that this witness Norng Chanphal was a detainee." Duch's national co-defense lawyer, Kar Savuth, confirmed that Duch did not. Nobody would defy Duch's orders and allow children to survive. Moreover, Kar Savuth noted, Norng Chanphal had been unable to find his mother's photograph at Tuol Sleng. Saying he was "certain on this matter," Duch said he believed that Norng Chanphal and his mother were detained elsewhere, though he was ready to acknowledge "any piece of S-21 documents confirming the identification of the mother."[50]

At this point, Bill Smith intervened. "Your Honor, just a brief comment," he began. "It appears that the defense position and the accused's position seem to change depending on what pieces of evidence are put before them. So, for example, prior to that biography being put to the Chamber, the accused was of the view that his father could not have been at S-21."[51] Once the document had been presented, however, Duch had changed his position. Now he was doing so again.

Six days later, National Deputy Co-Prosecutor Seng Bunkheang announced, "The prosecution would like to submit [evidence] concerning Mom Yauv, the mother of Norng Chanphal."[52] Following Norng Chanphal's testimony, he explained, DC-Cam had undertaken a search for documentation related to her. A staff member noticed that Norng Chanphal had pronounced his mother's name slightly differently from the spelling on her husband's biography.[53] This led her to look for alternative spellings of Mom Yauv's name, whereupon she found Mom Yauv's biography. This document, Seng Bunkheang stated, should satisfy Duch's demand for evidence, proving that Norng Chanphal and his mother were imprisoned at S-21.

When given the floor, Kar Savuth noted that Duch had "already confessed" and admitted to his involvement in crimes committed against more than 12,000 detainees. One more victim made little difference. "As long as Mom

Yauv was the mother of Norng Chanphal and that document was [authentic]," Kar Savuth said, "then we accept [it] with pleasure."[54] When asked for his observations, Duch said he accepted the document and "would like to seek forgiveness from Mr. Norng Chanphal."[55]

By this point, however, a new trial dynamic was evident. It appeared that, despite his admission of guilt and pleas for forgiveness, Duch would contest any evidence undercutting his defense and account of S-21, even if this meant challenging the claims of witnesses and victims. Just the day before, he had contested several claims made by a former guard. In the days that followed and as had been the case with M-13 witnesses, he would repeatedly contest incriminating testimony from former S-21 staff and victims.

Duch's motivation for making these contestations is uncertain. On the one hand he claimed he was challenging weak evidence to honor the truth. On the other hand Bill Smith's remark that Duch's position seemed to shift according to the evidence provided suggested a different explanation. It was as though Duch's depiction of events mirrored an S-21 confession, a mixture of truth and falsehood calibrated to meet the demands of the moment. If, in DK, everyone had to mold their ways of speaking and life-histories to accord with the Party line, so too was Duch remaking the past to fit the juridical present, reshaping events to accord with his legal argument that he was just a cog in the machine. To this end, his account foregrounded certain sorts of supporting evidence, such as the cover of Long Muy's confession, while editing out less favorable "facts."

When Duch's lawyers challenged the applications of a large number of civil parties and successfully argued that civil parties should not be allowed to fully participate in the portions of the trial devoted to character and sentencing, the tension between the civil parties and the defense only grew. A number of civil parties directly questioned Duch's claims, suggesting that he was lying about matters large and small and stating that they refused to accept his apologies.

| | | |

These events formed a key backdrop of the closing arguments given by Studzinsky and other civil party lawyers. If their remarks frequently invoked human rights, transitional justice, and the notion of humanity in the sense of universal suffering and repair, they also referenced Duch's perceived lies. The Trial Chamber, they noted, at times seemed insensitive to their clients' suffering and favored Duch in their rulings, especially with regard to denying their clients' right to speak on character and sentencing. This undercurrent of bitterness was perhaps most apparent in Studzinsky's close, even as she highlighted her clients' suffering.

Just as Jean Améry had remarked that a person tortured is never fully healed, Studzinsky told the court, so too had Bou Meng testified, "I will never become a healthy person again. . . . The visible and invisible scars remain forever and my mind and body [have been] destroyed."[56] The indirect victims in her group, in turn, wanted to know what happened to their loved ones and why. Her clients, she added, were "seeking justice," which meant, "among other things, finding the truth and getting answers to their excruciating and relentless questions which haunt them at night" resulting in "ghost-like visions" about their loved ones.[57]

To illustrate, Studzinsky briefly summarized the experiences of her clients who had not testified publically, since their stories "should be heard in public to memorialize and honour their loved ones who were tortured, dehumanized and finally killed at S-21. The crimes committed by the accused made their families incomplete. Not a day goes by without the memories of the horror suffered by loved ones."[58]

The first was the experience of a man who was just a child when his father joined the Khmer Rouge and later disappeared. He found his father's photograph on the walls of S-21 and was "plague[d] day and night" with questions about this father's fate. A woman whose husband had disappeared remained chronically ill, her life "destroyed and characterized entirely by pain and struggle."[59] Another woman who discovered her uncle's photograph at Tuol Sleng was haunted by the torture and suffering he likely endured.

The "emotional and moving" stories of these victims, Studzinsky continued, illustrated "the consequences that the crimes committed by the accused" have had and illustrated that "their suffering is on-going more than 30 years [later]."[60] They were exercising their participatory rights to seek justice and the truth, including an understanding of "how the DK regime worked and functioned . . . and the motivation for committing the crimes."[61] Even if her clients who testified had been nervous and forgotten part of what they wanted to say, they were nevertheless pleased that "the Trial Chamber allowed them to speak in Court about their experiences," an act that they had found "cathartic."[62]

Indeed, the themes of catharsis and transformation were a strong undercurrent of the civil party closing arguments, which invoked the "humanity lost" at S-21 and the attempt to regain it through the judicial process. As the civil party lawyers repeatedly emphasized, the S-21 victims had been thoroughly dehumanized, losing their dignity, rights, bodily integrity, and, with a few exceptions, lives.

To highlight this point, the French lawyer for Civil Party Group 3, Martine Jacquin, quoted Holocaust survivor Primo Levi's famous description of "the hollow man": "Imagine a man who is deprived of everyone he loves, and at the same time of his house, his habits, his clothes, in short, of everything he possesses: he will be a hollow man, reduced to suffering and needs, forgetful of dignity and restraint, for he who loses all often loses himself."[63] This experience, Jacquin added, was directly related to being viewed as "objects in the eyes of other human beings."[64]

This diminished humanity and the S-21 experiences that led to it were manifest in the tokens of injury repeatedly mentioned during the closings: traces, scars, suffering, trauma, hauntings, and silence. As such, the victims, like Duch, existed in a liminal state, contaminated by violation, relegated to a static space of defilement and degradation, plagued by dangerous and threatening emotions, and waiting for help in regaining their humanity. By extension, since the civil parties represented not just the S-21 victims but society more broadly, Cambodia itself was implicitly being depicted in these terms as suffering a lack as it sought a return to "civilization" and membership in the international community.

The court would serve as the vehicle of rehumanization and return. Legally, it afforded a status to the victims. Several civil party lawyers emphasized this distinct civil party role. Thus, the British lawyer Karim Khan, representing Civil Party Group 1, noted that Internal Rule 23 empowered civil parties to participate in the proceedings both in support of the prosecution and in order to seek "collective and moral reparations," a right that followed from "physical, material or psychological injury" that was a "direct consequence of the offence."[65] Their "unique perspective" would help the Trial Chamber ascertain the truth by providing "insights as to the impact of the alleged crimes upon their lives and the lives of their loved ones."[66]

Their testimony was also directly linked to reparation. In a legalistic sense, reparations would provide compensation for the injuries caused by a convict. On a symbolic level, however, this "return" was directly linked to the civil parties' rehumanization. Jacquin foregrounded this point by beginning her closing remarks with a quote from a Holocaust survivor who recalled that, at the end of World War II, the survivors returned "from a world where an attempt had been made to banish us from humanity. We wanted to tell of this but we came up against the incredulity and indifference of others. It was only years later that we found the courage to speak [out] because the world was listening."

At the ECCC, civil parties faced a similar situation. "As civil parties," Jacquin stated, "our first task is to speak out" about events that others, such as Duch, might prefer to forget.[67] The court was the enabling mechanism, creating a process through which "voice has been given to the voiceless. . . . We are enabling these sons and daughters of those who were tortured, disemboweled—these children of the horror are now allowed to be heard."[68] Bearing "the trace" of the violence, the civil parties wanted "to talk about the spectre that haunts them."[69]

Her French colleague, Philippe Cannone, also highlighted how the court gave voice to the victims, noting that they were engaged in a "universal fight" and following "percepts of the law" in order to "continue to be human" and "avoid sinking to the level of animals."[70] More broadly, Cambodians were "standing behind the values of progress and of liberty" as they undertook "the road . . . of reconstruction and reconciliation" that would "pass through this trial" and lead to Cambodia's "rebirth."[71]

Such remarks conferred status to the civil parties, and through them to Cambodian society as a whole, which paralleled that of Duch, who in turn stood for the Khmer Rouge more broadly. Though Duch was confined to the space of the dock and the civil parties were not, they shared with him a symbolic lack, dangerous emotionality, dysfunction, stasis, and a need for transformation. Through the juridical process, the civil parties were bestowed with liberal democratic rights and values, enacted through the participatory process of the trial. The court bequeathed the "gift" of "voice" that enabled this "rebirth," as the civil parties, and Cambodians more broadly, were allegedly "healed" and returned to humanity and civilization. In this transitional justice frame, so too did Cambodia undergo a similar process of transformation as it symbolically returned to the international community, ending its longtime status as a "failed state" characterized by savagery, violence, impunity, and authoritarianism.[72]

Even as it was repeatedly asserted, this juridical articulation of reordering and renewal through legal process was disrupted by events that complicated the narrative and therefore were edited out of the authoritative legal document, the verdict. Yet at times what had been redacted would suddenly come to the fore.

Sometimes this eruption happened subtly, as when Cannone alluded to the civil parties being denied the right to comment during the trial phases on character and sentencing. This decision, he suggested, had the potential to make the civil parties "revert to silence," becoming "icons of a kind; respectable, untouchable, but voiceless. Should we bury them again?" To do so risked creating the preconditions in which "a new Duch will arise."[73] More broadly, he noted, the civil parties were at times treated almost with "scorn," which constituted "a new form of dehumanization."[74] The international lawyer for Civil Party Group 4, Pierre-Olivier Sur, suggested there was even "complicity" between the Trial Chamber and Duch that enabled him to dominate the proceedings.[75]

Studzinsky offered the most direct critique of the Trial Chamber, which she lambasted for its insensitivity. Unlike other parties, she noted, the civil parties were rarely thanked for their testimony. When they testified, she continued, the judges often appeared disinterested. The Trial Chamber did intervene, however, whenever the civil parties, who Studzinsky noted were nervous and traumatized, became emotional. Instead of showing empathy, Studzinsky continued, the Trial Chamber advised the civil parties to "control their emotions," warning that if they did not, the Trial Chamber would not have "time to hear them later."[76] By ordering "the civil parties to suppress their tears and control their emotions," the Trial Chamber "did not contribute to a healing process" and suggested that civil party trauma was not relevant even though these "painful traumatic expressions are the result of the crimes committed by the defendant."[77]

To highlight this remark, Studzinsky discussed the case of civil party Mam Non. Mam Non, Studzinsky reminded the court, had overcome many obstacles and used "all her strength and courage to break the silence after 30 years" about her experiences as an S-21 medic. Before Mam Non testified, Studzinsky had pleaded with the Trial Chamber to be patient and not ask Mam Non to "control her emotions." This had drawn a rebuke from Judge Cartwright, who questioned Studzinsky's preparation and reprimanded her, emphasizing that the judges were "very experienced . . . and perhaps don't need the advice always that you give us."[78]

In her closing remarks, Studzinsky reminded the judges that Mam Non arrived at S-21 at the age of fifteen and witnessed Duch beating two of her uncles to death prior to herself being "arrested, interrogated, tortured and raped before being sent to S-24. Her father, mother and younger brother were killed at S-21." The Trial Chamber had raised many questions regarding her account, about which Duch had claimed "there is no evidence at all."[79] Studzinsky told the judges that Mam Non's statement "deserves more attention and needs a close assessment of credibility," given that she had testified that Duch personally killed people at S-21.

Studzinsky proceeded to lay out a series of "tools for credibility assessment of testimony," including the account's origin, delivery and affective style, motives for mendacity like "hatred or revenge," risk of self-incrimination, and content. In all these respects, Studzinsky argued, Mam Non's "statement is plausible, credible and convincing."[80] This conclusion was further supported by "the nonverbal reaction of the accused," who had "looked at the ceiling and acted uninterested" when Nam Mon described Duch's alleged execution of her uncles. He never directly denied her account, instead stating "there were no female medics at S-21."[81] Moreover, Mam Non later claimed that another witness, former guard Chhun Phal, had raped her at S-21, a charge that the Trial Chamber decided not to consider. Mam Non's testimony, Studzinsky suggested, was critical to the case against Duch, casting doubt on his credibility and defense.

While Studzinsky spoke, the judges sat solemnly, sometimes gazing at her, other times looking away. Their only response came after the lunch break, when Judge Nil warned that some civil party lawyer remarks had "strayed beyond the facts and legal matters" appropriate for closings.

As Studzinsky's remarks suggest, emotion had an uneasy place in the judicial process, a necessary marker of suffering and victimhood yet labile and potentially unsettling. On the one hand the emotions of victims were critical to the proceedings, a sign of violation and injury in need of remedy. This emotionality was important for the legitimacy of the court, providing a basis for its action and also helping to instantiate its key criminological binary of victim-perpetrator.

On the other hand emotions were also potentially contaminating, as the court was predominantly a space of rationality, epitomized by the judges, who usually sat with impassive expressions and rarely showed affect. This emphasis on rationality was in part meant to contain the potentially dangerous emotions circulating below the surface. If they erupted in an uncontained form, such emotions could threaten justice, which was idealized as a process transcending sentiments of vindictiveness that could threaten order. As the bearers of such emotions, civil parties constituted a potentially contaminating presence in the court.

Khan addressed this issue, noting defense suggestions that the civil parties "would like vengeance," as when Roux had stated "we are in a court of law not in a market square where one is pillorying . . . [and] stoning an accused."[82]

Despite all they had suffered, Khan assured the court, the civil parties had "not succumbed to the baser instincts of seeking revenge but have sought, quite properly, to avail themselves of the procedures put in place so that they can have a voice, so that they can have closure."[83] Cannone added that the key was to acknowledge this first "instinctive" reaction and then "transcend it. Then justice will be rendered and not savagery."[84]

Here again, Cannone portrayed the court as a vehicle of moral uplift and transformation. However, the discussion about the "base," "instinctive," and "savage" feelings of malice, even if fleeting, hinted at a parallel between the civil parties and "Duch the monster," one that undercut the victim-perpetrator binary and suggested the doubleness of the categories, each reflecting the other in ways that at times suggested both similarity and difference. More broadly, the foregrounding of alleged civil party antipathy toward Duch was part of a larger defense strategy to portray him as a victim. If Duch was the object of civil party malice, the defense suggested, he was also, in a sense, a victim of circumstance.

The civil parties attacked this argument. Cannone, for example, asked why Duch had chosen to recite a French romantic poem in a trial for crimes against humanity. The poem offered no hope for humanity, Cannon said, suggesting one has "to die without saying anything, while fulfilling your task in life." Admonishing Duch, Cannone continued, "We are not here in a trial dealing with elegancy. We are not here in a literary discussion. I am speaking to you about the 12,000 people who died at Tuol Sleng. Some say even 16,000. So where is the romanticism in this?"[85]

Several of the civil party lawyers stated that the evidence overwhelmingly demonstrated that Duch was not a mere pawn. Khan listed the many ways Duch had exercised autonomy and directly contributed to a spiral of violence through his annotations, analyses, and reports to the DK leaders.[86] He was ideologically committed to the revolution, Khan told the court, and had innovated continuously, "designing a cruel and callous system" at M-13 and then "perfecting it" at S-21. The evidence, Khan finished, demonstrated that Duch was seeking to "avoid the most awful parts of what happened" at the prison despite the strong "correlation between the activity of Duch and the suffering and activity in S-21."[87] He was trying, Khan argued, "to bluff this Court."[88]

Other civil party lawyers attacked Duch's claim to want to return to humanity. "What does it mean to be rehumanized?"[89] Pierre-Olivier Sur, the last civil party lawyer to speak, asked. Replying to his own question, Sur continued, "If we bring him back to our community of human beings, this means that we have to consider that he is part of our social group, that he is a member of the social contract that unites us all and that generates our society." In this capacity, Duch had a role, Sur stated, for which he had to be judged: "the role of a criminal, a criminal against humanity."

Duch's alleged contrition was critical to his claim to humanity. "Is your contrition sincere?" Cannone asked Duch at one point. Cannone noted that Duch had wept during the reenactment and that "weeping is a beginning of contrition." Apology, in turn, meant "the dawning of understanding and assumption of responsibility. . . . To look, to hear, to see those whom one caused to be tortured is to cease to consider people as objects. It means that the victims are allowed to regain their dignity."[90] Addressing Duch, Cannone continued, "So look at them, Duch. Look at these men and women that you sought to smash or whose parents, spouses or children you smashed. You can smash insects, animals. You cannot smash human beings."[91]

The civil party lawyers also discussed Duch's tears, in part because crying suggested contrition and, by extension, human feeling. If several Cambodian civil party co-lawyers described their client's suffering or offered ideas for reparations, Group 2 lawyer Kong Pisey touched on broader issues, including "the four pillars" of Duch's defense: obedience, lack of personal involvement, cooperation, and apology and remorse. Duch's "defense of being a victim" was insulting to the civil parties "and all other victims in Cambodia," and his frequent requests "for forgiveness, his apologies, and his expression of remorse toward the civil parties and their families . . . became more and more unctuous" and only "solidifies his guilt."[92] Duch, Pisey stated, cried "on cue, often around 4 P.M. at the end of the hearing" with what could only be described as "crocodile tears" that were "orchestrated and devoid of meaning." He had also failed to fully answer questions. Accordingly, Pisey's clients did not believe Duch's remorse was sincere and therefore could not forgive him.

As the notion of "crocodile tears" suggests, a number of civil party lawyers depicted Duch as calculating, manipulative, and lacking real affect, qualities associated with a "monster." Indeed, the "man or monster" issue repeatedly arose during the closings. Cannone, for example, stated that his clients were "trying to understand why a man—no worse than any other—can set up such barbarity. How a person—[a] basically ordinary person—can be at the same time respectable and terrifying."[93]

Repeatedly, the civil party lawyers sought without success to provide a clear picture of Duch, who came into focus for a moment and then suddenly blurred. In the final remarks of the day, Sur had highlighted a number of "paradoxes" that had emerged in the trial, including the paradox that "amongst our clients . . . are former victims but also former Khmer Rouge soldiers."[94] In addition, there were cultural issues, such as the tension between international justice and Buddhism, with its emphasis on karma, reincarnation, and forgetting. Even the court structure was paradoxical given the legal dissonance between civil and common law.[95]

And then there was Duch, who grew up in predominantly Buddhist Cambodia but was heavily inspired by Western ideas and French culture, as illustrated by his ability to recite de Vigny by memory. Then, after DK, Duch "converted to Christianity. So he, in a manner of speaking, re-Westernized himself."[96] Sur noted that Duch had also "monopolized the hearings and the Trial, sometimes assigning good and bad points at will, and so he is diametrically opposed in his approach to the families we represent." Moreover, his "difficulty in approaching sentiment and empathy, proximity, understanding of suffering that is experienced by other people" had caused Sur's clients "a great sense of discomfort."[97] After pointing out these unsettling tensions, Sur concluded by paying homage to "this extraordinary international justice which we are all serving here—the very noble mission of saying, and of judging that there are crimes against humanity that will not remain unpunished."[98] Paradox had been overcome by the ordering power of law, which would culminate in an articulation, the final judgment.

Throughout the day as the civil party lawyers spoke, Duch sat in the dock, staring at them at times, looking at his monitor or scribbling down notes on other occasions. During two of the breaks, he walked over to the glass wall dividing the courtroom from the public gallery and exchanged messages with a few audience members. After reading the notes, which had been pressed against the glass, he and his correspondents traded smiles. At the end of the day, he stood and politely greeted the chamber and audience. As he exited, Duch turned back to look at the audience. I gazed at him. We locked eyes.

Then Duch gave me a short salute.

Zealot

(PROSECUTION)

Culprit (Prosecution Closing Arguments, November 24–25, 2009)

The next morning, the courtroom was dominated by white, as hundreds of uniformed university students filled the gallery. A line of monks sat in the front row, a border directly behind the dock, their saffron robes a Buddhist symbol of earth, renunciation, balance, and equanimity.

I sat next to Chum Mey a few rows behind the monks, in an area filled with civil parties for whom there wasn't room inside the courtroom. Chum Mey tapped my knee, directing my gaze toward Duch, who was entering the courtroom wearing an oversized beige coat. "Duch's not telling the truth," Chum Mey remarked.

Duch glanced at the gallery and, when he saw Chum Mey, nodded in our direction. I moved my head slightly and then looked away. Chum Mey was upset. "Duch says he wants reconciliation. He weeps and apologizes. But I can't forgive him because he is not being honest. It makes me angry." I looked back at Duch, who was slumped in his chair.

"All rise," a voice suddenly commanded over the loudspeaker as the Trial Chamber judges entered the courtroom. Everyone stood, except the monks. "They're higher than the judges," another civil party explained to me in a whisper. After the judges sat, the parties and audience followed suit.

"The security personnel are now instructed to bring the accused to the dock," Judge Nil directed after confirming the parties were present. Duch stood and walked toward the dock. He bowed awkwardly to the civil parties. Several of them laughed. I glanced at Chum Mey, who looked angry. Then Chea Leang began the OCP's closing arguments.

| | |

"Yesterday," Chea Leang told the court, "you heard the voices of the victims . . . who reminded us of the never-ending impact of the accused's actions on the families and friends of those tortured and killed at S-21." Their suffering was like "a knife that continues to turn inside each and every one of them," giving them "hearts seized with anguish [chheu chap] that can never be still."[1]

The role of the prosecution, she continued, was to represent the victims and their friends and family, as well as Cambodians more broadly and "the world public." In representing this "public interest," the OCP respected "the rights of the accused" and were not "moved by calls for revenge or pleas of forgive and forget." Ultimately, Chea Leang noted, the OCP's role was "a legal one: to prove the facts in the indictment beyond reasonable doubt, and then ask that the law be applied fairly in sentencing, based on international standards of justice."[2] In contrast to the emotion of the day before, Chea Leang spoke in a flat monotone, reading prepared remarks spread out on a podium. Duch gazed at her, listening intently.

| | |

As Chea Leang stated, the OCP's duties revolved around the August 8, 2008, Closing Order indicting Duch. Most broadly, this indictment aimed to fulfill the OCP's duty to prosecute those falling within the ECCC's personal and temporal jurisdiction. To this end, the OCP "conducts preliminary investigations, prosecutes cases throughout the investigative, pre-trial, trial and appellate stages, processes victims' complaints, and participates in judicial investigations."[3]

Much of this work was geared toward producing an articulation based on a legal roadmap linking suspects to the commission of crimes by asserting "facts" calibrated to the crimes falling under the subject-matter jurisdiction of the court, listed in articles 3–8 of the ECCC Law. This frame was first laid out in the OCP's introductory submission. As the unit that opens an investigation, the OCP conducted a preliminary investigation to "determine if there is evidence showing that crimes within the jurisdiction of the ECCC were committed . . . [and] identify potential suspects and witnesses." If this is the case, the OCP then formally opened "a judicial investigation by sending an introductory submission, which makes reference to the facts, the type of offences alleged, the applicable law and, should the case arise . . . the name of any person to be investigated."[4]

The OCP's introductory submission began as an investigation of Duch and the four other suspects eventually charged in Case 002. Given the long lag time between the July 3, 2006, swearing in of the court personnel and the finalization of the ECCC's Internal Rules the following June, the OCP was able to conduct an unusually long initial investigation. As opposed to conducting time-consuming witness interviews, the OCP focused their investigation on scholarship and documentation supporting the "allegations we believed would ultimately be proven to be true."[5]

This set of factual allegations against five suspects—calibrated to qualify as crimes included in ECCC law and supported by the evidence gathered—formed the basis of the OCP's introductory submission, which provided the legal frame for the case. The alleged crimes included genocide, crimes against humanity, grave breaches of the Geneva Convention, torture, religious persecution, and homicide. "In support of their factual submissions," the co-prosecutors noted in a July 18, 2007 statement about their introductory submission, their office "transmitted more than 1,000 documents constituting over 14,000 pages, including third party statements and/or written record[s] of over 350 witnesses, a list of 40 other potential witnesses, thousands of pages of [DK era] documentation and the locations of over 40 undisturbed mass graves." The statement added: "These documents have all been digitalized and indexed in a database. Both electronic and hard copies of these documents have been provided to" the OCIJ.[6]

This documentation formed the backbone of the case file, or court dossier of materials related to the case, ranging from records of interviews to court transcripts. Each item in the case file is given an electronic record number. More broadly, the case file serves as an archive, the source material for the case as well as a symbolic mantle of authority, as it is passed from one office to the next as each unit takes the lead in the case. Once the OCP submitted its introductory submission, the OCIJ was given control of the case file as it took up its task of determining "whether the facts set out by the introductory submission amount to crimes within the jurisdiction of the ECCC and, at the same time, whether there is enough evidence to send the Charged Person to Trial for the crimes for which they have been charged."[7]

Within two weeks of beginning its investigation, the OCIJ arrested Duch, initially charging him with crimes against humanity. Almost immediately, they began to question him. Given Duch's cooperation, his agreement to many of the alleged facts, the narrow focus on S-21, and his long detention, the OCIJ separated his case, which they characterized as "uncomplicated and very simple," and designated it Case 001.[8]

In fulfilling its mandate to investigate the factual allegations, the OCIJ is empowered to question suspects, issue summonses, warrants, and orders, "interview Victims and witnesses and record their statements, [seize] exhibits, seek expert opinions and conduct on-site investigations."[9] As it carried out these actions, the OCIJ was assisted by legal research, analysis, and investigation teams.

Like the OCP, the OCIJ drew extensively on electronic databases like Case-Map, "a specialized case analysis program that assists in the collection and analysis of large volumes of information relating to witnesses, documents and legal issues."[10] All the while, the case file grew as new evidence and court documentation was added. Civil parties were also required to submit their applications to the OCIJ, which allowed them to become parties if the applicant demonstrated injury directly related to the alleged crimes—though this status could be challenged by the defense, as was the case in Duch's trial.

All of this activity was guided by the introductory submission, which contained the only factual allegations the OCIJ was charged with investigating and defined the parameters of civil party participation. By the time the OCIJ informed the OCP that they intended to close their investigation on May 15, 2008, six civil party applications had been accepted. At this juncture, the OCIJ transferred the case file back to the OCP to decide whether the case should proceed.

On July 18, 2008, the OCP filed its final submission, a 158-page document containing numerous alleged "material facts" that, the OCP argued, warranted indicting Duch for crimes against humanity, grave breaches of the Geneva Conventions of 1949, and violations of the 1956 Cambodian Penal Code.[11] The OCIJ largely concurred with the OCP in its August 8, 2008 Closing Order indicting Duch. While the OCIJ disagreed about the applicability of the legal doctrine of "joint criminal enterprise" to the Duch case (the OCP would appeal), its Closing Order was directly informed by the initial legal frame laid out in the OCP's introductory submission and more detailed final submission.

This indictment was a key backdrop to Duch's trial, an incipient juridical articulation linking alleged facts, applicable law, and criminal acts.

| | |

During closing arguments, the prosecution's comments centered on this articulation, as the OCP argued that the evidence proved that Duch had committed the crimes for which he had been indicted. Chea Leang noted that even though Duch had agreed to or not disputed many of the alleged facts, his admissions did "not remove the prosecutor's obligation to prove the case against the accused beyond a reasonable doubt." Moreover, there remained "inconsistencies and gaps."[12]

In particular, she noted, Duch had acknowledged that criminal acts took place but "admitted very little in relation to his criminal intent. In short, he has claimed that although he passed on the criminal orders, he did so only on the threat of death by his superior." Given that "criminal intent is as significant in determining responsibility for a crime as much as the act of the crimes itself," Chea Leang pointed out, "the omission of his agreement to full criminal intent . . . limits the effect of his agreement on the facts."[13]

She then provided an overview of the key facts Duch did acknowledge. She began with an implicit contrast, noting that he admitted that, during DK, "there were no proper legal structures in place . . . no proper justice system . . . no courts, no police force and no published law . . . [or] fair trials."[14] Instead of prisons, he had stated, the CPK ran "death chambers" from which there was no possibility of release, due to "a strict and discriminatory party policy to smash all 'enemies.'"

S-21 was directly involved, Chea Leang reminded the court, as she began to describe the prison's structure and operation. As she spoke, Chum Mey appeared tired and distracted, flipping through a court booklet and later closing his eyes, perhaps because he had arisen before dawn to meet a Japanese film crew. He looked up when Chea Leang said, "Perhaps the clearest way to illustrate these crimes is to retrace the prisoner's horrible journey from arrest to execution."

First Chea Leang mentioned Vann Nath's journey to S-21, recalling how he had "described how he lost his dignity" due to the abysmal conditions and way prisoners were like animals.[15] Chum Mey tapped my knee and nodded slightly as Chea Leang said, "Former prisoner and survivor Chum Mey was treated particularly badly. His experiences have deeply traumatized him.

The Trial Chamber witnessed firsthand, actually, how even now, more than 30 years on, it is agony for him to recount what happened."[16]

As she described his detention, interrogation, and torture, Chum Mey appeared on the verge of tears. Uncertain of what to do, I set aside my notebook and rested my hand on his knee. For about fifteen minutes, he inhaled sharply as he tried to compose himself. I glanced at Bou Meng, who sat at the other end of the row. He also looked upset as Chea Leang began to discuss his story. Both would later tell me they were glad to have their story acknowledged in court.

Duch, Chea Leang continued, played a central role in running this "systematic torture-killing centre." Among his many S-21 annotations was one on which he had written in red ink next to the name of a prisoner whose blood had been drained, "Smashed. Blood." At S-21, Chea Leang went on, "the cruelty toward the prisoners knew no limits," as they were placed in "squalid bestial conditions" before being killed at Choeung Ek, which has come to symbolize the "inhuman cruelty" of the DK regime."[17]

| | | |

Having summarized many of the key facts, Chea Leang next matched this evidence to the crimes in the indictment. She noted that the OCP had submitted a 158-page final submission, yet another iteration of the introductory submission, which updated the Closing Order by taking into account trial evidence. This document laid out the "Facts" of the case as well as their "Legal Characterization" and relationship to "Sentencing."[18]

"What crimes do these facts prove?" Chea Leang asked.[19] The facts, she continued, described acts that could be "properly qualified as criminal offences under the ECCC law" and the indictment. "I [will] now turn to each criminal classification in turn," she told the court.[20] While it was not proper to speak of a hierarchy of crimes, she observed, crimes against humanity were particularly salient because of "the impact that is felt not simply by individual victims and their direct family and friends, but by humanity as a whole." Moreover, Chea Leang continued, these crimes "involve an attack on the dignity of all human beings and on the very notion of mankind. . . . The barbaric acts committed at S-21 fall squarely within this category."[21]

Article 5 of the ECCC Law listed nine crimes against humanity for which suspects falling under the jurisdiction of the court could be tried.[22] The evidence clearly demonstrated, Chea Leang argued, that seven of the crimes against humanity had taken place at S-21: imprisonment, enslavement, torture, murder, extermination, persecution, and other inhumane acts. In order to fall within this legal category, the crimes had to satisfy given "jurisdictional elements" specified in the ECCC Law, constituting "acts committed as part of a widespread or systematic attack directed against any civilian population on national, political, ethnical, racial or religious grounds, as such."[23]

As the prosecution had initially done in their introductory submission, Chea Leang next described how the evidence proved that each of these "elements" was satisfied. The crimes at S-21, she began, were directly linked to the broader DK violence and were "systematic," following from CPK policy and involving an elaborate security apparatus of which S-21 was a central part. According to international law, she explained, an "attack" was defined as "conduct involving the commission of acts of violence." Within S-21, she contended, "tens or even hundreds of thousands of individual acts of violence" took place, including "beatings, torture, killings and other inhumane acts" perpetrated against civilians on political, ethnic, and religious "grounds."[24] Duch knew about the crimes and the CPK policy that drove them, fulfilling the requirement that a perpetrator had "knowledge of the existence of the attack."[25] As Chea Leang discussed each element, she provided numerous "facts" supporting the OCP's case.

Chea Leang did the same as she discussed each of the seven crimes against humanity alleged to have taken place at S-21. To prove each, the prosecution had to demonstrate that related elements were satisfied; these components were laid out in numeric lists in the OCP's final submission. Chea Leang turned to imprisonment first, which included three elements: "(1) an individual is deprived of his or her liberty; (2) the deprivation of liberty is imposed arbitrarily; and (3) the act or omission by which the individual is deprived of his or her physical liberty is performed by the accused, or a person or person for whom the accused bears criminal responsibility." The crime had to have been committed with intent. Imprisonment, in turn, was "defined as arbitrary where it is imposed without a justifiable legal basis and without due process."[26]

At S-21, Chea Leang stated, at least 12,273 people, and likely far more, had been detained, and "there can be no doubt whatsoever that all deprivation of liberty at S-21 was arbitrary. Prisoners were arrested because they were considered enemies."[27] Prisoners had no legal recourse since, during DK, "there was never a functioning legal system. As the commander of S-21, the accused arbitrarily deprived prisoners of their liberty." Duch had admitted that he knew "there was no legal basis for their detention, nor any means by which prisoners at S-21 could challenge their imprisonment."[28]

And so Chea Leang proceeded, delineating the elements of each crime against humanity and linking them to material facts from the trial. Then she turned to "war crimes" before concluding with a discussion of "murder" and "torture" as defined by the 1956 Cambodian Penal Code. The entire time Chea Leang had spoken, Duch had stared at her from the dock.

| | |

When Bill Smith took the floor, he turned to sentencing. "Our job as prosecutors," he told the Trial Chamber, in the same flat tone Chea Leang had used, "is to assist Your Honors in achieving a sense of justice that separates your judgment from . . . the 12,000 judgments that the accused gave at S-21."[29] This justice would be achieved by "applying the ECCC law, a law that demands a fair trial, a law that demands convictions based on facts only proved beyond reasonable doubt, and a law that demands your sentence is in accordance with international standards of fairness."

This sentence should not be based on "revenge but on retribution and deterrence. It's society's way of demonstrating that its people are worth protecting and their lives are worthy of respect. It's a way of sending a message to others who may be tempted to commit crimes like this." In the context of Duch's trial, Smith continued, "it's the Cambodian and international community's way of saying S-21 should never have happened and it should never happen again."[30]

"So what is a just sentence for this accused?" Smith asked. "It will depend on the gravity of the crimes, the impact on the victims and his role, the accused's role, in them. Do you believe him when he says that he was a hostage and a prisoner of the regime from 1971 until the mid-1990s?" As opposed to being a hostage, prisoner, or victim, Smith argued, Duch "was an idealist, a CPK revolutionary, a crusader who was prepared to sacrifice everything for his cause; prepared to torture and kill willingly for the good of the revolution, no matter how grotesquely misguided."[31] The Trial Chamber thus needed to resolve significant differences regarding intent. Following the OCP's final submission, Smith's closing arguments would highlight "the evidence of the extent and the nature of the accused's participation; and then, second, submit how his participation should be legally qualified under the law, and address [the] relevant factors we believe you should take into account when determining your sentence."[32]

He then began by summarizing the many facts suggesting Duch's criminality. Duch, Smith stated, was a "true believer" who was close to the apex of the CPK and enjoyed broad authority. "Nothing happened within S-21 without his knowledge or approval," in part because Duch was "meticulous, a logical man bordering on obsessive, a master of detail with a brilliant memory."[33] As opposed to being passive, Duch "implemented the extremist ideology of the CPK" in an "obsessive and merciless way."[34] At S-21, he was personally involved in the arrest and interrogation of prisoners like Ya and Koy Thuon. Documents demonstrated that Duch gave guidance and help catalyze the purges, a role further amplified by his analyses, reports, and summaries of confessions.

Duch's "indifference to the suffering of the victims," Smith told the court, reveals "a man who [had surrendered] himself so much to the purpose of S-21 that he could ignore one of the most human of impulses, to alleviate the pain of others."[35] In fact, Duch was "so hardened and absolute" that he "found no place for mercy for even his closest friends and associates." To illustrate this point, Smith reminded the court of how Duch's former teachers, Ke Kim Huot and his wife, Deum Sareaun, were "horribly tortured. Huot was beaten and forced to eat excrement. Sareaun was raped with a stick." Duch's denials about his role in such arrests were undermined by the fact that his "annotations [are] on the very pages describing the torture of Ke Kim Huot."[36] His mercilessness was further illustrated by Ya's interrogation, when Duch reassured Pon that if Ya died before confessing "it would not be a violation of revolutionary discipline."[37]

Duch's assertion that he simply relayed "information contained in the confessions" and passively followed orders was undercut by enormous evidence, including "documents containing the accused's direct written orders to kill. They are chilling in their unemotional, unapologetic, ruthless efficiency," with annotations like "Interrogate four; kill the rest" or simply "Smash."[38] Noting that Duch had admitted seeking to elevate the status of S-21, Smith asked: "How could someone be so proud [of] the reputation of such an evil place? It was because he believed."[39] Duch even chose to start a family at S-21, saying that he wanted his two children to join and "love the revolution."[40]

Duch, Smith suggested, was a zealot. On the last day of questioning, Duch had suddenly acknowledged this after François Roux asked, "Do you admit that in reality you were the man who, enjoying the trust of your superiors, implemented in a devoted and merciless fashion the persecution by the CPK of the Cambodian people in S-21?" Duch had replied, "Yes, I completely admit it."[41]

Finally, Smith suggested, Duch had "decided to admit the truth" in a "complete turnaround" from the defense's contention that he "hated his work, he lived in fear, he was forced to order the torture and killing with no choice." The change was "very late," and his lies had caused the civil parties "anguish." Duch needed to "set the record straight" and explain whether he was changing "his plea on motive."[42]

Ultimately, Smith said as he finished his comments on Duch's role and motivations at S-21, Duch had been a "willing participant" in the CPK crimes, a believer, "a perfectionist and a workaholic," fully aware of what was taking place. "We do not suggest that the accused is a monster nor do we say he is pathologically inhumane," Smith remarked. "However, we reject the suggestion he was a prisoner of the regime."[43] Moments later, Smith's words trailed into silence. He picked up his headphones, stood uncertain for a moment, and then sat down, with no sound.

Long ago, Duch had stopped looking at Smith. Slumped in his chair, Duch gazed at the ceiling, maybe in anger, perhaps ashamed, possibly praying to God.

| | | |

Due to technical difficulties, the proceedings were suspended until the next day, when Smith again took the floor. Smith—after arguing that Duch clearly met the indictment's charge of individual criminal responsibility as defined in article 29 of the ECCC Law (as someone who "planned, instigated, ordered, aided and abetted, or committed the crimes" at S-21)[44] and was part of a joint criminal enterprise—turned to sentencing.

Since the crimes were "unprecedented," Smith stated, Cambodian law offered little guidance. ECCC law simply specified a possible range for sentencing: five years to life.[45] Accordingly, the court needed to turn to international rules and precedent for direction. While aggravating and mitigating factors were relevant to sentencing, Smith noted that "it's widely accepted that the most important consideration in determining a sentence is the gravity or seriousness of the crime," which "is therefore, the starting point for the Chamber's deliberations."[46] In international law, three factors were central to assessing the gravity of a crime: "one, the nature of the crimes and the means by which they are committed; two, the extent of impact upon the victims; and three, the degree of participation of the accused."[47]

Smith took up each factor in turn, continuing the OCP's work of tying the facts and crimes to the legal frame laid out in the indictment and calibrating an appropriate sentence. The OCP's final submission provided a long list of factors linked to the nature and means of the crimes, including "the 'inherently shocking nature' or 'heinous character' of the crime; the number of victims, [and the magnitude and] scale of the crime."[48] Smith linked factual details from the case to each of these factors as he noted that at S-21 "more than 12,000 human lives were destroyed. A large percentage of these victims were brutally tortured. All suffered unspeakable conditions. Most significantly, these crimes . . . occurred daily, systematically and deliberately."[49]

For prisoners, Smith noted, "S-21 was a place of no return," one that had "permanently scarred" Vann Nath, Chum Mey, and Bou Meng. These three survivors, he continued, had "testified in graphic detail of their suffering," which had led to "emotional instability, anguish, anxiety, [and] nightmares," emotions also experienced by "a network of traumatized family members and friends" of S-21 victims that extended "across the entire world."[50]

With regard to the third component, gravity, Smith stated, participation could be direct or indirect in terms of superior orders—or both, in which case the gravity of the crime was more serious. This was also the case if a crime was committed knowingly and enthusiastically. In Duch's case, Smith held, all these factors were present. At S-21, Smith argued, Duch had "ordered his subordinates to interrogate and kill. By his own admission, he toured interrogation cells. He personally kicked and hit prisoners and caused prisoners to beat each other. His faith in the CPK was unqualified." Duch's crimes, Smith finished, "are rarely matched in modern history in terms of their combined barbarity, scope, duration, premeditation and callousness."[51]

In international law, Smith continued, aggravating and mitigating factors were also relevant to sentencing. Three aggravating factors applied to the Duch case. The first was "abuse of power." Instead of using his authority to fulfill his "legal and moral obligations to protect the rights of [his] detainees," Duch had instead overseen their "systematic mistreatment, torture and murder."[52] Moreover, S-21 was characterized by extreme "cruelty," a second aggravating factor, including crimes with a "particularly savage, sadistic or ruthless quality." To support his contention, Smith cited numerous facts, including "savage beatings," tortures, medical experimentation, and execution at Choeung Ek.

Ultimately, Duch's prisoners were "defenseless," the third aggravating factor. They were "starved, shackled, tortured, with no ability to defend themselves," Smith stated.[53]

Several mitigating factors—including duress, superior orders, cooperation, a guilty plea, remorse, illegal detention, and contribution to reconciliation—were central to Duch's defense, Smith said. While agreeing that Duch was entitled to a reduction in sentence for his illegal pretrial detention by the Cambodian Military Court starting in 1999, other mitigating factors were less relevant.

The defense, Smith noted, had repeatedly asserted that Duch had worked under duress and had to follow orders. Starting with Bizot's testimony about M-13, however, ample evidence demonstrated Duch was by no means "a hostage and prisoner of the CPK." As opposed to being "a victim of terror,"[54] he was one of its causes, "an enthusiastic and willing participant" who helped create the system of terror. Given his belief and "desire to advance the revolution and smash its enemies,"[55] Smith stated, Duch's claim of obedience to authority was without merit.

Continuing to link each mitigating factor to law and trial evidence, Smith turned to cooperation. Receiving credit for cooperation depended on "the quality and quantity of the information provided and whether it was given voluntarily and selflessly without asking for anything in return." If Duch deserved credit for his statements about the origins, structure, and implementation of CPK policy, he ultimately "only admitted part of the truth" about his personal responsibility by repeatedly invoking duress and superior orders.[56] This "lack of cooperation" in admitting responsibility, Smith argued, was reflected by a larger defense strategy that sought repeatedly to "limit the scope of the evidence and the ability of this Trial Chamber to review the relevant facts."[57]

This strategy, according to Smith, was evident from the start. During opening arguments, for example, the defense had challenged the court's jurisdiction even as it emphasized Duch's cooperation. During the M-13 trial phase, the defense objected to evidence suggesting that Duch "was an experienced, hardened torturer and killer well before arriving at S-21."[58]

To further hinder the flow of evidence, the defense had also sought to diminish witness testimony. They objected to the use of a reserve witness list that could "fill potential evidentiary gaps that may have been left if the scheduled witnesses suffered memory loss or were reluctant to tell the truth."[59] Relatedly, Smith went on, when the first of Duch's former staff members, Mam Nai (Chan), was about to testify, the defense "decided to take over the Court's role of advising [Mam Nai] . . . that if he testified" he might be tried in local courts—despite the fact this was unlikely. Moreover, this action "sent a message through the media to all remaining S-21 witnesses that testifying was a risky business."[60]

The defense also objected to the OCP's submission of detailed witnesses' summaries, a move "clearly motivated to ensure that the impact of the crimes and the role of the accused was less easily discoverable."[61] Smith noted that in international law, the use of such "comprehensive summaries of large amounts of evidence" was common and was meant to ensure "the focus is kept on key issues so that all the parties, including the Chamber, do not become lost in a sea of evidence. In effect, these tools are a road map to assist the Trial Chamber and the parties to understand the key issues."[62]

Smith's invocation of the "road map" alluded to the legal schema that underlay the OCP's closing arguments and the case more broadly. While the prosecution linked facts, law, and crimes to assert the legitimacy of its legal articulation in court, there was also a behind-the-scenes effort to make their case through the organization of information, much of it electronic. At various times, the parties made reference to databases like CaseMap, which allows facts and evidence to be coded and linked to the legal elements in the case.

Internally, the OCP sometimes referred to this legal data management system as the "issues tree," a metaphor connoting a legal trunk (the central legal argument that Duch committed crimes at S-21 with zeal), a crown (his particular crimes), and branches (the legal elements for each crime). "As each piece of evidence comes in, a document, transcript, or whatever," an OCP legal officer told me, a case manager will "create an entry in CaseMap" that is subsequently "tagged for all of the various branches to which it relates."[63] When someone clicks on a given "branch," he noted, CaseMap will show which of the 10,000–20,000 pieces of evidence have "been assessed as relevant to that issue."

Each of the court offices, he noted, worked with such databases, now common in international criminal law. Indeed, CaseMap and other databases provide a digital infrastructure to the legal articulation of the case, taking shape with the introductory submission and then modified as needed during the trial. Thus, the OCP jurist noted, when the Case 002 Closing Order had been issued, the OCP had to retag everything, a task that took several months. In many ways, the Closing Order, as well as the submissions, resembled an "issues tree."

As these comments suggest, in parallel with the courtroom contestations, there was a behind-the-scenes attempt to win the case through information management. Like the other offices, the OCIJ and the Trial Chamber have legal officers who use the same or similar databases. While there are rules separating the offices so they can't directly share databases, the OCP can seek to influence them by transferring the Excel lists of facts to the other offices, which can then import into their own version of CaseMap or whatever database they use.

More broadly, the OCP legal officer noted that one of the most important things in prosecuting a case was to present "a clear theory of the case. What do you say happened and how did it happen? Because it's only once you have that clear in your head that you can start to pitch it and to present it."[64] If Case-Map coding and data transfer constituted one part of the "pitch and presentation," so too did simplified summaries facilitating the analysis of evidence. One example was the creation of charts encapsulating enormous amounts of information in clear form. The witness summaries constituted a second example, particularly given that the judges selected witnesses. "So we have to convince them," the OCP jurist told me, that certain "witnesses should be heard or otherwise we can't get to the proof of things." It was critical to be "highly organized," which was why the OCP spent so much time translating "all that material . . . into something the judges can actually use."

| | |

The defense, Smith argued, had directly sought to impede the Trial Chamber's work by contesting the use of such summaries. This goal of obstructing the flow of information, he contended, extended to the introduction of trial evidence, as when the defense had objected to documentation in the Etcheson report. If the defense claimed such evidence was "unnecessary and repetitive," their actions "led to time-consuming and unnecessary argument before the Chamber." So, Smith asked, "What is the overall effect of the accused's cooperation with this Court?" If Duch provided information about the structure and functioning of S-21 and the CPK, he had been uncooperative "and not truthful about his role at S-21" and "less than co-operative by attempting to limit the evidence flow . . . to reduce this Chamber's ability to understand the full gravity and impact of the crimes and the accused's role in them."[65]

Smith turned to two other mitigating factors, admission of guilt and remorse. These interrelated factors required "a level of honesty and sincerity." Duch had exhibited neither; his conduct was better exemplified by his having been reproached by the Trial Chamber for "laughing, [for] gesturing and for [displaying] 'attitude' during questioning. The Chamber also censured the

Accused for using inappropriate language."[66] As illustrated by his refusal to accept Norng Chanphal's testimony, Duch had contested evidence and admitted only to actions for which there was clear proof. He generally lacked the ability to empathize, a trait noted in a report prepared by psychological experts. Critically, Duch's de facto guilty plea and expressions of remorse, Smith contended, were at odds with his failure to admit that he had "committed crimes as a devoted man with the enthusiasm and zeal of an ardent revolutionary."[67]

The last mitigating factor Smith discussed was reconciliation, to which the defense argued that Duch had contributed through his cooperation and remorse. While reconciliation was listed as a goal in the ECCC Agreement and could result in a reduction in sentence, Duch's contribution had been minimal. "The central purpose of this trial," Smith stated, "is to ascertain the truth, impose a just and proportionate sentence and end impunity . . . national reconciliation is a by-product of a criminal trial, not its purpose."[68] Duch's limited admissions, cooperation, and remorse, "while helpful," had not had "any discernable impact on peace in Cambodia or in the minds of the victims."[69] As opposed to giving Duch a reduced sentence, Smith stated, "the first step in righting the wrongs of S-21" was to make humanity "whole by sternly punishing one of its own for ignoring it so gravely."[70]

Bringing together the threads of his discussion, Smith concluded with the OCP's recommendation for sentencing. Duch, he noted, had been given "even-handed justice" and a fair trial that stood in stark contrast to the "brutality and inhumanity" the prisoners had endured at S-21. "The accused," Smith argued, "insured they were treated as animals. To him, they were enemies of the state who deserved no mercy and no compassion."[71] The conclusion of the OCP's final submission similarly stated that the brutality of the S-21 crimes "shocked the conscience of humankind to its core" and "defied comprehension," ranking among "the most extreme category of evil human beings are capable of inflicting."[72]

Despite his "repeated apologies and his tears" during the pretrial reenactment, Smith continued, Duch had sought to "minimize his role." He was not "a victim of the system," Smith went on, "but its loyal and dedicated agent," who made a choice and "abandoned his conscience. In fact, he abandoned every duty we, as human beings, owe to each other."[73] As opposed to being an ordinary man caught in a revolutionary machine he could not escape, Duch was "an extraordinary person" who "abandoned all moral concepts of right and wrong" and committed "monstrous crimes."[74]

Ultimately, Smith stated, "the primary focus of this trial must be the gravity of the crimes, the impact on the victims, and the accused's role in the infliction of that suffering. The sentence must reflect the destruction the accused perpetrated so willingly and enthusiastically."[75] Normally the appropriate sentence in such a situation would be life. Because of Duch's illegal detention, Smith said, the length of his sentence should be set at forty-five years, from which he deserved a limited five-year reduction due to mitigating factors. The appropriate sentence was therefore forty years.

Smith urged the Trial Chamber, in its deliberations, to "remember the stories" and suffering of the victims. "The whole of humanity," he continued, "demands a just and proportionate response to these crimes and this Court must speak on behalf of that humanity. It must punish the accused justly and send a clear message that crimes like these must never be perpetrated again."[76] The judgment of the Trial Chamber, Smith concluded, had to "speak for justice in finding this accused guilty and imposing the sentence we have recommended," one reflecting Duch's "criminal responsibility for more than 12,000 crimes. In imposing this penalty, you are not taking away the accused's humanity, but you are giving it back; back to the victims of S-21."[77]

Scapegoat
(DEFENSE)

Proof (Defense Closing Arguments, November 25, 2009)

"Objective."

With this word, Duch began to read his final remarks, titled "The continuous killing carried out by the Communist Party of Kampuchea (CPK)." Without looking up, he continued: "Ascertaining the general aspect from which a particular aspect can be derived in accordance with the general and particular principle, both being mutual contributors." This general aspect, he went on, "refers to the killing carried out by the CPK during its entire history, whereas the particular aspect refers to the crimes committed from 17 April 1975 to 6 January 1979, at S-21 in particular."[1]

Duch stood straight, hands at his sides, as he read. A different man seemed to be standing before the court from the slovenly-looking man who had sat slumped in his chair the day before. At times during the trial, he had seemed like a teacher; on other occasions he acted more like a lawyer than an accused. Today he took on the mantle of a jurist. He was ready to deliver his own verdict.

After thanking the Trial Chamber for the opportunity to speak, Duch, reading glasses on, raised his hands, two fingers from each supporting his handwritten statement. He would submit the document when he finished reading, his personal addition to the case file.

"Killings before 17 April 1975," Duch read. "One. The CPK began to kill people as soon as it began to carve out a liberated sector. Two . . ." The three-part list reminded me of Duch's annotations on Long Muy's confession. The pressed lettering was the same as that in Duch's communications to Pon regarding Ya's confession.

Duch, it quickly became apparent, was laying out an argument resembling something between a mathematician's proof and a legal judgment. It began with an axiom (the CPK killings were continuous) to be demonstrated. Given this axiom, and the fact that the general (the CPK's continuous killing) structured the particular (S-21 functioning from April 17, 1975, to January 6, 1979), it implicitly followed that the S-21 killing that took place was conditioned by the fact that the CPK killing was continuous, even if S-21 had a secondary influence on the process.

Duch's statement was devoted to proving this point, which would minimize his role in the violence. He proceeded by deduction, demonstrating the validity of his conclusion through a series of supporting facts backed by evidence, including CPK slogans and documents. Here his predilection for math converged with law, both of which drew on, but then ultimately stripped away, contextual detail in favor of the abstract (mathematical principles and law) so as to render articulations. Perhaps this similarity was part of the reason he had often seemed at ease in the courtroom, even if his level of comfort was uncanny—as were his final remarks.

The CPK killings, Duch stated, had begun as soon the CPK began to control territory, and were informed by an official policy of "smashing the enemy."[2] Initially applied to spies from areas under Lon Nol government control, the policy of killing soon extended to people living in Khmer Rouge zones who came under suspicion. "I was completely terrified at the destruction," Duch stated, "but I just did not know what I could do about it. The only option available to me was to devise a proper interrogation tactic."[3]

To do so, Duch recruited Pon and interrogated a former journalist. "We learnt on the job," Duch recalled. "It took us more than a month to complete that interrogation. Unexpectedly, my commitment and the skill Pon and I developed had plunged us deep into a criminal act. We were made to work endlessly. The work we were assigned was criminal."[4] Duch was using the passive voice.

The spiral of violence escalated as internal purges began, many of which, Duch contended, were catalyzed by Mok, whom Duch portrayed throughout as a key driver of the killings. As increasing numbers of prisoners arrived at M-13, the security office had no choice but to interrogate them. "Anyone the party identified as an 'enemy,' " Duch remarked, "had to be smashed. The Chief of [a] Police Office had no right to challenge such decision[s]." This command structure extended to the use of violence, as "physical torture was a method they made us use. Most often it was inevitable."[5] Duch named Chhay Kim Hor and Vorn Vet as the ones who ordered him to use torture.

Turning to "Killings after 17 April 1975," Duch described how the CPK organized the secret killing of former Lon Nol officials and high-ranking monks during the evacuation, even as they began to register people "to screen for elements to be smashed."[6] The second phase of violence lasted from the promulgation of the March 30, 1976 Decision, until the end of DK. Duch repeatedly made note of the four groups who were authorized to "smash" and therefore were most responsible for the violence.

Duch's statement detailed the purges, catalyzed by the April 2, 1976, grenade attack and Koy Thuon's arrest, which "terrified me" because "as a child of the north, I could do nothing to help."[7] Over time, Mok increasingly gained power, since the "CPK regarded Mok and his people as the top people who could solve every problem" because of their pure peasant origins.[8] In the end, the CPK "chose to use killing as [the] means to solve each and every problem."[9]

Having laid out this "general" principle of the CPK killing as continuous, Duch next turned to the particular: the individual security centers. S-21, he noted, was one of 196 such offices that operated in a similar manner. All were "under the clear organizational supervision of the Party" and under orders to extract confessions.[10] The use of torture "was mostly inevitable [and] a permitted tactic" that was "employed at all Santebal [Security] offices."[11] The violence was determined by the Party, since the security offices "had no right to smash."[12]

By the time Duch discussed what was "unique" about S-21, he was 24 pages into his statement. S-21 was distinct, he acknowledged, because it was the place where high-ranking cadre whom Pol Pot regarded as "thorns in his eyes" were sent.[13] Nevertheless, "all Santebal offices received orders to smash," and the head of S-21 had no greater power than the heads of other DK prisons. As for the "Crimes at S-21," Duch discussed his limited role under Nat, who, Duch noted, violated the party line by secretly arresting 62 people. Duch's only comment about the period he served as chairman was a single line: "I always and forever [will] be responsible for at least 12,380 lives."[14] He left it to the court to deliberate "other aspects" of the S-21 crimes.

Duch concluded with a brief statement titled "About my position and behavior." The "monumental destruction both within and outside the ranks," he declared, "is solely the crime committed by the" CPK and its leader, Pol

Pot.[15] Since he was a member of the CPK, Duch was "psychologically account-able" for this "mind-boggling" destruction. "A decision to choose which path to walk is made in a matter of seconds," he lamented, while the consequences of a "wrong choice will result in lifelong remorse."[16] Thus Duch had joined the revolution for noble reasons, only to find himself "serving a criminal organization which destroys its own people in an outrageous fashion. I could not withdraw from it. I was just like a cog in a running machine."[17]

Then Duch apologized again. "I am solely and individually liable," he said, "for the loss of at least 12,380 lives" and "wish to most respectfully and humbly apologize to the dead souls." He acknowledged his crimes "in the legal and moral context." Yet, as opposed to simply apologizing, he again seemed to offer a qualification. If he were responsible only in some ways, then in what ways was he not responsible? Regardless, he asked the victims "to kindly leave [the] door open" for forgiveness and hoped that one day others would "recognize me again as part of humankind."[18]

Although he had reached the end of his statement, Duch was not finished. He proceeded to read out his footnotes, one at a time, completely decontextualized. A man obsessed by procedure, meticulous and exact, lacked a fundamental awareness of context. As his final "proof" suggested, Duch the mathematician preferred abstract principles distilled from the messiness of real world detail. This orientation was well suited for the head of S-21, an institution where people were classified as enemies, impurities to be "smashed" for the sake of abstract principle and the Party line—a DK articulation that, to be asserted, demanded the erasure of human life. Duch, the man who had failed to recognize the humanity of his victims in implementing this vision, now pleaded, in an arena of abstract law, to be seen as human.

"Mr. President, I would like to submit this document to the court," Duch concluded, as he began reordering the loose pages of his statement, carefully tapping the edges of the stack until each made a clean, straight line.

Duch would speak again. Two days later, with a point of his finger, he made another choice that fundamentally changed the trial and perhaps his life, suddenly blurring an assumption everyone had thought was clear.

The Wrong Man (Kar Savuth, Defense Closing Arguments, November 25, 2009)

What Duch had argued with a math teacher's precision his lawyers framed in juridical terms.

Duch was a "scapegoat," co-defense lawyer Kar Savuth told the court, asking if this was the standard of justice the Trial Chamber wished to uphold. For, as Duch had suggested in his final remarks, S-21 was just one of at least 196 DK prisons and ranked just tenth in terms of the numbers killed.[19] "Why," Kar Savuth asked, raising his voice for emphasis, was only Duch being tried while the heads of the other prisons were "living free? Each prison used the same torture, the same murder under the same order from Angkar."[20] The Cambodian Constitution guaranteed equality, Kar Savuth stated, before asking: "Is the[re] equality here?"[21]

Kar Savuth's arguments reflected several defense objectives. The first, an OCP legal officer told me, was to "act according to their client's instructions . . . [and] present the defense the accused wants."[22] Accordingly, a defense lawyer might put forward a guilty plea or, if not guilty, challenge incriminating evidence. And, when possible, a defense lawyer's role was "to bring out evidence that might mitigate, to make [the act] more understandable, the action less serious by bringing other factors into account."[23]

In carrying out these tasks, the OCP legal officer noted, the defense had to ensure that "the rights provided to [an accused] under law," including fair trial rights, were being safeguarded. As with the OCP, the work of the defense was also structured in terms of the overarching legal frame in the introductory submission and closing order. In contrast to the goals of other offices, the objective of the defense lawyers, assuming that their client wanted to contest parts of the indictment, was to cast doubt on the evidence and on ways the prosecution was linking facts to law.

If the OCP had to prove its case beyond a reasonable doubt, the defense had nothing to prove. Another OCP legal officer told me: "It's more of a demolition job . . . than providing a coherent, clear structure. For them, it could be a job of picking your best battles and fighting them really hard [while] hoping to put enough holes in the walls of the prosecution's case to make it not stick."[24] Even as the defense was critical to pushing the case to a conclusion in the verdict, their role also opened the door to that which the prosecution's case had pushed out of sight and thereby provided a space in which the uncanny might suddenly erupt, as it did on the last day.

Both Kar Savuth's and Roux's closing arguments can be seen in this light. Thus Kar Savuth sought to question the legitimacy of the court to try Duch. The court was, he suggested, violating the Cambodian Constitution as well as the statute of limitations (by applying the 1956 Cambodian Penal Code).

Following what was implicit in Duch's statement, Kar Savuth challenged the court's jurisdiction by claiming that Duch was a scapegoat. On the one hand Duch was just one of almost 200 DK prison chiefs who had merely carried out superior orders. On the other hand authority was vested in a small group of criminal "masterminds" authorized to "smash" enemies.[25] Pol Pot, Nuon Chea, and Son Sen gave the orders, not Duch. For these reasons, Kar Savuth concluded, "Duch is not guilty . . . so I request that Your Honors acquit Duch and drop the charges."[26]

Duch, Kar Savuth had just told the court, should be freed.

A tension at the heart of Duch's defense, underlying the simultaneous claim that he was a scapegoat and was a person who accepted responsibility for the S-21 crimes, suddenly broke into the open. Many observers were shocked, particularly given that Duch had just apologized. Perhaps stunned as well, François Roux asked if he could delay his closing remarks until the following day.

Human (François Roux, Defense Closing Arguments, November 26, 2009)

The next morning, Roux apologized.

"For reasons that will be clear to legal practitioners," he began, "we have had to review the entire plan of our proceedings because of Mr. Kar Savuth's pleadings yesterday."[27] As everyone could see, Roux acknowledged, "our team has not labored without disagreements."[28] Roux left it to Kar Savuth to reply to some of his co-lawyer's "exceptional objections that are not admissible," including Kar Savuth's challenge to the court's jurisdiction.[29] Nevertheless, the court was now confronted with a contradictory defense. "We cannot, on the one hand, ask for the acquittal of the accused, which would mean that he is not guilty," Roux noted, "as well as enter a guilty plea. This has been expressed publicly. The accused will not plead guilty."[30]

Before turning to his substantive arguments, Roux thanked his legal team and announced that, after thirty-seven years, "this will be my last pleading as a lawyer."[31] His closing remarks, he said, were dedicated to his grandchildren and the younger generation. While he had "stood tall" in carrying out the "noble" task of defending an accused, he was still, "beneath the gown . . . a human being," deeply disturbed by what the victims endured.

Because of "my compassion and my respect as a human being," Roux continued, he was pleased by this "first step on the road to catharsis . . . this little drop of water [that] will come to cool the suffering" and should be celebrated.[32] So, too, should the extent of civil party participation in the trial, a "first" in international justice. Despite the difficulties, "here we are," Roux said. "We've done it."[33]

Nevertheless, Roux went on, a golden opportunity had been missed. The defense had "sought to maintain dialogue with the [OCP]," a discussion that could have been a "historical moment for this country" as the defense and prosecution worked together to "build the truth" with "an accused who recognizes his guilt" and who had, in his final remarks just the day before, "apologize[d] on his knees."[34] There was a strong model for such cooperation, Roux contended, at the International Criminal Tribunal for the Former Yugoslavia, where a former officer had admitted his responsibility and cooperated with the prosecution. Roux asked that a film clip from that trial be played and then discussed the ways the officer, Mr. Obrenovic, had helped with the truth-seeking process, peace, and reconciliation.

"This is what this trial should have been," Roux told the court.[35] Instead of welcoming this opportunity, the OCP had "missed its date with history."[36] By suggesting that Duch was not telling all, the prosecutors had contributed to the frustration of the victims. "What a waste," Roux lamented.[37]

The OCP had responded to this historic opportunity with a conventional argument, Roux claimed, one asserted at the Nuremberg Trials and "whose underlying philosophy is as follows. This man is a monster even though they said 'I am not saying this man is a monster.' In fact, the attempt was to portray him as such." Instead of asserting such trite arguments, "we must go further, we must try to understand the mechanisms that lead a man, who is a decent man by all accounts, [to become] a torturer."[38] The defense, he promised, would grapple with the underlying problems that led this to happen.

In some ancient societies, Roux noted, a scapegoat "was loaded with all the evils, with all the suffering of a society. All of this was loaded onto the head of a goat. Amongst the Hebrews, the goat was sent into the desert so that social group could be reformed because they would say, 'This goat bears all our wrongdoings.'"[39] Duch should not be used as a scapegoat, left to "bear on his head all the horrors of the Cambodian tragedy. No, Duch is not the person you described, Mr. Co-Prosecutor."[40]

Civil party lawyer accusations that Duch was shedding "crocodile tears" or "enjoyed converting human beings into torturers" were similarly misdirected.[41] Given the relatively small number of people who perished at S-21, it was outlandish to try to amplify Duch's guilt to encompass killings all over the country. "How dare you," Roux admonished the prosecution, while noting, in contrast, "I will not use suppositions, not untruths, not exaggerations, not truncated quotations."[42]

Instead, Roux said, he would highlight key aspects of the trial. From the beginning, he noted, Duch had admitted most of the facts in the case. In the defense's final submission, the defense team had claimed that this admission, in which Duch had only disputed 33 of the 132 paragraphs in the Closing Order, amounted to a confession.[43] This 19-page submission also mirrored the Closing Order in being divided into sections on "The Facts," "The Law," and "Sentence." The document argued that the prosecution had not proven beyond a reasonable doubt the disputed facts, including the assertion that Duch had had the authority to arrest people or had himself tortured and executed prisoners. Along these lines and echoing Duch's final statement, Roux argued that it was a "rewriting of history" to assert that Duch had the power to influence the larger events of DK. Duch, Roux told the court, had "no choice" and was forced to carry out the "terrible, sinister task [he] was given."[44] Authority lay with his superiors, as illustrated by the March 30, 1976 Decision.

Great weight, Roux argued, should be given to mitigating factors. In addition to agreeing to most of the facts, Duch had repeatedly admitted his responsibility. When Judge Lavergne had asked if Duch acknowledged degrading and dehumanizing the terrified prisoners, Roux reminded the court, Duch had replied that he did.[45] Similarly, Duch had affirmed his cowardice, saying "I closed my eyes; I closed my ears. I did not want to see."[46] He likewise admitted that he had acted in a "devoted and merciless manner."[47] His cooperation extended to the pretrial reenactment, to which he had agreed voluntarily, despite the difficulty of returning to Tuol Sleng and Choeung Ek and meeting his former victims. He had shown his remorse at this time. On seeing the tree against which children were bashed at Choeung Ek, for example, Duch fell on his "knees and [honored] the souls of those who perished."[48]

The defense, Roux continued, had one advantage that the prosecution lacked: direct contact with Duch. "We meet with the accused person in his prison cell in private moments when he is able to . . . speak freely from the heart," Roux told the court. "We see what you . . . are unable to see," including moments when Duch had collapsed in tears. "That is what we bear witness to," Roux stated. "And that is what I testify to today."[49]

Roux had slipped into the role of witness.

"The problem," Roux continued, returning to how Duch came to commit his crimes, is that he "was the perfect disciple of the Party line as had been defined and perfected by his superiors,"[50] a young revolutionary drawn to the movement's ideals who sought to fulfill the tasks he was assigned, even if they were abhorrent. The Khmer Rouge cultivated such cadre, Roux went on, by seeking to destroy their personalities, which were regarded as counterrevolutionary and individualist. "I can only believe [Duch]," Roux asserted, "when he says to me, 'I did not want to be the head of S-21.' And by the way, did you ever ask yourselves, Mr. Co-Prosecutors, gentlemen, if [Duch] was the man that you are describing?"[51] Ultimately, Duch was a "slavish servant," whose identity was transformed and who lost the ability to feel empathy, serving at the behest of "his masters."

To understand Duch, Roux argued, these sorts of factors need to be taken into account. Doing so was uncomfortable, since it was easier "to consider Duch as a monster, as someone who is perverse, someone that we're going to alienate from society" by giving him what was effectively a life sentence, as the prosecution had proposed. Duch was guilty and needed to be sentenced. But ultimately, to stop such crimes from recurring, it was necessary to examine "with lucidity the phenomena that lead a normal man to become one day an executioner. This phenomenon is . . . [the] crime of obedience."[52]

For more than three decades, Roux stated, he had defended cases of civil disobedience. Disobedience, he noted, was not easy and had to be learned, a point that historian David Chandler had made during his testimony and that was suggested by experimental evidence, including the Milgram shock experiments in which "sixty percent of the people, just like you, just like me . . . obeyed the orders of the [authority figure] wearing the white smock, pressed the [shock] button all the way down to the mortal [danger level]."[53]

Obedience, Roux continued, is something that is a part of our everyday lives, as we receive orders from bosses and give orders to others in our institutional worlds. "That's how we all operate," Roux claimed.[54] We needed to ask ourselves, if we were placed in a situation like the one Duch faced, "What would I have done?" In the last sentence of his book on S-21, Chandler had offered an insight that, Roux contended, should have been a key understanding emerging from a constructive dialogue between the OCP and the defense. Chandler states: "To find the source of the evil that was enacted at S-21 on a daily basis, we need look no further than ourselves."[55] This idea, Roux asserted, was "far removed from the very easy explanation of identifying a scapegoat."[56]

After a brief discussion of legal and evidentiary issues, Roux returned to Duch's personality. A number of character witnesses had described him as "a humble man, a simple man, a generous man, a respectful man. He was an honest man. He was a calm man. He was a sweet man. He was a nice man.

Words like that can be found in their testimony."[57] It was necessary to see the "journey on which the accused person finds himself,"[58] one that, the psychological experts who had evaluated Duch had explained, was difficult and a prolonged process. Moreover, people suffering from trauma have a tendency to avoid painful recollections about traumatizing events. This could lead to "partial amnesia" or even "total emotional insensitivity." Perhaps, Roux suggested, this had something to do with the reluctance Duch had sometimes shown when speaking about painful memories, such as the arrest of his teachers. "I do not know any more than you," Roux claimed. "I am only noticing."[59]

"What is the point of the sentence?"[60] Roux queried as his closing argument drew to an end. If punishment was an obvious aim, rehabilitation was also important. And banishment was not rehabilitation. Instead, Roux suggested, the Trial Chamber should consider creative options, such as "turning Duch into a simple gardener, yes, I [can] see him at Choeung Ek . . . explaining to the younger generations what should not be done" and how it is possible to make a decision you forever regret.[61] "So can Duch still be useful to humanity?" Roux asked the judges. "That is the question that you will [need to] ask yourselves."[62]

Duch, Roux noted, had already been imprisoned for 10 years and was a fugitive on the run for 20 more. "Please take this into account," he pleaded. Roux recalled a conversation with a Cambodian man who told him that "Buddhists say that the evil that you do, you'll receive it in return and he said, 'Duch has already paid for the evil that he committed. Send him back home' . . . that's what I heard. He paid. He paid for the evil that he committed. Please send him home."[63]

To conclude, Roux recounted a Cambodian story about a wise man who, Roux said, had a universal message. Roux continued, "It could be the story of an old imam, an old rabbi, a philosopher, a priest or a pastor or—in this country—a Buddhist monk."[64] One day the wise man asked his disciples, "How do we know that we are moving from night to day, from the shadows to the light?" The first discipline replied, "When we begin to distinguish the colour of the mango leaves." The second said, "When you begin to see the [mountains] in the distance." The third one got it right when he said, "When you can recognize your brother in another's eyes."[65]

"Duch," Roux said to his client, "all your victims were your brothers and sisters in humanity." Roux continued: "You said that you had been cowardly and that you did not go to see them while they were in detention. In human eyes, you will never be absolved of these crimes and the eyes of those you did not wish to meet will remain on you forever."

"What about us, Your Honours?" Roux asked the Trial Chamber. "Are we prepared to look Duch in the eye and see him for the fellow human that he is?" Are you, Roux continued, ready to "bring back Duch into the fold of humanity?"

"Duch is dead," Roux finished.[66]

Mathematician (Rebuttals, November 26–27, 2009)

Then the rebuttals began. Everyone, Judge Nil warned, needed to keep their remarks focused on a common object, the judgment. Civil party co-lawyer Karim Khan was the first to take the floor.

After acknowledging Roux's "last occasion in robes" and his "elegant statements," Khan said, "there will not be any philosophy from me and nor will my statements be anywhere near as erudite."[67] "My task," he continued, was "to focus on some evidence that may assist Your Honors in determining the truth"[68] and that supported the claims of Khan's clients. Accordingly, the proceedings should be focused "on the conduct, the character, the evidence and the guilt or otherwise of the gentleman that sits in the dock."

"Now, Your Honors," Khan stated, "there's no soft way to put this, but it is my respectful submission that the accused in this case has sought to ride two horses."[69] The day before, "at the last possible moment . . . things changed" when the accused switched from a de facto guilty plea to a demand to be released.[70]

Khan noted that Roux had "with his usual charm and verve" claimed that the prosecution had missed its date with history. In fact, it was Duch who had "missed an important opportunity to actually speak clearly, unequivocally, spontaneously, candidly to the Court." His attitude was illustrated by the way he had "physically turned away during the important part of the submission of the Co-Prosecutor."[71] Instead of responding to the "pain and plight of the civil parties" in his final statement, Duch had given "a carefully scripted, carefully constructed, paragraph by paragraph, footnote by footnote statement."

Ultimately, the Trial Chamber would need to "gaug[e] the demeanor" of the accused and, "after reviewing all of the evidence, to make an objective and dispassionate assessment as to his genuineness of remorse."[72] Such contrition and truthfulness were valuable to the civil parties. "Indeed," Khan stated, "it is the only thing that the gentleman in the dock can offer those civil parties . . . whose lives have been torn, shattered and smashed because of [Duch]."

Roux had sought to prove Duch's contrition, Khan noted, when Roux asked, "Well, who can dispute [Duch's] tears?" Tears, however, were not "determinative" of remorse. Moreover, Duch had only cried three times during a lengthy trial. In contrast, Khan noted the emotional struggles of the civil parties. "At the end of the day," Khan contended, a person cannot "peer into the heart of another individual."[73]

As for when "my learned friend lifted the veil of legal privilege and sought to give an account of the accused's demeanor in private consultations," Khan said, the court rules specified that "the only evidence that is probative and admissible is the evidence that has been tested and put before the Chamber."[74] If Roux's account had been "eloquent [and] riveting," it was "legally irrelevant" and unsubstantiated. "This is a court of law," Khan stated, "not a forum for unsupported hypotheses to be brought like a conjurer's rabbit out of the hat at the last moment."[75]

Recalling Duch's comment that a decision about "which path to walk" is made in a moment while the consequences could last a lifetime, Khan contended that this assertion was inaccurate since Duch had made numerous choices. With regard to the 12,380 victims, "there were 12,380 moments when the accused could have done the right thing." Moreover, despite the overwhelming evidence in the case, Duch remained, as his final remarks attested, "content to leave matters opaque, contradictory and ambiguous."[76] The civil parties, in contrast, wanted "the truth, they want their lives back, they want some kind of closure and it is simply unacceptable from every angle that we are left in this chaotic state of affairs," with Duch pleading not guilty yet accepting responsibility and expressing contrition.[77]

Lawyers from the other civil party teams added to the criticisms of the defense. Studzinsky complained that Duch's sudden change was "a slap in the face of the civil parties," leading to "serious additional traumati[zation]."[78] The civil parties, she said, were more than ever convinced of Duch's duplicity. He had been "playing a game," and the "time has come to shed the sheep's clothing."[79]

Martine Jacquin, in turn, told Duch, "You are not a scapegoat. . . . But you are a symbol . . . [of] the denegation of responsibility."[80] Her colleague Philippe Cannone added that instead of "true contrition," the civil parties had only heard from Duch a "litany of administrative details." Perhaps, Cannone pondered, "this gentleman has not understood a single thing," stuck in his "methodical mind set. He is still lost in his footnotes."[81]

"Your Honours," Bill Smith said the next morning as the OCP began its rebuttals, "the prosecution take[s] great exception to the remarks by the defense made yesterday that we have been representing this case by untruths, stating things that are not based on the evidence." He invited the court to look at the OCP's "final submission with 1,000 footnotes, [158] pages which support everything we have said about this case from beginning to end."[82] He trusted the Trial Chamber would "scrutinize these claims by the defense by actually looking at the evidence, rather than the rhetoric."

The court, Smith claimed, had been "grossly misled by the defense." After proceeding throughout the trial with a de facto guilty plea, which everyone had been taking for granted, it was unacceptable that, at the very end of the trial, the defense suddenly "asked for an acquittal for this accused, for a man that says he's co-operating."[83] To avoid an appeal, the court needed to clarify "whether or not this accused instructed his counsel to ask for an acquittal . . . this needs to be resolved before we leave the courtroom."[84]

After Chea Leang rebutted a number of the defense's legal claims, Smith again took the floor to finish. He noted that Duch's trial differed fundamentally from the Obrenovic trial, which had involved an "upstanding military officer," not someone who, Smith noted, had told Bizot that he beat prisoners "until I'm out of breath."[85]

The defense, Smith pointed out, kept saying that the S-21 crimes were acts that anyone might commit. "Well," Smith continued, "ordinary people don't commit these types of crimes."[86] As for Duch's argument that he was a minor "cog in the machine" who had no choice, Smith again directed the judges' attention to Duch's annotations, teaching about torture, and proposals to make further arrests.[87] This evidence, Smith argued, provided "a clear photograph of the state of mind of the accused back in 1975 to 1979."[88]

In his final statement, Smith went on, Duch had an opportunity to publically acknowledge his crimes. He might have turned to the civil parties and said " 'Yes, I did believe in the CPK. It was madness. I did terrible things but I believed in it. I believed it was a means to an end.' That's what the evidence says. That's what the hundreds and hundreds of annotations say."[89] Instead of doing this, Duch "shut the door" on the victims. Ultimately, the case was not about revenge but "about respecting the humanity of this accused . . . [and] the victims at S-21." Smith urged the judges to render "a judgment to be proud of rather than the ones handed down by the accused many years ago."[90]

| | | |

When the defense next took the floor, Kar Savuth and Roux reiterated many of their points, with Kar Savuth again asserting that Duch was a scapegoat who did not fall within the court's jurisdiction. "Release my client," Kar Savuth urged. "Allow him to go home."[91]

Roux noted that the defense lawyers had not built an independent strategy but instead had sought "to convert into a legal framework what the accused has been saying since 1999 when he was arrested."[92] This framework was reflected in Duch's final remarks as well as Roux's rebuttal that Duch was "just a link in the chain of command that went from Pol Pot down to the smallest ranking guard at S-21." Duch was trapped in this system, Roux contended, in which "each one in his way passed on orders and each one imposed upon his subordinates to enforce these orders." Roux advised, "Never forget the decision from March 30, 1976."[93]

Duch had nevertheless believed in the regime and followed orders. This was, Roux stated, Duch's "tragedy." Yet, Roux said, "with or without Duch, S-21 would have continued," since it was ultimately a "killing machine in the hands of Son Sen." After joining the revolution for good ends, Duch became "lost." He was now seeking his way back to humanity.

It had not been an easy journey. A psychological report, Roux reiterated, had stated that "before dehumanizing their victims the executioners" were themselves dehumanized, as was the case with Duch, whose personality was refashioned by the Khmer Rouge. "No one is born an executioner," Roux went on; "one becomes so, and we can also be re-humanized," even if this involves a difficult path.[94]

While it could never "repair the suffering of the victims," a sentence, Roux said, raising his voice for emphasis, should "take into account all of the restorative aspects of justice," including apologies, contrition, a guilty plea, and a defendant's character and process of transformation."[95] This was particularly important since criminal justice was no longer on a "primitive level" that followed "the eye-for-eye and tooth-for-tooth law."[96] It was also fair, since there were former Khmer Rouge "who had more blood on their hands than the accused" and were not being tried. "Let's be fair," Roux urged. "Your decision should take all of this into account. It is the only means not to turn Duch, in-deed, into a scapegoat."[97]

"Yesterday," Roux recalled, "I said to you Duch is dead."[98] During the trial, Duch had noted how he was transformed "from an ordinary person to a communist person. That was during 1964 through my training and temper-ing. And the Party recognized me . . . [as] a Party member. So I was a new Duch, who was so different from Kaing Guek Eav, who was a math profes-sor in school."[99] The case file, Roux concluded, contained ample evidence to confirm that this revolutionary "Duch is dead and that we are now facing again Mr. Kaing Guek Eav."[100]

Almost immediately, Bill Smith stood up. "We note the international Co-Prosecutor is on his feet," Judge Nil said. "You may proceed."[101]

"The defense," Smith stated, "has evaded your question in relation to why this change of plea." It was unacceptable, he continued, for the defense to effectively run two defenses at the same time, asking for both mitigation and acquittal. Smith suggested Duch be asked directly if he had instructed his counsel to enter pleas of acquittal on all charges. "Otherwise you will leave this courtroom with two defenses" and the possibility of appeal. The trial was "a very, very costly exercise, Your Honour," Smith cautioned. "I would ask that [this issue] be resolved now."[102]

Despite Roux's protestation that the prosecution did not have the right to speak after defense rebuttals, the Trial Chamber decided to give the floor to Duch. Duch reiterated that he had fully cooperated during the proceed-ings, answering all the questions posed by the OCIJ and OCP. "The records of the interviews at the ECCC are . . . evidence and proof," he said. He had also apologized, expressed remorse, and admitted his guilt as a member of the CPK and the head of S-21, he said, even if he was not one of the top leaders. "I [have] been detained from 8th of May 1999 until now, it has been 10 years al-ready—10 years, six months, 18 days," Duch ended, "So I would ask the Cham-ber to release me."[103]

The judges huddled once more, and then Judge Nil asked Duch, who was sitting in the dock, to stand. "What made you ask for the release?" Judge Nil asked. "Would you ask the Chamber to acquit all charges against you or would you want the Court to reduce the sentence, based on your co-operation? . . . Could you please clarify?"[104]

"My ability to analyze is limited," Duch replied. "I would like the Chamber to release me and if Your Honours may, please allow my co-counsel, Mr. Kar

Savuth, to say a few more words."[105] Faced with two legal paths, Duch had decisively made his choice.

The proceedings, Judge Nil commented, had become "rather strange." Since Duch had "point[ed] to his national co-lawyer for help," Judge Nil continued, "the chamber would allow Mr. Kar Savuth to clarify."[106]

Duch, Kar Savuth told the court, his voice booming as he waved his hands in the air, had not been a senior leader and, as illustrated by the March 30, 1976 Decision, had not had "the right and authority to smash." Duch had "only obeyed the CPK. So the CPK was the culprit.... That's why my client asked that he be released."[107]

"Do I infer from your last comments," Judge Cartwright asked Kar Savuth, "that the accused is seeking an acquittal?"

"Thank you, Your Honour," Kar Savuth replied. "Release means acquittal."[108]

The Accused

(TRIAL CHAMBER JUDGMENT)

"Detention Guards, bring the accused, Kaing Guek Eav, alias Duch, to the dock."

On July 26, 2010, Judge Nil gave these instructions at the start of the culminating moment in Duch's trial, the verdict. As he spoke, the security guards escorted Duch to the court's wooden dock, made up of two horseshoe-shaped beams connected by posts.

I thought of the iron bar windows at Tuol Sleng.

| | | |

The similarity was not coincidental. In the Western legal tradition, especially the British legal tradition, docks have long referred to enclosures for those on trial, and the term is thought to be etymologically related to slang for an animal pen or cage.[1]

This sense of domestication is captured by other meanings. "Dock" can refer to a type of coarse weed or the "solid fleshy part of an animal's tail."[2] A related verb form of "dock" means to cut short, as in docking an animal's tail or reducing wages. In both cases, "dock" suggests reduction from excess. Relatedly, "dock" suggests transformation, a notion highlighted by perhaps the term's most common usage, "dock" as a low-water berth connected to a pier where ships load or unload cargo or receive repairs. "To dock" thus suggests the reconnection of the wild (rivers and oceans) with the civilized (cultivated land as in a port). The courtroom dock retains these connotations, signifying a space in which the wild and dangerous—a criminal defendant—is placed in a secure berth connecting the accused with the civilized, which is epitomized by law and domesticates through legal process.

The judges oversee this process of purification, which has the aura of the sacred. At the ECCC, Judge Nil and his colleagues wore robes and sat on a raised dais across from Duch. An empty space, "the well," lay between them. While the court was in session, it was usually taboo to traverse this area, which metaphorically suggests purity (a place where untainted substances, such as spring water, are accessed) and revelation (as that which lies hidden below is brought to the surface). All the court personnel remained at their "stations" during the proceedings, rising from their seats only to pay respect when the Trial Chamber entered or left the court ("all rise") or when they sought "standing" from the judges, who metonymically stood for "the court," to speak. Everyone is expected to display deference toward the Trial Chamber, as is illustrated by the honorifics used.

Those who violated court etiquette might be sanctioned, both through verbal reprimands (chastising a lawyer for tone or language), formal sanctions (holding someone "in contempt of court" or ordering his or her microphone turned off), or nonverbal actions (ignoring an unruly lawyer). All these actions took place during ECCC proceedings.

The court's authority in such matters, large and small, was symbolized by the ECCC logo, which was prominently displayed on the wall behind the judges. This insignia was omnipresent at the court, affixed as a badge on the robes of the judges and lawyers, placed on every official ECCC document, even stenciled into the armrests of the seats in the public gallery. This authority is reinforced by the presence of blue-shirted security personnel in the courtroom and public gallery, where spectators who fall asleep, chat, or put their feet up are quickly reprimanded.

To reach the public gallery requires crossing through a roadside checkpoint, registering at a security gate, passing through an X-ray machine, handing over electronic devices, and being searched prior to entering the public gallery, which is separated from the courtroom by a wall of presumably bulletproof glass. Before a session begins, a recording instructs participants on proper behavior, including the need to remain seated while the court is in session. By the time the curtain opens as the judges enter, everyone in the gallery is primed to rise. The movement of visitors is highly restricted, as they are cordoned into two areas, the public gallery and an outside courtyard that is fenced and guarded. Moving outside these spaces requires permission.

If these security precautions ensure the safety of the defendant and court personnel, they also signify the authority of the court and, by extension, the state and international community. The high level of security creates a sense of unease, a feeling heightened by the spatial context of the court (located on the outskirts of Phnom Penh in a secure compound adjoining a headquarters of the National Police) and by monitoring from at least three points.

First, omnipresent security officers constantly scan for misbehavior. Second, court cameras record the proceedings. The footage, which shifts in perspective and includes background shots of the audience, is displayed on screens in the public gallery. Inside the courtroom, the feed runs on monitors placed before the participants, who also have a computer allowing access to key files. There is also a monitor on a small desk inside the dock, at which Duch sometimes glanced. Trial footage is shown on TV and on the Internet. Such "recordings" always involve a redaction, as a single shot comes to stand for the proceedings as a whole, erasing what transpires in the gallery and court spaces out of sight.

Finally, the Trial Chamber has a dominant gaze during the proceedings. From their raised dais by the back wall of the court, the judges have the clearest view of the courtroom and public gallery. When they see signs of disruptive behavior, they may contact security. They also "rule" the court. If a point is contested, the parties appeal to the judges, who might confer, retire to chambers, or defer or render a decision, referred to as a "ruling."

The judges monitor the proceedings in more mundane ways, ranging from ensuring that the proceedings stay on track and parties remain within their time allocations, part of the frequently invoked need for "time management" to ensure fair trial rights. Beyond this institutional monitoring, the court itself was observed by monitoring groups, the media, and NGOs.

As opposed to being neutral, then, the space of a court asserts an order and structures the proceedings in various ways. Positioning demarcates a classification and status. The empty space of the courtroom is filled with desks, chairs, and objects like cameras and checkpoints, which create borders and demarcate status and difference—ranging from the raised dais of the judges, signifying the court's authority and hierarchical preeminence, to the barred dock of criminality and contagion.

The prosecution and defense are positioned opposite one another, separated by the gulf of the well. Civil parties sit next to the prosecution, with whom they are allied in proving the guilt of the accused. Each team is afforded rights and obligations to be exercised within the parameters of the court procedures, regulations, and rules. Indeed, the first thing the legal personnel did on the launch of the tribunal was to establish internal rules, which were periodically modified to address problems that arise. During the proceedings, each person remains at their station unless authorized by the Trial Chamber to move, such as when Judge Nil requested that the guards bring Duch to the dock.

As he sat in the dock, Duch entered a spatial matrix that asserted a conceptual order (the classificatory status of the participants), authorized and constrained a set of practices (their actions during the proceedings), and informed lived experience (ranging from bodily movements and postures to speech acts and events that occurred therein).[3] This frame enabled a performance through which articulations of the "international community" and "rule of law" were asserted—along with Cambodian state authority.

This spatial frame and the juridical apparatus and articulations it supported, however, were sometimes disrupted by complexities they could not fully contain, order, or redact. Duch, the crimes of which he was accused, the brutality of the prison he ran, and his trial had illustrated this point in unsettling and haunting moments during the proceedings. Duch himself was an uncanny presence, familiar yet strange, situated in the dock at the border of humanity and inhumanity.

These issues had circulated as Duch sat in the dock, an enigma each of the parties sought to solve. He upended these efforts throughout his trial, up to and including his remarkable last-minute request for acquittal.

| | | |

"The Chamber will now read its disposition."

With these words Judge Nil, who had spent the morning reading a summary of the written version of the Trial Chamber's 275-page judgment, initiated the Trial Chamber's final act: proclaiming the verdict.

The day had begun with an absence: François Roux was not in court. Just weeks before, Duch requested Roux's withdrawal, stating that he had "lost confidence" in this lawyer.[4] No public explanation was given, though the fact that Duch had suddenly dropped a lawyer who, since 2007, had devoted an enormous amount of time to his case was not lost on some observers. One suggested that Roux had been "backstabbed" by Kar Savuth and that Duch "never did like meeting face-to-face those he was betraying."[5] Others suggested that Kar Savuth's close connection to Prime Minister Hun Sen might have had something to do with the dramatic change at the end of the trial.[6]

As the July 26, 2010 proceeding commenced, Kar Savuth sat in the defense section; a dozen civil parties crowded into seats on the opposite side of the courtroom. Bou Meng and Chum Mey sat near the courtroom's glass partition, watching intently.

Judge Nil's statement about the disposition was a declaration of the court's authority, one that had been asserted frequently during the proceedings. Judge Nil, for example, referred to himself and his colleagues not as individuals but as "the Chamber" or "the Trial Chamber." If the authority of the Trial Chamber was symbolically affirmed through ritual behaviors (everyone standing whenever the judges entered or exited the courtroom) or symbolic space (their raised dais), the Trial Chamber's authority was also asserted through such speech acts.

Thus, to commence the rendering of the verdict, Judge Nil noted the Trial Chamber's bureaucratic control by stating the numeric case file information and then the legal basis of its authority, including the name and age of the accused, the crimes with which the accused was charged, the law establishing the ECCC, and the temporal jurisdiction of the court. In its introductory remarks, the Trial Chamber also avowed the jurisdiction of the court, noting its agreement with the OCIJ that Duch was one of those "most responsible" for the DK crimes, thus dispensing with one defense argument.[7]

Before reading the summary, however, Judge Nil asserted the Trial Chamber's authority through two regulatory behaviors that had been performed at the start of each trial session. First, he asked the court clerk to confirm the attendance of the parties, which was necessary for the session to proceed but also marked the Trial Chamber's managerial control. Second, Judge Nil instructed the detention guards to bring Duch to the dock.

By so doing, Judge Nil operationalized the symbolic space and ordering power of the court. Now, the court would undertake the culminating act, rendering a final decision, or "disposition" in legal discourse. While the word "disposition" may refer an inclination emerging from a psychological arrangement of mind or feeling, it broadly connotes ordering and regulation, as suggested by its etymological link to the Latin word *disponere*, a combination of *dis-* (apart) and *ponere* (to put, place).[8] A disposition, then, connotes a regulatory act in which that which is out of place is controlled, ordered, and classified in an articulation.

The Accused (Trial Chamber Judgment) | 233

In the context of the trial, the accused, Duch, was the subject of this juridical discipline, as illustrated by his placement in the liminal space of the dock, a space of containment from the threat of contamination and disorder he represented. His confinement in "detention" performed a similar function, as detention suggests restraint, a "holding back" of something threatening to disrupt order. As the civil parties and prosecution had claimed during closings, Duch's crimes suggested a wild and "savage" violence that seemed "beyond comprehension," "shocked the conscience," was an attack on "humanity," and "shook the very foundation of society." As the vehicle that tamed and regulated this wildness, the Trial Chamber performed a key restorative, protective, and transformative role by—through its ultimate "disposition"—reestablishing order, contributing to deterrence, and healing a violated humanity.

Even as it confined Duch in the dock, the Trial Chamber convened a larger symbolic space. On the one hand the Trial Chamber oversaw an administrative bureaucracy, most visibly evoked by the row of court clerks sitting immediately below the raised dais of the judges, creating yet another barrier between the Trial Chamber and the rest of the participants. On the other hand the Trial Chamber also exercised regulatory control over the different parties, with the defense, prosecution, and civil parties each placed behind metaphoric "bars," which were frequently invoked by participants.

Here an interesting doubleness came into play, as the interaction of the parties also contains a threatening wildness, in particular anger and the desire for revenge that can potentially upset the proceedings. As emotional beings who, besides suffering, potentially bear malice toward an accused, the civil parties also manifest a wildness that must also be contained by a barrier, the "bar" behind which the parties are restrained. Indeed, all movement is highly regulated within the court, with the Trial Chamber even determining who has "standing."

In contrast to the threatening emotionality of the parties, the judges remain largely impassive, symbolic guardians of rational justice. The blindfolded Lady Justice provides an idealized model of how a Trial Chamber should function as it administers impartial justice (Lady Justice's blindfold) with the authority of law (the sword she holds in one hand) and by rationally assessing the evidence (the scales she holds in the other). Similarly, the ECCC logo invokes the authority of justice, even if justice is meted out by a high-ranking official—or, in the eyes of some Cambodians who view the logo through a religious lens, a *tevoda* or guardian spirit.

During the proceedings, this juridical role of the Trial Chamber was invoked in various ways. It was sometimes likened to a protector, a notion referenced by metaphors of the Trial Chamber as "guardians of justice" or by lawyers acknowledging that a matter was "in your hands." With regard to the scales of justice, the Trial Chamber was sometimes described as "weighing" or giving "weight" to different evidentiary factors, as well as seeking to "balance" the rights of the parties.

At different times, various parties commented on the obligations of the Trial Chamber, as did the OCP's final submission, which stated that the "Chamber's primary responsibility [is] to assess the relevance, reliability and probative value of the individual pieces of evidence as they relate to the factual allegations in the Closing Order."[9] Along these lines, the Trial Chamber was sometimes described as the "triers of the facts," and the introduction to their Judgment notes that "over the course of 72 trial days, the Chamber heard the testimony of 24 witnesses, 22 civil parties and nine experts. Approximately 1,000 documents were put before the Chamber and subjected to examination."[10]

The metaphor of the "chamber" is revealing here. While the word "chamber" may refer to a formal meeting hall, it has a more abstract sense of a small, enclosed space, often private and removed from public interchange. A bedroom, a bathroom, even the offices of a judge are sometimes called "chambers."[11] These usages are derived from the term's etymological link to the French *chambre*, which in turn emerges from the Latin *camera*, which can refer to an enclosed or vaulted space.

This etymological connection to the word "camera" offers a suggestive way of thinking about the "Trial Chamber." Typically, a camera includes an opening through which light is refracted by a lens into an enclosed chamber, forming an inverted replica of the image outside. This inverted image may be reversed to its original form using a mirror, a trick early camera obscuras deployed. The clarity of an image, in turn, could be enhanced by the modification of the lens, which could bring it "into focus."

The Trial Chamber works in a loosely analogous manner, as alleged facts and evidence are, as is often said in court, "put" to it, just as light enters the camera opening. These facts, like the light, are then refracted by the framing "lens" of law, which brings them into focus, eliminating ambiguity. In the end, the Trial Chamber has to come to a decision, a truth that is black and white, all shades of gray pushed out of sight. The notion of the mirror, which converts the inverted image into something similar to but still different from the original image, captures this process of the transformation of a wide array of evidentiary information into a singular articulation / "disposition."

The judgment is just such a legal articulation. It operates through a process of disambiguation, in which the complexity of real-world details is edited down to a more singular narrative calibrated to accord with a framing set of abstract parameters (law)—just as a psychological expert's report provided an articulation of Duch's character in terms of the frame of psychological theory, and S-21 confessions were calibrated in terms of the frame of the party line. Each of these articulations is produced in a camera-like chamber with different lenses (law, psychology, the party line). Each renders a distinct reading of person and subjectivity, involving a particular constellation of self, identity, body, and society. Complicating detail is pushed out of sight in order to produce truths situated in particular matrices of knowledge and power.

In constructing the verdict, the Trial Chamber followed the legal and factual trail of the indictment, a requirement specified in the ECCC's Internal Rules. The sequence of the proceedings loosely paralleled the structure of the closing order, with evidence "put" to the Trial Chamber along the way. Using the lens of law, the Trial Chamber then evaluated the evidence, determining its relevance to the facts of the case and the corresponding law and criminal charges. Like the OCP, legal officers in the Trial Chamber almost certainly used case management software, gathering data for their own "issues tree" to order the facts and charges in the indictment and the corresponding evidence that was "put" to the Trial Chamber during the trial.

Although much of the decision-making process remains opaque, traces of it appear in the questions the judges posed as well as their verdict. The judgment notes that in making its determinations, the Trial Chamber held a high standard of proof that, in keeping with the right to be presumed innocent, required "sufficient evidence" to prove a fact: "any doubt as to guilt was accordingly interpreted in the Accused's favor."[12] This task was made easier since Duch admitted or did not contest the majority of these facts.

But at times the evaluation process of the Trial Chamber can be seen. Under one of the numeric "branches" discussing "Facts Relevant to Crimes against Humanity Committed at S-21" (2.4), for example, the judgment enumerates "Torture, including rape (2.4.4)," a subbranch of which is "Specific Incidents of Torture" (2.4.4.1.2). The Judgment notes that the "accused has denied the use of techniques such as plunging detainees in a water jar or suspending them by their hands tied behind their back, as shown in one of Witness Vann Nath's paintings." A supporting footnote refers to Vann Nath's testimony. "The Chamber," the judgment goes on, "finds however that the testimony of Witness Vann Nath, who saw and painted this scene, is consistent and reliable and meets the standard required to prove torture."[13] Nothing more is said, as the Judgment moves on without explaining why it favored the testimony of a single witness over Duch's claims.

For the most part, the Judgment resembles the closing order and thus, more loosely, the legal frame originally asserted by the OCP—except that now what was alleged is transformed into either proven and thus factual or not proven and thus, by implication, false or at least questionable.

| | | |

"The accused, Kaing Guek Eav, stand."[14]

Judge Nil's reading of the summary had drawn to a close. He was prepared to announce the Trial Chamber's disposition.

Duch rose from his chair in the dock and stood motionless, arms straight at his sides, as if at attention. He had assumed his "student Duch" posture, his face drawn.

"The Chamber finds Kaing Guek Eav guilty."

I heard a gasp in the gallery. A few people quietly wept.[15] Bou Meng looked upward, perhaps thinking of his wife's soul.

Duch stood straight. His only visible reaction was a shift of the eyes, a slight turn of the head.

| | | |

Duch, the Trial Chamber found, was a zealot.

He had exercised his authority actively, innovating, managing S-21, recruiting and training staff, participating in arrests, and reporting about and annotating confessions. "The accused," Judge Nil had said, "knew of the criminal nature of the S-21 system and acted with the intent to further its criminal purpose . . . having planned, instigated, ordered, and aided and abetted the crimes committed at S-21."[16] Given the systematic character of the crimes committed at S-21, they could also be considered a "joint criminal enterprise."

Duch's claims of duress fell short, since he had "willingly and actively participated" in implementing the CPK system of terror, carrying out his duties with
"a high degree of efficiency and zeal."[17]

On the one hand, Judge Nil explained, Duch had committed crimes
against humanity, which the Trial Chamber defined as "persecution on political grounds," a crime that "subsum[ed] the crimes against humanity
of extermination (encompassing murder), enslavement, imprisonment,
torture (including one instance of rape), and other inhumane acts."[18] In
situations where there are multiple, overlapping convictions, Judge Nil explained, international law allows lesser crimes to be subsumed by more
serious ones.[19]

The Trial Chamber's written judgment stated that the court "in essence
found that any individual detained at S-21, considered rightly or wrongly to
be connected to any political group other than the CPK and typically with
some class background to which it objected, was a target of discrimination."[20]
Given the zeal and willingness with which Duch admittedly implemented
CPK policy, the Trial Chamber stated, he had demonstrated the requisite discriminatory intent to be convicted of political persecution, a crime against
humanity which, because of its gravity and extent, subsumed other sorts of
crimes against humanity.

The oral judgment did not mention a dissent by Judge Cartwright, who
had argued that the evidence did not conclusively prove that Duch himself held the requisite discriminatory intent. Through this act of juridical
subsumption, the Trial Chamber asserted an articulation of the violence
at S-21 as a singular phenomenon—an act of political persecution that was
part of a joint criminal enterprise—which at once had broader explanatory
power while editing out complicating details, as Judge Cartwright's dissent
suggested.

If the vast majority of the violent acts Duch committed at S-21 were crimes
against humanity, the Trial Chamber also agreed with the OCP that he was guilty
of grave breaches of the Geneva Conventions of 1949 for atrocities committed
against civilians and prisoners during the war with Vietnam. The crimes, Judge
Nil explained, included "willful killing, torture and inhumane treatment, willfully causing great suffering or serious injury to body or health, willfully de-
priving a prisoner of war or civilian of the rights of a fair and regular trial, and
unlawful confinement of a civilian."[21] Due to a split within the Trial Chamber,
it did not rule on whether Duch had committed the crimes of murder and

torture under the 1956 Cambodian Penal Code—one of the only decisions where defense arguments prevailed.

| | |

Most observers had been confident Duch would be convicted, given his admissions and the enormous evidence against him. For them, the biggest question revolved around his sentence. Was it possible that, as the defense had requested, he would be allowed to walk free? Would the Trial Chamber find that his cooperation and unlawful detention merited his return to society?

On finding Duch guilty of crimes against humanity and grave breaches of the 1949 Geneva Conventions, Judge Nil continued, the Trial Chamber had considered "the entirety of circumstances of the case" to determine the "appropriate sentence." On the one hand there were "a number of aggravating features, including the shocking and heinous character of the offences, which were perpetrated against at least 12,273 victims over a prolonged period." The gravity of the crimes warranted "a substantial term of imprisonment."[22]

On the other hand the Chamber acknowledged "significant mitigating factors which mandate a finite term of imprisonment rather than one of life imprisonment," which the crimes might otherwise merit. This mitigation stemmed from Duch's "cooperation with the Chamber, admission of responsibility, limited expressions of remorse, the coercive environment of [DK], and the potential for rehabilitation." The sentence had emerged from a consideration of the relative weight of these factors, Judge Nil's comments suggested, as the scales of justice had tilted in one direction or the other.

"On the basis of the foregoing," Judge Nil continued, rarely glancing up from his prepared text, "the majority of the Chamber sentences Kaing Guek Eav to a single sentence of thirty-five years of imprisonment."

Due to Duch's illegal detention, Judge Nil explained, his sentence would be reduced by five years. And Duch would receive credit for the eleven years he had already spent in prison since he was first detained in 1999.

| | |

With Duch's guilt and sentence established, the Trial Chamber could consider civil party claims. Once again, trial evidence was taken in by the "Chamber"

The Accused (Trial Chamber Judgment) | 239

and projected into a "disposition" that set things into place. The first part of this ordering exercise was to assess civil party status. A claim to this status required proof of identity and direct or indirect injury from Duch's crimes. The judgment noted that sixty-six civil parties, including four direct survivors (Bou Meng, Chum Mey, and two survivors of S-24) and sixty-two indirect victims had satisfied this criteria. Judge Nil read the names of all sixty-six of the civil parties while making brief note of their victimization. The claims of the remaining twenty-four civil parties, Judge Nil noted in passing, were denied.[23] He did not name them.

In its longer written judgment, the Trial Chamber did list these civil parties and discuss the reasons for the rejection of their claims. Nam Mon, whose case Studzinsky discussed during her closing arguments, was one of them. Nam Mon's assertion that she was an S-21 medic and prisoner, the written judgment noted, was undermined by "inconsistencies between the information contained in her Civil Party application and her in-court statements and subsequent submissions."[24] In addition, she was not able to provide much detail about S-21 or to prove her relationship to the relatives she said were imprisoned and killed there. While acknowledging her suffering and "even allowing for the impact of trauma and the passage of time,"[25] the Chamber did not have sufficient evidence to grant her civil party status and therefore rejected her claim. Here again, the "Chamber" worked to sort and filter evidence, which it inflected, through the framing lens of law, into an articulation of juridical truth or, by rejection, implicit falsity.

Those civil parties whose claims had been accepted, Judge Nil noted, were entitled to "moral and collective" reparations, about which the Trial Chamber had invited the civil parties to make suggestions. Their proposals included memorials, educational initiatives, medical and psychological care, a national commemoration, the inscription of the victims' names at Tuol Sleng, and the preservation of Choeung Ek and Tuol Sleng.[26]

The Trial Chamber, Judge Nil stated, was limited in its powers of enforcement and implementation. In addition, Duch had been declared indigent and could not make reparative payments. As a result, the Trial Chamber had granted only two civil party reparation requests. First, the names of the civil parties were to "be included in the final judgment, including a specification as to their connection with the crimes committed at S-21." In addition, the court would compile and publish Duch's apologies. The Trial Chamber, Judge Nil said, otherwise "rejects all civil party claims."[27]

"The trial proceedings in this case have now come to an end," Judge Nil announced. "Guards, take the criminal, Kaing Guek Eav alias Duch, back to the Detention Center."[28]

With these words, the trial had come to a close.

Duch stood, impassive. He looked down briefly and then gave a stiff *sampeah* before quickly departing. He was carrying a Bible.

| | | |

The Trial Chamber had completed its evaluation of the evidence to ascertain the facts. Like the light flowing into the chamber of a camera, inflected by the framing lens of law, a new image was being projected. In it, Duch, the man stranded in the dock, had undergone a transformation from suspect to "the accused" and now convict, a fact highlighted by Judge Nil's new reference to Duch as "the criminal" as opposed to "the accused," which he had used throughout the trial. Duch was a criminal of a particular sort, one who, like the civil parties, had been invested with rights granted by law. The juridical process had not just produced an articulation of the liberal, rights-bearing being, it was a performance of a liberal order. The process also rendered a social order, through a "disposition" that set things properly into place, an articulation that, like math, edited out complicating detail in favor of abstract truth. In law, like math, there was just black and white, guilt or nonguilt; no gray.

"Please rise," a voice instructed.

Everyone stood as the Trial Chamber judges, led by Judge Nil, exited the courtroom through a side passage, walking slowly in a neat, single-file line.

| | | |

Outside the court, things began to unravel.

Some observers, including Vann Nath, said they were satisfied with the verdict. At long last, a former Khmer Rouge leader had been brought to justice. Duch's trial had been conducted in accordance with international standards.[29]

Other people were visibly upset. If Duch had been sentenced to thirty-five years in prison, sixteen years were to be taken off this total, eleven for time served and five for his illegal imprisonment. This meant that he would remain imprisoned for nineteen years. Since Duch was sixty-eight, he could walk free at the age of eighty-seven, a disturbing possibility to many.

A number of civil parties expressed anger and even outrage, making comments that became the focus of newspaper headlines. Theary Seng, a civil party in Case 002 and civil society leader, was quoted by *Time* as saying, "If you can kill 14,000 people and serve only 19 years—11 hours per life taken—what is that? It's a joke."[30] A *New York Times* story titled "Prison Term for Khmer Rouge Jailer Leaves Many Dissatisfied" was accompanied by a photograph of Theary Seng comforting a sobbing Hong Savath amid a media crowd.

Hong Sarath had joined as a civil party after seeing a photograph of her uncle on the walls of Tuol Sleng in 2008. Later it emerged that she had been gang-raped and had witnessed her father's execution during DK. Like other civil parties, Savath had only discovered her civil party status had been rejected when she did not hear her name among those of the admitted civil parties announced during the reading of the judgment.[31]

Chum Mey also became agitated, angrily telling reporters, "I am not satisfied! We are victims two times, once in the Khmer Rouge time and now once again. His prison is comfortable, with air-conditioning, food three times a day, fans and everything. I sat on the floor with filth and excrement all around."[32] Cracks were beginning to emerge in the Trial Chamber's carefully crafted judgment, as what had been redacted by its articulation suddenly appeared in a torrent of emotion and criticism.[33] Vannak Huy, a television news director, noted the limits of law in prosecuting mass murder. "Even if we chop him up into two million pieces," he said, "it will not bring our family members back."[34]

Two days later, I asked Bou Meng his thoughts on Duch's verdict. I knew he was upset, since he had told reporters immediately afterward, "I felt it was like a slap in the face."[35] He was still angry and said he had added his thumbprint to a civil party petition requesting an appeal. Soon all the parties would file formal appeals, with Duch again asking for release. Bou Meng noted that the Trial Chamber had rejected the status of many civil parties and ignored their suggestions for reparations. The civil party lawyers would appeal these decisions as well. As for Duch, Bou Meng said, "45 years, 35 years, whatever the sentence, it should be life. He should die in jail."

Invoking a Cambodian saying, Bou Meng added, "It's not possible to cleanse white paper that has been stained with black."[36]

Redactic

(FINAL DECISION)

February 3, 2012 (Night)

Charcoal gray, the old fortress stands alone, a perfect square of stone rising from the barren landscape. No plant cracks the hard dirt that surrounds the structure. Nothing living can be seen or heard. The air is still. No light breaks through the clouds. It is neither day nor night.

Suddenly, someone is here with me, a presence familiar yet strange, perhaps friendly, but clearly dangerous. This person lingers on the border of shadow and light, compels me to go into one of the square stone turrets placed on each corner of the unadorned fortress walls.

I stand on the ground floor of one of the windowless turrets. In the center, a narrow staircase encased by light spirals steeply into the shadows. The stairs and walls are etched with spider webs.

"Go," the faceless man demands.

Slowly, I ascend the steps. I worry that the man will attack me from behind, try to shove me over the handrail. I can no longer see the ground below, just the beam of light surrounding the stairwell that blurs and gradually fades into the darkness above and below.

I finally reach the top. The staircase leads to a dead end, where thick and impenetrable concrete forbids access to where I want to go above, onto ramparts set against a moonless sky. Blocked, I turn to go back down.

"Why don't you go first?" I ask the man, who I never clearly see.

"No," he replies sharply. "Proceed."

One by one, I climb the stairwells inside the fortress turrets. They look the same. Each has an identical end.

As I mount the last stairwell, I am completely alone. I want to flee, run back as fast as I can. I press on. My fear and anxiety build. The light fades. Ahead, I can only see dense cobweb tangles and handwriting on a wall, the print too faint to read.

February 4, 2012 (Daybreak)

I wake with a start, disoriented, then certain I had dreamed of S-21.

Yesterday, the Supreme Court Chamber (SCC) had ruled on the various appeals, including the defense's appeal for Duch's release. This morning, I am supposed to meet Bou Meng at Tuol Sleng to discuss the SCC's final decision.

If the details, at first clear, begin to fade, I still feel the dream's strong emotional pull as I depart for Tuol Sleng. I know I must revisit Building D and take another look at the defaced photograph of Duch. How will I see it now at the end of his long trial?

Over the course of the week, as I try to understand Duch, the prison he had run, and the path I might take to write about his trial, I return to Tuol Sleng again and again.

| | | |

My *tuk-tuk* taxi pulls up at the entrance to Tuol Sleng, which has recently been moved to the corner of the compound next to Building A. I stop at the new ticket kiosk, pay the $2 fee, and am given a brochure. It has long been rumored that part of the ticket fees, paid only by foreigners, are pocketed by officials, perhaps one reason the compound is run-down.

Despite the early hour, Tuol Sleng is teeming with visitors who, on entering, follow the far edge of Building A to the "The Victims' Graves," a memorial with white stone coffins of the last corpses discovered at S-21. In 2010, a memorial was erected nearby to commemorate the first anniversary of the designation of the Tuol Sleng archive as a UNESCO "Memory of the World" site, an event roughly coinciding with the start of Duch's trial.[1] The red base is already heavily chipped and at odds with the decorated gold border and etched lettering that includes the UNESCO seal.

The establishment of the memorial, marking the site as part of not just Cambodian history but world heritage, is the culmination of a process of transformation that began with the opening of Cambodia during the period of the United Nations Transitional Authority in Cambodia (UNTAC). Tourism in Cambodia has since risen dramatically.

| | | |

I begin walking the path to Building E, where prisoners were once processed at S-21. Opposite the old entry gates, now closed tight, Bou Meng has created a stand on the front countertop of the Building E terrace. Blindfolded, Bou Meng and his wife crossed this threshold during DK as they were taken to be photographed in a room behind Bou Meng's booth. Bou Meng is usually at his kiosk selling his book, but now all I see is a long, rectangular banner, held in place by red brick weights that look like bricks from the small cells in Building C.

One side of the banner has an image of the cover of Bou Meng's biography. On it, Bou Meng grimaces, as if about to cry, his wrinkled face half in shadow. On the other side, there is an S-21 photograph of a woman, with the number "331" affixed to her shirt by a pin. A caption explains, "MA YEOUN BOU MENG'S WIFE. This is Bou Meng's Wife Former Victim at S21 (Tuol Sleng Prison) Was Killed at the killing field (Choeung Ek)." The center of the banner reads, in large print:

> I am bou meng
> Former Victim at S 21
> (Tuol Sleng Prison)
> bou meng's Document
> Book is 10$ per 1

Since the book's publication in 2010, Bou Meng has sold copies to tourists almost every day.

A handful of workers sit on benches and chairs inside the open-air terrace. "Aunt, do you know where Bou Meng is?" I ask a middle-aged woman. "He went to a Victims Association meeting," she replies, adding, "Chum Mey went, too."

I glance at the courtyard in front of Buildings C and D. Two days earlier, on the day before the SCC's final decision, Bou Meng, Chum Mey, Studzinsky, and other outreach and civil party officials had gathered under an open tent to speak about victims' participation and the SCC's impending decision on the appeals. Perhaps a hundred people, ranging from civil parties to members of the media, attended.

Chum Mey had sat in the front row next to Bou Meng, who spoke first. "I can't accept the thirty-five-year sentence," Bou Meng had repeated several times. "I'm very upset." Chum Mey, wearing a white shirt and gold tie, added, "The sentence should be forty-five years or even life. Duch's sentence of thirty-five years means he could be released at the age of eighty-six. That's unjust."

An audience member later asked what would happen if the expectations of the civil parties were not met in the SCC's final judgment. Studzinsky, the one foreigner on the panel, replied that the civil parties were unable to request a sentence and had to hope that the OCP's appeal to increase the sentence to 45 years would be successful. She did not mention that Duch had appealed for release.

Studzinsky did note that the rejected civil parties had filed appeals that included additional documentation supporting their claims. Nevertheless, she cautioned, the civil parties needed to prepare for the possibility that the SCC might again reject their appeals. She remembered clearly, Studzinsky continued, how shocked and upset everyone had been after the Trial Chamber ruling. She added that she hoped the SCC would grant their appeal for additional reparations. But she wanted everyone to be ready so they were not "too shocked tomorrow [if our] expectations are not met. . . . The judgment tomorrow will be final. There is no appeal."

After the session had ended, I had spoken briefly with Bou Meng. He had handed me an invitation, in Khmer with English translation. "House Warming Party / Mr. Bou Meng and Mrs. Doung Chhunny," the invitation began. "We have a great honor to invite excellencies, Ladies, and Gentlemen to participate our HOUSE WARMING PARTY Which will be held on Sunday 12th February 2012, at 1:00 P.M. at the New House . . . Kohthom District, Kandal Province / (Please see the map) Thanks!"

The cover included the image of a carefully landscaped Western ranch house with a wraparound porch, an odd contrast to the house he had built, a two-story cement villa. The house had cost $30,000 to construct; Bou Meng had paid for it using earnings from selling his book at Tuol Sleng. "From two years selling my biography, I saved $30,000," Bou Meng had told a reporter. "I've been selling up to 10 books a day for at least $10 each and will keep doing this until I die."[2] He later told me, "Tourists will sometimes give me $20. When I tell them I don't have change, they often tell me I can just keep it. People have even given me a hundred dollars."

In a photo from the party, Bou Meng, wearing a formal blue suit with gold buttons and a red string around his wrist, sits beside Chum Mey.[3] Several of Bou Meng's paintings of Choeung Ek, including one of a baby being tossed into the air and impaled, hang in the background.

Beyond the courtyard grass where the civil party forum had been held, I notice a row of dark spaces, doorways to the Building D exhibitions. My eyes move to the second-floor room where I had first seen Duch's defaced photograph. Inside, all I can see is a single line of squares, beams of light cast through lattice airways onto pitch-black walls. Is the defaced photograph of Duch still hanging there? If so, how will I see it now?

I imagine a new word scrawled across his chest: "convict."

| | | |

Before going there, I walk to Building B to see the large photograph of Chan Kim Srun holding her infant. The day before, I had traveled to the ECCC compound with a group of Cambodians participating in a DC-Cam outreach program. The group included former S-21 guards and interrogators, teachers who worked with Duch in the 1990s, and Sek Say, the eldest daughter of Chan Kim Srun. At an informational meeting at DC-Cam before the final decision, Sek Say had sat next to an interrogator who had testified during Duch's trial. Had she wondered if he had tortured her mother? After the SCC's ruling, she had traveled to Tuol Sleng, where, on seeing her mother's photograph, she had wept.

"Chan Kim Srun—Sang 462." The white letters are printed on a rectangular slate affixed by string to the collar of Chan Kim Srun's black shirt. In the almost life-size photograph, Chan Kim Srun stares at the viewer, eyes marred by creases in the aging photo. She cradles an infant boy swaddled in white. The baby is still. A tear in the photograph paper cuts across the infant's forehead, a jagged scar.

As I prepare to take a shot of the photograph, I see fragments reflected in the protective glass of the display: white and beige tile, the bars of a window, the eyes of another prisoner photograph from across the room. I notice a silhouette in the frame, a man, dressed in dark trousers and a white short-sleeved sports shirt holding a camera. I snap the shot and look at the digital picture. My outline is part of the image.

I look closer. While I had missed it so many times before, I see a small triangular object above Chan Kim Srun's right shoulder, a shadow almost indistinguishable from her black shirt. An adjacent exhibition photograph reveals what was previously out of sight: a profile shot of Chan Kim Srun and her baby. Chan Kim Srun sits in a measurement chair, her back against a metal frame, her head set in place by the end of a prod pressed against the back of her skull. At the bottom, in tiny print, a caption reads, "This chair was used for taking photographs of the victims." A second caption states, "The wife of Sek Sath, secretary of region 25 South-west." No further information is given.

Tourists pass through the room, looking at Chan Kim Srun's photograph. No one reads the captions. Their gaze is fixed on the baby and, especially, Chan Kim Srun's eyes. A guide leads a group of solemn students, mostly women, into the room. They say little, speaking only in whispers.

"And now we look at this photo," the guide says. "This is a special chair for the victim to sit on and take photographs for documentation. If a prisoner tried to escape, [S-21] would have photograph and documentation." He pauses, "But no one prisoner can escape from this place." Directing the group's attention to the large photograph of Chan Kim Srun, he says, "And about the baby . . ." Lowering his voice, he continues, "The baby could not cry. If the mother cannot keep quiet, the guards will kill by [smashing against a] coconut tree." He adds, "One more way, toss the baby up, use a gun with knife, put through when body fall down. This way Khmer Rouge keep the children quiet."

Every guide stops at Chan Kim Srun's photograph, giving different inflections to a similar narrative focusing on victimization and the suffering of women and children. "Those are tears," a guide says pointing to Chan Kim Srun's eyes. "And see the other photo, a lot of tourists are confused about it. They think it's a killing tool or death chair. It's not that. It's just a chair for taking the victim's photos to get the proper documentation. It was made in China." Another guide, telling the story of how babies were smashed on coconut trees, directs his group's attention to the courtyard outside: "You may still find bones in the grass."

I study other display cases, which contain long rows of small prisoner photographs, a blur of humanity. Looking closer, details emerge: bandages; ripped clothing; surprised, hopeless faces. A few people look defiant. Others appear terrified. There are a handful of larger photographs in the room, including a display of foreign prisoners, suggesting the universality of the S-21 crimes.

This theme continues in the next room, which includes enlarged photographs of children. In one, a boy with thick dark hair glares, defiant. Bruises suggest he has been punched in the face. A large, black chain is wrapped around his neck. A white tag, affixed by a pin to his shirt, identifies him by a number, "1," printed in black. There is no caption, date, or name. His is simply a victim, a child.

I stand almost directly underneath the Tuol Sleng archive, the source of the photographs. No sign directs tourists to the archive, located in several rooms on the second floor of Building B. Up a flight of stairs, the archive is marked only by a metal gate, sometimes cracked open, sometimes locked shut, and the warning "NO ENTRY."

Once I had gained entry here. I passed through the gate and walked the pathway to a closed door. My escort, who had worked at Tuol Sleng for many years, led me into a classroom that had been used as a cell during S-21 and was now an archive. An air conditioner with a UNESCO logo struggled to cut the heat as an employee scanned documents; the sudden hum of the machine was the only sound in the room. My chaperone led me to a second, larger room, where the light was dim, blocked by tinted windows and tall wooden bookcases. The shelves were filled with black boxes, some in plain sight, others masked by shadow.

"Do you want to see?" my host whispered. He selected a box and set it on a table. Glancing at the front office to make sure no one was watching, he opened the lid, revealing a stack of S-21 confessions. He gingerly took one out. I only caught a glimpse of the script before my host quickly placed the confession back inside the box, replaced the lid, and returned it to the shelf. The confession, like Long Muy's, was covered with annotations. My host then led me to a file cabinet and, after another glance at the front office, pointed to the small boxes within. "Those are the photographs," he informed me. Before we exited, he quickly opened one of the boxes. It was filled with black-and-white negatives, the images of S-21 prisoners.

In traditional photography, a negative is formed when light passes through a lens into a chamber, where the filtered image is captured on film. As light is impressed on the surface of the film, an image that reverses light and shade is formed, one that can be used to create a duplicate, the positive. More abstractly, the word "negative" suggests negation, reversal, and absence.[4]

Along these lines, the negative is invested with a doubleness, an opposition that it both reflects and coconstitutes. This doubleness also runs in two directions. The first act of doubling is the creation of the negative through the photographic act, the snapshot. But it is an act that filters light in a particular way, unable to show what is blocked out of the frame.

Chan Kim Srun's measurement chair underscores this point, as it is almost completely unseen, even as it structures the image by positioning the prisoner. By itself, a photograph provides little information about the context of its origin, such as the reasons it was taken. Yet the measurement chair suggests one answer, as it was part of a bureaucratic process in which prisoners were disciplined, controlled, and classified in accordance with the thick frame of the DK party line.[5] At S-21, a prisoner entered a liminal space in which his or her status as "revolutionary" was recast as that of "prisoner" or, in Khmer, "guilty person" [neak toas]. The photograph both exercised a form of control and produced this new identity, one further manufactured during the confession process as this new articulation, prisoner, was asserted.

At S-21, the photographs were linked to prisoner identity; they were inflected quite differently at Tuol Sleng—as part of a mass of victimhood and suffering, epitomized by mother and child. This is the second doubling of the negative, as it is replicated in a positive, like the photograph of Chan Kim Srun. Here the photograph is invested with a different set of meanings, situated in the PRK atrocity and global human rights frames of the Tuol Sleng Genocide Museum. The curators make decisions about the size and placement of the photograph, as well as whether and how to caption it.

Through these choices, the photograph as exhibit becomes part of a larger articulation of the past, as suffering and human rights victimization—just as the photo was part of a carceral articulation at S-21 and a juridical articulation at the ECCC. Different audiences may "read" the exhibition differently (for example, tourists identifying as global citizens versus Chan Kim Srun's daughter or a Buddhist domestic audience), and these readings may change depending on the person and the time—as they did from the creation of Tuol Sleng to its dramatically increased post-UNTAC interfacing with global tourism and the thick frame of human rights.

Each of these articulations involves redaction, a point illustrated by the large photograph of Chan Kim Srun. This photograph shows little trace of the measurement chair, which is masked by the angle. It is suddenly revealed in the adjacent photograph, which adds meaning and detail about Chan Kim Srun's experience and the larger disciplinary context at S-21. This doubleness and excess of meaning add to the power of the S-21 photographs and their capacity to be foregrounded in very different articulations.

This point was further highlighted to me when I traveled into the Cambodian countryside to interview one of Ke Kim Huot's sons in the hope of finding out what had happened to his family and, especially, his thoughts about Duch. While Ke Kim Huot's son remained vague about DK, perhaps because of their family's revolutionary past, he readily spoke about Duch's trial, which he had followed closely. He was aware of the discussions of his father's torture. The interrogator annotations, he told me, show that his father struggled long and hard against his captors, refusing to admit betraying the revolution even when tortured.

In 1980, the son had traveled to Phnom Penh and discovered photographs of his father and mother hanging at Tuol Sleng. He had hired a photographer to take a close-up of the photographs, which he had enlarged. Afterward, he placed the large replications on his bedroom wall, so he could see the faces of his parents each day when he awoke or was going to bed. During Duch's trial, several civil parties had invoked the prisoners' photographs, a trace of the spirits of their lost loved ones.

Similarly, Chan Kim Srun's daughter, Sek Say, brought a distinct set of meanings to her encounter with her mother's photograph after the final decision when she saw her mother's photo and began to cry. "This was my first visit to the ECCC," Sek Say told a DC-Cam staffer after the decision.[6] "I had heard that Duch was previously sentenced to 35 years imprisonment. I did not follow the Duch trial very often, for I was busy earning a living." Her discussion quickly turned personal, as she recalled: "During the KR time, I was too young to remember anything. I can only recall that when I was separated from my mother, I cried and went around searching for her. However, I could not find her. Later on, I found out that my mother, Chan Kim [Srun], and my brother were brought to Tuol Sleng and executed." Sek Say noted, with regret, "If my mother had lived, I would have had a chance to go to school."

| | | |

Now, I turn to leave. As I walk down the steps to the courtyard path leading to Building D, I see three log benches and a table, smooth polished surfaces obscuring jagged bark backs. Above the benches and table, a large mango tree rises into the sky, its tangles of leaves and branches offering relief from the heat. If you sit there facing Building B, you can see banks of photographs through the iron-barred windows, the eyes of prisoners staring.

This is where Savina Sirik and a colleague from DC-Cam had brought Sek Sey to comfort her after she had broken down on seeing the photograph of her mother. "We sat together and just held her hand, letting her talk," Sirik recalled.[7] Sek Say had told Sirik that seeing the photograph had made her think about her mother and brother and what they had endured, as well as the fact that the death of her parents had left her an orphan. "I had no one left," Sek

Say had told Sirik, before describing how she was adopted and later wed in an arranged marriage. Seeing the photograph reminded Sek Say of her loss. She also wondered about her mother's and brother's fates. Her brother, she thought, "was probably thrown up and killed with a bayonet. It was terrible to imagine how they were killed, how horrible it had been, how horrified they must have felt."

| | |

"I pay my respects to the Buddha, Dhamma, and Sangha."[8]

The chanting of monks grows louder as I approach Building D. In the middle of a street in back of Tuol Sleng—a space that, like the area around the museum, was once part of S-21—a tent encased in long white drapes has been set up for a ceremony. At the front of the narrow tent, above the front entrance, a black sign with white lettering announces: "Seven Day [Death] Ceremony Dedicated to the Soul of Theng." As I climb the steps leading to the second floor, the chanting rises in pitch; "Please forgive me in case I have done anything wrong [in violation of] the Buddha, Dhamma, and Sangha [monastic order]." The monks suddenly stop, signaling the end of their sermon, and there is silence.

On the second-floor corridor, I go straight to the fourth doorway, which opens into the room where Duch's photo hung when I went to Tuol Sleng at the beginning of the trial. I pause; then, as I step across the threshold, what was dim suddenly comes into focus.

| | |

Duch's defaced photograph hangs there. "Evil" is still written in black ink across the collar of his white shirt. His eyes remain aglow. But there is more graffiti now, markings left by other passersby. An arrow slashes across Duch's torso and points to a hole inside a small heart. Another person has drawn devil-like horns on the top of Duch's head. Perhaps some of this was there before, but I have forgotten. Or perhaps I just didn't see.

I stare at Duch's photograph and think of Chan Kim Srun. Her image was taken in a burst a light, the flash illuminating her face for a moment in brilliant white, leaving just a trace of the measurement chair. The measurement chair bears a similarity to the dock, marking the occupant as transitional and subject to thick frames that will rearticulate their identity. Thus, at S-21, the measurement chair asserted her status as a prisoner, an enemy being revealed, controlled, confined, regulated, and categorized by the state in accordance with the frame of the party line.

In the photograph, I notice that Duch sits at a microphone. Near the tip of the narrow cylinder, a small band glows red, signaling activation. It looks like a court microphone, a first clue. The caption does not list a time or place but provides a source: "Photo: Documentation Center of Cambodia Archive." A DC-Cam staffer would later inform me that the photograph was taken on November 20, 2007, by a Cambodian photojournalist.[9] This was the date of Duch's pretrial detention hearing.

The first line of text in the official transcript from that day is an ellipsis, the hint of something missing through three words in parentheses: "(Photographers enter courtroom)."[10] There is no mention of their exit or of what happened. On the second day of the hearing there is another absence: eight pages stricken from the public record, their presence hinted at by another parenthetical: "(At this point of the proceedings, a portion of the transcript [pages 38 to 45] was extracted and kept under separate cover, as the proceedings were conducted in camera)":[11] a gap in pagination between pages 37 and 46, and two-thirds of a page left blank.

What unfolded? When I search the ECCC's online media archive, I find ten photographs from this date.[12] One reveals that the hearing was held before the Pretrial Chamber and in a different courtroom, one lined with brown curtains and crammed with people, not the spacious venue where Duch's trial took place. Kar Savuth and François Roux sit side by side in another shot. There is still another photo of Duch standing. His white polo shirt is uncharacteristically untucked, a detail unseen in the defaced photograph.

Duch stands before a throng of journalists, who raise their video and photo cameras high, trying to get a clear shot, each capturing Duch's likeness from a slightly different angle. On one of the video camera screens, Duch's blurry image can just be made out, his image doubled. A last photograph shows him sitting in the dock by the microphone. The suited person whose torso can be seen in the defaced photograph is revealed; it is Rupert Skilbeck, the first head of the ECCC Defense Support Section.

Like Chan Kim Srun in the measurement chair, Duch sits in the dock. If Chan Kim Srun was immediately assumed to be guilty, Duch has been labeled a suspect, a person invested with rights and presumed innocent until proven guilty. Nevertheless, this juridical status places him in a machinery of discipline, as he also is contained, controlled, regulated, and categorized by the legal apparatus. In both cases, there is an aspect of spectacle, as Chan Kim Srun and Duch's entry into these disciplinary frames are recorded and displayed as evidence and as part of the enactment of a larger regulatory and judicial process about to unfold.

Supreme Court Chamber (February 3, 2012)

A day earlier, Duch's image had again been illuminated by the flash of cameras prior to the start of the SCC's announcement of its decision on the appeals. In the official court transcript from the day, there is no official record of when the photographs were taken. Doing so had become routine.

But there is a trace, the notes I took while sitting in the audience, fragments written in a composition notebook: my fieldwork archive. It records (brackets now added): "curtain [rises]" / "greffier on rules [tells audience rules of decorum]" / "photographer takes shots [of Duch, the courtroom, and crowd]" / "CPs Chum Mey by window [closest to the gallery] in yellow shirt" / "Duch looks at audience" / "[bell] ring—all stand (but monks don't stand) [higher status than judges and 'above politics']." This is where the official court transcript begins, recording words and framing images, even as I try to make sense of what I am seeing, to notice some of the things being edited out.

| | | |

The bell rings. "All rise," says the greffier. We stand. The judges walk into the court, ready to deliver the final judgment. The seven SCC judges are new, but they are garbed in the same red-and-black robes as the Trial Chamber judges, enter in the same measured manner, and, following the lead of SCC president Kong Srim, sit down together on the same elevated dais the Trial Chamber used.

"Please be seated," Kong Srim begins, as he puts on his reading glasses and headphones. Then, just as Judge Nil did a year and a half before, Kong Srim looks down and begins reading prepared remarks in a flat monotone: "On behalf of the Cambodian people and the United Nations, today, Friday 3, 2012, the Supreme Court Chamber of the ECCC [is holding] a public hearing pronouncing the Final Judgment in Case 001 . . ."[13]

After confirming the attendance with the court clerk, the SCC president directs: "Security guards, you are instructed to bring the accused Kaing Guek Eav, alias Duch, to the dock." Duch rises and walks briskly to the dock, escorted by two detention guards. He pauses for a moment to greet the judges, clasping his hands in a *sampeah*, and then sits. Directly behind him, in the first rows of the gallery, are two lines of saffron-robed monks, ECCC informational booklets open on their laps.

In the gallery, several video monitors are positioned against the glass wall dividing the spectators from the courtroom. Thick vertical beams of steel, cross-cut by a single horizontal bar, frame the glass, making the court resemble a cage or jail cell. I look at one of the monitors, which displays a full view of the courtroom and gallery, the sort of view the SCC judges have. In the gallery, we observe the courtroom proceedings from the rear, leading many audience members to watch the proceedings from the monitor instead of looking at what is taking place before them. All the parties in the courtroom, including Duch, have monitors on their desks, at which they also often stare. I watch as Duch looks at one of his two monitors. Seeing that the camera is focused on him, he turns away, lips pressed tight.

I glance back and forth through the glass wall, from the gallery video monitor to the courtroom. Then, as Duch sits in the dock, I notice a figure in the fourth row of the gallery. He wears a white polo shirt and is left-handed. He sits in back of the monks in the right section of the court, where I am sitting. The figure watches Duch's greeting and then writes something in a notebook.

It's me.

That morning I wrote in my notebook: "Duch to dock (see me in background)," "[Duch's] eyes look glassy," and "as judge starts to read D's face tightens." But even now I can't be certain. Two years later, as I draft this chapter, I review the online footage and watch the figure who I think is me peering at his own image on the courtroom monitor and then writing something down. I see an image of the image of someone looking at an image. I look at it again and again. I'm almost positive. But the picture is slightly blurred.

| | |

"Summary of the Appeal Judgment. A. Introduction," Kong Srim begins,[14] briefly describing the procedural history of the case before turning to each of the appeals. "B. Personal Jurisdiction," he continues, moving to the key basis of Duch's appeal. To ensure a fair trial, he states, an accused retains the right to challenge a court's jurisdiction at any point. "In the absence of bad faith or a showing of unsound professional Judgment," however, the Chamber "has no power to review [decisions regarding personal jurisdiction that] . . . are exclusively policy decisions for which the Co–Investigating Judges and

Co-Prosecutors, not the Chambers, are accountable. The accused's appeal on personal jurisdiction is accordingly rejected."[15]

As Kong Srim dismisses the appeal on personal jurisdiction, Duch, who has been watching unmoving, suddenly fidgets and pulls the edges of his unzipped jacket closer. With a frown, he glances at his lawyers. In my notebook I write: "What is Duch thinking? / does not look happy / D knows / must be considering future / looks mad." On the video monitor, the robes of monks can be seen through the glass just above Duch's head, a saffron curtain.

Duch loses again on the sentence, which the defense had argued should have a maximum of 30 years. Kong Srim continues reading until finally, after an hour and a half, he glances up and orders: "Mr. Kaing Guek Eav, stand in order to listen to the Disposition."[16]

Once again, Duch stands in the dock as his status is transformed by the Chamber's disposition. Like the Trial Chamber, the SCC has undertaken legal analysis, used databases linking evidence to crimes, and reviewed court transcripts and the case file. This information has been filtered, like light, through the lens of law and into a chamber, where once again an image has been formed—one that has reedited the Trial Chamber's verdict, creating a double both familiar and strange.

The SCC, Kong Srim tells the court, as Duch stands frowning, "quashes the Trial Chamber's decision to subsume under the crime against humanity of persecution the other crimes against humanity for which it found Kaing Guek Eav responsible." His conviction for persecution is affirmed, but the totalizing articulation of the Trial Chamber crumbles, as the newly revised SCC judgment includes piecemeal convictions for "enslavement, imprisonment, torture, and other inhumane acts."[17] In legal parlance, "quashing" is a form of redaction, a legal "smashing" that erases what has been, reediting the text to create a revised articulation of fact and law.

The quashing continues. Granting the OCP's appeal, the SCC "quashes" the Trial Chamber's sentence of 35 years. Earlier, Kong Srim has explained that the SCC agreed with the OCP that the Trial Chamber "attached undue weight to mitigating circumstances and insufficient weight to the gravity of crimes and aggravating circumstances."[18] Duch's crimes were of a "particularly shocking and heinous character," involving over 12,000 dead, and "among the worst in recorded human history."

At the "factory of death" Duch ran, Kong Srim continues, crimes were committed that are "an affront to all of humanity, and in particular to the Cambodian people, inflicting incurable pain," whose reverberations continue. Accordingly, Duch's crimes warrant "the highest penalty available to provide a fair and adequate response to the outrage these crimes invoked in victims, their families and relatives, the Cambodian people, and all human beings."[19] Duch glances down, perhaps in shame, maybe in anger. Given the gravity of the crimes, the SCC, in a split decision, exceeds even the OCP's request of 45 years.

It sentences Duch to life.

With this new sentence imposed, Kong Srim turns to the civil parties. After reviewing the appeals of civil parties whose applications were rejected, the SCC admits 10 additional civil parties. Hong Savath, the woman who had sobbed in front of reporters after the Trial Chamber verdict, is one of them. So, too, is Nam Mon.[20] As for reparations, the SCC rules that, while sympathetic to the civil party appeals, the judges have a limited mandate and so are dismissing the additional claims.

"The appeal proceedings in this case have come to an end," Kong Srim announces. "Security guards, take the convict, Kaing Guk Eav, back to the detention facility."[21] Duch perfunctorily raises his hands to *sampeah* the judges, then leaves the court, detention guards behind and before him. He doesn't look at the audience as he passes the glass wall. He looks as if he might cry. "All rise," the court clerk instructs as the judges, led by the president, exit next.

In the courtroom, the prosecutors are smiling.

If the SCC had been in the courtroom with Duch for the nine months of trial hearings, I wonder, would its ruling have been different? Instead, they had only interacted with him at a remove, a distance that perhaps led them to view him more punitively. Or perhaps his personality and Roux's elegant words had persuaded the Trial Chamber. We will never know. There is only the outcome, a filtering of light, a redacted judgment, conviction, a sentence of life.

In the gallery, 500 people stand, push through a single exit, walk down a flight of stairs, and spill into the ECCC courtyard, where hundreds more have watched the proceedings on video monitors. Journalists search for people to interview, gathering in circles around prominent officials, civil society actors, and survivors.

Many Cambodians are pleased. "I'm proud, so proud, with this Supreme Court Chamber," Chum Mey tells a reporter. "It is the absolute justice [for which] I had hoped . . . for more than three decades. I am at ease now."[22] Bou Meng likewise states he is largely satisfied, even if somewhat troubled by the reparations decision.[23] These sorts of comments will be incorporated into official court publications, including the monthly English-language periodical the *Court Report*, largely aimed at the international community, especially donor countries.[24]

| | | |

But, as happened after the 2010 Trial Chamber judgment, cracks immediately began to emerge in the Supreme Court's legal articulation, as issues redacted by the highly constrained parameters of the courtroom "chamber" were suddenly revealed. Most centered on political influence. While welcoming the conclusion of Duch's trial as "an important step towards achieving accountability for the mass crimes of the Khmer Rouge," Amnesty International's Cambodian officer stated: "the decision to overturn the legal remedy for Duch's unlawful detention and to provide no alternative may be perceived as a case of public opinion trumping human rights."[25]

For many, the SCC's reversal of the decision to give Duch credit for his illegal detention time, a decision from which two of the three international SCC judges had dissented, suggested an attempt to protect the reputation of the Cambodian state and its judiciary, which had long been criticized for corruption and political influence. Even if a life sentence was warranted, Duch's rights needed safeguarding.

Along these lines, some further criticized the SCC for failing to give Duch appropriate credit for his cooperation and apologies. In contrast to the Trial Chamber, the SCC ruled that Duch's cooperation was "incomplete, selective and opportunistic," while noting his "belated request for appeal," as well as the fact that he "spent almost the entire time given to him for his final statements seeking to minimize his responsibility by placing it upon 'senior leaders' . . . while his reference to remorse and apology was limited to a few sentences."[26]

In a public statement issued on the day of the SCC's judgment, civil society leader Theary Seng said that while she agreed with the life sentence, she found the SCC's rulings "extremely disturbing," since they had "dangerous consequences for the Cambodian national court system in the embedding of persistent violation of fair trial rights and due process, especially on the violation of pre-trial detention rights which is an abhorrent and pervasive problem."[27]

Theary Seng, who had withdrawn as a civil party in Case 002 after calling the ECCC an "irredeemable political farce," added that the Cambodian government was attempting to "make Duch, a small fish (not a senior KR leader)" a scapegoat as part of the government's attempt to "re-write history according to its resources and brute power, that is, to be known as the regime which put the KR on trial and in the process whitewashed its own KR history and crimes."[28]

Theary Seng's claims dovetailed with a second stream of criticism focusing on the SCC's ruling on personal jurisdiction, one interpreted by some as politicized. The determination of "senior leaders" and "those most responsible" was a matter of "investigatorial and prosecutorial policy," the SCC had ruled, and therefore an action at the discretion of the OCP and OCIJ. As such, barring bad faith, the determination of personal jurisdiction was "a nonjusticiable issue before the Trial Chamber."[29] This decision, which effectively diminished the scope of the Trial Chamber's oversight of a critical issue, stood out given recent events.[30]

From the beginning, a dispute over the jurisdiction of the court had been simmering in the shadows of juridical process. The terms "senior leaders" and "those most responsible" were never clearly defined, and members of the Cambodian and UN sides appeared to have had different assumptions about how many people would be tried. Hun Sen and other Cambodian government officials were open about their view that the number would be limited to the first five suspects indicted in Cases 001 (Duch) and 002 (Nuon Chea, Khieu Samphan, Ieng Sary, and Ieng Thirith).

While repeated many times, this position was perhaps most directly stated in an October 2010 meeting during which Hun Sen informed UN secretary-general Ban Ki-moon that there would be no additional cases. Cambodian foreign minister Hor Namhong told the media: "Samdech [Hun Sen] clearly affirmed that Case 003 [and Case 004] will not be allowed. We have to think about peace in Cambodia or the court will fail."[31]

Such government statements appeared to directly influence the actions of the ECCC's national staff. When, in December 2008, International Co-Prosecutor Petit sought to introduce introductory submissions against additional suspects in what would become Cases 003 and 004, his national counterpart, Chea Leang, disagreed, citing "Cambodia's past instability and the continued need for national reconciliation," as well as the ECCC Law, which her office interpreted as envisioning "only a small number of trials."[32]

In accordance with ECCC procedure, their dispute was sent to the five-person Pre-Trial Chamber for adjudication. In an August 18, 2009, decision, just as the proceedings of the trial of Duch were drawing to a close, the Pre-Trial Chamber issued a decision split along national and international lines—with the Pre-Trial Chamber's national judges arguing that the introductory submission request should not go forward and the international judges stating that it should. In accordance with ECCC law, the introductory submission was sent to the OCIJ, since the threshold of a four-person supermajority decision had not been reached.[33] The dispute would intensify.

Once the introductory submission for Cases 003 and 004 reached the OCIJ, little seemed to happen. The OCIJ did not issue any arrest warrants, and only a limited number of investigations into Case 003 took place in 2010, largely at the behest of Judge Lemonde, who headed the international side of the OCIJ.[34] Judge Lemonde resigned at the end of November 2010, whereupon he was replaced by the reserve OCIJ judge, Siegfried Blunk. The controversy further intensified in April 2011, when Judge Blunk and his Cambodian counterpart, Judge You Bunleng, announced that they had concluded the Case 003 investigation.[35]

Andrew Cayley, the international co-prosecutor who had replaced Robert Petit, then took the unusual step of requesting additional investigations, even as he released detailed information about Cases 003 and 004. He argued that doing so was in accordance with his duty to keep victims and witnesses informed and to ensure that the charges were "fully investigated."[36] Apparently, the OCIJ had neither interviewed the two suspects in Case 003 nor even formally informed "suspects that they were under investigation. Witnesses were not interviewed. Crime sites were not examined."[37]

Cayley's statement generated a great deal of publicity, playing into reports that the court was plagued by corruption and political influence. While again emphasizing the importance of "national reconciliation, stability, peace and security," Chea Leang responded by issuing a statement saying that "the suspects mentioned in the Case File 003 were not either senior leaders or those most responsible" during DK and therefore did "not fall within jurisdiction of the ECCC."[38] The OCIJ, in turn, complained about false rumors while demanding that Cayley retract his statement, which revealed confidential information.[39]

A number of international OCIJ staff began to quit in protest over the failure of their office to fully investigate Cases 003 and 004.[40] Then, on October 10, 2011, Judge Blunk issued a statement noting recent remarks made by Cambodian government officials, including this one: "If they want to go into Case 003 and 004, they should just pack their bags and leave." Shortly thereafter Judge Blunk resigned, amid allegations of OCIJ procedural irregularities, including the "falsification of evidence, including witness tampering, and the back-dating of orders."[41]

When the international reserve co-investigating judge, Laurent Kasper-Ansermet, announced his intention to begin work in a December 6, 2011, statement, You Bunleng immediately issued a statement claiming that Kasper-Ansermet had to wait until he was officially appointed and therefore that "any procedural action taken by Judge Laurent Kasper-Ansermet is not legally valid."[42] For the next four months, as Kasper-Ansermet sought to push forward the investigations into Cases 003 and 004, he was systematically thwarted, not just by his Cambodian counterpart but by the Cambodian president of the Pre-Trial Chamber as well as by administrative personnel. Before resigning on May 4, 2012, Kasper-Ansermet issued a document complaining about Judge You Bunleng's pervasive obstructionism, the refusal to allow Kasper-Ansermet to place documents on the case file, the impeding of internal and case-related investigations, and even the denial of Kasper-Ansermet's use of the official OCIJ seal.[43]

Some observers read the SCC's decision on personal jurisdiction in the Duch case in light of these ongoing events, since it effectively placed the decision about personal jurisdiction under the aegis of the OCP and the OCIJ where, potentially, it was more subject to political influence. For many years, international observers had speculated that Hun Sen wanted to restrict the number of cases for fear that an expanding number of cases would implicate members of his party, perhaps including himself, who were former Khmer Rouge and who, during DK, had held midlevel positions comparable to those of suspects in Cases 003 and 004.[44]

These ongoing events unsettled the legitimacy of the court. If "the Chamber" rendered a Judgment as the evidence was filtered through the lens of law to establish the truth, then the flagrant political interference in Cases 003 and 004, influence that appeared pervasive and deep, undermined its very purpose, which, as one observer noted, was "to make decisions independently on the facts and the law."[45]

Even as the SCC asserted its juridical articulation and ordering of "the facts," then, a number of issues that this articulation pushed out of sight nevertheless burst forth. These issues included questions about the personal and temporal jurisdiction of the court, who was being tried and who was not, and a perceived political skew to "the truth" that failed to provide a more complete picture—one that included an accounting of the role of midlevel Khmer Rouge and of members of the CPK, as well as of some donor countries, who had "benevolently" provided funding to the ECCC even as, due to the courts limited temporal jurisdiction, their own involvement in the events before, during, and after DK as redacted.

Yet it would be a mistake to simply dismiss the court as "corrupt." The very focus on the independence of the court, while important, may play into long-standing stereotypes about countries like Cambodia that say something not just about the observed but about the observers. Throughout the trial of Duch, I gave interviews to the media. Almost invariably, Western journalists asked questions about court scandals, ranging from kickbacks to political influence. I mentioned this tendency to a few reporters, who explained that their audiences and media outlets were concerned with these issues. The enormous attention paid to the controversies surrounding Cases 003 and 004 underscores this point. This is not to say that the media should ignore such stories. The point is to ask what is being foregrounded and backgrounded.

For, once again, these patterns reveal something about how a community (such as the "international community") not only looks at a place like Cambodia and the trial taking place in it but also constitutes itself through its ways of seeing—just as observers who gaze at the defaced Duch photo filter it through different lenses, articulate meanings in various ways. Moreover, the focus of this gaze also raises questions about what is not seen.

From a human rights perspective, one inflection of which is the "transitional justice imaginary," Cambodia prior to international peace-building intervention is often viewed as a "failed state," a country beset by authoritarian rule, violence, human rights abuses, and backwardness.[46] As a mechanism of transition, the tribunal is portrayed as a way to help Cambodia develop from this state of backwardness to one of progress, democracy, justice, civil society, peace, and the rule of law. Indeed, this set of human rights values is clearly laid out in the ECCC Agreement and was invoked in myriad ways during Duch's trial.

A related set of human rights understandings informs remarks written in the comment books in the room with Duch's defaced photograph. Visitors often invoke idioms of atrocity or humanitarian sentiment that assert the importance of universal human rights and the imperative to intervene to prevent senseless atrocity. Various comments made during the course of Duch's trial similarly foregrounded human rights violations, suffering victims, deterrence, prevention, and humanity as important reasons to hold the court. The Tuol Sleng photographs provide emotionally powerful images affirming these values—even if, as noted, there are other ways of reading such photos (for example, through the Khmer Rouge carceral lens, the Buddhist understandings of family members of the victims, or the juridical frame of the court).

And then there is the defaced photograph of Duch, stenciled with the word "evil" and adorned with devilish eyes, horns, and goatee. In 2012, people would write on his shirt "Die Slowly" and "BURN IN HELL!!!"—comments suggesting the fate of such a supposedly evil person. Many observations in the comment book parallel the graffiti, highlighting the seemingly incomprehensible violence, cruelty, and barbarity of S-21/Tuol Sleng. These ideas dovetail with the trope of "Duch the Monster" and related discourses on savagery. Duch, the "evil" and "cruel" savage, stands through metonymy as a representative of conflict-ridden Cambodia, the "failed state" plagued by a sort of Hobbesian "war of all against all" or the "Heart of Darkness," a metaphor used by Joseph Conrad in the context of Africa but easily transposed onto "savage" places like Cambodia—as illustrated by the film *Apocalypse Now*, in which the destination is Cambodia.

When we gaze at Duch, we stare at ourselves as we bring to bear our moral frames and articulations of self and other. At the ECCC, human rights frames and the transitional justice imaginary constitute such a powerful gaze, one that easily slips into long-standing stereotypes of the Oriental "other" that simultaneously constitutes an "us."[47] The "savage" plays a central role in this discursive formation, as the "civilized" in its various permutations (such as "the international community" or "humanitarians") is placed in the dominant position of the "savior" who comes to the rescue—preventing, intervening, assisting, donating, and uplifting a backward society by bringing democracy, justice, the rule of law, and human rights.[48] This discursive formation could be seen at the ECCC, where the "international community" was assisting Cambodia's transition from authoritarianism and savagery to civilized democracy, a process in which "the civilized" served as "donors" bestowing, with humanitarian benevolence, the "gift" of human rights, democracy, and civilization.

As I have illustrated repeatedly in this book, such articulations of the other inevitably redact, pushing complicating detail out of sight through the assertion of a monolithic representation. In the context of Cambodia and the ECCC, this articulation may obscure unsettling pasts. Thus, Cambodia is sometimes implicitly depicted as being rescued from a "failed state" of savagery by a set of "donors," including the United States, France, and China, who played a role in Cambodia's civil wars. This historical role—one critical to a more complete understanding of the past, the causes of the Khmer Rouge rise to power, and the "failed state" that followed DK—is redacted from the court narrative, due to a restricted temporal and personal jurisdiction that these very actors demanded before agreeing to allow the trial to take place.

The media focus on corruption and political influence likewise runs the risk of obscuring the longer history of Cambodia, which is often portrayed as jumping from DK to the early 1990s (the Paris Peace Agreements and 1993 UN elections) or the early- to mid-2000s (the establishment and start of the

ECCC). Some critics, including scholars, journalists, and even defense lawyers in Case 002, have sought to bring these complicated histories to light as the tribunal has proceeded.[49] But, again, this discussion often takes place within the context of the "international community" or "the West." What other sets of understandings, we might ask, also mediate the ways Cambodians view the trials?

February 4, 2012 (Morning)

Standing in the Building D room where the defaced photograph of Duch hangs, I adjust my gaze and look away from it to see what else is on the wall. Duch's photograph is part of a bank of photographs of DK leaders. A photo of Nuon Chea is placed directly below Duch's. It, too, has been graffitied, the text all in Khmer. Someone has struck a line in black marker across Nuon Chea's eyes. Nearby, someone else has drawn swirls on Ieng Sary's head, as if to signify a crazed mind. But I choose not to linger on these images.

Instead, I look for the exhibition placard titled "Justice and Responsibility."

It's still there, though the print has faded. I reread the five paragraphs describing the historical events leading to the creation of the trial, including some that took place between 1979 and 1993 and have been pushed out of sight at the ECCC due to its limited temporal jurisdiction. But the text, which I wrote in 2006, is no longer familiar. It is as if I am reading someone else's words. Seeing myself named as author of the "Justice and Responsibility" panel, my name and my words separated from Duch's defaced photo by just a meter of space and the bar of the placard's black frame, remains uncanny. So, too, would the experience of returning to the room in 2013 to find the defaced photograph of Duch gone, marked only by the two nail holes and the trace outline of the missing frame.

The text I wrote for the "Justice and Responsibility" panel asserted, of course, an articulation of Cambodia's past, as does what I now write about Duch's trial. I, too, am a "graffiti artist" and a redactor. This book is my articulation. Like the trace outline of Duch's missing photograph, my articulation is inevitably leaving out much, a fact that is disconcerting. For whatever we write invariably has gaps, as we selectively edit, foreground, background, frame, push that which is discordant out of sight.

Originally, I planned to write a different book, one examining how, in the context of Duch's trial and the ECCC, Western notions of justice were operationalized on the local level as institutions and ideas were adapted, modified, ignored, and transformed on the ground. I even had a title for the book, "Justice in Translation," one I may use for a companion volume. But this project took a different turn as I became caught up in the flow of Duch's trial. There are traces of this shift in my fieldwork notebooks, my own small archive, fragments of text providing an authority of sorts, a claim to "being there" and "having seen or heard," which I have selectively used and edited to write the story of Duch's trial.

Two days after the SCC's final decision, for example, I attended a Case 002 hearing. On the first page of my fieldnotes, I wrote things like, "Chum Mey / Bou Meng argument" and "Gaze at court emblem → yesterday Bou Meng says Buddhist" (the words "Gaze" and "BM says Buddhist" are circled). At the bottom of the notebook page, however, are quickly jotted notations forming a rudimentary diagram that lays out a chronological sequence of book chapters: "Preface (DC-Cam) / Apology (view of court, CPs vs Duch, history of court) / M-13 (perpetrators, how [they] come to do it, psychology) / S-21 (Him Huy? Prak Khan?) / Civil Parties (Bou Meng) / Norng Chan Phal (evidence, Case 002, DC-Cam) / Appeal / Verdict." Underneath, I wrote "types of redaction." I had been waiting until the trial of Duch concluded to start writing my book, and here, just two days later, I began to settle on a sequential structure that would follow the course of the trial as well as one of the conceptual frames, the redactic, which would inform my articulation.

While I had closely followed the proceedings of the trial of Duch to their conclusion, I decided to undertake a writing process that mirrored the narrative of the trial, composing each chapter based on what was being said in court at the time and not looking ahead at later court transcripts. I soon found that I was writing something along the lines of an ethnodrama, a genre less frequently found in anthropology, despite what it allows through the use of performative techniques. I wanted a style that would foreground the language in the transcripts and background my own voice of ethnographic authority, even if, of course, it remained present in the articulation I created and the redactions I made.

I have long been convinced that anthropologists and scholars in general can do much more in their writing, experimenting and making or reinforcing their ideas, experiences, and points through the use of literary techniques. Accordingly, as I have written this book, I have tried to bear in mind the creative writing imperative "Show, don't tell." Because of my academic training, I have struggled with this imperative throughout the writing process. Even here, I am "saying it," though doing so, perhaps, in a manner that disrupts that which is often pushed out of sight in academic books—the process of writing and, especially, redacting.

My use of literary techniques, such as poetic form, is directly linked to the ethnodramatic approach I decided to take. Thus, I placed an abecedarian about Duch at the start of this book. I found it possible to evoke in a few short pages—and often in a more interesting manner—what would take many more pages to convey through traditional exposition. Poetic form allows for the use of juxtaposition, sequencing, and imagery, which is difficult to do in traditional academic prose. Similarly, literary techniques provide a distinct way of capturing a moment and being attentive to voice, testimony, and the fragmentary. Along these lines, I sought to disrupt a more traditional style of expository voice by blending narrative styles, including directly placing myself into the text through first person narrative.

I have also provided an erasure, a poetic form based on redaction. In erasures, portions of an existing text are edited out to foreground both presence and absence. The erasure poem I created from the text of Duch's apology, sought to foreground Duch's use of "I" and the way his act of apology involved redaction as it pared down the enormity of the S-21 violence, masking it within the juridical context. The erasure form also suggests the unease Duch's repeated apologies created for some civil parties. Furthermore, the erasure form dovetailed with my attempt to highlight the tension of articulation and redaction, the creation of text through editing, a process that foregrounds by acts of erasure.

Likewise, my use of a cento, a poetic form juxtaposing text from different sources, fits with the thematic of reconstruction, even as it, too, involves redaction. There is more, such as my attempt to use imagery—passages, interiors and exteriors, geometric shape, optics, silence, darkness and light, and even a dream. But I am straying far from "Show, don't tell."

My use of such literary techniques and imagery circulates around the redactic, the tension that emerges when, during the process of framing, calibration, and conversion involved in articulation, we necessarily edit and erase. This notion is at the heart of this book and ultimately suggests something about all of us. To navigate the world, we frame, calibrate, and articulate. In doing so, we redact. This point is seemingly self-evident. But we must be wary of the maskings and obfuscations that are always present and that underlie the banality of everyday thought, including those related to the more structured—and often highly politicized—"thick frames" that are epitomized by the DK party line as well as the politics of memory after DK, ranging from the PRK atrocity frame to the human rights and juridical frames circulating at the time of Duch's trial. Political power is often naturalized and masked by such thick frames, not just in the extreme case of DK and S-21, but even in seemingly more neutral contexts like the ECCC and transitional justice more broadly, which are also linked to geopolitical hierarchies, categorizations, obfuscations of the past, and redactic renderings of a singular truth.

This situation is fraught because people readily attend to the articulation, which is structured by thick frames and related taken-for-granted and even naturalized understandings—not the redaction and potentially related maskings of power. The redactic is frightening, uncanny, something familiar that threatens to disrupt the understandings that structure our thought and behavior and thereby provokes anxiety. It may also hint at something "at stake" that is just out of sight, ranging from political contestations to deeply held convictions.

Complicated philosophical questions emerge here, not just about political power but also about belief. What is belief? How does it structure our being? In anthropology, such questions have often been grappled with through the notion of culture, or the sets of institutions and beliefs mediating our interactions with one another and the world—interactions that can also mean the difference between death and life, that enable us to adapt, love, hate, trade, feel, think, and understand, that make us human.

While anthropologists and other scholars have traditionally been quick to discuss these structures of knowledge, they have sometimes been less ready to grapple with the redactic, or that which has been pushed out of sight, remains unsaid and silenced, or has been obscured by the salient cultural models, "thick framings," and political power. Why, again, do we so readily turn to explication? How might we also highlight ambiguity, tension, what doesn't fit with our articulations, what has been edited out?

In psychology and philosophy, scholars have in different ways discussed what I am calling articulation and redaction. Freud's notion of the uncanny provides an illustration of this point, with its attunement to the familiar and the strange, the return of the repressed, and the double—notions that have been threaded throughout this book. Derrida and Lacan picked on some of these ideas, using them in new ways.[50]

The uncanny, for example, is found in Lacan's notion of the Real, the sudden eruption of something almost familiar that is nevertheless beyond our comprehension and terrifying and leads us to avert our gaze. Relatedly, Lacan viewed the sense of self as fragmentary and anxiety-provoking, something we strive to articulate even as a coherent self is impossible to achieve and our efforts fall short, threatening and haunting our sense of being. This notion of the self as illusory and fragmented dovetails with Buddhist understandings as well. Such ideas regarding the uncanny, the self, and anxiety resonate with the articulation-redaction dynamic that undergirds much of this book.

As an anthropologist, I am methodologically inclined to the experience-near—in this case back to S-21, DK, and Duch's trial. Everywhere we turn in this situation, we find framing, calibration, articulation, and redaction: confessions and revolutionary stances calibrated to accord with the party line, assessments of character framed in terms of psychological function, judicial judgments calibrated in terms of legal frames. All involve articulation and the redactic, as what has been pushed out of sight may suddenly emerge in unsettling ways—in hauntings, slippages, traces, and ambiguities.

What is distinct about the party line and genocidal ideologies are the manner in which violence is utilized to assert an articulation, to erase categories of being that don't fit with this vision, and to prevent that which has been pushed out of sight from reemerging. In its most extreme form, the genocidal imaginary seeks to accomplish this by completely eradicating difference so that there is no possibility of return—even if what has been redacted inevitably returns in a trace, a haunting, a double, a moment in which what has been hidden suddenly dehisces, as illustrated by the Cambodian proverb Duch mentioned: "If you break open the crab you'll show the shit."

If it is not possible to escape framing, calibration, articulation, and redaction, the extremity of genocide and S-21 perhaps suggest responses. If one is the need to unmask what has been redacted, another is a stance of openness. It is a response I was thinking of when, during one of Duch's trial sessions, I wrote in a notebook: "Face of the other/perpetrator." The notion of attuning to the "face of the other" is often linked to the philosopher Levinas, even if scholars, dating back to Herodotus, have grappled with the ways "the other" is seen and, along these lines, respected, feared, hated, tolerated, ignored, resented, embraced, stereotyped, purged, and killed. How, then, do we see the other? Do we recognize their humanity? How does the way we see "them" help create an "us"? Such issues are strong undercurrents of Duch's trial, sometimes implicit, on other occasions explicit.

These are some of the questions I have asked while writing this book. "Seeing the face of the other" requires an acknowledgment of different ways of knowing, alternative sets of values and norms, various ways of seeing the world. There are, in short, different articulations of reality, ones that may clash with and unsettle our deepest beliefs. As opposed to resorting to killing, "seeing the face of the other" requires that we do our best to understand different articulations, consider what is redacted from our own, remain open to "recalibration," and attempt to find points of a shared humanity, even if defined as a shared space of being-in-the-world, since the concept of "the human" may vary.

I have built this tension regarding "seeing the face of the other" into this book. It is manifest in the redactic binary of "man or monster," two competing visions of Duch that ran throughout the trial. Thus I emphasized passages highlighting how constructions of "Duch the man" and "Duch the monster" were asserted. François Roux, for example, repeatedly argued for the humanity of Duch, acknowledging his profound mistakes and awful choices but nevertheless stressing circumstance, his own supposed dehumanization within the DK system, and his capacity for change. For others, as expressed most strongly by some of the civil parties, Duch had lost his claim to humanity when, day after day, he presided over torture, suffering, pain, and mass death. The victims had been dehumanized, and the trial process and Duch's conviction potentially provided a path for them to regain their humanity, in part through civil party testimony.

This dilemma, and the broader question of how we "see the face of the other," is the reason I chose to foreground the defaced photograph of Duch. For it clearly highlights that there are different ways to "graffiti" Duch. In English, Duch is labeled "evil." But another set of interpretations is implicit in the Khmer text, annotations an English speaker may overlook. Duch's eyes highlight this point, as, in one frame, they suggest the demonic. From a Cambodian Buddhist perspective, however, they may also convey ignorance, the state of being that leads to sinful action. When an English-speaker gazes at Duch's photograph, this alternative articulation of Duch remains unseen.

Even as we offer articulations, we must remain open to alternative framings. This is one critical point a study of the Khmer Rouge reveals. They, like other groups that have committed mass murder, offered a singular vision of the world that made sharp demarcations between us and them. Rather than being open to "the other," the Khmer Rouge regime sought their elimination. The paradox, of course, is that ultimately the struggle is against an other that is a double, an inverted image of an identity that is constituted by the way the other is imagined.

While prisoners lie on the floor of the torture cell, their humanity is diminished and remains unseen, even as their identity is recalibrated in terms of the dominant articulation, their past recast as a history of deviant action, malicious motive, and treason—the qualities of an "enemy," however so defined.

Complicating pasts and characteristics of the detainee are redacted. The "face of the other" is pushed out of sight. This process does not just emerge in the extremity of genocide—it pervades our everyday lives. The problem is that these articulations become taken-for-granted, making it more difficult to see what has been redacted. The erasure form dramatically illustrates this point.

Duch's photograph and trial offer us lessons about this process of calibration, articulation, and redaction. How, we must ask, do we see and "graffiti" the other? What does this say about ourselves, our own belief systems, the banality of our everyday thought, and the moral economies we circulate? Ultimately, the consideration of such questions may be deeply unsettling and lead to uncomfortable answers. For who wants to acknowledge that, in gazing at a "monster" like Duch, we catch glimpses of ourselves?

But it is the attempt at attunement, an openness to "the other" and their humanity, which may provide one with an ethical position in the face of violence. This stance is not easy. It is something with which I have grappled. When I gaze at Duch's photo and consider who I am looking at, I struggle not to simply see him as a monster and present him as such. Perhaps I have done so. This possibility is unsettling.

| | |

My own preconceptions in this regard emerged when, after Duch's trial, I traveled to Long Muy's hometown. I wanted to ask Long Muy's brother, Long Tai, what he thought about the fact that Duch had used his brother's confession as part of his defense. I thought Tai would be outraged and condemn "Duch the monster." But Tai didn't say much in this regard. He did talk about how he, Long Muy, and other members of his family had joined the Khmer Rouge during the civil war. He noted that the family used to jump into trenches when the area was carpet-bombed by US planes, though he insisted that Sihanouk's appeal was the main reason they had joined the revolution.

Tai didn't remember Long Muy well, though he recalled that he liked to play soccer, was honest, and had become a revolutionary to save the country. He also recounted how, during Long Muy's last visit home, Long Muy had given the family the photograph of himself standing in front of Wat Phnom in the heart of Phnom Penh. Tai showed me this photograph along with a blurry childhood shot of Long Muy.

After DK, the family received no news about Long Muy. "I did dream about him a few times," Tai said. He told me that in his dream, "I said to my brother

Long Muy at Wat Phnom, c. 1976. Photo courtesy of the DC-Cam / SRI Archives.

'I thought you were dead,' but he said 'No, I survived, I'm still alive.'"[51] Tai only learned of Long Muy's death in 2000, after a local official read a story about Long Muy in a DC-Cam magazine. By this time, their parents had passed away. Later, he read Long Muy's confession. "Some things, perhaps 30 percent of the confession, were true, particularly his description of events prior to 1970," Tai said. "But other parts were not true at all. He just wrote things down to avoid torture." Tribunal outreach staff had asked if he wanted to become a civil party, but Tai declined, saying he just wanted to forget.

"Did you know that Duch used your brother's confession as part of his defense?" I asked. Tai responded that his wife had seen this on TV. "Duch did this to prove that he was working under Son Sen and Pol Pot and was only following orders," he replied. "People who do wrong don't admit it; they point their finger at someone else to escape the charges." As we conversed I was surprised, because I had thought Tai would be outraged by Duch's use of Long Muy's confession. Instead, he spoke in a quiet monotone, his sentences short and clipped.

"Can you forgive Duch?" I asked. Tai was quiet for a moment and appeared close to tears. Finally, he said, "I have forgotten these things because they happened long ago. But I can't forgive him."

On the drive back to Phnom Penh, I reflected on this moment. I had entered this interview with an expectation of outrage. Indeed, it was one of the reasons I had traveled far into the countryside to meet with Tai and to try to recuperate some of Long Muy's lost history, which had been redacted first at S-21 and then during the trial, when Duch had used Long Muy's confession as part of his defense. But Tai did not appear outraged. Instead, he seemed more inclined to forget the events and spoke with little passion about Duch. There was just that one moment when he almost began to cry. I could easily have made that moment the focus of a description of this encounter, a dramatic crescendo around which my narrative would be structured.

But this articulation would redact his silences, his marginal interest in the court, the many times his affect had been flat. It would also foreground my own biases regarding human rights while pushing away alternative frames, such as the Buddhist or Cambodian-Chinese understandings mediating Tai's response.

This is just a single moment in the over two hundred interviews I conducted during my research on Duch's trial. Most of the interview material never figured directly in this book; the parts I have used are selective and have been edited to help create this account. I have asserted articulations. I have redacted. I invite you to flip through the pages of this text, look in the shadows, consider what has been pushed out of sight. As you do so, consider your own articulations and redactions.

Ultimately, all of our analyses are articulations. We redact as we weave together our narratives. What is difficult is to see our own biases, what we may have left out—our own ethical stance in relationship to spaces of violence and the difficulties involved in confronting our biases and encounters with the other, an encounter that reveals much about ourselves and the moral economies undergirding our gaze. We articulate, we redact, we erase. We need to consider what we have blackened out, to seek the face of the other, to search for what has been pushed out of sight.

To acknowledge this point does not entail giving up explanation. On the contrary, retaining a self-critical openness toward the redactic, a point I discuss further in the epilogue, enables us to develop more nuanced understandings of given phenomenon—even if an awareness of the redactic suggests the impossibility of there being one overarching singular "truth," a point highlighted in this book in contexts ranging from the torture chambers of S-21 to the juridical rendering of a verdict to the imposition of a reductive frame such as "man or monster."

February 5, 2012, Tuol Sleng Prison (Midday)

Blood spurts as a cadre dressed in black with a Mao cap drags a knife across the throat of a blindfolded and bound victim. The cadre looks at ease, casually glancing down as he grips the prisoner's hair and yanks back his victim's head to better expose the neck. A second cadre, holding an AK-47, observes the execution with a pleased look from a few yards away. He stands in a field of grass; behind him, a thicket of green bamboo stalks rises toward a light blue sky.

After a moment of shock at seeing the scene, I notice that at the very front edge of the painting, just below the skin of the victim's lower legs, the corpses of several recently killed prisoners lie in a mass grave. A green bamboo club is on the ground by the prisoner's side. The end is covered in blood.

"That's my wife, Ma Yeoun."[52] Bou Meng explains after we ascend a set of steep stairs leading to a second-story flat he is renting, kitty-corner from Tuol Sleng. The oil canvas painting of his wife's execution, leaning against a wall, is the first thing I see on reaching the landing of the spare flat. A single mattress lies on the floor next to a few piles of clothes and Bou Meng's art. Accustomed to seeing such scenes within the walls of Tuol Sleng, but not expecting to see such a painting inside a person's home, I am startled.

"It's Choeung Ek," Bou Meng continues. "It's the place where they clubbed the prisoners and then cut their throats to make sure they were dead." The executioner, he tells me, is Him Huy, the S-21 cadre who oversaw the executions. Bou Meng explains that the painting, which he completed after the Trial Chamber's judgment, is based on Duch's testimony. "I want to show the world that my wife, Ma Yeoun, was killed at the killing fields of Choeung Ek, not Tuol Sleng."

Eventually our conversation shifts to the SCC's final decision. "I'm 100 percent satisfied," Bou Meng states. "It was appropriate given his crimes, violation of human rights, and mass murder at [S-21] . . . the sentence was fitting: he reaped what he sowed." Bou Meng goes on to explain that the ECCC will serve as "a model for the world" that can be used to bring future despots to justice. He notes that Cambodian law doesn't allow for the death penalty. "In truth," Bou Meng says, "given the extent of his guilt, Duch should have been shot and killed." He pauses for a moment then repeats, "Yes, he should have been shot."

I am not surprised when Bou Meng tells me that he can't forgive Duch.

Duch's crimes, Bou Meng explains, are just too serious, and he "didn't tell the truth. He always said he was following the orders of others. . . . But he was the one who taught the interrogators and, along with the other Khmer Rouge leaders, did so many cruel things and committed genocide." Duch, Bou Meng notes, "acted so that it seemed like he had a polite character. But his heart is really savage. From the outside, his face looked good. But inside, his heart was bad. . . . There is an old Khmer saying, 'You can know a person's face, but you can't know their heart.' "

The situation is different, Bou Meng stresses, for lower-level cadre like Him Huy, who just carried out Duch's orders. Duch is ultimately responsible for the "savage acts" that took place at S-21. "Duch used them to kill," Bou Meng continues, "so the guilt falls on him. The life sentence was like cutting off the head of a snake so it can no longer bite and kill." Accordingly, even though Him Huy beat Bou Meng at S-21, Bou Meng is still willing to reconcile with him and accept his apology—though Him Huy has not apologized.

When Duch's sentence was announced, Bou Meng said, he thought of his wife. Indeed, he explained that her spirit is constantly on his mind. On the day he testified, Bou Meng asked Duch where his wife had been killed. Bou Meng did so because he wanted to perform a ceremony for her. After Duch replied that his wife was likely killed at Choeung Ek, Bou Meng had taken a small amount of dirt from Choeung Ek, after praying to the God of the Earth, "My wife died here. I didn't see it. But you, Earth, were a witness. So I request permission to take this earth so that I can use incense and make offerings to the soul of my wife."

Later, after bringing the earth home, he performed a Buddhist ceremony in which he made offerings to monks who recited scriptures transferring the merit to "my wife, Ma Youen, so that she would receive the benefit [phal]. If she had been reborn in the Buddhist Hells, this would help her rise back up [to higher realms]." Bou Meng hopes she will be reborn as a Buddhist angel or human being, not a person who would die by having "someone cut her throat." Bou Meng uses *phal*, the same Khmer Buddhist term for "benefit" (or "yield," "consequence") that he used when stating that Duch had received the just result of his actions, a life sentence, commensurate with the magnitude of his bad deeds.

Much of what Bou Meng tells me is framed by his deeply Buddhist perspective, as is the case with other civil parties and Cambodians who interpreted Duch's trial using articulations that often differed from the assumptions of the transitional justice imaginary and Western conceptions of justice. While Bou Meng speaks about human rights, international justice, and prevention, he more readily invokes Buddhist understandings. During the final judgment, Bou Meng prayed to the Buddha to deliver a just verdict. When he saw the official court emblem, he thought the figure depicted was a Buddhist *tevoda*, not an ancient Angkorean official.

After the final judgment, Bou Meng went with other civil parties to Choeung Ek, where a ceremony was held to transfer the result to the spirits of their dead relatives. Bou Meng lit incense and prayed, "'I sought justice and now have it. Duch received a life sentence. Please, my dear Youen, receive this verdict, receive justice.' I also prayed like this at Tuol Sleng, sending the good result to her." Bou Meng said a prayer for Vann Nath, who had died a few months earlier.

The Buddhist notion of "return" (*sâng*) also figures in Bou Meng's remarks during our meeting in his flat. It is implicit in his discussion of action and result. But he also invokes this idea directly. After recalling the story of a follower of the Buddha who received the result of a bad deed, Bou Meng reflects, "Maybe in a past life, I did something like this to despicable Duch and now he has sinned back. So we have returned [sâng] malicious deeds to one another. [The vindictiveness] won't end until we stop being entangled by this [cycle of debt and return]."

"Can I speak to you about the documents?" Bou Meng asks at the end of the interview. "There are two people but just one document. Is that good or bad?" I don't know what he is talking about and ask him to clarify. "There's just one book," he replies. It turns out he is referring to a growing tension with Chum Mey.

A dozen yards away from Bou Meng's stand, Chum Mey sells copies of a DC-Cam magazine article about his experiences at S-21. Chum Mey had entered into a partnership with a vendor, whose kiosk stands under the shade of a metal overhang and nearby tree. While Chum Mey's magazine story is not as eye-catching as Bou Meng's book, Chum Mey sells other books about DK on a small folding table behind which he sits in a chair. In contrast to Bou Meng, he has no signs.

There appear to be two problems. The first is the problem of "the documents," by which Bou Meng means that only one of them, Bou Meng, has a biographical book to sell. This isn't fair, Bou Meng says, because Chum Mey has a complicated story, one that includes torture. Having just one book is "not balanced." However, he notes, it also isn't fair that Chum Mey's table is set closer to Building D, from which most tourists exit after finishing their tour. On the way out, tourists pass Chum Mey's stand first, giving Chum Mey a sales advantage.

As Bou Meng speaks, I glance at a second large painting hanging in the room, one depicting Bou Meng and Chum Mey smiling, arms on each other's shoulders, as they stand with a large group of Australian youths in front of the barbed-wire mesh of Building C. Bou Meng wears the same dark green jacket depicted in the painting.

I noticed tension between them when I first arrived at Tuol Sleng. I saw Chum Mey sitting on a bench and went to sit by him while I waited for Bou Meng to arrive. Chum Mey smiled and patted my knee as we began to speak. But when Bou Meng arrived, Chum Mey's smile disappeared, though he remained polite.

"Do you think you can help?" Bou Meng asks.

He is seeking the sort of third-party intervention to which Cambodians often turn to resolve a dispute. Courts, notorious for corruption, are usually a last resort. I am in an awkward position, caught in the middle of a growing dispute between two longtime informants and friends. "I'm just a foreigner," I reply after a pause. "This is Cambodia and maybe it would be better to get a Cambodian to assist since I am less familiar with local customs."

As we walk back down the steep stairs, Bou Meng doesn't say much or smile. I recall that, during the interview, he said that while satisfied with the verdict, things are not fully resolved for him because he lost his wife and children. "I still get headaches when I think about them," he said, adding: "I also am forgetful, get dizzy, have spikes in my blood pressure, and am quick to anger." I think of the many times I have seen Bou Meng rubbing his forehead or applying tiger balm. His psychological problems, Bou Meng explained, are directly related to the torture, cruelty, and loss he suffered at S-21.

| | |

In the early afternoon, I return to Tuol Sleng to meet Chum Mey. The vendor informs me that he has just eaten and will come back shortly. I notice that Chum Mey's little table has been moved to the far side of the kiosk, closer to Bou Meng's stand, though still first on the pathway leading from Building D. I wonder if this is a compromise. Or perhaps the table has been moved out of the sun.

After watching tourists pass through the room with Chan Kim Srun's photograph, I return to the old entrance. Chum Mey has not yet returned, but Bou Meng is there with a young woman. She tells me in English that she is Bou Meng's translator and works for a local English-language newspaper. She holds an open copy of Bou Meng's book, trying to catch the attention of tourists and make a sales pitch. She tells a group that Bou Meng lost his teeth because he was tortured here. Bou Meng points to his mouth and opens wide.

I wonder about the circuits of money that must be flowing behind the scenes. Bou Meng, who speaks no English, likely has a commission system with the journalist. Someone later tells me that Bou Meng pays $200 a month to sell his book at Tuol Sleng, perhaps a kickback to the officials there. Chum Mey may have a similar arrangement with the vendors in the kiosk, who do their best to facilitate his sales. There is something disconcerting about the commodification of their suffering and the fact these S-21 survivors now sell their stories at Tuol Sleng in a commercial transaction. Indeed, their stories are written in English and sold primarily to English-speakers. Many tourists who purchase their stories ask to take photos of themselves with Bou Meng or Chum Mey, which they sometimes post on blogs.

While it is easy to condemn this sort of "dark tourism," the money provides Bou Meng and Chum Mey with a livelihood and greatly increases their income. A Cambodian civil society staffer working on tribunal outreach once suggested to me that the money is like a reparation—precisely the financial sort that the court has been unable to provide to civil parties. Ultimately, it is their decision whether or not to sell their stories (Vann Nath chose not to), the sort of choice they were denied at S-21.

"I want to give you this," Bou Meng says with a smile.

It is an 11- by 17-inch reproduction of the painting depicting the cutting of his wife's throat at Choeung Ek. Even though I am taken aback, I politely thank him. I wonder what the hotel staff will think when I return with this graphic image. We start talking. His anger has passed, and he is eager to show me the different items in his stall. He has a stack of perhaps a dozen of his books, as well as a faded black-and-white photo of the S-21 survivors.

| | |

Over time, both he and Chum Mey would refine their sales operations. Both would print large stacks of business cards, which they would hand out each time they made a sale or met someone of interest. Both would advertise their books with large banners. Bou Meng's new one would headline "SURVIVOR" before explaining, in smaller print: "I'm Bou Meng, Artist and a Former prisoner of S-21 / Ma Youen, Bou Meng's wife, She was arrested, tortured here / and killed on August 16–1977 at Killing fields."

Below the text would be four images: the cover of Bou Meng's book and reproductions of three of his paintings with captions. The first painting, with the caption "They Tortured me," would show him being whipped and beaten. The second would depict how "They washed [my wounds] with salt water." The third—a reproduction of Bou Meng's painting of Him Huy cutting his wife's throat, the one he gave me—would read "They killed my wife." Bou Meng would kept reproductions of some of his paintings relating to S-21 in plastic wrap, including one depicting Hum Huy riding him like an animal up the steps of S-21, an incident discussed during Duch's trial.

Chum Mey would get a larger table lined with banners. The main one announced, "I am Chum Manh called 'Chum Mey' / Former victim / at S.21 / (Tuol Sleng Genocide museum)." The banner would have two captions, one telling of Chum Mey holding his hand up as he was being beaten. Over time, Chum Mey and Bou Meng would develop their sales pitches as they engaged in a low simmer capitalist competition. Tour guides, perhaps receiving a small commission, would bring large groups of tourists to their stands. At times, they would be able to sell ten, twenty, or even more copies of their stories to a group, earning considerable amounts of cash. One Cambodian NGO worker told me he estimated that on a good day, they could make as much as $1,000, a considerable sum in Cambodia.

| | | |

When Chum Mey returns, he explains he is late because he has been at a DC-Cam meeting with the director, Youk Chhang, and Seth Mydans, the longtime *New York Times* reporter who will help Chum Mey write his biography. So Chum Mey will also have a book. He smiles as he invites me to sit on a white plastic chair behind his table.

Like Bou Meng, Chum Mey is pleased with the SCC's final decision. "I filed as a civil party because I watched too many innocent Cambodians killed. I observed the trial closely for 77 days, listening to what the different parties said. I remember everything."[53] He is "100 percent satisfied" with the life sentence, though, he warns, he could not have accepted a sentence of 35 years or less and would have withdrawn as a Case 002 civil party if that had come to pass. He hopes the defendants in that case will also be sentenced to life (a wish that will be fulfilled). Given the need for peace and reconciliation, he tells me, echoing the government's position, only the five senior leaders indicted in Cases 001 and 002 should be tried. He adds that when Duch heard the life sentence, Duch's "face darkened."

Chum Mey says he cannot forgive Duch and still views his statements and apologies with suspicion. If Bou Meng compared Duch to a snake, Chum Mey likens Duch to a crocodile that cannot be trusted. Duch shed tears in court, but they were not sincere and could never compensate for the tears and suffering of thousands of victims. Duch, Chum Mey states, apologized to the court for the killings, but "never apologized directly to my face, Vann Nath, or Bou Meng. . . . If he had I would have been pleased." Instead, Duch, placing his hands in his pants pockets in an arrogant manner, gazed at the civil parties in the gallery.

"Have you seen the photograph of Duch on the second floor of Building D?" I eventually ask. "Where they have drawn on his face," Chum Mey affirms, chuckling. "People did this because they really hate [Duch,] Ieng Sary, Nuon Chea, and the other [Khmer Rouge bosses]." When I ask Chum Mey why someone has scribbled out Duch's eyes, Chum Mey explains that it signifies Duch's blindness, his inability to tell right from wrong. "Duch can't see the people and understand their stories, telling what is false and true. So someone scribbled out his eyes, making him blind."

I pause, considering how I first interpreted the graffiti on Duch's eyes as a demonic glow, a sign of "evil" linked to the Judeo-Christian tradition, with its association of Satan, hell, and the diametrical opposition of good and evil. In Khmer, however, there is no exact gloss for "evil." It is perhaps most readily translated as "bad" (*akrak*) or "sin" (*bap*). As Chum Mey's remark highlights, he reads the graffiti through a Cambodian Buddhist lens, one that, as with Bou Meng, deeply mediates his interactions with the court, even if he is able to invoke language linked to the transitional justice imaginary.

Duch's scribbled-out eyes, Chum Mey informs me, are directly tied to Buddhism. "According to Buddhism," he says, noting a common Buddhist adage, "those who act sinfully will receive sin, those who act meritoriously will receive merit." He continues: "Thus, Buddhist dhamma holds that those who act correctly receive a correct result [phal], while those who don't act correctly and do bad things [akrak] will receive a bad result [phal akrak]. If not in this life, then the person will receive this bad result when they are reborn." In making these statements, he uses the same term for "result" or "consequence" (phal) that Bou Meng invoked to discuss the transfer of merit to the dead, a point Chum Mey also makes. With regard to Duch's graffitied eyes, Chum Mey explains: "The execution of prisoners was an act in which the eyes did not see [properly]. Because the eyes are special, allowing us to know right and wrong. . . . If the eyes are blind [as in the Duch photo], it means that a person can't see right from wrong."

This Buddhist lens informs Chum Mey's interpretation of other parts of the graffiti. In Khmer, across Duch's cheeks and nose just below his scribbled-out eyes, someone has written "despicable cruel one" (a-chochov), a term mentioned frequently during Duch's trial. Chochov can be translated as "mean, ferocious, cruel, violent."[54] But it suggests a cruelty and wildness (brei) that comes from that beyond the social universe, the "cultivated" and domesticated order (srok). A person who is chochov does not abide by the law or the moral prescriptions of Buddhism.

Thus, Duch was chochov due to his status as someone who has transgressed the law during DK. His trial, from this perspective, is a way of returning him to the sociomoral order. This position on the edge of the wild and the domesticated, the brei and the srok, the water and the land, is a liminal one, placing Duch in a site of transformation—his location in the "dock"—as he is domesticated through the juridical process. But this position makes him all the more uncanny, as he is familiar yet unfamiliar, like "us" yet one of "them," a "man" who also seems a "monster."

With regard to Buddhism, Chum Mey says, after a pause, the chochov graffitied across Duch's face means "he doesn't have dhamma inside himself. . . . A person who has dhamma inside won't kill others for fear of sinning. But despicable [Duch] didn't have dhamma inside, his heart was extremely cruel [chochov]." For Chum Mey, Duch's cruelty and non-Khmer "otherness" is further illustrated by his ethnicity and religious belief. "Duch was born Chinese, and we don't know if he is also Buddhist. But later he converted to Christianity . . . because the Christian God can help if you are guilty"—a point noted during the trial. In Buddhism, Chum Mey continues, such sins cannot be washed away, since "those who do wrong will receive a bad result and those who act correctly will receive a good result [phal]."

The Buddhist notion of the inevitable "return" of the consequences of one's actions, good or bad, informs Cambodian understandings of the term "justice" (*yuttethoa*)—a term that itself is a compound suggesting "that which is in accordance" (*yutte*) with *dhamma* (*thoa*). From this Cambodian Buddhist perspective, justice implies a cosmic balancing, as a proper "return" or "yield" following a given act.

Indeed, balance is a key Cambodian idiom, mediating a variety of domains, from health to social relations to law. Bou Meng illustrated this point when explaining the meaning of justice by moving his index fingers back and forth, like the sides of a scale, to demonstrate how karma, the Buddhist law of action and consequence, works. Chum Mey notes that the monks who attended Duch's judgment were there because they "wanted to know the truth about whether the court was proper and in accordance with Buddhism" and with *yuttethoa*, which involved properly determining right from wrong.

From this perspective, Duch's sentence can be seen as a form of rebalancing in terms of the karmic consequences of his bad actions. As Bou Meng pointed out, Duch's acts entangle him in a cycle of "return" with his victims, living and dead. The imbalance caused by violent deaths unsettles the spiritual order, preventing the souls from having a proper rebirth. Chum Mey notes that when the civil parties went to Choeung Ek to dedicate the SCC judgment to the souls of their relatives, "this helped the dead by quieting their hearts [sgnop chhet], making it so that they did not want to continue being angry and tied in a karmic cycle of vindictiveness with Duch." He continues: "So we performed the ceremony, lighting incense and sending [the result/verdict/justice] to the [souls of the dead], saying 'Now the court has sentenced him and we have 100 percent justice . . . so please quiet your hearts.'"

As Chum Mey and Bou Meng's comments suggest, the juridical experience of the victims during Duch's trial was heavily mediated by this Buddhist lens of karma and (im)balance. His actions had created an imbalance that needed to be righted, as he properly received the consequences of his actions, and through the "result" (*phal*), symbolized by the verdict, the souls of the dead were quieted, as were the lives of the victims, whose own relations to the dead had been unsettled and whose state of health had been compromised by the S-21 violence.

Indeed, both Bou Meng and Chum Mey say that Duch's sentence makes them feel more at ease and helps alleviate psychological problems that have long afflicted them. While courts do not invariably "heal" as the transitional justice imaginary suggests, such trials may, on a case-by-case basis, help some victims, albeit in ways mediated by local frames of understanding—including

Cambodian Buddhist and ethnopsychological beliefs that may diverge sharply from universalizing Western biomedical understandings about post-traumatic stress disorder.

| | |

"You have a lot of guests," a young man working at the kiosk with an older woman, perhaps his mother, says to Chum Mey. The vendor's tone borders on disrespectful, more so because of youth. His comment seems like a reprimand. I wonder what sort of business arrangement Chum Mey has with the owners of the stall, perhaps entailing an obligation. I look over at a group of Cambodian youths sitting in the courtyard between Buildings A and B on the edge of the raised white coffin memorial to the last S-21 victims. They write intently in notebooks, perhaps recording their teacher's lecture. They sit in the sun underneath a leafless tree.

"I'm doing an interview," Chum Mey replies. He doesn't seem concerned as he returns to our conversation, which is drawing to a close. The young man starts sifting through a stack of postcards. We finish a short time later, and I ask Chum Mey if I can take his photo. He agrees with a smile and picks up a copy of the magazine with his story and image on the cover, which he sells to tourists for $10 a copy. I take a photo as he holds the magazine against his maroon short-sleeved dress shirt. I think for a moment of the tag that was pinned to his chest when he entered S-21. A European tourist sees what I'm doing, quickly takes out his camera, and snaps a shot. I say goodbye as Chum Mey gets back to work.

I turn and see Bou Meng sitting at his kiosk as his journalist-partner works to catch the attention of passing tourists. I walk up, and Bou Meng greets me warmly. He smiles and encourages me to attend his housewarming party, telling me that the food will be plentiful and delicious. I thank him but apologize, saying him that I will have departed by then. I clasp my hands to make a *sampeah* and say farewell. Unexpectedly, he closes his hands over mine and gives me a blessing for a safe journey home.

February 11, 2012, Tuol Sleng (Afterglow)

I decide to have one last look. Each time I went to Tuol Sleng during my 2012 research trip, I thought it would be the last. But I found myself returning again and again.

A few hours before I am supposed to fly back home, I pass through the entrance of Tuol Sleng once more. The complex is teeming with tourists, some in groups led by guides, others traveling with just a companion or two.

I walk to a cement bench in the courtyard between Buildings A and B and sit beneath a mango tree, the branches creating a cool shade. The tree is laden with green fruit, not yet ripe.

Tuol Sleng. "Hill of the Poisonous Tree." It's hard to imagine now. Small birds flutter on the ground, pecking for worms or seeds, their chirping almost peaceful.

I glance toward Chan Kim Srun's photo in Building B. Through a barred window, I can make out checkered rows of black-and-white prisoner mug shots. I also see a large photo of two prisoners handcuffed together. One man stands looking into the camera; his companion leans out of the picture frame, only his bare torso visible.

Tourists sit on nearby benches. A pair of young women, wearing shorts, examine maps of Phnom Penh in their guidebook. Nearby, an older European woman wearing a crimson hat stares into the distance, lost in thought.

A Cambodian teenager and his grandmother sit at the log table and benches where Chan Kim Srun's daughter cried after seeing her mother's photograph. The grandmother wears a traditional silk dress, while he is dressed casually in a T-shirt that reads in English and Khmer "Build Solidarity." She tells the boy, "That's where they beat people." After a moment of silence, they rise and walk toward Building B.

A few minutes later, two young Cambodian girls run up and sit at the table. The younger one has a Teletubbies purse. "ANGER" is emblazoned across the top of her shirt, which features two Angry Birds from the popular videogame. They giggle as they peel the skin of a fruit, then leave.

The woman in the hat joins a group of perhaps twenty older tourists. A Cambodian guide speaks to them in German. I follow them toward Building C, where Chum Mey stands waiting. "Hello, Sir," I greet him politely. He doesn't recognize me at first, then breaks into a wide smile. "I'm with this group of Germans," he tells me. "They are paying me $100."

He takes off with authority, leading the group into Building C. "This is where I was imprisoned by the Khmer Rouge," he tells the Cambodian guide, who translates. "They kept me here with almost no food or water. We had to sleep shackled on the ground, wearing only shorts." He lies down in a small brick cell, illustrating how he was shackled. "They tortured me day and night." The tourists take photos. Their video cameras are recording.

I ascend the stairs to the second story of Building D, intent on taking a final look at Duch's defaced photograph. As I start down the exterior corridor, I notice three Cambodian students gathered around a comment book.

One writes, "When I understood what happened here, I got a headache and became dizzy. I never could have imagined such cruel [chochov] and savage things. I really hate this [Khmer Rouge] regime. And I don't want this to happen again. . . . Please sentence the perpetrators who did these things in an appropriate manner." It is signed "a group from Preah Sisowat High School." I think of how Bou Meng and Chum Mey suffer from such symptoms of imbalance also linked to their experiences at S-21.

I enter the room the students had just visited. It has panels about Khmer Rouge perpetrators. I see one of Him Huy from 1977, when he was twenty-three and working at S-21. He wears a Mao cap, face serious. I think of Bou Meng's painting of his wife's execution.

Duch's photo hangs in the next room. My attention is immediately drawn to the glow of the scratches across his eyes, which through a Judeo-Christian frame, articulate this man as a demonic monster, a mass murderer epitomizing evil. Then my glance falls on the epithet "despicable cruel one" (a-chochov) written in Khmer across his face. This phrase suggests a different articulation of Duch, one framed by Cambodian Buddhist understandings of dhamma, karmic return, balance, and the blindness that led Duch to oversee so much death and suffering. Besides the symbolism of the eyes, there are other Buddhist-related markings on his photo. Someone has written "hell fiend"; another person has scribbled the hope that the Guardian of the Buddhist Hells will never forgive Duch.

Other texts are there as well, though some print is illegible.[55] Someone has written "Die quickly, despicable one" in thick black marker lettering, using the term applied to animals for "die." Other graffiti reads "despicable dog" and "Deserves to Hang." A couple of markings reference the court, including the line "Duch, you dog, you deserve life imprisonment."

I think of all the terms applied to Duch: man, monster, teacher, torturer, executioner, suspect, accused, convict, son, student, revolutionary, father, stoic, brute, repentant, man of God, savage, evil, dog, witness, victim, perpetrator, bystander, pervert, servant, commandant, cog in the machine, criminal. The terms suggest articulations, redacting as they assert orders of meaning. Moral economies of understandings circulate as observers, like me, gaze at Duch's Building D photo, some choosing to inscribe their thoughts on his likeness or in the comment books. Other articulations of meaning, ranging from the transitional justice imaginary to personality types to judicial decision, circulated in the court as Duch sat in the dock. I pause for a moment and wonder: "What do Duch's eyes really look like?" I can't recall.

Turning, I go back out onto the second-floor balcony of Building D. Below, Chum Mey slowly walks across the yellow-and-red pathway and sits on a bench. Most likely he has just come from an exhibition featuring a photo of him and the other survivors of S-21, the same one Bou Meng keeps at his kiosk, where he tells tourists about the group's escape at the end of DK. I follow his gaze to the compound walls, still topped with barbed wire, and toward the city life just beyond.

I walk through the rooms of Building D, watching the tourists. In the last room, three Cambodian students slowly examine cases filled with the skulls and bones of the dead. One girl wears a surgical mask; her friend's shirt says "Love." Looking one last time at the golden memorial in the center of the room, I leave Building D and head for the exit.

Halfway there, I pass the old entrance where S-21 prisoners were photographed and Bou Meng now has his stall. Chum Mey stands in silence in the open-air entry terrace of Building E as the German tour leader speaks to the group about the significance of S-21 and the connections to their country's genocidal past and human rights present. Occasionally the Cambodian guide offers a few words of translation to Chum Mey. The German tourists thank him and depart.

Across the path, Bou Meng's kiosk sits empty. Chum Mey invites me to his table and tells me that Bou Meng has left to prepare for the housewarming party, noting how much money Bou Meng has made from selling his book.

We talk about the tourists and the trial. I mention that Him Huy and Norng Chanphal led an educational seminar in a Tuol Sleng classroom the previous day. "Do you know Norng Chanphal?" I ask. In response, Chum Mey picks up a DC-Cam book, *On Trial*. "Look," he says as the shows me the back cover, which has a photograph of the ECCC set above photos of Duch and the Case 002 defendants.

"Nuon Chea. Ieng Sary. Khieu Samphan. Ieng Thirith." Pointing at their photos, Chum Mey slowly names each defendant. "If they are put in prison," he continues, "we will have justice. If not, there is no justice." Opening the book, he flips to a photo of Norng Chanphal and his brother standing naked in front of a large metal gate, a few days after the Khmer Rouge fled. "There he is in 1979."

"How do you and Him Huy get along now?" I ask. "Is there still tension?" "It's okay now," he replies, picking up a different book and flipping to a Khmer Rouge era photograph of Him Huy, rifle slung over his shoulder.

We gaze at the photos in silence before Chum Mey speaks, repeating what he told me days before: "Look, now that Duch has received a life sentence, we have justice. It is an example for Cambodia and for the world. If Duch had not received a life sentence, it would not have been just."

"So you and Him Huy no longer have a conflict?"

Chum Mey's smile disappears for a moment, and he furrows his brow. "Now that Duch has received a life sentence," he tells me, "the prisoners and the perpetrators can reconcile. We can understand one another and shake hands. The verdict brings us peace and reconciliation." He pauses, "But if Duch had not received a life sentence. It would have been different. I would have stopped coming to the court." His smile returns. "But now [that Duch has received a life sentence] I will continue to go to the court for Case 002, though I am very busy here," he says, motioning toward the table of books and copies of the magazine with his story.

As our conversation turns back to Bou Meng's housewarming party, an Australian woman walks up to the folding table. The woman running the kiosk begins to show her books and directs her attention to Chum Mey. "Survivor," she says in heavily accented English. "Oh!" the woman exclaims. "Wow!" With me translating, Chum Mey tells her how he was arrested, imprisoned, and tortured.

When Chum Mey describes how his fingernails and toenails were extracted, she covers her mouth with her hand and calls over her husband and two young children. Chum Mey tells the family how he was electrocuted and fell unconscious. "How awful!" the woman says, then asks, "Did they beat him on the body?" Chum Mey replies that he was beaten all over his body, which was extremely swollen afterward. They take a photograph. The daughter reaches out and touches Chum Mey. Then they leave without purchasing anything.

I excuse myself, telling Chum Mey that I have to leave for the airport. He smiles, places his hands over mine, and, just as Bou Meng did, gives me a small blessing. "May you have a safe journey home . . ."

We stand directly behind the old gates of Tuol Sleng, the spot where prisoners, shackled and blindfolded, began to lose all hope. It has become a place where a blessing can be given.

I walk slowly toward the exit, then turn to take one last look. Two monks, who have just exited Building D, move toward the stall where Chum Mey sits. Their saffron robes fire against the grey and white walls of Tuol Sleng. Slowly they approach Chum Mey's stand and the old entrance to S-21, robes billowing, walking step-by-step along the path, tracing new beginnings in this place that once was, for so many, the end.

Man or Monster?
(CONVICTION)

Man or Monster?

This question is foregrounded in the title of this book as a provocation. It is meant, in accordance with the Latin root of the term, "to call" (*vocare*) "forth" (*pro*), in a "challenge" (*provocare*) to the reader: to "stimulate a reaction" by "provoking" thinking about the question itself and what, ultimately, it suggests about Duch's trial and the banality of everyday thought.[1] For the question "Man or monster?" is highly redactic, suggesting an articulation of Duch, and by implication perpetrators of genocide and mass violence in general, as either "a monster" or an ordinary "man."

This frame, as I have illustrated throughout this book, recurred frequently during Duch's trial, providing a key undercurrent of the arguments of the prosecution and defense as well as civil party and expert testimony. François Bizot struggled with this question as he contemplated the seeming discrepancy between the man with whom he had established a rapport and who had secured Bizot's release and the monster who ran a camp where atrocities took place and who admitted to having beaten prisoners until he was out of breath. If, in his testimony and books, Bizot ultimately came down on "the man" side of the argument, he did so with hesitation and ambivalence, since the question suggested a troubling potentiality residing in himself and all of us.[2]

The position that Duch was an ordinary man, which was at the core of Roux's defense arguments, was elucidated by David Chandler, who argued in his testimony and pioneering book *Voices from S-21*, that ordinary men like Duch commit atrocities not because they are "evil" but because they share with us a human potential for unquestioning obedience to authority (as illustrated by the Milgram "shock experiments"), for giving in to the situational constraints and incentives amplified in a "total institution," for projection, and for susceptibility to craving for group belonging and terror of group exclusion. To discover the origins of the S-21 violence, Chandler states in the last sentence of his book (a quotation Roux highlighted): "We need look no further than ourselves."[3]

To further bolster his arguments about Duch "the man," Roux also drew on the assessments of two psychological experts. If Duch evinced some psychological tendencies—including disempathy, rationalization, obsessiveness, and repression—that facilitated his entry into the revolutionary movement, the experts found, he was not pathological. His actions were better understood as a process of becoming that was heavily mediated by the radical ideology and policies of the DK regime. "Before becoming a torturer who dehumanizes his victims," the French psychologist testified, "the torturer has always first been dehumanized himself."[4] The psychological articulation of "Duch the man" in this report and the parallel arguments of Chandler and Roux have also informed journalist Thierry Cruvellier's and researcher Terith Chy's accounts of Duch.[5]

While acknowledging Duch's humanity, other accounts of him have at times leaned more toward an articulation of him as a "monster." Journalist Robert Carmichael, for example, even as he stresses the importance of understanding Duch and draws on Chandler's work and the psychological report to do so, also describes him in passing as "a bully and a sadist" and "the prince of his dark domain."[6] Similarly, filmmaker Rithy Panh explicitly states that Duch is "no monster" and is "human at every instant,"[7] even as his portrayal of Duch, both in a book and a film, at times suggests someone lacking in humanity who has sociopathic tendencies (a person who lies and manipulates with cold calculation). This deviance is suggested by the highlighting of Duch's appearance and mannerisms, including his distinctive, seemingly almost maniacal laugh, a trait that was mentioned in Rithy Panh's book and related film, during trial testimony, and in the title of another book about Duch.[8]

The articulation of "Duch the monster" is more pronounced in other accounts, including prosecution descriptions of him and the prison he ran as "savage," "barbaric," "sadistic," and "ruthless," qualities the prosecutors also highlighted with their choices of evidence. Roux noted this undercurrent when he chastised the OCP for submitting a "conventional, traditional argument whose underlying philosophy is . . . this man is a monster."[9] Articulations of Duch the monster have circulated more freely in public, ranging from his graffitied photo at Tuol Sleng to media stories that freely drew on words like "monster" or "evil" when describing Duch. At times civil parties also characterized him along these lines.

Like others who have written about Duch, I have struggled with the reductive "man or monster" framing. I chose an ethnodramatic and more literary style, including the use of first person narrative voice, in an attempt to render the complexities this framing obscures. By placing myself more directly into the narrative than usual in a scholarly book, I have sought to render a more polyphonic account, to use imagery, language, and juxtaposition to convey key concepts in the book and to highlight my positioning in the narrative I construct and thereby foreground some of what is often edited out of "authoritative" academic and journalistic accounts.

So, after writing this book, what is my response to the question "Man or monster?" The question itself is haunted. It suggests an answer, but not the one that first comes to mind. For the question, in its apparent framing, is redactic, whittling a complex human life down to two narrow possibilities: Duch the monster or Duch the man. This is the same sort of reductive categorization that took place during DK as people were transformed into "enemies." The title thus suggests a key point: the parallels between what took place at S-21 and the banality of everyday thought, including an "either-or" framing of the question "Man or monster?"

Even as such reductive articulations are asserted, they are unsettled by the complexities they redact. These complexities haunt the articulation, a latent potentiality that may suddenly burst forth in a dehiscence. The "Man or monster" question is therefore haunted by its double, a second, less apparent question that calls into doubt the binary that is asserted ("Man or monster" as statement) and then is destabilized by the question mark ("Man or monster?" as query). This second sense of the phrase haunts the straightforward "either-or" articulation that demands a choice of Duch as man or monster.

To articulate is to render in a "clear" and "distinct" manner, as when speaking.[10] But "articulate" may also mean "to connect" or "unite by a joint," such as the joints between bones or even between the assembled segments of skeletal remains, a ghostly image. A joint is a point both of connection and separation;[11] it gives the appearance of a seamless unity but involves a construction of pieces separated by gaps. I have been using the word "articulation" in this sense to connote a simplified rendering that gives the appearance of clarity but is nevertheless riddled by gaps, the haunting obscured spaces from which the redactic bursts forth.

This is part of the reason Duch was such a haunting and uncanny presence during the trial. As people sought to fix his identity (for example, as "man or monster"), the complexities of his humanity would emerge and undercut these articulations. Bizot grappled with this issue, noting that Duch was a man even as this possibility raised unsettling questions. He faced someone who had joined the revolution in the name of the good and had gone on to do horrible things for this cause. Bizot testified that his awareness of this "ambiguity in [Duch's] humanity" had deeply impacted his life and remained "my personal tragedy," one Bizot had difficulty understanding and "I cannot rid myself of."[12]

Rithy Panh struggled with this ambiguity as well, acknowledging Duch's humanity even as he refused the idea that Duch was just a "cog among other cogs in a killing machine" and that "we're all potential torturers."[13] Many people I spoke with found Duch's actions at the trial ambiguous and unsettling, often noting the many contradictory roles he occupied at times: Duch the man, teacher, lawyer, judge, defendant, victim, perpetrator, repentant, monster, and so forth. The chapter headings in this book play on this ambiguity as well. Duch's graffitied photo at Tuol Sleng suggests this haunting in another way, through both its uncanny appearance and its multiplicity, with inscriptions clear and unclear, distinct and faded, in English and in Khmer, each seeking to articulate Duch's identity through a single word or phrase.

Duch's trial was haunted in other ways, as when what had been pushed out of view by foregrounded articulations dehisced. The very attempt to render justice for the crime of mass murder highlighted this point. As soon as the Trial Chamber had delivered its verdict, precisely ordered in terms of a clear decision based on evidence and law, questions emerged about the limits of law. Theary Seng highlighted this point with her comment that Duch had been sentenced to serve 11 hours for each person killed at S-21. Her remark suggests one of the limits of law, which is unable to impose a sentence befitting the magnitude of crimes like genocide and extermination.

Likewise, as was quickly revealed at Nuremberg, law falls short in its categorization of the acts committed, seeking to classify horrific events through an abstract formulation that trims away complexity, detail, and ambiguity.[14]

This process is epitomized by the ultimate decision of "guilt or nonguilt," which pushes aside all shades of gray.

Such dissonance between abstract law and the experience of mass violence was also highlighted by the civil parties' participation. Their complicated and devastating stories often overwhelmed the dry legalistic proceedings. At times it became clear that an excess of meaning was circulating in the court, as when civil party Chhin Navy highlighted a Buddhist conception of justice, potentially at odds with legalism, by invoking a related saying to illustrate how she viewed people like Duch who do bad deeds: "If you plant a hot chili pepper, you'll get a hot chili pepper. . . . Whatever a person does, that person will receive the result."[15]

Another civil party, Neth Phally, held up a black-and-white photo of his brother and called out: "My Brother, whose soul remains even if you died at S-21, please Brother, know that this trial is being done for you."[16] He added: "It's like my elder brother is sitting here by me in this court watching as the accused is tried. . . . Please Elder Brother, the soul of my brother, always remain with me and in this photograph, so that I can pay my respect and perform ceremonies to send merit to you whenever I have the opportunity."[17] Neth Phally's address to his brother seemed out of place in the court, a sudden intrusion of something familiar yet strange that had been pushed out of sight. Everyone was aware that an unspoken absence, the spirit of the dead, was a presence in the court and in the photograph itself.

If allowing a space for these unexpected moments, the trial process ultimately redacted such potentially dissonant remarks and the rich and complicated life histories in which they were embedded, narrowing and recasting this "testimony" in a more rigid legalist fashion. Besides deciding which details were "relevant" and reducing them to a truncated and standardized form in its ultimate Judgment, the Trial Chamber also judged the authenticity of civil party claims—an act that provoked upset and furor over the denial of civil party status to people who had participated throughout and sometimes even told their stories during the trial.

The implicit rational, unbiased, and balanced nature of justice was also thrown into question by politics, which formed a key backdrop rarely mentioned during the proceedings, even if it was hinted at by the defense's suggestions that Duch was a scapegoat.[18] Indeed, the scapegoat argument pointed toward another limit of law, which is focused on the individual and thereby potentially redacts group-level responsibility, structural factors, complicity, and politics, issues that may give rise to allegations that the proceedings are a "show trial."[19]

During and after the Duch trial, political controversies that were back-grounded in the courtroom—including a corruption scandal, allegations of political influence, and suggestions about the potential culpability of former Khmer Rouge associated with Prime Minister Hun Sen's government—periodically burst forth in the media and in statements made by trial observ-ers (such as Amnesty International and Human Rights Watch) and by the Cambodian government (such as Hun Sen's repeated declaration that only five people would be tried). Journalist Stéphanie Giry's account of the Duch trial and the ECCC picked up on this line of analysis in articles with titles like "Necessary Scapegoats? The Making of the Khmer Rouge Tribunal."[20]

The question "Man or monster?" is haunted in yet another way: in its more apparent "either-or" sense, it demands conviction. If "conviction" refers to the proving of legal guilt, it also means "a firmly held belief or opinion." Both of these senses are related to the term's etymological connection to the word "convince," which is derived from the Latin *convincere*, or to "wholly" (*con-*) "conquer" (*vincere*).[21] Along these lines, "conviction" may refer to a strong investment in an articulation that is asserted to the exclusion of alternatives, which are "conquered" by the conviction at hand. Thus, a criminal conviction, such as Duch's conviction at the ECCC, involves a singular articulation of his identity in terms of criminality, depending on whether he is found guilty or not guilty.

The apparent sense of the question "Man or monster?" likewise demands a singular response, a haunting "either-or" choice. Many scholars now adhere to the "ordinary men" thesis, which suggests that almost anyone, given the right circumstances, might participate in genocide and mass murder.[22] But this explanation has a potential insipidness, suggesting a modal personality type that is "with no distinctive features; normal or usual."[23] While a corrective to reductive psychological theories of psychopathy, including those suggesting that perpetrators are "monsters," the notion of "ordinariness" tends to flatten out the complex dynamics of human lives. It also has ethical implications, sug-gesting that situations define and shape the actions of perpetrators, thereby potentially mitigating their agency and responsibility.[24]

Rithy Panh seems to have been reacting against such implications of the "or-dinary man" thesis when he argued against the idea that Duch was one among many cogs and that we are "all a fraction of an inch . . . from committing a great crime."[25] Instead, he argued that it was necessary to focus on the trajectory of individual lives, the process of becoming that the psychological experts and Roux also highlighted during the trial. Moreover, Rithy Panh noted that Duch, as opposed to being "ordinary," was an intellectual, "a thinking man," who made choices that led him to S-21 and continued as he ran the prison.

If Duch was a "thinking man," he was also a man of conviction, a deeply committed revolutionary. It was a point on which almost everyone in the trial agreed, even if the defense and prosecution interpreted his conviction in different ways. Duch himself frequently referenced his conviction in relation to his willingness to sacrifice everything for revolutionary ideals and to liberate his people and country from oppression. His conviction was perhaps nowhere more clearly on display than when he described his induction into the Party, a moment he recalled vividly and with passion and highlighted by his giving a revolutionary salute.

In colloquial speech, describing a person as "having conviction" may have positive connotations. Duch's trial, however, suggests the opposite side, the danger of what might be called "effacing conviction." For if Duch had conviction, it was most often manifest in singular articulations that "conquered" alternative possibilities. First he served the revolution; later he served God. The psychological experts commented on this tendency, reporting that Duch had a strong need for ideals, even as he "can only deal with one belief or idea at a time."[26] During DK, the party line, including the Party Statutes, provided such a singular ideal. Perhaps this is also part of what appealed to him about math, which, like the party line, offers clear abstract principles and methods for determining truth, eliminating shades of gray.[27]

This desire for singular belief—combined with his meticulousness and what the psychological experts characterized as a lack of empathy—meshed well with the task of running S-21, where effacing conviction was institutionalized. By "effacing conviction" I mean the assertion of singular articulations that efface difference and alternative perspectives. To efface is to "rub out, obliterate" something "so as to leave no distinct traces," including the erasure of words or sentences from a text, an act of redaction.[28] Etymologically, the term suggests "rubbing out the face" (*effacer*). At S-21, the distinctive identities of prisoners were effaced as their biographies were refashioned to accord with the thick frame of the DK party line and the highly simplified articulations of "the enemy" it afforded.

As redactions, these articulations of the other remain haunted and are unsettled, as the complexity of the real world pushes back—as when a respected former comrade or teacher suddenly stands accused. Duch faced this situation repeatedly, as Ke Kim Huot, Deum Sareaun, Chhay Kim Hor, Vorn Vet, and other revolutionary mentors and associates passed through the gates of

S-21. Duch claimed to have been increasingly haunted by such arrests, even as he appears to have nevertheless regarded them with an effacing conviction. It was an attitude that the DK leadership also demanded and institutionalized through its ideology and security apparatus—as have other regimes that have carried out genocide and mass murder.

If Duch's trial warns about the dangers of conviction, it also suggests, if not a remedy, an alternative. In English, it is difficult to find an antonym of effacement. There is, however, a somewhat obsolete term that comes close, "aface," which suggests "facing" as in "before a person's face" or "to face another person or thing."[29] Along these lines, "afacement" would involve a process of recognizing the distinctiveness of another person. An "afacing conviction," in turn, would be one that, even when deeply held, involves reflexive articulation, or maintaining a recognition that a more singular articulation is being made and not just acknowledging different possibilities but actively exploring and thinking critically about—instead of seeking to "conquer"—them.

Such a perspective parallels my earlier discussion of Arendt's emphasis on thoughtlessness as well as the banality of everyday thought, or the reductive and redactic articulations we constantly use to navigate our social worlds. As Rithy Panh notes, Duch is clearly "a thinking man." But Duch is also "thoughtless" in the sense of approaching the world with an attitude of effacing conviction, uneasy with messiness, disorder, and the discomfort that afacement may entail.

Afacement requires an openness to alternatives that may trouble deeply held assumptions and beliefs, the bases of singular articulations and the banality of our everyday thought. An afacing orientation demands "thoughtfulness," a willingness to think critically and remain open to difference and the real-world complexities that we are inclined, by our existential anxieties and the banality of everyday thought, to pare down, edit, and redact.

Duch's invocation of the proverb "If you break open the crab you'll show the shit" might be rethought in this regard, suggesting the importance of doing exactly this—all the more so in contexts where thick frames of power are operative, masking the unsaid and "the natural" while foregrounding singular articulations of the other. Indeed, this saying might be doubled and recast as "If you break the shell of articulation, you'll see what has been pushed out of sight," a metaphor that speaks to the redactic and the metaphor of "unloosening," "undoing," or "unpacking" that is central to analysis and critical thinking.[30] This is an insight that emerges from Duch's trial and also speaks to my attempt to unpack the "man or monster" articulation.

If the title of this book is a provocation, then, it is a haunted one that has a less apparent sense and is meant to spur critical thinking and self-reflection. The Duch who appeared on stage at the ECCC is our double, someone who, as we all do, passes through the gray zones of everyday life.[31] His trial asks us to consider when and how we navigate this unsettling messiness and the anxiety it arouses by calibrating and ordering it through simplifying articulations that are foregrounded by frames, including thick frames of political power, and that are part of the banality of everyday thought.

Duch chose to do so from a "thoughtless" stance of effacing conviction, a perspective reflected by his mathematics background, ideological rigidity, hyperrationality, tendency to strip away complicating detail to assert a narrower, categorized vision of the world, disempathy, and desire for "black and white" truth. If this orientation did not predetermine his path to becoming a torturer and executioner, it likely predisposed him to do so in a context like DK. His superiors appear to have selected him to run M-13 and S-21— institutions structured to produce, in accordance with the thick frame of the DK party line, singular articulations of the enemy other—in part for this reason.

Duch's experience cautions us about where the banality of everyday thought may lead. Like him, we constantly render articulations of self, other, and the world. And like him, we have a choice about whether to do so with effacing conviction or afacement. For me, this is the key lesson we can take from Duch's trial, one that, like the title of this book, is provocative, haunted, and haunting.

Acknowledgments

One of the first lessons I learned about studying transitional justice and trials, in particular, is that they take time. My research for this book began in 2008, beginning in full with the start of the Duch trial. I only began writing this book in 2012, after the appeals in the case had been decided. Many people and institutions have helped me along the way as I undertook and completed this project.

First, I'd like to recognize my wife, Nicole, and our daughters, Meridian and Arcadia, who have put up with long hours of writing and talking about the project. Nicole read and commented on many drafts and provided support in so many ways. Thank you! I also want to acknowledge other family members, including my father, Ladson, as well as my late mother, Darlene, and my brothers, Ladson and Devon, and my in-laws, Peter, Jacki, and Susan, Carolee, and Alissa.

I'd also like to recognize my colleagues and the Rutgers Center for the Study of Genocide and Human Rights (CGHR), particularly the members of the CGHR Executive Board and the UNESCO Chair on Genocide Prevention, Nela Navarro and Stephen Eric Bronner. Nela and Steve, as well as Tom LaPointe, have been great colleagues for many years and have helped to create a vibrant intellectual atmosphere in which to consider issues related to the concerns of this book.

A special thanks also goes to Youk Chhang and his staff at the Documentation Center of Cambodia (DC-Cam)/Sleuk Rith Institute (SRI), who have provided a "home away from home" while I did research in Cambodia. I continue to appreciate our close collaborations. As always, Youk provided invaluable help with this project, including granting permission to use photographs from the DC-Cam/SRI archive.

Thanks also go to many other colleagues and students at CGHR and Rutgers. The Rutgers University Research Council, Division of Global Affairs,

Faculty of Arts and Science, Department of Sociology and Anthropology, and Centers for Global Advancement and International Affairs also provided sabbatical time and grants to help support this research, as did the United States Institute of Peace (USIP) (the ideas and conclusions in the book are, of course, my own and do not necessarily reflect the view of the USIP). I greatly appreciate their assistance.

I was also fortunate to spend time at the Institute for Advanced Study (IAS) in Princeton. It is difficult to describe what a wonderful space they provide to scholars, including a place to take risks and branch out in new directions, as I hope I have done a bit in this book. Didier Fassin was unwavering in his support and encouragement. I'd also like to recognize the other faculty in the IAS School of Social Sciences, Joan Scott, Michael Walzer, and Danielle Allen as well as other Fellows at the IAS including Jens Meierhenrich, Nancy Scheper-Hughes, Kimberly Theidon, and Jarret Zigon.

Once written, the book needed to find a publishing home. In this regard, I very much appreciate all that my editor, Gisela Fosado, has done to support the publication of this book. Indeed, she is perhaps the most efficient editor with whom I have had the pleasure of working. A number of anonymous reviewers provided important feedback and suggestions, which is much appreciated. Different staff members at Duke have also provided critical assistance, including Lydia Rose Rappoport-Hankins, Sara Leone, Heather Hensley, Martha Ramsey, Christopher Robinson, and other members of the editorial, marketing, and production staff. I appreciate Duke University Press publishing a book that is written differently from many academic books.

Finally, this book has been shaped in more indirect ways through different talks I have given at different academic and professional institutions. I thank the audiences for their remarks and the hosts for providing me with a space to experiment with my ideas. My colleagues at the International Association of Genocide Scholars deserve special note, as do the coorganizers and participants in the "Rethinking Peace Studies" seminars that cohosted with the International Christian University (ICU) in Japan and the Japan ICU Foundation, including Paul Hastings, David Vickner, Giorgio Shani, Mark Flanigan, and Jeremiah Alberg.

Many other people provided support, encouragement, and suggestions during the course of this project. I would like to express my appreciation to David Chandler and Victoria Sanford for their detailed comments on the manuscript and to Samphors Huy for her research assistance. The late Reach Sambath and his colleague Lars Olsen from the ECCC Public Affairs office also provided enormous help along the way, including providing key documents and some of the images in this book.

In addition, I thank Joyce Apsel, Fredrik Barth, Kurt Bredenberg, Rob Borofsky, Bou Meng, Terith Chy, John Ciorciari, Chum Mey, Jean-Marc Coicaud, Khamboly Dy, Craig Etcheson, Kok-Thy Eng, Daniel Feierstein, Jacqueline Finkelstein, Louis Harrison, Vannak Huy, Helen Jarvis, Julia Spicher Kasdorf, Lauren Kaplan, Andrew Kinney, Judy Ledgerwood, Ann Martin, Sally Merry, Pheaktra Neth, Carolyn Nordstrom, Charles Nuckolls, Devin Okay, Finola O'Sullivan, Robert Paul, Clement Price, Eileen Quam, Joanna Regulska, Steven Riskin, Tony Robben, Sirik Savina, Sophat Morm, Bradd Shore, Greg Stanton, Mark Urken, Ernesto Verdeja, Dawn Wilson, Andrew Woolford, and Carol Worthman. I have no doubt left many other deserving people off this brief list of acknowledgments, and my thanks go out to them as well. Finally, I'd like to thank the informants who spoke to me, often for hours at a time, during interviews and conversations. Many, especially those working at or with the tribunal itself, asked to remain anonymous.

| | | |

"Erasure—Duch's Apology" previously appeared in the *Mekong Review* 1, no. 4 (August-October 2016): 20. The text this erasure uses is from ECCC, "Compilation of Statements of Apology Made by Kaing Guek Eav alias Duch during the Proceedings," 3.

Timeline

1942	Duch born in Kompong Thom Province
1953	Cambodian independence from France; Prince Sihanouk dominates Kingdom of Cambodia until 1970
Mid-1960s	Duch meets Son Sen, his future patron and Khmer Rouge leader; starts teaching math and revolutionary activities
1967	Duch joins the Communist Party of Kampuchea and is jailed the next year; Khmer Rouge begin armed struggle against Prince Sihanouk
1970	General Lon Nol coup against Sihanouk; Khmer Republic established; Duch released from jail, rejoins Khmer Rouge; Sihanouk joins the Khmer Rouge in united front
1971	Duch appointed head of M-13 security center
1975	Khmer Rouge, led by Pol Pot, topple Khmer Republic; Democratic Kampuchea (DK) established; Duch appointed deputy head of S-21
1976	Duch appointed head of S-21; Khmer Rouge purges begin to intensify
1979	Vietnamese-backed army topples DK regime; socialist Peoples Republic of Kampuchea (PRK) established; Duch and his men flee into the forest to join Khmer Rouge leaders; S-21 discovered and turned into Tuol Sleng museum; new civil war begins
1986–1988	Khmer Rouge send Duch to teach in China; peace negotiations begin, eventually resulting in 1991 accord

1993	UN-backed elections held; Royal Government of Cambodia formed
Mid-1990s	Duch's wife killed during robbery (1995); Duch converts to Christianity (1996); Khmer Rouge defections begin and movement begins to implode; discussions to hold international tribunal commence (1997)
1999	Duch arrested by Cambodian government; Khmer Rouge movement ends following Pol Pot's death (1998)
2003	UN and Cambodia reach agreement to hold tribunal
2006	Extraordinary Chambers in the Courts of Cambodia (ECCC) open
2007	Duch arrested by ECCC
2009–2012	Duch trial proceedings (2009); judgment (2010); final decision (2012)

Abbreviations

CPK	Communist Party of Kampuchea (Khmer Rouge party organization)
DC-Cam	Documentation Center of Cambodia
DK	Democratic Kampuchea (period of Khmer Rouge rule in Cambodia, April 17, 1975 to January 6, 1979)
ECCC	Extraordinary Chambers in the Courts of Cambodia (Khmer Rouge Tribunal)
ICC	International Criminal Court
ICTR	International Criminal Tribunal for Rwanda
ICTY	International Criminal Tribunal for the former Yugoslavia
M-13	Security office run by Duch during the Cambodian civil war
OCIJ	Office of the Co-Investigating Judges
OCP	Office of the Co-Prosecutors
PTC	Pre-Trial Chamber
PRK	People's Republic of Kampuchea (government that ruled Cambodia for a decade following DK)
S-21	Security center run by Duch during DK
PTC	Pre-Trial Chamber of the ECCC
SCC	Supreme Court Chamber of the ECCC
TC	Trial Chamber of the ECCC

Notes

Foreground. Monster

1. ECCC, "Kaing Guek Eav."
2. ECCC, "Transcript of Proceedings—'Duch' Trial Public." Hereafter the specific transcript will be indicated by the trial day and transcript page number if in English, or, if in Khmer, "Khmer" will be specified, followed by the transcript page numbers: in this case, Duch Trial Day 4, 48; Khmer-language transcript, 38, which is shortened to "Day 4, 48; Khmer, 38."
3. Day 4, 48; Khmer, 38.
4. Day 4, 49; Khmer, 38.
5. Day 4, 49; Khmer, 39.
6. Day 4, 51; Khmer, 39.
7. Day 4, 51; Khmer, 40.
8. Day 69, 40.
9. Day 69, 41.
10. Day 69, 41–42.
11. Dunlop, *Lost Executioner.*
12. Thayer and Dunlop, "Duch Confesses," 18–19.
13. Day 10, 47.
14. Christophe Peschoux, interview with Kaing Guek Eav, also known as Duch, chairman of S.21, April 28–29 and May 4–6, 1999, David Chandler Cambodia Collection, Monash University Library, Melbourne, http://arrow.monash.edu.au, accessed November 4, 2015; Day 10, 45ff.
15. Reang, "Man or Monster?"
16. Headley, *Cambodian-English Dictionary,* 760.
17. Chandler, *Tragedy of Cambodian History.*
18. Military Court, "Record of Interrogation," 3.
19. "Frame," OED *Online.*
20. The use of the metaphor of the frame in social science dates back at least as far as the pioneering work of Bateson, *Steps to an Ecology of Mind,* and Goffman, *Frame Analysis.*
21. For these events and the pioneering study of S-21, see Chandler, *Voices from S-21.* On the history of the museum, see also Caswell, *Archiving the Unspeakable;* Ledgerwood, "Cambodian Tuol Sleng Museum of Genocidal Crimes."

22. The text in the signs at Tuol Sleng are here reproduced verbatim, without correcting the English-language errors.

23. On the history of civil war and DK, see Chandler, *Tragedy of Cambodian History*, and *Voices from S-21*; Hinton, *Why Did They Kill?*; Kiernan, *Pol Pot Regime*.

24. Chandler, *Voices from S-21*; Hinton, *Why Did They Kill?*; Kiernan, *Pol Pot Regime*.

25. See Locard, *Pol Pot's Little Red Book*, 211.

26. See Criddle and Mam, *To Destroy You Is No Loss*, 99.

27. Day 35, 39; Khmer, 32.

28. Gottesman, *Cambodia after the Khmer Rouge*, 60.

29. Gottesman, *Cambodia after the Khmer Rouge*; Ledgerwood, "Cambodian Tuol Sleng Museum of Genocidal Crimes."

30. Ledgerwood, "Cambodian Tuol Sleng Museum of Genocidal Crimes," 82.

31. The following quotations from Heng Samrin's speech are cited in Gottesman, *Cambodia after the Khmer Rouge*, 7–8; see also SPK Radio, "Front Issues Declaration," H3, H7.

32. Gottesman, *Cambodia after the Khmer Rouge*.

33. See Kamm, "Aide Says Pol Pot Regime Is Ready to Join Old Foes against Vietnam."

34. See, for example, Fawthrop and Jarvis, *Getting Away with Genocide*, 86ff.

35. See Ledgerwood, "Cambodian Tuol Sleng Museum of Genocidal Crimes."

36. See, for example, Laqueur, "Bodies, Details and the Humanitarian Narrative," 176–204.

37. Comment book, Tuol Sleng Genocide Museum, January 15, 2011. On tourist conceptions of Tuol Sleng, see Hughes, "Dutiful Tourism." See also Caswell, *Archiving the Unspeakable*.

38. Comment 506 (December 22, 2005), comment book, Tuol Sleng Genocide Museum, January 15, 2011.

39. Comment book, Tuol Sleng Genocide Museum, March 2011.

40. Hinton, "Transitional Justice Imaginary."

41. Initial Hearing, Day 1, February 17, 2009, 113.

42. Initial Hearing, Day 1, February 17, 2009, 113.

43. Comment, February 12, 2005, comment book, 2005–2006, Tuol Sleng Genocide Museum.

44. Peaktra and Barton, "Memories of Evil Stir as Duch Trial Opens," 1–2; Shears, "Monster of the Killing Fields"; Bernstein, "At Last, Justice for Monsters."

45. Arendt, *Eichmann in Jerusalem*. On the comparison of Eichmann and Duch, see also Chy et al., *When the Criminal Laughs*.

46. Clearly, there are multiple dynamics involved in the genocidal process, ranging from socioeconomic upheaval to structural constraint. For a detailed discussion in terms of DK and S-21, see Chandler, *Voices from S-21*, and Hinton, *Why Did They Kill?*

47. Veneciano and Hinton, *Night of the Khmer Rouge*.

48. Freud, *Uncanny*, 126, 132–33. See also "Uncanny," *OED Online*; Hinton, "Black Holes, Uncanny Spaces and Radical Shifts in Awareness."

49. Comments 680, 831, comment book, 2005–2006, Tuol Sleng Genocide Museum.

50. Hinton, "Justice and the Redactic." See Douglas, *Memory of Judgment*, on the didactic and legalism.

51. "Redact," *OED Online*.

52. "Dehiscence," *OED Online*. See also Derrida, "Signature, Event, Context," who uses the word "dehiscence" to refer to ruptures associated with iteration.

53. The anthropological focus on performance and drama goes back at least as far as Victor and Edith Turner's pioneering work; see, for example, Turner and Turner, "Performing Ethnography." On ethnodrama and performative ethnography, see Saldaña, *Ethnotheatre* and *Ethnodrama*.

54. See, for example, Marcus and Fischer, *Anthropology as Cultural Critique*; Clifford and Marcus, *Writing Culture*.

55. A modest literature on the trial of Duch has emerged, which is discussed in the epilogue and offers articulations of Duch from a variety of perspectives, including Bizot (former prisoner of Duch, trial witness, and scholar), *Facing the Torturer*; Carmichael (journalist), *When Clouds Fell from the Sky*; Cruvellier (journalist), *Master of Confessions*; Rithy Panh (filmmaker and Cambodian genocide survivor), *Elimination*; and Chy et al. (civil society researchers), *When the Criminal Laughs*. See also Chandler, *Voices from S-21*; Dunlop, *Lost Executioner*; and Peschoux, interview with Kaing Guek Eav, also known as Duch, chairman of S.21, April 28–29 and May 4–6, 1999.

Chapter 1. Man

1. ECCC, "Compilation of Statements of Apology Made by Kaing Guek Eav alias Duch during the Proceedings," 3.

2. While Duch was not charged with genocide, the defendants in Case 002 have been. And Tuol Sleng is called a "genocide museum." On the applicability of the term "genocide" to the Cambodian case, see Hinton, *Why Did They Kill?*

3. ECCC, "Judge Nil Nonn (President)."

4. Pike, "Battambang."

5. Defense, "Ieng Sary's Application to Disqualify Judge Nil Nonn Due to His Purported Admission That He Has Accepted Bribes"; Atlas Project, "Transitional Justice in Cambodia," 51–52.

6. United Nations Commission on Human Rights, "Situation of Human Rights in Cambodia."

7. See, for example, Amnesty International, "Cambodia: Cambodians Deserve International Standards of Justice"; "Cambodia: Fair Trial and Due Process."

8. Open Society Justice Initiative, "Corruption Allegations at Khmer Rouge Court Must Be Investigated Thoroughly"; Goldstone, "Letter to the Editor on Corruption Charges at Khmer Rouge Court."

9. Human Resources Management, "Results of the Special Review Made Public." Munthit, "Cambodian Genocide Tribunal Faces Allegations"; Veasna, "UNDP."

10. Victims Unit, "Historical Achievement in International Criminal Law."

11. ECCC, "ECCC Emblem."

12. UNCHR, "Situation of Human Rights in Cambodia."

13. United Nations, "Report of the Group of Experts for Cambodia established pursuant to General Assembly Resolution 52/135," para. 5. On the history of the negotiations leading to the ECCC, see Ciorciari and Heindel, *Hybrid Justice*;

Etcheson, *After the Killing Fields*; Fawthrop and Jarvis, *Getting Away with Genocide*; Ramji and Van Schaack, *Bringing the Khmer Rouge to Justice*.

14. United Nations, "Report of the Group of Experts for Cambodia Established Pursuant to General Assembly Resolution 52/135," paras. 10, 6.

15. See Etcheson, "A 'Fair and Public Trial,'" 8–9; United Nations, "Report of the Group of Experts for Cambodia Established Pursuant to General Assembly Resolution 52/135," 3.

16. ECCC 2003. On the structure and functioning of the ECCC, see Ciorciari and Heindel, *Hybrid Justice*.

17. Extraordinary Chambers in the Courts of Cambodia, "Transcript of Proceedings— 'Duch' Trial Public." Hereafter the specific transcript will be indicated by the trial day and English transcript page numbers and in some cases Khmer transcript page numbers: in this case, Duch Trial Day 1, English-language transcript, 2–5.

18. ECCC, "Agreement between the United Nations and the Royal Government of Cambodia Concerning the Prosecution under Cambodian Law of Crimes Committed during the Period of Democratic Kampuchea," "Law on the Establishment of the Extraordinary Chambers in the Courts of Cambodia," and "Internal Rules," Version 1, June 12, 2007.

19. The material in this paragraph is based on OCIJ, "Closing Order Indicting Kaing Guek Eav alias Duch (Public Redacted Version)," 3.

20. "Closing Order Indicting Kaing Guek Eav," 4.

21. This and the below quotations from Chea Leang's remarks are from Day 2, 2.

22. ECCC, "Ms. Chea Leang."

23. OCP, "Statement of the Co-prosecutors," January 5, 2009.

24. Day 2, 2–3.

25. Day 2, 5.

26. The following statistics on S-21 are taken from Day 2, 29–30. See also OCIJ, "Closing Order Indicting Kaing Guek Eav alias Duch (Public Redacted Version)," 13–14.

27. ECCC, "Mr. Robert Petit."

28. Giry, "Necessary Scapegoats?"

29. Kauth, "Robert Petit."

30. Day 2, 35.

31. Day 2, 36.

32. Day 2, 36.

33. Day 2, 36.

34. Day 2, 42.

35. Day 2, 35.

36. ECCC, "Chart Presented by Craig Etcheson."

37. Day 2, 47.

38. Day 2, 56.

39. Day 2, 62.

40. Day 2, 62.

41. Day 2, 64.

42. Day 2, 64.

43. ECCC, "Compilation of Statements of Apology," 1; see also Day 2, 66ff.; Khmer, 52ff.

44. ECCC, "Compilation of Statements of Apology," 1.
45. ECCC, "Compilation of Statements of Apology," 2.
46. ECCC, "Compilation of Statements of Apology," 3.
47. ECCC, "Compilation of Statements of Apology," 3.
48. ECCC, "Compilation of Statements of Apology," 4.
49. ECCC, "Compilation of Statements of Apology," 4.
50. Day 2, 88.
51. Giry, "Cambodia's Perfect War Criminal."
52. Day 2, 74.
53. Day 2, 75.
54. Day 2, 78, 80.
55. Day 2, 83.
56. Day 3, 19.
57. Gée, "Interview with Phung Guth Sunthary."
58. Special Tribunal for Lebanon, "Head of Defense Office—François Roux."
59. ECCC, "Compilation of Statements of Apology," 2.
60. Day 2, 87.
61. Day 2, 89.
62. Day 2, 90.
63. Day 2, 91.
64. Day 2, 91.
65. Day 2, 91.
66. Day 2, 91–92.
67. Day 3, 4.
68. Civil Parties before the Extraordinary Chambers in the Courts of Cambodia, "Civil Party Lawyer Silke Studzinsky."
69. Day 3, 5.
70. On the origins and development of civil party rights at the ECCC, see Thomas and Chy, "Including the Survivors in the Tribunal Process."
71. ECCC, "Internal Rules," Version 1, June 12, 2007, 18.
72. Victims Unit, "Historical Achievement in International Criminal Law."
73. Thomas and Chy, "Including the Survivors in the Tribunal Process," 234.
74. Public Affairs, "Media Alert."
75. Day 1, 2.
76. Civil Parties before the Extraordinary Chambers in the Courts of Cambodia, "Civil Party Lawyer Silke Studzinsky."
77. Kahn and Rudy, "Right of Civil Parties to Participate v. the Right of the Accused to a Fair and Expeditious Trial," 2.
78. Day 13, 50. See also RFI Staff, "Apology of Prison Chief Met with Skepticism.
79. Day 3, 21.
80. Day 3, 23.
81. Day 3, 26.
82. Day 3, 37.
83. ECCC, "Internal Rules," Version 3, March 6, 2009, 59.
84. Day 3, 38.

85. Day 3, 50.

86. Day 3, 41.

87. Day 3, 41, 42.

88. ECCC, "Ms. Martine Jacquin."

89. Day 3, 44.

90. Day 3, 44.

91. Day 2, 95.

92. Day 2, 96.

93. Day 3, 45.

94. Day 4, 5.

95. Day 3, 52–53.

96. Day 3, 62.

97. Day 3, 79.

98. Day 3, 93.

99. Day 3, 94.

100. Day 3, 99.

101. Day 3, 99.

Chapter 2. Revolutionary

1. ECCC, "Transcript of Proceedings—'Duch' Trial Public." Day 4, 7.

2. Day 4, 15; Khmer, 13.

3. Day 4, 16; Khmer, 13.

4. Chandler, *History of Cambodia*, 194ff.

5. Chandler, *History of Cambodia*, 194ff.

6. Pol Pot, "Long Live the Nineteenth Anniversary of the Communist Party of Kampuchea," 24.

7. Pol Pot, "Long Live the Nineteenth Anniversary of the Communist Party of Kampuchea," 24.

8. Pol Pot, "Long Live the Nineteenth Anniversary of the Communist Party of Kampuchea," 28–29.

9. Day 67, 67–68; see also Dunlop, *Lost Executioner*, 29; TC, "Trial Chamber Judgment, Announced on 26 July 2010, Case 001, Kaing Guek Eav alias Duch," 43.

10. OCIJ, "Closing Order Indicting Kaing Guek Eav alias Duch (Public Redacted Version)," 40.

11. Day 4, 16; Day 67, 21.

12. Day 67, 21.

13. Dunlop, *Lost Executioner*, 29–30.

14. Dunlop, *Lost Executioner*, 48.

15. Dunlop, *Lost Executioner*, 56.

16. Associated Press Staff, "Khmer Rouge Prison Chief to Face Charges."

17. Day 68, 52ff.

18. Dunlop, *Lost Executioner*.

19. Day 68, 55–56. Associated Press Staff, "Khmer Rouge Prison Chief to Face Charges."

20. Day 4, 17.

21. Day 4, 17.

22. Day 4, 18; Khmer, 14. See also Cruvellier, *Master of Confessions*, 5, on this moment.
23. Day 4, 49–50.
24. Day 4, 39ff.
25. Pol Pot, "Long Live the Nineteenth Anniversary of the Communist Party of Kampuchea," 37.
26. Pol Pot, "Long Live the Nineteenth Anniversary of the Communist Party of Kampuchea," 32.
27. Day 4, 28.
28. Day 4, 51.
29. Day 4, 66.
30. Day 4, 89.
31. Day 5, 48.
32. Day 4, 24.
33. Day 5, 20.
34. Day 5, 39.
35. Day 5, 20.
36. Owen and Kiernan, "Bombs over Cambodia."
37. Day 6, 32.
38. Day 6, 33.
39. Day 6, 35.
40. Day 6, 35.
41. Day 4, 79.
42. Day 5, 22.
43. Day 6, 46.
44. Day 4, 82.
45. Day 6, 39.
46. Day 6, 50.
47. Day 71, 70.
48. I thank Ladson Hinton for making this connection between Duch, de Vigny, and the assertion of civility.
49. Day 62, 24.
50. Day 6, 98.
51. Day 6, 47.
52. Day 6, 49.
53. While what follows is primarily based on Bizot's testimony on Days 6 and 7 of the trial of Duch, it also adds details, at times, from Bizot's memoirs (*The Gate* and *Facing the Torturer*) about his experience of being imprisoned at M-13 and testifying at the ECCC.
54. Bizot, *Facing the Torturer*, 25.
55. Bizot, *The Gate*, 45; Day 7, 34.
56. Bizot, *The Gate*, 40.
57. Bizot, *The Gate*, 41.
58. Day 7, 6, 15.
59. Day 4, 66.
60. Day 6, 86.

61. Bizot, *The Gate*, 48–49.
62. Bizot, *Facing the Torturer*, 32.
63. Day 6, 64.
64. This and the following quotation are from Bizot, *Facing the Torturer*, 35.
65. Bizot, *The Gate*, 75.
66. Bizot, *The Gate*, 75–76.
67. See Ponchaud, "Social Change in the Vortex of Revolution," 154, 173.
68. Bizot, *The Gate*, 86.
69. Bizot, *The Gate*, 86.
70. Bizot, *The Gate*, 105.
71. See Day 7, 27, and Bizot, *The Gate*, 61 (on *dhamma*) and 108 (on discipline and renunciation). On the link between Khmer Rouge ideology and Buddhism, see also Ponchaud, "Social Change in the Vortex of Revolution," and Hinton, *Why Did They Kill?*
72. Bizot, *The Gate*, 109.
73. Day 6, 70; see also Bizot, *The Gate*, 85.
74. Day 6, 70.
75. The material quoted in this paragraph is from Bizot, *The Gate*, 112. See also Day 6, 70ff.
76. Day 6, 71.
77. Day 6, 71.
78. Bizot, *Facing the Torturer*.
79. Day 7, 24.
80. Bizot, *Facing the Torturer*, 55.
81. Day 7, 46.
82. Day 7, 47.
83. Bizot, *The Gate*, 138; Day 7, 48.
84. Day 4, 64.
85. Day 4, 41.
86. Day 4, 42.
87. Day 4, 39. On Duch being beaten on the head, see Bizot, *The Gate*, 83.
88. Dunlop, *Lost Executioner*, 52, 65.
89. Day 5, 12.
90. Day 5, 63.
91. Day 5, 64.
92. Day 6, 102.
93. Unless otherwise indicated, what follows is based on Uch Sorn's testimony on Day 5, 51ff.
94. Day 9, 85–86.
95. Day 7, 70.
96. Day 7, 70.
97. Day 7, 70.
98. Day 7, 67.
99. Day 7, 69.
100. Day 7, 84–85.
101. Rasy Pheng Pong, "Security System of Special Zone's Office M-13," 3–9.

102. Day 8, 12.
103. Day 8, 12.
104. Day 8, 38.
105. Day 8, 13.
106. Day 8, 15.
107. Day 8, 63.
108. Day 8, 39.
109. Day 8, 45.
110. Day 9, 94.
111. Day 9, 94–95.
112. Day 8, 23.
113. Day 8, 26–27.
114. Day 8, 104.
115. Day 8, 98.
116. Day 8, 105.
117. Day 8, 105.
118. Day 8, 101.
119. The material in this paragraph is taken from Day 9, 9ff.
120. Day 9, 10.
121. Day 9, 42.
122. Day 9, 81.
123. Day 9, 82–83.
124. Day 9, 84.

Chapter 3. Subordinate

1. ECCC, Day 10, 70.
2. OCIJ, "Written Record of Interview of Charged Person," April 29, 2008, 3. See also Day 5, 56ff.
3. Day 14, 26–27; Khmer, 20.
4. Day 4, 69ff.
5. Day 14, 27; Khmer, 20.
6. Day 14, 27; Khmer, 20.
7. Day 14, 27; Khmer, 20.
8. Day 13, 41; Khmer, 29.
9. Day 13, 42.
10. Day 13, 42; Khmer, 30.
11. Day 13, 42; Khmer, 30.
12. Day 15, 9; Khmer, 6.
13. See Hinton, *Why Did They Kill?*
14. Day 15, 8; Khmer, 6.
15. OCIJ, "Written Record of Interview of Charged Person," April 29, 2008, 3.
16. OCIJ, "Written Record of Interview." See also Day 10, 71.
17. Day 13, 5.
18. Phnom Penh Domestic Service, "We Build and Defend the Country by Always Upholding the Traditional Characteristics of the Cambodian Revolution."

19. Phnom Penh Domestic Service, "Remarkable Morals of our Brother Combatants and Cadres of a Unit in Phnom Penh."
20. See Huy, *Khmer Rouge Division 703*, 32ff.
21. Phnom Penh Domestic Service, "Society of New Cambodia Is Just and Clean and Unprecedented in Our History."
22. Phnom Penh Domestic Service, "Society of New Cambodia."
23. Day 13, 3. See also Day 14, 82.
24. Chandler, *Voices from S-21*, 19. Day 4, 74.
25. TC, "Trial Chamber Judgement," 43.
26. Huy, *Khmer Rouge Division 703*, pp. 36ff.
27. Day 10, 88; see also Chandler, *Voices from S-21*, 19.
28. Chandler, *Voices from S-21*, 19.
29. See Hinton, *Why Did They Kill?*, 96ff.
30. Day 10, 73; TC, "Trial Chamber Judgement," 45.
31. Day 10, 78; Khmer, 58. See also Chandler, *Voices from S-21*, 3.
32. Day 10, 74; Khmer, 55.
33. On the role of Division 12/703 in the capture, evacuation, and "cleanup" of Phnom Penh, see Huy, *Khmer Rouge Division 703*.
34. Day 10, 76.
35. Day 10, 74.
36. Day 13, 46; Khmer, 33.
37. Day 13, 46–49.
38. Day 10, 76.
39. Day 10, 77.
40. Day 12, 42.
41. Day 12, 43; Khmer, 33.
42. Day 11, 14.
43. Day 11, 14; OCIJ, "Closing Order Indicting Kaing Guek Eav alias Duch (Public Redacted Version)," 7–8.
44. See Day 12, 43ff.
45. Chandler, *Voices from S-21*, 23; Huy, *Khmer Rouge Division 703*, 82.
46. Day 12, 18–19.
47. Day 12, 20–21; Khmer, 16.
48. Chandler, *Voices from S-21*, 23; Day 12, 23–24.
49. Day 12, 24.
50. Day 14, 40.
51. Day 10, 81; see also Chandler, *Voices from S-21*, 24.
52. Day 5, 96.
53. Day 11, 16.
54. TC, "Trial Chamber Judgement," 46; Day 30, 68.
55. Day 10, 80; Khmer, 49.
56. See Headley et al., *Cambodian-English Dictionary*, 586, 573.
57. Day 15, 3; Khmer, 3.
58. Day 14, 18; Khmer, 13.
59. Day 30, 27, 4; Day 14, 39; Day 13, 21.

60. Day 13, 21; Khmer, 14.
61. Day 14, 24; Khmer, 17.
62. Day 14, 14; Khmer, 10–11.
63. Day 12, 91; Khmer, 70.
64. Day 15, 11; Khmer, 8.
65. Day 30, 77.

Chapter 4. Cog

1. ECCC, Day 12, 51; Khmer, 40.
2. CPK, "Decision of the Central Committee Regarding a Number of Matters." See also Chandler et al., "Pol Pot Plans the Future."
3. Day 10, 89; Khmer, 66.
4. Day 10, 87.
5. Day 12, 47; Khmer, 37.
6. Day 12, 48; Khmer, 37.
7. Day 12, 48; Khmer, 37.
8. The following translations from Long Muy's confession are adapted from Day 12, 52–53, and ECCC, "Colour Copy Excerpt of Confession of Long Muy."
9. Chandler, *Voices from S-21*, 65–66.
10. Ly, "Long Muy, Known as Chuon," 6.
11. Phnom Penh Domestic Service, "We Build and Defend the Country by Always Upholding the Traditional Characteristics of the Cambodian Revolution," H1.
12. Kiernan, *Pol Pot Regime*, 316ff.
13. Kiernan, *Pol Pot Regime*, 321.
14. Chandler, *Voices from S-21*, 52.
15. On the arrest of Chakrei and those implicated in his confession, including the designations using roman numerals, see Chandler, *Voices from S-21*. See also Kiernan, *Pol Pot Regime*, 324.
16. Kiernan, *Pol Pot Regime*, 324.
17. Day 13, 21; Khmer, 14.
18. Day 13, 22; Khmer, 14.
19. Chandler, *Voices from S-21*, 47; Short, *Pol Pot*, 355.
20. Day 11, 26.
21. Day 14, 86.
22. Day 11, 22; Day 12, 44.
23. Day 15, 2–3; Day 13, 37; Khmer, 26.
24. Day 11, 29.
25. Day 12, 35; Khmer, 27.
26. Day 12, 35–36, 73.
27. OCIJ, "Written Record of Interview of Charged Person," April 1, 2008, 2; see also Day 14, 6; Khmer, 5.
28. OCIJ, "Written Record of Interview of Charged Person," April 1, 2008, 2; see also Day 14, 8; Khmer, 6.
29. Day 24, 3; Khmer, 27.
30. Day 24, 36; Khmer, 27.

31. Day 24, 47–48.
32. Day 24, 9.
33. Day 25, 43.
34. Day 25, 38; Khmer, 27.
35. Day 15, 21.
36. Day 24, 9–10.
37. Day 24, 74.
38. Day 24, 77; Khmer 57.
39. Day 24, 38. See also Day 15, 30–31.
40. Day 15, 45. See also Day 24, 10.
41. The quotations in this paragraph are from CPK, "Communist Party of Kampuchea Statutes," 3.
42. "Communist Party of Kampuchea Statutes," 3.
43. Day 15, 33.
44. Day 15, 34–35.
45. Day 15, 35.
46. Day 15, 36. See also Day 25, 3ff.
47. Day 15, 44.
48. Phnom Penh Domestic Service, "Constitution of Democratic Kampuchea," H4. See also Dy, *History of Democratic Kampuchea*, 21.
49. Day 25, 8.
50. Day 25, 8.
51. Day 15, 37.
52. Day 25, 9.
53. Day 25, 10.
54. Day 15, 13; see also Day 15, 38.
55. Day 15, 37.
56. Day 25, 37–38.
57. Day 25, 12.
58. Day 15, 39.
59. CPK, "Communist Party of Kampuchea Statutes," 13–14.
60. "Communist Party of Kampuchea Statutes," 13–14.
61. Day 15, 52.
62. Day 15, 53–54.
63. CPK, "Communist Party of Kampuchea Statutes," 5.
64. "Communist Party of Kampuchea Statutes," 5.
65. "Communist Party of Kampuchea Statutes," 10.
66. "Communist Party of Kampuchea Statutes," 12.
67. "Communist Party of Kampuchea Statutes," 12.
68. Day 15, 48–49.
69. Day 16, 45.
70. Day 16, 45.
71. Day 28, 25.
72. Day 16, 47–48.
73. Day 24, 8.

74. Day 24, 104.

75. Day 25, 16.

76. Day 25, 16–17.

77. Day 25, 17.

78. The Duch quotations in this paragraph are from ECCC, "Compilation of Statements of Apology Made by Kaing Guek Eav alias Duch during the Proceedings," 5.

79. Day 32, 13.

80. ECCC, "Compilation of Statements of Apology Made by Kaing Guek Eav alias Duch during the Proceedings," 5.

81. Day 32, 13.

82. Day 28, 38.

83. Day 31, 71.

84. ECCC, "Compilation of Statements of Apology Made by Kaing Guek Eav alias Duch during the Proceedings," 5; OCIJ, "Written Record of Interview of Charged Person," April 2, 2008, 6.

85. Day 16, 67.

86. Day 18, 25.

87. Day 16, 73–74.

88. Day 16, 85.

89. CPK, "Decision of the Central Committee Regarding a Number of Matters," 6.

90. This and the following quotation are from Day 16, 80.

91. Day 19, 28.

92. See also Hinton, *Why Did They Kill?*

93. See Hinton, *Why Did They Kill?*

94. See, for example, Day 32, 29.

95. Day 14, 36.

96. Day 15, 35; Khmer, 26.

97. Day 12, 83, 85.

98. Day 12, 85–86; Khmer, 66.

99. See, for example, Duch's discussion of Comrade Tuy, Day 32, 16.

100. Day 12, 86.

101. On the historical origins and dynamics of patronage in Cambodia, which continues into the present, see Chandler, *History of Cambodia*; Hinton, *Why Did They Kill?*

102. Day 12, 91; Khmer, 70.

103. Day 14, 11.

104. Day 21, 46.

105. OCIJ, "Written Record of Interview of Charged Person," April 2, 2008, 4.

106. Day 17, 5.

107. Day 17, 6; see also Chandler, *Voices from S-21*, 62.

108. Day 17, 8.

109. Day 17, 9.

110. Day 17, 40.

111. Day 17, 44.

112. Day 17, 45.

113. Day 14, 24.

114. CPK, "Minutes of the Meeting with the Organization's Office, 703 and Sâ-21."
115. CPK, "Minutes of the Meeting with Comrade Tal Division 290 and Division 170."
116. Day 19, 58.
117. Day 19, 59.
118. Day 21, 52.
119. Day 21, 54.
120. Day 21, 55.
121. Day 21, 55.
122. Day 24, 83; Khmer, 60.
123. Day 25, 50–51.
124. Day 23, 91.
125. Day 23, 92.

Chapter 5. Commandant

1. ECCC, "Transcript of Proceedings—'Duch' Trial Public." Day 32, 19.
2. Day 31, 76.
3. Day 31, 53ff.
4. Day 32, 20.
5. Day 31, 56.
6. Day 31, 56.
7. Day 31, 58.
8. Day 31, 52; see also 49.
9. Day 31, 52.
10. Day 31, 48.
11. Day 31, 58.
12. Day 34, 33.
13. Day 34, 34.
14. Day 31, 47.
15. Day 33, 9ff.
16. Day 33, 19.
17. Day 32, 18. See also OCIJ, "Written Record of Interview of Charged Person," March 27, 2008.
18. Day 33, 17.
19. Day 33, 47; Day 44, 43; Day 28, 20, 17.
20. Day 28, 16.
21. OCIJ, "Closing Order," 18, 20–21, 240.
22. OCIJ, "Closing Order," 240; Day 28, 15.
23. Day 28, 16, 80.
24. OCP, "Revised S-21 Prisoner List" (Long Muy is prisoner 4856 on the list).
25. Day 28, 26.
26. For Duch's description of the detention conditions, see Day 28, 36ff.
27. Day 28, 86.
28. Day 28, 55.
29. Day 28, 63.
30. Day 28, 56.

31. Day 28, 32.
32. Day 28, 59.
33. Day 31, 82–83.
34. Day 31, 85.
35. See, for example, Day 28, 42–43, 64.
36. Day 28, 86–87.
37. The material on the structure and operation of the interrogation process are largely based on Day 29, 13ff.
38. Day 29, 15.
39. Day 29, 16.
40. Day 29, 15–16.
41. Day 29, 17, 50.
42. Day 29, 21.
43. Day 29, 22.
44. Day 29, 22.
45. Day 29, 20.
46. Day 29, 27.
47. Day 29, 18.
48. Day 29, 14, 44.
49. Day 29, 44. See also Day 13, 72.
50. Day 31, 85.
51. Day 31, 24.
52. Day 29, 18.
53. Day 29, 57.
54. Day 29, 36, 56.
55. Day 29, 57.
56. Day 29, 58.
57. Day 29, 16.
58. Day 29, 42.
59. Day 32, 16.
60. Day 32, 42.
61. Day 29, 58.
62. Day 29, 56, 88.
63. Day 29, 45.
64. Day 32, 15.
65. Day 32, 15. On interrogators learning by observation, see Day 31, 117, and Day 32, 2.
66. Day 29, 25.
67. Day 29, 25, 26.
68. Day 24, 51–52.
69. Day 24, 46, 50–51.

Chapter 6. Master

1. ECCC, "Torture Manual."
2. ECCC, "Statistics List."
3. ECCC, "Statistics List," 14.

4. ECCC, "Statistics List," 3.

5. ECCC, "Statistics List," 6–7.

6. ECCC, "Statistics List," 5–7.

7. ECCC, "Statistics List," 10.

8. ECCC, "Statistics List," 9.

9. ECCC, "Statistics List," 9–10.

10. ECCC, "Statistics List," 13.

11. ECCC, "Statistics List," 13.

12. ECCC, "Statistics List," 14.

13. ECCC, "Statistics List," 14.

14. ECCC, "Statistics List," 13.

15. ECCC, "Statistics List," 13.

16. ECCC, "Statistics List," 16.

17. ECCC, "Statistics List," 12.

18. ECCC, "Statistics List," 16.

19. ECCC, "Statistics List," 15.

20. ECCC, "Statistics List," 15.

21. ECCC, "Statistics List," 15.

22. ECCC, "Statistics List," 17.

23. ECCC, "Statistics List," 17.

24. ECCC, "Statistics List," 17.

25. ECCC, "Statistics List," 18.

26. ECCC, "Statistics List," 18.

27. ECCC, "Statistics List," 19.

28. ECCC, "Statistics List," 19.

29. ECCC, "Statistics List," 18.

30. ECCC, "Statistics List," 20, 21.

31. ECCC, "Statistics List," 22.

32. ECCC, "Statistics List," 22.

33. ECCC, "Statistics List," 9.

34. ECCC, "Statistics List," 11.

35. ECCC, "Statistics List," 20, 30.

36. ECCC, "Statistics List," 20.

37. ECCC, "Statistics List," 20.

38. ECCC, "Statistics List," 21, 24.

39. ECCC, "Statistics List," 29.

40. ECCC, "Statistics List," 26.

41. ECCC, "Statistics List," 17.

42. ECCC, "Statistics List," 19.

43. Author interview with Prak Khan, Cambodia, January 10, 2006.

44. ECCC, "Transcript of Proceedings—'Duch' Trial Public." Day 29, 79.

45. Day 29, 68.

46. Day 29, 68.

47. Day 29, 68.

48. Day 29, 69.

49. Day 29, 79.

50. OCP, "Revised S-21 Prisoner List," 142.

51. ECCC, "Situation of Interrogating Ke Kim Huot," 5. See also Chandler, *Voices from S-21*, 110.

52. ECCC, "Situation of Interrogating Ke Kim Huot," 9–10.

53. ECCC, "Situation of Interrogating Ke Kim Huot," 10.

54. ECCC, "Situation of Interrogating Ke Kim Huot," 10.

55. Day 29, 87.

56. ECCC, Ke Kim Huot Confession, n.d.

57. ECCC, Ke Kim Huot Confession, March 7, 1978.

58. OCP, "Revised S-21 Prisoner List," 535.

59. Day 29, 88.

60. Day 29, 51, 53, 58, 60.

61. Day 29, 37.

62. Day 29, 80.

63. Day 29, 80.

64. Day 28, 46.

65. Chandler, *Voices from S-21*, 57. See also Colm and Sim, "Anatomy of an Interrogation."

66. Day 31, 31.

67. Day 31, 33.

68. Colm and Sim, "Anatomy of an Interrogation," 2–3.

69. Chandler, *Voices from S-21*, 57.

70. Day 31, 30.

71. ECCC, "Pon Note to Ya," September 23, 1976. See also Colm and Sim, "Anatomy of an Interrogation," 3.

72. ECCC, "Duch Letter to Ya," September 24, 1976.

73. ECCC, "Duch Letter to Ya," September 24, 1976.

74. ECCC, "Duch Letter to Ya," September 24, 1976.

75. ECCC, "Letter from Pon to Duch," September 25, 1976.

76. ECCC, "Letter from Pon to Duch," September 25, 1976.

77. Day 31, 36.

78. Colm and Sim, "Anatomy of an Interrogation," 5.

79. Colm and Sim, "Anatomy of an Interrogation," 5; see also ECCC, "Confession of Ya, Version Two."

80. ECCC, "Confession of Ya, Version 3"; see Colm and Sim, "Anatomy of an Interrogation," 6.

81. ECCC, "Letter from Pon to Ya," September 29, 1976; see also Colm and Sim, "Anatomy of an Interrogation," 6.

82. ECCC, "Ya Response to Pon Letter"; Colm and Sim, "Anatomy of an Interrogation," 6.

83. ECCC, "Memo from Pon to Ya."

84. Day 31, 37.

85. ECCC, "Memo from Pon to Ya."

86. ECCC, "Confession of Ya, Version Four."

87. ECCC, "Confession of Ya, Version Four."

88. ECCC, "Confession of Ya, Version Four."

89. ECCC, "Confession of Ya, Version Four."

90. ECCC, "Confession of Ya, Version Four."

91. ECCC, "Letter from Duch to Pon," September 30, 1976.

92. ECCC, "Letter from Duch to Pon," October 1, 1976.

93. ECCC, "Letter from Duch to Pon," October 1, 1976.

94. Day 31, 39, 40.

95. Day 31, 39, 40.

96. ECCC, "Confession of Ya, Version Five."

97. Colm and Sim, "Anatomy of an Interrogation," 7.

98. Colm and Sim, "Anatomy of an Interrogation."

99. ECCC, "Chan Notebook."

100. ECCC, "Chan Notebook."

101. ECCC, "Tuy Pon Notebook."

102. ECCC, "Tuy Pon Notebook," 17.

103. ECCC, "The Last Joint Plan."

104. ECCC, "The Last Joint Plan," 5.

105. ECCC, "The Last Joint Plan," 8.

106. ECCC, "The Last Joint Plan," 9.

107. ECCC, "The Last Joint Plan," 11.

108. ECCC, "Chan Notebook," 16.

109. ECCC, "Chan Notebook," 15.

110. Kiernan, *The Pol Pot Regime*, 432–33.

111. ECCC, Confession of Long Muy alias Chuon.

112. OCP, "Revised of S-21 Prisoner List," 212.

113. Choung, "An Interrogator at S-21 Was Arrested," 9. I thank Youk Chhang and Kok-Thay Eng for their help in determining that Vong Oeun may have been Long Muy's interrogator, though we remain uncertain.

114. ECCC, "Statistics List," 6.

115. What follows is based on "Confession of Long Muy alias Chuon," handwritten manuscript, Documentation Center of Cambodia, Phnom Penh; Ly, "Long Muy, Known as Chuon," 5–7; Choung, "Long Muy, a Translator of the Chinese Language, Is Accused by the Khmer Rouge of Disloyalty to the Revolution and Executed," 4–7.

116. Choung 2005, 5.

117. Choung 2005, 6.

118. Choung 2005, 7.

119. Ly, "Long Muy, Known as Chuon," 7. The following paragraphs on the DC-Cam interview of Long Muy's family are based on Sophal Ly's account in this article.

120. Ly, "Long Muy, Known as Chuon," 7.

121. Day 30, 6; Day 28, 36.

122. OCP, "Revised S-21 Prisoner List," 212.

123. Day 30, 65.

124. Day 30, 17, 46–48.

125. Day 30, 46.

126. Day 30, 19.

127. Day 30, 18.

128. See Day 17, 50ff; see also Keo and Yin, "Fact Sheet."

129. Day 29, 96.

130. Day 29, 99.

131. Day 29, 94.

132. Day 29, 82.

133. Day 29, 91.

134. Day 12, 66.

135. Day 10, 84.

136. Day 30, 37, 28–29.

137. Day 30, 29.

138. Day 30, 12.

139. Day 30, 69–71.

140. Day 30, 34.

141. Day 30, 36ff.

142. Day 30, 45.

143. Day 30, 52–53.

144. Day 30, 75.

145. Day 30, 16.

146. Day 30, 89–90.

147. Day 30, 91.

Chapter 7. Villain

1. ECCC, Day 73, 36.

2. Day 73, 36–37.

3. Day 73, 37.

4. Day 73, 38.

5. Day 35, 64.

6. Day 35, 23.

7. Day 35, 25.

8. Day 35, 26.

9. Day 35, 68.

10. Day 35, 98.

11. Day 35, 67.

12. Day 34, 100.

13. Day 35, 36.

14. Day 35, 76.

15. Day 35, 39.

16. Day 35, 46.

17. Day 35, 57.

18. Day 35, 95.

19. Day 35, 58.

20. Day 36, 9–10.

21. Day 36, 10.

22. Day 36, 72.

23. Day 36, 11. See also 24–25.

24. Day 36, 11; Khmer, 9.

25. Day 36, 53.

26. Day 36, 11; Khmer, 9.

27. Day 36, 11; Khmer, 9.

28. Day 36, 12; Khmer, 10.

29. Day 36, 12; Khmer, 10.

30. Day 36, 12; Khmer, 10.

31. Day 36, 12–13; Khmer, 10.

32. Day 36, 13, 67; Khmer, 11, 55.

33. Day 36, 13; Khmer, 11.

34. Day 36, 13; Khmer, 11.

35. Day 36, 14; Khmer, 11.

36. Day 36, 78; Khmer, 63.

37. Day 36, 24.

38. Day 36, 29.

39. Day 36, 84.

40. Day 36, 48.

41. Day 36, 78; Khmer, 63.

42. Day 37, 13.

43. Day 37, 31–32.

44. Day 37, 13.

45. Day 37, 19, 36.

46. Day 37, 64.

47. Day 37, 38.

48. Day 38, 29, 52.

49. The quotations in this paragraph are from Day 38, 83–84.

50. Day 38, 87.

51. Day 38, 88.

52. Day 41, 1.

53. Cryder, "Investigative Inertia during the ECCC Trial Phase," 9.

54. Day 41, 3.

55. Day 41, 4–5.

56. Day 73, 40.

57. Day 73, 41.

58. Day 73, 49.

59. Day 73, 44.

60. Day 73, 50.

61. Day 73, 50.

62. Day 73, 50.

63. Day 73, 92; Levi, *Survival in Auschwitz*, 34.

64. Day 73, 93.

65. ECCC, "Internal Rules," Version 1, June 12, 2007.

66. Day 73, 5, 7.
67. Day 73, 84.
68. Day 73, 87.
69. Day 73, 94.
70. Day 73, 78.
71. Day 73, 83.
72. Hinton, "Transitional Justice Imaginary."
73. Day 73, 79.
74. Day 73, 78.
75. Day 73, 115.
76. Day 73, 51.
77. Day 73, 51–52.
78. Day 42, 53.
79. Day 43, 54.
80. Day 73, 57.
81. Day 73, 57.
82. Day 73, 4–5.
83. Day 73, 5.
84. Day 73, 75.
85. Day 73, 82.
86. Day 73, 119–20.
87. Day 73, 33.
88. Day 73, 32, 34.
89. Day 73, 119.
90. Day 73, 77.
91. Day 73, 77.
92. Day 73, 70.
93. Day 73, 77.
94. Day 73, 113.
95. Day 73, 114.
96. Day 73, 115.
97. Day 73, 115.
98. Day 73, 123.

Chapter 8. Zealot

1. ECCC, Day 74, 2; Khmer, 2.
2. Day 74, 2.
3. OCP, "Office of the Co-prosecutors."
4. OCIJ, "Co–investigating Judges."
5. Interview, OCP official, Phnom Penh, February 26, 2013.
6. OCP, "Statement of the Co-prosecutors." The structure of the introductory submission is outlined by Internal Rule 53, which states it should include "a summary of the facts; the type of offence(s) alleged; the relevant provision of the law that defines and punishes the crimes; [and] the names of any person to be investigated" (ECCC Internal Rule 53).

7. OCIJ, "Co–investigating Judges."

8. OCIJ, "Separation Order."

9. Internal Rule 55.5 (ECCC, "Internal Rules," Version 3, March 6, 2009).

10. OCIJ, "Co–investigating Judges."

11. OCP, "Public Information by the Co-prosecutors Pursuant to Rule 54 Concerning the Rule 66 Final Submission Regarding Kaing Guek Eav alias 'Duch.'"

12. Day 74, 13.

13. Day 74, 13–14.

14. Day 74, 14.

15. Day 74, 21.

16. Day 74, 23.

17. Day 74, 29.

18. OCP, "Co-prosecutors' Final Trial Submission with Annexes 1–5."

19. Day 74, 29.

20. Day 74, 30.

21. Day 74, 30.

22. ECCC, "Law on the Establishment of the Extraordinary Chambers in the Courts of Cambodia."

23. ECCC 2004; Day 74, 31.

24. Day 74, 33.

25. OCP, "Co-prosecutors' Final Trial Submission with Annexes 1–5," 86.

26. OCP, "Co-prosecutors' Final Trial Submission with Annexes 1–5," 86–87.

27. Day 74, 37.

28. Day 74, 37–38.

29. Day 74, 62.

30. Day 74, 62.

31. Day 74, 63.

32. Day 74, 63.

33. Day 74, 67.

34. Day 74, 69.

35. Day 74, 78.

36. Day 74, 78–79.

37. Day 74, 79.

38. Day 74, 84, 86.

39. Day 74, 93.

40. Day 74, 94.

41. Day 72, 43; Day 74, 97.

42. Day 74, 97–98.

43. Day 74, 99.

44. ECCC, "Law on the Establishment of the Extraordinary Chambers in the Courts of Cambodia"; Day 75, 2.

45. ECCC, "Law on the Establishment of the Extraordinary Chambers in the Courts of Cambodia"; Day 75, 7.

46. Day 75, 8; OCP, "Co-prosecutors' Final Trial Submission with Annexes 1–5," 121.

47. Day 75, 8.

48. ocp, "Co-prosecutors' Final Trial Submission with Annexes 1–5," 122.
49. Day 75, 8; ocp, "Co-prosecutors' Final Trial Submission with Annexes 1–5," 122–23.
50. Day 75, 9.
51. Day 75, 12.
52. Day 75, 13.
53. Day 75, 15.
54. Day 75, 17.
55. Day 75, 19.
56. Day 75, 22.
57. Day 75, 22.
58. Day 75, 23.
59. Day 75, 24.
60. Day 75, 25.
61. Day 75, 24.
62. Day 75, 24.
63. Author interview, ocp staff member, Phnom Penh, March 25, 2014.
64. Author interview, ocp staff member, Phnom Penh, March 25, 2014.
65. Day 75, 27–28.
66. ocp, "Co-prosecutors' Final Trial Submission with Annexes 1–5," 146–47.
67. Day 75, 29–30.
68. Day 75, 30–31.
69. Day 75, 31.
70. Day 75, 31–32.
71. Day 75, 34.
72. ocp, "Co-prosecutors' Final Trial Submission with Annexes 1–5," 154.
73. Day 75, 35, 36.
74. ocp, "Co-prosecutors' Final Trial Submission with Annexes 1–5," 156, 157, 158.
75. Day 75, 36.
76. Day 75, 37.
77. Day 75, 38.

Chapter 9. Scapegoat

1. Kaing Guek Eav, "Continuous Killing Carried Out by the Communist Party of Kampuchea (cpk)," 39.
2. Kaing Guek Eav 2009, 1.
3. Kaing Guek Eav 2009, 3.
4. Kaing Guek Eav 2009, 4.
5. Kaing Guek Eav 2009, 4, 6.
6. Kaing Guek Eav 2009, 8.
7. Kaing Guek Eav 2009, 14.
8. Kaing Guek Eav 2009, 15.
9. Kaing Guek Eav 2009, 19.
10. Kaing Guek Eav 2009, 21.
11. Kaing Guek Eav 2009, 24.

12. Kaing Guek Eav 2009, 23.

13. Kaing Guek Eav 2009, 24.

14. Kaing Guek Eav 2009, 27.

15. Kaing Guek Eav 2009, 28.

16. Kaing Guek Eav 2009, 28.

17. Kaing Guek Eav 2009, 29.

18. Kaing Guek Eav 2009, 30.

19. ECCC, Day 75, 104, 105. Savuth's figures appear to have been based on mapping research conducted by the DC-Cam (http://www.dccam.org), Phong-Rasy, "DK Prison," "Burial."

20. Day 75, 76, 77.

21. Day 75, 103.

22. Author interview with OCP legal officer, Phnom Penh, February 26, 2013.

23. Author interview with OCP legal officer, Phnom Penh, February 26, 2013.

24. Author interview with OCP legal officer, Phnom Penh, March 25, 2014.

25. Day 75, 110.

26. Day 75, 114, 117; Khmer, 84.

27. Day 76, 2.

28. Day 76, 8.

29. Day 76, 8.

30. Day 76, 9.

31. Day 76, 3.

32. Day 76, 4.

33. Day 76, 5.

34. Day 76, 10.

35. Day 76, 16.

36. Day 76, 18.

37. Day 76, 18.

38. Day 76, 18.

39. Day 76, 19.

40. Day 76, 20.

41. Day 76, 20.

42. Day 76, 21, 22.

43. Defense, "Final Defense Written Submission," 18.

44. Day 76, 44.

45. Day 76, 24.

46. Day 76, 25.

47. Day 76, 32.

48. Day 76, 28.

49. Day 76, 28.

50. Day 76, 60.

51. Day 76, 62.

52. Day 76, 64.

53. Day 76, 66.

54. Day 76, 67.

55. Chandler, *Voices from S-21*, 155.

56. Day 76, 69.

57. Day 76, 73.

58. Day 76, 73.

59. Day 76, 75.

60. Day 76, 77.

61. Day 76, 78.

62. Day 76, 79.

63. Day 76, 80.

64. Day 76, 81.

65. Day 76, 82.

66. Day 76, 82.

67. Day 76, 84.

68. Day 76, 85.

69. Day 76, 85.

70. Day 76, 86.

71. Day 76, 87.

72. Day 76, 88.

73. Day 76, 90.

74. Day 76, 88–89.

75. Day 76, 89.

76. Day 76, 91.

77. Day 76, 94.

78. Day 76, 95, 101.

79. Day 76, 95.

80. Day 76, 102.

81. Day 76, 105.

82. Day 77, 2.

83. Day 77, 4.

84. Day 77, 4.

85. Day 77, 20.

86. Day 77, 21.

87. Day 77, 25.

88. Day 75, 25.

89. Day 77, 26.

90. Day 77, 28.

91. Day 77, 38.

92. Day 77, 40.

93. Day 77, 45.

94. Day 77, 47.

95. Day 77, 48, 47.

96. Day 77, 48.

97. Day 77, 50.

98. Day 77, 50.

99. Day 34, 51; see also Day 77, 50.

100. Day 77, 50.
101. Day 77, 50.
102. Day 77, 52.
103. Day 77, 59.
104. Day 77, 60.
105. Day 77, 60.
106. Day 77, 61.
107. Day 77, 62.
108. Day 77, 62.

Chapter 10. The Accused

1. "Dock," OED Online.
2. "Dock," OED Online.
3. On the spatial matrix, see Lefebvre, *Production of Space*. On legal space, see Butler, "Critical Legal Studies and the Politics of Space"; Eltringham, "Spectators to the Spectacle of Law."
4. Rogers, "Request by Mr. Kaing to Withdraw Co-lawyer Francois Roux."
5. Cruvellier, *Master of Confessions*, 311.
6. Giry, "Cambodia's Perfect War Criminal."
7. TC, "Judgement," 4.
8. "Disposition," OED Online.
9. OCP, "Co-prosecutors' Final Trial Submission with Annexes 1–5," 9.
10. TC, "Judgement," 2.
11. "Chamber," OED Online.
12. TC, "Trial Chamber Judgement, Announced on 26 July 2010, Case 001, Kaing Guek Eav alias Duch," 15.
13. TC, "Judgement," 89.
14. TC, "Judgement," 29; Khmer, 23.
15. Saliba and Nims, "Duch Sentenced to 35 Years in Prison," 3.
16. TC, "Judgement," 18, 19.
17. TC, "Judgement," 20.
18. TC, "Judgement," 29.
19. TC, "Judgement," 20.
20. TC, "Trial Chamber Judgement, Announced on 26 July 2010, Case 001, Kaing Guek Eav alias Duch," 135.
21. TC, "Judgement," 29.
22. TC, "Judgement," 30.
23. TC, "Judgement," 24.
24. TC, "Trial Chamber Judgement, Announced on 26 July 2010, Case 001, Kaing Guek Eav alias Duch," 223.
25. TC, "Trial Chamber Judgement, Announced on 26 July 2010, Case 001, Kaing Guek Eav alias Duch," 224.
26. TC, "Trial Chamber Judgement, Announced on 26 July 2010, Case 001, Kaing Guek Eav alias Duch," 233–237.
27. TC, "Judgement," 31.

28. TC "Judgement," 31.
29. See, for example, Cambodian Center for Human Rights, "Duch Trial."
30. Friedman, "Quotes."
31. AsianScientists Staff, "Trial of Cambodia Khmer Rouge Jailer Duch Exerted Mental Toll on Survivors."
32. Mydans, "Prison Term for Khmer Rouge Jailer Leaves Many Dissatisfied."
33. For a discussion of the response to the Eichmann and Nuremberg trials, see Douglas, *Memory of Judgment.*
34. Mydans, "Prison Term for Khmer Rouge Jailer Leaves Many Dissatisfied."
35. Mydans, "Prison Term for Khmer Rouge Jailer Leaves Many Dissatisfied."
36. Author interview with Bou Meng, July 28, 2010, Phnom Penh.

Background. Redactic

1. Kong, "Torture Center Marks First Year as 'Memory of the World.'"
2. Di Certo and Titthara, "S-21 Survivor Plays Host."
3. Di Certo and Titthara, "Bou Meng Housewarming."
4. "Negative," OED Online.
5. See also Caswell, *Archiving the Unspeakable.*
6. Sirik, "Duch Final Judgement," 19–20.
7. Author interview with Savina Sirik, February 6, 2012, Phnom Penh.
8. Translation from Pali. Samphors Huy, personal communication, July 31, 2014.
9. Terith Chy, personal communication, July 21, 2014.
10. PTC, "Appeal Hearing," November 20, 2007, 1.
11. PTC, "Appeal Hearing," November 21, 2007, 2.
12. Public Affairs, "Photo Archive."
13. SCC, "Transcript of Appeal Judgement," 1.
14. SCC, "Transcript of Appeal Judgement," 2.
15. SCC, "Transcript of Appeal Judgement," 8.
16. SCC, "Transcript of Appeal Judgement," 33.
17. SCC, "Transcript of Appeal Judgement," 34.
18. SCC, "Transcript of Appeal Judgement," 17.
19. SCC, "Transcript of Appeal Judgement," 20.
20. SCC, "Appeal Judgement," 263–65.
21. SCC, "Appeal Judgement," 35.
22. Seiff and Naren, "Duch Sentenced to Life in Prison by Khmer Rouge Tribunal," 9.
23. Naren and Foster, "Ten Duch Victims Celebrate Civil Party Status," 2.
24. Public Affairs, "Kaing Guek Eav Sentenced to Life Imprisonment."
25. Amnesty International, "Cambodia: Khmer Rouge Judgment Welcome, but Raises Human Rights Concerns."
26. SCC, "Appeal Judgement," 168–69.
27. Seng, "Duch Final Pronouncement."
28. Khmer Rouge Victims in Cambodia, "Phnom Penh: Khmer Rouge Victims in Cambodia." Seng, "Duch Final Pronouncement."
29. SCC, "Appeal Judgement," 41.
30. See Giry, "Necessary Scapegoats?"

31. Sokha and O'Toole, "Hun Sen to Ban Ki-moon."

32. OCP, "Statement of the Co-prosecutors," January 5, 2009.

33. PTC, "Public Redacted Version—Consideration of the PTC Regarding the Disagreement between the Co-prosecutors Pursuant to Internal Rule 71."

34. Open Society Justice Initiative, "Recent Developments at the Extraordinary Chambers in the Courts of Cambodia" (November).

35. OCIJ, "Statement from the Co-investigating Judges," April 29, 2011.

36. OCP, "Statement from the International Co-prosecutor regarding Case File 003."

37. Open Society Justice Initiative, "Recent Developments at the Extraordinary Chambers in the Courts of Cambodia" (June), 10. Sou Meth died, a suspect but untried, in mid-2013.

38. OCP, "Statement by the National Co-prosecutor regarding Case File 003."

39. OCIJ, "Statement from the Co–investigating Judges," May 18, 2011.

40. Radio Free Asia Staff, "Khmer Rouge Tribunal Staff Quit."

41. Gillison, "Justice Denied."

42. OCIJ, "Statement of the National Co–investigating Judge."

43. OCIJ, "Note of the International Reserve Co–investigating Judge to the Parties on the Egregious Dysfunctions within the ECCC."

44. Giry, "Necessary Scapegoats?"

45. Stephen Rapp, US ambassador-at-large for war crimes issues, quoted in Gillison, "Justice Denied."

46. Hinton, "Transitional Justice Imaginary."

47. Said, *Orientalism*.

48. See, for example, Mutua, "Savages, Victims, and Saviors." On Cambodia as a "failed state," see, for example, Helman and Ratner, "Saving Failed States."

49. See, for example, Fawthrop and Jarvis, *Getting Away with Genocide*.

50. See, for example, Derrida, "Force of Law"; Lacan, *Écrits*.

51. Author interview with Long Tai, Peareang district, Prey Veng province, March 24, 2014.

52. The following text is based on the author's interview with Bou Meng, February 5, 2012, Phnom Penh.

53. The following text is based on the author's interview with Chum Mey, February 5, 2012, Phnom Penh.

54. Headley et al., *Cambodian-English Dictionary*, 148.

55. I thank Terith Chy for helping me to discern some of the more illegible graffiti, even if it wasn't always possible to make out what was written.

Epilogue. Man or Monster?

1. "Provoke," OED Online.

2. Bizot, *The Gate*, and *Facing the Torturer*.

3. Chandler, *Voices from S-21*, 155; ECCC, "Transcript of Proceedings—'Duch' Trial Public," Day 55, 120; Day 76, 69.

4. Day 67, 34; Day 76, 51ff.

5. Cruvellier, *Master of Confessions*; Chy et al., *When the Criminal Laughs*.

6. Carmichael, *When Clouds Fell from the Sky*, 162.

7. Rithy Panh, *The Elimination*, 34, 57.

8. Rithy Panh, *The Elimination*, 2, 133; Chy et al., *When the Criminal Laughs*.

9. Day 76, 18.

10. "Articulate," OED *Online*.

11. I thank Nicole Cooley for noting this point.

12. Day 6, 97.

13. Rithy Panh, *The Elimination*, 57, 243.

14. See Douglas, *The Memory of Judgment*.

15. Day 63, 76; Khmer, 65.

16. Day 60, 109–10; Khmer, 84.

17. Day 60, 110; Khmer, 84.

18. This was not true during Case 002, where some defense lawyers have sought a strategy of rupture that questions the legitimacy of the court.

19. See Koskenniemi, *Between Impunity and Show Trials*.

20. Giry, "Cambodia's Perfect War Criminal," and "Necessary Scapegoats?"; see also Gillison, "Justice Denied."

21. "Conviction," OED *Online*.

22. The term "ordinary men" was popularized by Browning, *Ordinary Men*.

23. "Ordinary," OED Online.

24. On recent legal decisions undercutting the criminal defense of superior orders, see article 7 of the International Criminal Tribunal for the Former Yugoslavia Statutes and TC, "Trial Chamber Judgement, Announced on 26 July 2010, Case 001, Kaing Guek Eav alias Duch," 190.

25. Rithy Panh, *The Elimination*, 57, 243.

26. Sironi-Guilbaud and Ka, *Psychological Assessment Report*, 26.

27. On this point, see also Carmichael, *When Clouds Fell from the Sky*.

28. "Efface," OED *Online*.

29. "Aface," OED *Online*.

30. "Analysis," OED *Online*.

31. On the "gray zone" and the dangers of simplification, see Levi, *Drowned and the Saved*.

Bibliography

Amnesty International. 2002. "Cambodia: Cambodians Deserve International Standards of Justice." Press release. November 19. http://www.amnesty.org.

Amnesty International. 2003. "Cambodia: Fair Trial and Due Process Are Not Up for Negotiation." Press release. April 25. http://www.amnesty.org.

Amnesty International. 2012. "Cambodia: Khmer Rouge Judgment Welcome, but Raises Human Rights Concerns." Amnesty International News, February 3. https://www.amnesty.org/en/latest/news/2012/02/cambodia-khmer-rouge-judgment-welcome-raises-human-rights-concerns/.

Arendt, Hannah. 2006. *Eichmann in Jerusalem: A Report on the Banality of Evil*. New York: Penguin.

AsianScientist Staff. 2012. "Trial of Cambodia Khmer Rouge Jailer Duch Exerted Mental Toll on Survivors." *AsianScientist*, February 3. http://www.asianscientist.com/2012/02/features/cambodia-trial-khmer-rouge-tuol-sleng-prison-kaing-guek-eav-duch-life-sentence-mental-toll-2012.

Associated Press Staff. 2009. "Khmer Rouge Prison Chief to Face Charges." March 27. http://www.msnbc.msn.com.

Atlas Project. 2010. "Transitional Justice in Cambodia: Analytical Report." October. http://projetatlas.univparis1.fr.

Badgley, Lya. 1993. "Archives at Tuol Sleng Imperiled." *Phnom Penh Post*, June 18.

Bateson, Gregory. 1972. *Steps to an Ecology of Mind: Collected Essays in Anthropology, Psychiatry, Evolution, and Epistemology*. Chicago: University of Chicago Press.

Bernstein, Richard. 2009. "At Last, Justice for Monsters." *New York Review of Books*, April 9.

Bizot, François. 2002. *The Gate*. New York: Vintage.

Bizot, François. 2011. *Facing the Torturer: Inside the Mind of a War Criminal*. London: Rider.

Browning, Christopher R. 1992. *Ordinary Men: Reserve Police Battalion 101 and the Final Solution in Poland*. New York: HarperCollins.

Butler, Chris. 2009. "Critical Legal Studies and the Politics of Space." *Social and Legal Studies* 18(3): 313–32.

Cambodian Center for Human Rights. 2010. "The Duch Trial—A Good Example for the Cambodian Courts." Press release. July 26.

Carmichael, Robert. 2015. *When Clouds Fell from the Sky: A Disappearance, A Daughter's Search and Cambodia's First War Criminal*. Bangkok: Asia Horizons Books.

Caswell, Michelle. 2014. *Archiving the Unspeakable: Silence, Memory, and the Photographic Record in Cambodia*. Madison: University of Wisconsin Press.

Chandler, David P. 1991. *The Tragedy of Cambodian History: Politics, War and Revolution since 1945*. New Haven: Yale University Press.

Chandler, David P. 1999. *Voices from S-21: Terror and History in Pol Pot's Secret Prison*. Berkeley: University of California Press.

Chandler, David P. 2007. *A History of Cambodia*. Boulder, CO: Westview.

Chandler, David P., Ben Kiernan, and Chanthou Boua. 1988. *Pol Pot Plans the Future: Confidential Leadership Documents from Democratic Kampuchea, 1976–1977*. Monograph series 33. New Haven: Yale University Southeast Asia Studies.

Choung, Sophearith. 2000. "Long Muy, a Translator of the Chinese Language, Is Accused by the Khmer Rouge of Disloyalty to the Revolution and Executed." *Searching for the Truth* 3 (March): 4–7.

Choung, Sophearith. 2000. "An Interrogator at S-21 Was Arrested." *Searching for the Truth* 12 (December): 6–9.

Choung, Sophearith. 2001. "The Reasons behind Prisoner Kang's Suicide." *Searching for the Truth* 23 (November): 29–31.

Chy, Terith, Pechet Men, Kok-Thay Eng, and Savina Sirik. 2014. *When the Criminal Laughs: The Past Is His Enemy*. Phnom Penh: Documentation Center of Cambodia.

Ciorciari, John D., and Anne Heindel, eds. 2009. *On Trial: The Khmer Rouge Accountability Process*. Phnom Penh: Documentation Center of Cambodia.

Ciorciari, John D., and Anne Heindel. 2014. *Hybrid Justice: The Extraordinary Chambers in the Courts of Cambodia*. Ann Arbor: University of Michigan Press.

Civil Parties before the Extraordinary Chambers in the Courts of Cambodia. N.d. "Civil Party Lawyer Silke Studzinsky." Civilparties.org.http://www.civilparties.org /Civil-Party-Lawyer-Silke-Studzinsky.htm.

Clifford, James, and George E. Marcus. 1986. *Writing Culture: The Poetics and Politics in Ethnography*. Berkeley: University of California Press.

Colm, Sara, and Sorya Sim. 2007. "Anatomy of an Interrogation: The Torture of Comrade Ya at S-21." *Phnom Penh Post*, November 2–15.

CPK. 1970. "Communist Party of Kampuchea Statutes." January 1. ECCC Doc. E3/214. http://www.eccc.gov.kh/en/document/court/statute-cambodiancommunist-party.

CPK. 1976. "Decision of the Central Committee Regarding a Number of Matters." March 30. ECCC Doc. E3/1. http://www.eccc.gov.kh/en/document/court /corrected-1-decision-central-committee-number-problems.

CPK. 1976. "Minutes of the Meeting with Comrade Tal Division 290 and Division 170." September 16. ECCC Doc. E3/88. http://www.eccc.gov.kh/sites/default/files /documents/courtdoc/00381484–00381486_E3_822_EN.TXT.pdf.

CPK. 1976. "Minutes of the Meeting with the Organization's Office, 703 and Sâ-21." September 9. ECCC. ECCC Doc. D64-Annex 04. http://www.eccc.gov.kh/en/document /court/annex-04-minutes-meeting-organization's-office-703-and-s-21.

Criddle, Joan D., and Teeda Butt Mam. 1987. *To Destroy You Is No Loss: The Odyssey of a Cambodian Family*. New York: Anchor.

Cruvellier, Thierry. 2014. *The Master of Confessions: The Making of a Khmer Rouge Torturer*. New York: Ecco.

Cryder, Spencer. 2009. "Investigative Inertia during the ECCC Trial Phase: The 1979 'S-21 Video' and Child Survivor Norng Chanphal." *Searching for the Truth*. July.

Defense. 2009. "Final Defense Written Submissions." November 11. ECCC Doc. E159/8. http://www.eccc.gov.kh/en/documents/court/final-defence-written -submissions.

Defense. 2012. "Ieng Sary's Application to Disqualify Judge Nil Nonn Due to His Purported Admission That He Has Accepted Bribes & Request for a Public Hearing or in the Alternative for Leave to Reply to Any Submissions Presented by Judge Nil Nonn in Response to This Application." January 14. ECCC Doc. E5. www.eccc.gov.kh /en/documents/court/ieng-saryrsquos-application-disqualify-judge-nil-nonn-due -his-purported-admission-li.

Democratic Kampuchea. 1976. "Statement of the Government of Democratic Cambo-dia Condemning the Ferocious and Barbaric Aggression by U.S. Imperialist Planes against Siem Reap Town on 25 February 1976." Phnom Penh Domestic Service, Foreign Broadcast Information Service, Asia and Pacific, February 27, H1.

Derrida, Jacques. 1977. "Signature, Event, Context." *Glyph* 1: 172–97.

Derrida, Jacques. 1990. "The Force of Law: The 'Mystical Foundation of Authority.'" *Cardozo Law Review* 11: 920–1045.

Di Certo, Bridget, and May Titthara. 2012. "Bou Meng Housewarming." Documenta-tion Center of Cambodia, February 13. http://d.dccam.org/.

Di Certo, Bridget, and May Titthara. 2012. "S-21 Survivor Plays Host." *Phnom Penh Post*, February 13. http://www.phnompenhpost.com.

Douglas, Lawrence. 2001. *The Memory of Judgment: Making Law and History in the Trials of the Holocaust*. New Haven: Yale University Press.

Dunlop, Nic. 2005. *The Lost Executioner: A Story of the Khmer Rouge*. London: Bloomsbury.

Dy, Khamboly. 2007. *A History of Democratic Kampuchea (1975–1979)*. Phnom Penh: Documentation Center of Cambodia.

Ea, Meng-Try, and Sorya Sim. 2001. *Victims and Perpetrators? Testimony of Young Khmer Rouge Cadres*. Phnom Penh: Documentation Center of Cambodia.

ECCC. 2003. "Agreement between the United Nations and the Royal Government of Cambodia Concerning the Prosecution under Cambodian Law of Crimes Com-mitted during the Period of Democratic Kampuchea." June 6. www.eccc.gov.kh /en/documents/legal/agreement-between-united-nations-and-royal-government -cambodia-concerning-prosecutio.

ECCC. 2004. "Law on the Establishment of the Extraordinary Chambers in the Courts of Cambodia for the Prosecution of Crimes Committed during the Period of Demo-cratic Kampuchea" (amended version). October 27. www.eccc.gov.kh/sites/default /files/legal-documents/KR_Law_as_amended_27_Oct_2004_Eng.pdf.

ECCC. 2007. "Internal Rules." Version 1. June 12. http://www.eccc.gov.kh/en /documents/legal/internal-rules.

ECCC. 2009. "Transcript of Proceedings—'Duch' Trial Public." Case file no. 001/18–07–2007-ECCC/TC. http://www.eccc.gov.kh/en/case/topic/1.

ECCC. 2009. "Internal Rules." Version 3. March 6. www.eccc.gov.kh/en/documents /legal/internal-rules-rev3.

ECCC. 2009. "Chart presented by Craig Etcheson during the hearing of 28 May 2009." ECCC Doc. E72. www.eccc.gov.kh/en/documents/court/chart-presented-craig -etcheson-during-hearing-28-may-2009 /.

ECCC. 2012. "Compilation of Statements of Apology Made by Kaing Guek Eav alias Duch during the Proceedings." ECCC Doc. F28.1. www.eccc.gov.kh/en/document /court/correctedıcompilation-statements-apology-made-kaing-guek-eav-alias-duch -during-procee.

ECCC. N.d. "Case Information Sheet, Kaing Guek Eav, alias Duch." January 24, 2012.

ECCC. N.d. "The Chan Notebook." ECCC doc. E3/231.

ECCC. N.d. "Colour Copy Excerpt of Confession of Long Muy alias Chuon Annota-tion." September 2, 1977, ERN 32/IV-Annex 74. www.eccc.gov.kh.

ECCC. N.d. "Confession of Long Muy alias Chuon." Handwritten manuscript. Docu-mentation Center of Cambodia Collection, Phnom Penh.

ECCC. N.d. "Confession of Ya, Version Two." September 27, 1976, ECCC Doc. E3/372.

ECCC. N.d. "Confession of Ya, Version Three." September 28, 1976 with September 29, 1976 notation by Duch. ECCC Doc. E3/372.

ECCC. N.d. "Confession of Ya, Version Four." September 29, 1976, ECCC Doc. E3/372.

ECCC. N.d. "Confession of Ya, Version Five." October 1, 1976, ECCC Doc. E3/372.

ECCC. N.d. "Duch Letter to Ya," Ya Confession. September 24, 1976. ECCC Doc. E3/372.

ECCC. N.d. "ECCC Emblem." www.eccc.gov.kh.

ECCC. N.d. "Extraordinary Chambers in the Courts of Cambodia: ECCC at a Glance," ECCC, April 2014.

ECCC. N.d. "Judge Nil Nonn (President)." www.eccc.gov.kh.

ECCC. N.d. "Kaing Guek Eav." www.eccc.gov.kh.

ECCC. N.d. "Ke Kim Huot confession." March 7, 1978. E3/369, ECCC Doc. E3/369.

ECCC. N.d. "Ke Kim Huot confession." N.d. ECCC Doc. E3/369.

ECCC. N.d. "The Last Joint Plan." July 7, 1978. ECCC doc. E5/2.29.

ECCC. N.d. "Letter from Duch to Pon." September 30, 1976. ECCC Doc. E3/372.

ECCC. N.d. "Letter from Duch to Pon." October 1, 1976. ECCC Doc. E3/372.

ECCC. N.d. "Letter from Pon to Duch." September 25, 1976. ECCC Doc. E3/372.

ECCC. N.d. "Letter from Pon to Ya." September 29, 1976. ECCC Doc. E3/372.

ECCC. N.d. "Memo from Pon to Ya." September 29, 1976. ECCC Doc. E3/372.

ECCC. N.d. "Mr. Robert Petit." www.eccc.gov.kh.

ECCC. N.d. "Ms. Chea Leang (National Co-prosecutor)." www.eccc.gov.kh.

ECCC. N.d. "Ms. Martine Jacquin." www.eccc.gov.kh.

ECCC. N.d. "Pon Note to Ya," Confession of Ya. September 23, 1976. ECCC Doc. E3/37.

ECCC. N.d. "The Situation of Interrogating Ke Kim Huot alias Sot, July 22." ECCC Doc. E3/369.

ECCC. N.d. "The Statistics List." DK Interrogation Notebook. ECCC Doc. E3/426.

ECCC, N.d. "The Torture Manual." ECCC Doc. E3/426.

ECCC. N.d. "Tuy Pon Notebook." ECCC Doc. E3/73.

ECCC. N.d. "Ya Response to Pon Letter." September 29, 1976, ECCC Doc. E3/372.

Eltringham, Nigel. 2012. "Spectators to the Spectacle of Law: The Formation of a 'Validating Public' at the International Criminal Tribunal for Rwanda." *Ethnos* 77(3): 425–45.

Etcheson, Craig. 2005. *After the Killing Fields: Lessons from the Cambodian Genocide.* Westport, CT: Praeger.

Etcheson, Craig. 2006. "A 'Fair and Public Trial': The Political Origins of the Extraordinary Chambers." In *The Extraordinary Chambers,* ed. Stephen Humphreys and David Berry, 7–24. New York: Open Society Justice Initiative.

Fawthrop, Tom, and Helen Jarvis. 2004. *Getting Away with Genocide: Cambodia's Long Struggle against the Khmer Rouge.* London: Pluto.

Freud, Sigmund. 2003. *The Uncanny.* New York: Penguin.

Friedman, Megan. 2010. "Quotes: Senior Khmer Rouge Official's Prison Sentence." *Time,* July 26. http://newsfeed.time.com.

Gée, Stephanie. 2008. "François Roux: The Lawyer and Convinced Human Rights Activist." Ka-Set, Information Website about Cambodia, April 16. http://cambodia.ka-set.info.

Gée, Stephanie. 2009. "Interview with Phung Guth Sunthary: When a Civil Party Looks at Duch's Trial." *Ka-set News,* May 15. http://cambodia.ka-set.info.

Geertz, Clifford. 1983. *Local Knowledge: Further Essays in Interpretive Anthropology.* New York: Basic Books.

Gillison, Douglas. 2011. "Justice Denied." *Foreign Policy,* November 23. www.foreignpolicy.com.

Giry, Stéphanie. 2010. "Cambodia's Perfect War Criminal." Blog entry. *New York Review of Books,* October 25. www.nybooks.com.

Giry, Stéphanie. 2012. "Necessary Scapegoats? The Making of the Khmer Rouge Tribunal." Blog entry. *New York Review of Books,* July 23. www.nybooks.com.

Goffman, Erving. 1974. *Frame Analysis: An Essay on the Organization of Experience.* New York: Harper and Row.

Goldstone, James. 2007. "Letter to the Editor on Corruption Charges at Khmer Rouge Court." *Cambodia Daily,* March 7.

Gottesman, Evan. 2003. *Cambodia after the Khmer Rouge: Inside the Politics of Nation Building.* New Haven: Yale University Press.

Hall, John A. 2008. "A Tribunal Worth Paying For." *Wall Street Journal Online,* July 16. http://online.wsj.com.

Headley, Robert K., Jr., Kylin Chhor, Lam Kheng Lim, Lim Hak Kheang, Chen Chun 1977. *Cambodian-English Dictionary,* Vols. 1 and 2. Washington, DC: Catholic University of America Press.

Helman, Gerald B., and Steven R. Ratner. 1992–93. "Saving Failed States." *Foreign Policy* 89 (Winter): 3–20.

Hinton, Alexander Laban. 2005. *Why Did They Kill? Cambodia in the Shadow of Genocide.* Berkeley: University of California Press.

Hinton, Alexander Laban. 2012. "Justice and the Redactic." Paper presented at workshop "The Trial of Adolf Eichmann: Retrospect and Prospect," Centre for Jewish History, University of Toronto, September 10.

Hinton, Alexander Laban. 2014. "The Transitional Justice Imaginary: Uncle San, Aunty Yan and Victim Participation at the Khmer Rouge Tribunal." In *Justice for Victims: Perspectives on Rights, Transition and Reconciliation,* ed. Inge Vanfraechem, Antony Pemberton, and Felix Mukwiza Ndahinda, 247–61. New York: Routledge.

Hinton, Ladson. 2007. "Black Holes, Uncanny Spaces and Radical Shifts in Awareness." *Journal of Analytical Psychology* 52:433–47.

Hughes, Rachael. 2008. "Dutiful Tourism: Encountering the Cambodian Genocide." *Asia Pacific Viewpoint* 49(3): 318–30.

Human Resources Management. 2008. "Results of the Special Review Made Public: ECCC Human Resource Management Passes Scrutiny Test Successfully." March 27. ECCC. www.eccc.gov.kh.

Human Rights Watch. 2002. "Cambodia: Khmer Rouge Tribunal Must Meet International Standards." December 19. hrw.org.

Huy, Vannak. 2003. *The Khmer Rouge Division 703: From Victory to Self-Destruction.* Phnom Penh: Documentation Center of Cambodia.

Kahn, Karim A. A., and Daniella Rudy. 2010. "The Right of Civil Parties to Participate v. the Right of the Accused to a Fair and Expeditious Trial: Challenges at the ECCC?" Oxford Transitional Justice Research working paper. June 10. http://otjr .crim.ox.ac.uk.

Kaing Guek Eav. 2009. "The Continuous Killing Carried Out by the Communist Party of Kampuchea (CPK)." November 23. ECCC Doc. E159/10. www.eccc.gov.kh.

Kamm, Henry. 1979. "Aide Says Pol Pot Regime Is Ready to Join Old Foes against Vietnam." *New York Times,* June 1, A1.

Kauth, Glen. 2009. "Robert Petit: A Divergent Path." *Canadian Lawyer,* July. http:// www.canadianlawyermag.com.

Keo, Dacil Q., and Nean Yin. 2011. "Fact Sheet: Pol Pot and His Prisoners at Secret Prison S-21." Phnom Penh: Documentation Center of Cambodia.

Khmer Rouge Victims in Cambodia. 2011. "Phnom Penh: Khmer Rouge Victims in Cambodia." Press release. November 15. http://ki-media.blogspot.com.

Kiernan, Ben. 2008. *The Pol Pot Regime: Race, Power, and Genocide in Cambodia under the Khmer Rouge, 1975–79.* New Haven: Yale University Press.

Kong, Sothanarith. 2010. "Torture Center Marks First Year as 'Memory of the World.'" *Voice of America Khmer,* August 9. http://www.voacambodia.com.

Koskenniemi, Martti. 2002. "Between Impunity and Show Trials." *Max Planck Yearbook of United Nations Law* 6: 1–35.

Lacan, Jacques. 2007. *Écrits.* New York: Norton.

Lacquer, Thomas. 1989. "Bodies, Details and the Humanitarian Narrative." In *The New Cultural History,* ed. Lynn Hunt, 176–204. Berkeley: University of California Press.

Ledgerwood, Judy. 1997. "The Cambodian Tuol Sleng Museum of Genocidal Crimes: National Narrative." *Museum Anthropology* 21(1): 82–98.

Lefebvre, Henri. 1991. *The Production of Space.* Oxford: Blackwell.

Levi, Primo. 1989. *The Drowned and the Saved.* New York: Vintage.

Levi, Primo. 1996. *Survival in Auschwitz.* New York, Touchstone Books.

Locard, Henri. 2004. *Pol Pot's Little Red Book: The Sayings of Angkar.* Chiang Mai, Thailand: Silkworm.

Ly, Sophal. 2007. "Long Muy, Known as Chuon: Head Khmer-Chinese Translator at K-16." *Searching for the Truth* (Special English Edition, Fourth Quarter), 5–7.

Macau Daily Times Staff. 2008. "Chief of Personnel Removed from KRouge Court." *Macau Daily Times,* August 13. http://www.macaudailytimesnews.com/.

Marcus, George E., and Michael M. J. Fischer. 1999. *Anthropology as Cultural Critique: An Experimental Moment in the Human Sciences.* Chicago: University of Chicago Press.

Military Court. 2002. "Record of Interrogation." Phnom Penh: Royal Government of Cambodia, June 5.

Munthit, Ker. 2008. "Cambodian Genocide Tribunal Faces Allegations." Associated Press, August 6. http://www.washingtonpost.com.

Mutua, Makau. 2001. "Savages, Victims, and Saviors: The Metaphor of Human Rights." *Harvard International Law Journal* 42(1): 201–45.

Mydans, Seth. 2010. "Prison Term for Khmer Rouge Jailer Leaves Many Dissatisfied." *New York Times,* July 27, 2010, 4.

Naren, Kuch, and Alice Foster. 2012. "Ten Duch Victims Celebrate Civil Party Status." *Cambodian Daily,* February 4–5.

OCIJ. 2007. "Separation Order." September 19. ECCC Doc. E18.

OCIJ. 2008. "Closing Order Indicting Kaing Guek Eav alias Duch (Public Redacted Version)." Case 001. August 8. ECCC Doc. D99/3/3.

OCIJ. 2008. "Written Record of Interview of Charged Person." March 27. ECCC Doc. E3/380. www.eccc.gov.kh.

OCIJ. 2008. "Written Record of Interview of Charged Person." April 1. ECCC Doc. E3/5. www.eccc.gov.kh.

OCIJ. 2008. "Written Record of Interview of Charged Person." April 2. ECCC Doc. E3/117. www.eccc.gov.kh.

OCIJ. 2008. "Written Record of Interview of Charged Person." April 29. ECCC Doc. E3/3. www.eccc.gov.kh.

OCIJ. 2010. "Closing Order." Case 002. September 15. ECCC Doc. D427. www.eccc.gov.kh.

OCIJ. 2011. "Statement by the International Co-investigating Judge." October 10. ECCC. www.eccc.gov.kh.

OCIJ. 2011. "Statement from the Co-investigating Judges." April 29. ECCC. www.eccc.gov.kh.

OCIJ. 2011. "Statement from the Co-investigating Judges." May 18. ECCC. www.eccc.gov.kh.

OCIJ. 2011. "Statement of the National Co-investigating Judge." December 6. ECCC. www.eccc.gov.kh.

OCIJ. 2012. "Note of the International Reserve Co-investigating Judge to the Parties on the Egregious Dysfunctions within the ECCC Impeding the Proper Conduct of Investigations in Cases 003 and 004." March 21. ECCC Doc. D114. www.eccc.gov.kh.

OCIJ. N.d. "The Co-investigating Judges." ECCC. www.eccc.gov.kh.

OCP. 2007. "Statement of the Co-prosecutors." July 18. ECCC.

OCP. 2008. "Public Information by the Co-prosecutors Pursuant to Rule 54 Concerning the Rule 66 Final Submission Regarding Kaing Guek Eave alias 'Duch,'" July 18. ECCC. www.eccc.gov.kh.

OCP. 2009. "Co-prosecutors' Final Trial Submission with Annexes 1–5." November 11. ECCC Doc. E159/9.

OCP. 2009. "Statement of the Co-prosecutors." January 5. ECCC. www.eccc.gov.kh.

OCP. 2011. "Statement by the National Co-prosecutor regarding Case File 003." May 10. ECCC. www.eccc.gov.kh.

OCP. 2011. "Statement from the International Co-prosecutor regarding Case File 003." May 9. ECCC. www.eccc.gov.kh.

OCP. N.d. "Office of the Co-prosecutors." ECCC. www.eccc.gov.kh.

OCP. N.d. "Revised S-21 Prisoner List." ECCC Doc. E68.1.

Open Society Justice Initiative Staff. 2007. "Corruption Allegations at Khmer Rouge Court Must Be Investigated Thoroughly." February 14. http://www.justiceinitiative.org.

Open Society Justice Initiative. 2011. "Recent Developments at the Extraordinary Chambers in the Courts of Cambodia." New York: Open Society Justice Initiative, June.

Open Society Justice Initiative. 2011. "Recent Developments at the Extraordinary Chambers in the Courts of Cambodia." New York: Open Society Justice Initiative, November.

Owen, Taylor, and Ben Kiernan. 2006. "Bombs over Cambodia: New Information Reveals That Cambodia Was Bombarded Far More Heavily Than Previously Thought." *Walrus*, October. http://www.walrusmagazine.com.

Peschoux, Christophe, and Haing Kheng Heng. 2016. *Itinerary of an Ordinary Torturer: Interview with Duch, Former Khmer Rouge Commander of S-21.* Chiang Mai, Thailand: Silkworm.

Pheaktra, Neth, and Cat Barton. 2009. "Memories of Evil Stir as Duch Trial Opens." *Phnom Penh Post*, February 18.

Phnom Penh Domestic Service. 1975. "The Remarkable Morals of our Brother Combatants and Cadres of a Unit in Phnom Penh." Foreign Broadcast Information Service, Asia and Pacific, June 8.

Phnom Penh Domestic Service. 1975. "The Society of New Cambodia Is Just and Clean and Unprecedented in Our History." Foreign Broadcast Information Service, Asia and Pacific, May 10.

Phnom Penh Domestic Service. 1975. "We Build and Defend the Country by Always Upholding the Traditional Characteristics of the Cambodian Revolution." Foreign Broadcast Information Service, Asia and Pacific, June 25.

Phnom Penh Domestic Service. 1976. "The Constitution of Democratic Kampuchea." Foreign Broadcast Information Service, Asia and Pacific, January 5.

Pike, Amanda. 2002. "Battambang: The Judge" (reporter's diary, entry 4). "Cambodia—Pol Pot's Shadow, October, 2002" (documentary). PBS *FrontlineWorld*. www.pbs.org/frontlineworld/stories/cambodia/diary04.html.

Pol Pot. 1977. "Long Live the Nineteenth Anniversary of the Communist Party of Kampuchea: Speech by Pol Pot, Secretary of the Central Committee of the Kampuchean Communist Party. September 29, 1977." Phnom Penh: Democratic Kampuchea Ministry of Foreign Affairs.

Ponchaud, François. 1992. "Social Change in the Vortex of Revolution." In *Cambodia 1975–1978: Rendezvous with Death*, ed. Karl D. Jackson, 151–77. Princeton: Princeton University Press.

Pong-Rasy, Pheng. 2008. "Burial." Phnom Penh: Documentation Center of Cambodia.

Pong-Rasy, Pheng. 2008. "DK Prison." Phnom Penh: Documentation Center of Cambodia.

PTC. 2007. "Appeal Hearing." November 20. ECCC.

PTC. 2007. "Appeal Hearing." November 21. ECCC.

PTC. 2008. "Public Decision on the Co-lawyers' Urgent Application for Disqualification of Judge Ney Thol Pending the Appeal against the Provisional Detention Order in the Case of Nuon Chea." February 4. ECCC Doc. C11/29. www.eccc.gov.kh.

PTC. 2009. "Public Redacted Version—Consideration of the PTC regarding the Disagreement between the Co-prosecutors pursuant to Internal Rule 71." August 18. ECCC Doc. www.eccc.gov.kh.

Public Affairs. 2007. "Photo Archive. November 20, 2007." ECCC. www.eccc.gov.kh.

Public Affairs. 2008. "Media Alert." November 6. ECCC. www.eccc.gov.kh.

Public Affairs. 2012. "Kaing Guek Eav Sentenced to Life Imprisonment." *Court Report*, February 10.

Radio Free Asia Staff. 2011. "Khmer Rouge Tribunal Staff Quit." *Radio Free Asia*, June 12.

Ramjii, Jaya Ramji, and Beth Van Schaack, eds. 2005. *Bringing the Khmer Rouge to Justice: Prosecuting Mass Violence before the Cambodian Courts*. Lewiston, NY: Edward Mellen.

Rasy Pheng Pong. 2003. "The Security System of Special Zone's Office M-13." *Searching for the Truth* (Special English Edition, 2nd Quarter), 3–9.

Reang, Putsata. 2007. "Man or Monster?" *Guardian*, December 16.

RFI Staff. 2009. "Apology of Prison Chief Met with Skepticism," *Radio France International*, April 1. http://www.rfi.fr/actuen/articles/112/article_3357.asp.

Rithy Panh. 2012. *The Elimination: A Survivor of the Khmer Rouge Confronts His Past and the Commandant of the Killing Fields*. New York: Other Press.

Rithy Panh. 2013. "Duch: Master of the Forges of Hell." New York: First Run Features.

Rogers, Richard J. 2010. "Request by Mr. Kaing to Withdraw Co-lawyer Francois Roux." Defense Support Section, ECCC, July 5.

Said, Edward. 1979. *Orientalism*. New York: Vintage.

Saldaña, Johnny, ed. 2005. *Ethnodrama: An Anthology of Reality Theater*. Walnut Creek, CA: Rowman and Littlefield.

Saldaña, Johnny. 2011. *Ethnotheatre: Research from Page to Stage*. Walnut Creek, CA: Left Coast Press.

Saliba, Michael, and Tyler Nims. 2009. "Duch Sentenced to 35 Years in Prison; Will Serve only 19." *Cambodia Tribunal Monitor*, July 26.

SCC. 2012. "Transcript of Appeal Judgement—Kaing Guek Eav 'Duch' Public." Case File No. 001/18–07–2007-ECCC/TC/SC." February 3.

SCC. 2012. "Appeal Judgment," February 3. ECCC Doc. F28. www.eccc.gov.kh/en/document/court/case-001-appeal-judgement.

Seiff, Abby, and Kuch Naren. 2012. "Duch Sentenced to Life in Prison by Khmer Rouge Tribunal." *Cambodia Daily*, February 4–5.

Seng, Theary. 2012. "Duch Final Pronouncement." KI Media, February 3. ki-media .blogspot.com.

Shears, Richard. 2013. "Monster of the Killing Fields: The Torturer Who Murdered 16,000 for Pol Pot Faces Justice at Last." *Mail Online*, February 17. http://www.dailymail.co.uk.

Short, Philip. 2005. *Pol Pot: Anatomy of a Nightmare*. New York: Holt.

Sirik, Savina. 2012. "Duch Final Judgement: Justice and Humanity." Phnom Penh: Documentation Center of Cambodia, February 2–3.

Sironi-Guilbaud, Françoise, and Sunbaunat Ka. 2008. *Psychological Assessment Report*. ECCC.

Sokha, Cheang, and James O'Toole. 2010. "Hun Sen to Ban Ki-moon: Case 002 Last Trial at ECCC." *Phnom Penh Post*, October 27. www.phnompenhpost.com/national /hun-sen-ban-ki-moon-case-002-last-trial-eccc.

Sophal Ly. 2007. "Long Muy, Known as Chun: Head Khmer-Chinese Translator at K-16." *Searching for the Truth.*

Special Tribunal for Lebanon. N.d. "Head of Defense Office—François Roux." www.stl -tsl.org/.

SPK Radio. 1978. "Front Issues Declaration." Foreign Broadcast Information Service, Asia and Pacific, December 4, H3, H7.

TC. 2010. "Trial Chamber Judgement, Announced on 26 July 2010, Case 001, Kaing Guek Eav alias Duch." July 26. ECCC Doc. E188.

TC. 2010. "Judgement." Transcript of Trial Proceedings—Kaing Guek Eav "Duch" Public. July 26. ECCC.

Thayer, Nate, and Nic Dunlop. 1999. "Duch Confesses." *Far Eastern Economic Review,* May 16, 18–20.

Thomas, Sarah, and Terith Chy. 2009. "Including the Survivors in the Tribunal Process." In *On Trial: The Khmer Rouge Accountability Process,* ed. John D. Ciociari and Anne Heindel, 214–93. Phnom Penh: Documentation Center of Cambodia.

Titthara, May. 2012. "A Tuol Sleng Interrogator Speaks Out." *Phnom Penh Post,* May 10. www.phnompenhpost.com.

Turner, Victor. 1975. *Dramas, Fields, and Metaphors.* Ithaca, NY: Cornell University Press.

Turner, Victor, and Edith Turner. 1982. "Performing Ethnography." *Drama Review* 26(2): 33–50.

United Nations. 1997. "Report of the Special Representative of the Secretary-General for Human Rights in Cambodia, Mr. Thomas Hammarberg, Submitted in Accordance with Commission Resolution 1996/54." UN Economic and Security Council. E/CN.4/1997/85. http://www.unhchr.ch.

United Nations. 1999. "Report of the Group of Experts for Cambodia Established Pursuant to General Assembly Resolution 52/135." U.N. General Assembly Security Council, 53rd session. UN Doc. A/53/850. February 8. www.unakrt-online.org.

United Nations Commission on Human Rights. 1997. "Situation of Human Rights in Cambodia." UN Commission on Human Rights Resolution 1997/49. April 11. http://www.unhchr.ch/Huridocda/Huridoca.nsf/TestFrame.

United Nations Development Programme (UNDP). 2007. "Audit of Human Resources Management at the Extraordinary Chambers in the Courts of Cambodia (ECCC)." UNDP report no. RCM0172. June 4. http://www.unakrt-online.org.

Veasna, Mean. 2008. "UNDP: Government Won't Probe Tribunal Allegations." *Voice of America,* February 21. http://www.voanews.com.

Veneciano, Jorge Daniel, and Alexander Hinton, eds. 2007. *Night of the Khmer Rouge: Genocide and Justice in Cambodia.* Newark, NJ: Paul Robeson Gallery.

Victims Unit. 2008. "Historical Achievement in International Criminal Law: Victims of Khmer Rouge Crimes Fully Involved in the Proceedings of the ECCC." February 4. ECCC. www.eccc.gov.kh/sites/default/files/media/Victim_Unit_Press_Release.pdf.

Index

afacement, 295–96

Améry, Jean, 176–77, 189

Amnesty International, 258, 293

Annan, Kofi, 48

Apocalypse Now (film), 26

Arendt, Hannah, 31, 35, 295

articulation, 9–10, 24, 29–37, 92, 98, 116, 143, 158–59, 182, 191, 196, 198, 201, 209, 214, 216, 232–33, 236, 240–42, 250, 256, 258, 261–72, 275, 284, 290–96; Man or Monster, 34, 68, 76–77, 82–83, 86, 284, 288–90; reflexive, 35

atrocities: as human rights violations, 26–32, 33, 262; PRK frame, 23–26, 28, 33, 250, 266; in S-21, 13–14, 55, 61, 238, 288–89. *See also* Choeung Ek execution center; torture

Avocats Sans Frontières, 63, 65

banality of everyday thought, 31, 34–36, 266, 270, 288, 290, 295–96

banality of evil, 31, 35

Ban Ki-moon, 259

Bates, Alan, 92, 127–28

Bizot, François, 68, 78–83, 84, 86, 288, 291

Blunk, Siegfried, 260

Bou Meng, 12, 63, 64, 176–77, *178*, 180, 181, 184–86, *185*, 189, 202, 207, 233, 242, 245–47, 257, 273–86

Brother Number One. *See* Pol Pot

Buddhism, 268, 269, 279–81

calibration, 33, 35, 92, 159, 161, 182, 188, 198, 199, 207, 236, 266, 268–70, 296

Cambodian Code of Criminal Procedure, 62

Cambodian Human Rights Action Committee, 63

Cambodian Penal Code (1956), 200, 204, 217, 238–39

Cannone, Philippe, 191–92, 194, 195, 196, 224

Cartwright, Silvia, 2, 48, 125, 152, 187, 192, 228, 238

CaseMap case analysis program, 200, 209–10

Cayley, Andrew, 260

CD-Cam. *See* Documentation Center of Cambodia

Central Zone, 122

Chan (Mam Nai), 83, 100, 131, 137, *138*, 159, 208

Chan Chakrei, 108, 117–18, 124, 127, 128

Chandler, David, 137, 221, 289

Chan Khan, 85, 88

Chan Kim Srun, 20, 21, 247–48, 251, 253–54, 283

Chan Voeun, 86–88

Chhang, Youk, 32, 278

Chea Leang, 2, 52–54, 65, 198, 201–4, 225, 260

Cheng An, 91–92, 121, 123

Chhay Kim Hor, 6, 8, 71–72, 73, 74, 84, 102, 121, 123, 215, 294

Chhin Navy, 292

Chhit Iv, 140

Chhouk. *See* Suas Neou (Chhouk)

Chhun Phal, 193

Chiang Kai-shek, 160

Choeung Ek execution center, 55, 166–67, 202, 220, 245, 247, 271, 273, 274, 275, 277

Chum Mey, 52, 63, 64, 139–40, 152, 176–77, 178, 181–84, 197, 201, 207, 233, 242, 245–47, 257, 275–86
Chuon. *See* Long Muy (Chuon)
Chy, Terith, 289
Cold War, 25
Communist Party of Kampuchea (CPK), 6, 57; Central Committee, 104, 153; extremist ideology, 205, 207, 225, 237–38; obeying and protection within, 123; Office 870, 134; origins of, 70; policies, 72, 111–12, 143, 153, 177, 201, 203, 208, 238; purges, 114, 126, 127, 201, 213–16; Standing Committee of the Central Committee, 16, 55, 117–18, 122, 124, 125; statutes, 70, 112–13, 115, 117, 119
confessions. *See under* torture; specific individuals
Conrad, Joseph, 263
conviction, afacing and effacing, 288–96
corruption, 18, 45–46, 94, 258, 260–62, 263, 276, 293
Court Report (periodical), 257–58
CPK. *See* Communist Party of Kampuchea
Cruvellier, Thierry, 289

dark tourism, 277
DC-Cam. *See* Documentation Center of Cambodia
"Decision of the Central Committee Regarding a Number of Matters." *See* March 30, 1976 Decision
dehiscence, 24, 92, 290–91
Democratic Kampuchea (DK): class structure, 117, 122–23; collapse of, 121; framing, 11; ideology, 95–96; nepotism in, 123; purges, 124–25; security policy, 104; social engineering by, 53; symbols, 114
Derrida, Jacques, 267
Deum Sareaun, 42, 139, 149–50, 152, 205, 294
Division 170, 127, 144
Division 290, 127
Division 310, 125
Division 450, 125
Division 502, 125
Division 703, 91, 94, 95–96, 99–100, 101, 108, 110–11, 123, 133, 137, 140
Division 920, 164

DK. *See* Democratic Kampuchea
Documentation Center of Cambodia (DC-Cam), 32, 63, 163, 247
Doeum Saroeun, 139
Duch (Kaing Guek Eav), 17, 47, 132; abecedarian, 41–43; apology, 44–45, 57, 67, 168, 195, 216, 218, 240, 258, 279; arrest of, 200; articulation of conspiracies, 158–67; backdrop of trial, 45–52; closing arguments, civil parties, 176–96, 239–40; closing arguments, defense, 213–28; closing arguments, prosecution, 197–212; defense of S-21, 188; on executions, 164–67; fact sheet, 1–2; final decision, 254–73; foreground, 3–37; framing, 9–11; interrogation training, 55, 74, 113, 131, 137, 141, 145–52, 274; judgment, Trial Chamber, 223, 229–42; justice and humanity, 52–61, 190, 203, 289–91; lead-up to S-21, 91–95; at M-13 camp, 69–89, 91; marriage, 93; as mathematician, 67, 214, 216, 223–28; as monster, 30, 33–34, 81–89, 195, 262–63, 289–90; motives, 205–6; on name change, 5–6; as ordinary man, 288–96; paradoxes of, 8, 68, 80, 195–96; pedagogy, 9; personal qualities, 6–7, 55, 221–22, 284–85; photograph of, 23, 28, 131, 252–53, 279–80; reparations claims, 62–63, 65, 190, 195, 240, 242, 246, 257; at S-21 camp, 95–102; S-21 functioning, 130–41; S-21 policy and implementation, 103–29; as scapegoat, 58–59, 217–18, 219, 221, 226–27, 258–59, 292; seeking forgiveness, 44, 57–58, 60–61, 64, 65, 67, 188, 195, 197, 216, 272; self-portrayal, 8; survivor stories, 177–96; as teacher, 6, 69–72, 75, 91, 111, 213; testimony on purge incidents, 117–21; timeline, 301–2; on torture training, 142–47, 225; trial as ethnodrama, 265–66; voice in trial, 61–67, 191
Dunlop, Nic, 7, 15

East Zone, 106, 108, 118, 124, 125, 127, 133, 143, 158, 160, 164
ECCC. *See* Extraordinary Chambers in the Courts of Cambodia
effacing conviction, 294–96
Eichmann, Adolf, 14, 30–31

erasure, 33, 37, 168, 266, 270, 294. *See also* redaction

Etcheson, Craig, 121–22, 124–26, 128–29, 210

ethnodrama (ethnotheater), 35–36, 265–66, 290

ethnography, 35–37; ethnographic authority, 36, 265; experimental writing, 36, 265; literary techniques/poetic form), 36, 41–43, 168, 171–75, 266

evil, 3, 4, 10, 26, 27, 29–31, 33, 35, 37, 67, 176, 205, 211, 219, 221, 222, 252, 262–63, 269, 279, 284, 289–90

Extraordinary Chambers in the Courts of Cambodia (ECCC), 4, 29, 46, 47, 49–50, 191, 198–99, 230, 261, 263; Internal Rules, 62, 63, 65, 190, 6232. *See also* Pre-Trial Chamber; Supreme Court Chamber; Trial Chamber

First Party Congress, 70

frames/framing, 9–35, 37, 264–66, 272, 288; Buddhist, 275, 281, 284; CPK (DK Party line), 143, 159, 182, 236, 250, 252–53, 268, 294, 296; human rights, 26–33, 250, 258, 263; thick, 11, 34, 35, 143, 182, 250, 252, 266–67, 294–96; juridical (legal), 55, 198–200, 207, 217, 226, 232, 236–37, 254, 262, 266, 268; PRK atrocity, 23–26, 28, 33, 250, 266; psychological, 236, 268, 281; transitional justice, 191, 263

Free Khmer network, 143–44

Freud, Sigmund, 32

Front Union of Salvage National Kampuchea, 14

Gang of Four, 114

Gao Laing, 113

Geneva Conventions (1949), 51, 199, 200, 238

genocide, 25, 34; as naturalized, 30

geopolitics, 28

global citizenship, 26

Hang Pin. *See* Duch

Hazan, Pierre, 27

Heng Nath. *See* Vann Nath

Heng Samrin, 24

Herodotus, 268

Him Huy, 22–23, 23, 273, 274, 284, 285–86

Ho Chi Minh, 124, 140–41

Hoeung Song Huor. *See* Pon (Hoeung Song Huor)

Hong. *See* Nget You (Hong)

Hong Kimsuon, 63, 136

Hong Savath, 242, 257

Hor (Khoem Vat), 96, 99, 134, 138, 183

Hor Namhong, 259

human rights frame, 26–32, 250, 258, 263

Human Rights Watch, 293

Hu Nim, 117

Hun Sen, 23–24, 48, 53, 233, 259, 261, 293

Iem Chan, 178

Ieng Sary, 15, 16, 24, 25, 28, 70, 73, 259, 264, 285

Ieng Si Pheng. *See* Yann Pheng (Ieng Si Pheng)

Ieng Thirith, 18, 112, 259, 285

In Lorn. *See* Nat (In Lorn)

International Civil Party, 61

interrogation: collaboration with prisoners, 82–83, 119, 159; interrogators, 8, 132, 137–41, 138, 166, 247; at M-13, 74, 79, 83; process, 137–41; at S-21, 83–84, 96, 98–102, 104, 108, 110, 137, 153–57, 160–61, 205, 214–15; survivor stories, 177–96; techniques, 80, 182, 214; training, 55, 74, 113, 131, 137, 141, 145–52, 274. *See also* torture

Jacquin, Martine, 65–66, 190, 191, 224

Johnson, Lyndon B., 140–41

Kaing Guek Eav. *See* Duch (Kaing Guek Eav)

Kao Bun Heang, 84

Kar Savuth, 2, 58–59, 60, 128–29, 187–88, 216–18, 226, 227–28, 232–33, 253

Kasper-Ansermet, Laurent, 260–61

Ke Kim Huot (Sot), 8, 42, 71, 150–52, 158, 164, 205, 294

Keo Meas, 153, 154, 158–59

Ke Pauk, 28

Khan, Karim, 63, 89, 190, 193–94, 223–24

Khieu. *See* Son Sen (Khieu)

Khieu Samphan, 24, 28, 48, 70, 259

Khmer Rouge, 7, 22, 24–25, 28–29, 134, 242;
    capture of Phnom Penh, 75; documents,
    112; end of, 48; ideology, 95, 112, 114, 129,
    269; policy on married couples, 133; pris-
    ons, 59; purges, 54, 124, 258, 269; rise of,
    53, 69–70, 263; Rule (1975–1979), 2, 3–4;
    secrecy principle, 75–76; social engineer-
    ing program, 15–18, 53; "Statistics List,"
    142; tempering by, 19; on U.S. imperial-
    ism, 73, 95
Khmer sayings, 116–17, 166, 242, 274
Khmer Serei network, 158
Khoem Vat. See Hor (Khoem Vat)
Khoun. See Koy Thuon (Khoun)
Kiev. See Duch (Kaing Guek Eav)
Kim-suon Hong, 63
Kok Min Tang (KMT), 159–60, 162, 163
Kong Pisey, 195
Kong Sophal, 121
Kong Srim, 254–57
Koy Thuon (Khoun), 107, 109, 114, 119–21, 120,
    122, 124–25, 134, 140, 158–59, 164, 205, 215
Kuomintang. See Kok Min Tang

Labor Party of Kampuchea, 163
Lacan, Jacques, 267
"Last Joint Plan, The," 158–59
Lavergne, J-M, 2, 48, 86, 152, 167
Lemonde, Marcel, 2, 51, 260
Levi, Primo, 190
Levinas, Emmanuel, 268
Li Chriel, 162
Li Phel (Phan), 109, 117–18
Long Muy (Chuon), 90, 103–7, 117, 122, 135,
    160–64, 270–72, 271
Long Tai, 270–72
Lon Nol, 15, 56, 74, 75, 94, 96, 97, 99, 101, 104,
    114, 140, 214–15
Ly Phen, 108
Ly Vay, 108

M-13 prison camp, 4–5, 68, 69–89
Mam Nai. See Chan (Mam Nai)
Mam Non, 192–93
Mao Zedong, 114
March 30, 1976 Decision, 104, 107–8, 111, 112,
    117, 122, 128–29, 136, 164, 215, 220, 226, 228
Ma Yeoun, 273

memory sickness, 19
Meng, 180
Milgram shock experiments, 221, 289
Ministry of Commerce, 120, 124, 125
Ministry of Energy, 125
Ministry of Industry, 91, 93
Ministry of Public Works, 125
Ministry of Railways, 125
Ministry of Social Affairs, 165
Mok, 214–15
Mom Yauv, 187–88
Mony Thou, 2
moral economies, 31, 36, 270, 272, 284
Moussaoui, Zacarias, 60
Mydans, Seth, 278

Nai Non, 149
Nam Mon, 193, 240, 257
Nat (In Lorn), 73, 95, 97, 98, 99, 100–102,
    107, 109, 118, 121, 123–24, 128, 137, 140, 165,
    166–67, 215
New York Times (newspaper), 242, 278
Ney Saran. See Ya (Ney Saran)
Nget Sambon, 83–84
Nget You (Hong), 121, 159
Nhet Phally, 292
Nil, Judge. See Nonn Nil
Noeun, 138
Nonn Nil, 2, 5, 45–48, 69, 91, 96, 128, 151–52,
    180, 183–84, 187, 193, 198, 223, 227, 229–30,
    232–33, 237–41
Norng Chanphal, 63, 186–88, 211,
    285–86
Norodom Ranariddh, 48
Northeast Zone, 150, 153
Northern Zone, 107, 114, 117–18, 120–21, 122,
    124–25
Northwest Zone, 121, 125
Nun Huy, 132, 133–34, 135, 139
Nuon Chea, 15, 16, 29, 48, 55, 104, 121, 123,
    134, 165, 259, 264, 285
Nuremberg Trials, 176, 219, 291

OCIJ. See Office of the Co-Investigating Judges
OCP. See Office of the Co-Prosecutors
Oeun. See Vong Oeun
Office of the Co-Investigating Judges (OCIJ),
    50–51, 199–200, 260

Office of the Co-Prosecutors (OCP), 50, 121, 199, 203, 209, 211, 219, 238, 256
Open Society Justice Initiative, 46
otherness, 263, 268–70
Ottara You, 48

Pang, 134–35
Panh, Rithy, 289, 291, 293–94, 295
Paris Bar Association, 63
patronage, Cambodian, 122–23
Peng, 99, 180
People's Republic of Kampuchea (PRK), 7, 11, 28; atrocities frame, 23–26, 28, 33, 250, 266; formation of, 23–24
People's Revolutionary Tribunal, 25
Peschoux, Christophe, 7–8
Petit, Robert, 2, 52, 54–56, 66, 259, 260
Phal, 99
Phan. *See* Li Phel (Phan)
Phan Than Chan, *178*
Phnom Penh, 11, 75, 93, 108
Pisey, Kong. *See* Kong Pisey
Pol Pot, 15, *16*, 58, 70–71, 215–16, 218; on class structure, 114–15; clique, 13–14, 24, 25–26, 28; death, 29, 48; on DK violence, 157; genocide conviction, 25; on imperialism, 73; influence on Duch, 141; as intellectual, 8; K offices and, 122; lectures, 112–13; paranoia, 117; poison plot, 165; portraits, 179, 186; resignation, 153; on S-21, 7, 96, 104–6, 165–66, 215
Pon (Hoeung Song Huor), 100, 131, 137, *138*, 153–57, 205, 214
Prak Khan, 149, 171–75
Pre-Trial Chamber (PTC), 49, 62, 65, 66, 259–60
Prey Sar re-education camp, 55, 83, 133–34
PRK. *See* People's Republic of Kampuchea
Prok Khoeun, *132, 133*
PTC. *See* Pre-Trial Chamber

Real, notion of, 267
redactic, 32–37, 98, 243, 265–69, 273, 288, 290, 291, 295, 306n50, 339
redaction, 1–2, 32–37, 92, 97–98, 107, 116–17, 143, 156, 159, 191, 231, 250, 257, 263–73, 290–91, 294–95

Roux, François, 2, 27, 56, 58, 59–61, 64–65, 67, 75–76, 121, 129, 193, 205–6, 218–23, 224, 226–27, 232, 253, 289–90
Ruy Neakong, *178*

S-21 security prison, 4, 54, *98, 138, 178–79*; atrocities in, 13–14, 55, 61, 238, 288–89; death totals, 3; dream of, 243–44; establishment of, 95–102; executions, 164–67; functioning of, 130–41; interrogation at, 83–84, 96, 98–102, 104, 108, 110, 137, 153–57, 160–61, 205, 214–15; interrogation training, 55, 74, 113, 131, 137, 141, 145–52, 274; interrogators, 8, 132, 137–41, *138*, 166, 247; naming of, 96; policy and implementation, 103–29; purges, 117–26; torture in, 14, 20–21, 55, 83–89, 101, 118, 144–45, 153–57, 160–61, 181, 183–86, 192, 198, 201–8; torture training, 142–47, 180; as uncanny, 32–33; women and children, treatment of, 136, 167, 186–88, 248. *See also* Tuol Sleng Genocide Museum (Phnom Penh)
S-24. *See* Prey Sar re-education camp
Sao Phim, 108, 118, 124, 125, 143, 156, 158
Savina Sirik, 251–52
Savuth, Kar. *See* Kar Savuth
SCC. *See* Supreme Court Chamber
Sek Sath, 248
Sek Say, 247, 251–52
Seng, 182, 183, 184
Seng Bunkheang, 187
Shawcross, Hartley, 176
Siet Chhe (Tum), 105, 118, 128, 140, 158–59, 160
Sihanouk, Prince, 15, 70, 74, 96
Skilbeck, Rupert, 253
Smith, William (Bill), 111, 131, 136, 187, 204–8, 210–12, 225–26, 227
social engineering program, 18, 53
Sok, 12, 77–78, 84, 123
Sok An, 53
Sokhan Ya, 2, 48
Son Sen (Khieu), 6, 8, 15, *16*, 55, 71, 73, 74, 91, 95–97, 102, 104, 106, 110, 112, 122–23, 124, 126, 128, 131, 160, 165
So Phim, 108
Sot. *See* Ke Kim Huot (Sot)
Sou Met, 129

Sous Sopha, 152
Special Zone, 91–92, 95, 121
"Statistics List of Security Office S-21, The,"
    142, 145, 161
Statutes of the Youth League, 144
Studzinsky, Silke, 61–62, 176, 177, 188–89,
    192–93, 224, 245–46
Suas Neou (Chhouk), 108, 118, 124, 127,
    143, 154
Supreme Court Chamber (SCC), 49, 244,
    254–73
Sur, Pierre-Olivier, 192, 194–95, 196–97

Tal, 127, 128
Ta Mok, 29, 48, 91, 112, 115, 214–15
TC. See Trial Chamber
Tet, 183, 184
Thayer, Nate, 7
Theary Seng, 242, 258–59, 291
Time (magazine), 242
torture: abecedarian on, 41–43; as common-
    place, 74, 83; confessions from, 9, 42, 105,
    107, 140, 146, 149, 161, 271; as dehuman-
    izing, 53, 54, 61, 105–6, 190, 216, 220, 226,
    269, 289; faith in humanity and, 176–77;
    manual of, 142, 145; as obligation, 77–78;
    practices, 20, 85–86, 139–41, 145, 183, 185,
    216–17; in S-21, 14, 20–21, 55, 83–89, 101,
    118, 144–45, 153–57, 160–61, 181, 183–86,
    192, 198, 201–8; survivor stories, 177–96;
    training, 55, 142–47, 180, 225. See also
    atrocities; interrogation
Toy, 140, 141, 151
traces, 20, 34–35, 190, 191, 236, 250–52, 254,
    264, 265, 268
transitional justice, 27, 49, 188, 267; tran-
    sitional justice frame, 191; transitional
    justice imaginary, 27, 262, 263, 275, 279,
    281, 285

Trial Chamber (TC), 5, 47, 49, 51, 61, 65, 68, 69,
    109, 188–89, 192–93, 202, 204, 208–12, 217,
    222–23, 225, 227, 229–42, 256–57, 259, 291–92
Tum. See Siet Chhe (Tum)
Tuol Sleng Genocide Museum (Phnom
    Penh), 3, 4–23, 12, 27, 244–53, 273–78,
    282–87. See also S-21 security prison
Ty Srinna, 63

Uch Sorn, 84–86
uncanny concept, 32–33, 35, 77, 143, 267
Ung Pech, 178
United Nations: Commission of Human
    Rights, 46; negotiations with Cambodia,
    48–49, 59

Vannak Huy, 242
Vann Nath, 4, 12, 20, 22, 23, 52, 63, 177–81, 178,
    201, 207, 241
Vietnamese: invasion of Phnom Penh
    (1979), 11; withdrawal from Cambodia
    (1989), 28
Vigny, Alfred de, 76–77
Vong Oeun, 160–61
Vorn Vet, 6, 16, 72, 74, 91–92, 95, 121, 123,
    134–35, 139, 294

Werner, Alain, 63
West Zone, 164
Workers' Party of Kampuchea (WPK),
    158–59, 163
Workers' Party of Vietnam, 154
WPK. See Workers' Party of Kampuchea

Ya (Ney Saran), 153–57, 158–59, 182, 205
Yann Pheng (Ieng Si Pheng), 105, 162, 163
Yet Chakriya, 157
You Bunleng, 2, 51, 260–61
Yun Yat, 112, 223